PURSUING
THE
AMERICAN
DREAM

PURSUING THE AMERICAN DREAM

KENNETH S. KNODT

La Salle College

PRENTICE-HALL, INC. *Englewood Cliffs, New Jersey*

Library of Congress Cataloging in Publication Data
Main entry under title:

Pursuing the American dream.

    1. College readers. 2. Readers—United States—
Civilization. I. Knodt, Kenneth S., 1940–
PE1122.P8   808'.04275   75-26608
ISBN 0-13-742742-5

Printed in the United States of America

10 9 8 7 6 5 4 3 2

PRENTICE-HALL INTERNATIONAL, INC., *London*
PRENTICE-HALL OF AUSTRALIA, PTY. LTD., *Sydney*
PRENTICE-HALL OF CANADA, LTD., *Toronto*
PRENTICE-HALL OF INDIA PRIVATE LIMITED, *New Delhi*
PRENTICE-HALL OF JAPAN, INC., *Tokyo*
PRENTICE-HALL OF SOUTHEAST ASIA (PTE.) LTD., *Singapore*

CONTENTS

THE MINORITY EXPERIENCE

PART TWO
THE PURSUIT OF SUCCESS 103

THE SUCCESS ETHIC

THE BUSINESS OF AMERICA

PART THREE
THE SHAPING OF THE LAND   173

RHETORICAL CONTENTS

FICTION

Romantic

Horatio Alger, Jr., "Frank Is Offered a Position"
James Fenimore Cooper, from *The Deerslayer*
Edward L. Wheeler, "Barkin' Up the Wrong Tree"

Realism and Naturalism

William Faulkner, "That Evening Sun"
Sherwood Anderson, "Sophistication"
Hamlin Garland, "Under the Lion's Paw"
Edith Wharton, "Mrs. Manstey's View"
John Updike, from *Rabbit Redux*

Impressionism

Stephen Crane, "The Bride Comes to Yellow Sky"

Social Protest

Upton Sinclair, "The Stockyards"
John Steinbeck, from *The Grapes of Wrath*

Satire

John Cheever, "O Youth and Beauty!"
Joseph Heller, "Milo"

Symbolic

Ralph Ellison, "Battle Royal"
Harvey Swados, "Joe, The Vanishing American"

Experimental

John Dos Passos, "Tin Lizzie"

POETRY

PREFACE

When a reader of the 1970s searches for contemporary analyses of the American character, he inevitably encounters the American "dream." This book helps define those essential concepts which have shaped —and still are shaping in one way or another—this dream, as suggested through the recurrent themes of our literary, historical, and political heritage. The selections provide many balances. First, there is a balance among fields suggesting the broad appeal of this book in English thematic and composition courses, American studies, humanities, history, U. S.-centered political science, and mini-semester courses. Second, the book provides a balance in terms of optimism and pessimism as seen in the dream, showing that neither view has at any time totally dominated American thought. Last, the book balances the classic and the new, the pre-twentieth century selections with twentieth century ones, in order to provide a chronological perspective on the American dream.

Many aids have been provided for the exploration of ideas in the forms of an introduction to each section, headnotes, questions for discussion, other suggested readings, and a rhetorical table of contents. The teacher's manual provides questions on rhetoric and literary analysis, writing and research suggestions, and discussions to help teachers approach the selections.

I want to thank the many people whose ideas have helped make this a better book: James Butler, Hilma Cooper, Keith Cooper, John Keenan, Barbara Millard, Caryn Musil, and Robert Musil. Lilian Tonkin of the Library Company was quite helpful in locating many of the sources in rare books. My special thanks go to my wife Ellen who has helped immensely in the development of this book through her knowledge, insight, and effort.

Philadelphia   KENNETH S. KNODT

ACKNOWLEDGMENTS

WHAT IS AN AMERICAN?: From Letter III of *Letters from an American Farmer* (1782).

THE DECLARATION OF INDEPENDENCE: The text is that authorized by the State Department: *The Declaration of Independence, 1776* [1911].

THE PURITAN: From *V-Letter and Other Poems,* copyright 1944 by Karl Jay Shapiro. Reprinted by permission of Random House, Inc.

CIVIL DISOBEDIENCE: Originally delivered as a speech in 1848 and first published in 1849 in *Aesthetic Essays* and entitled "Resistance to Civil Government."

FOR YOU O DEMOCRACY: From *Leaves of Grass* (1891 edition).

From **PASSAGE TO INDIA:** From *Leaves of Grass* (1891 edition).

SOMETHING'S HAPPENING OUT THERE: From *Family Circle,* copyright January 1973. By permission of the publisher and author.

A POPULIST MANIFESTO: From *A Populist Manifesto: The Making of a New Majority* by Jack Newfield and Jeff Greenfield. Originally in New York Magazine, July 19, 1971. Copyright 1971 by Jack Newfield. Reprinted by permission of the Sterling Lord Agency.

DISSENTING OPINION, DEFUNIS V. ODEGAARD (1974): In *Official Reports of the Supreme Court,* Vol. 416, Part I. Government Printing Office, Washington, D.C.

THE CONSTITUTION IS ALIVE AND WELL: From the Op-Ed page of The New York Times, August 11, 1974. Copyright 1974 by The New York Times Company. Reprinted by permission.

A SLAVE'S LIFE: From Chapter 10 of *Narrative of the Life of Frederick Douglass* (1845).

INVISIBLE MAN: From *Invisible Man,* copyright 1947 by Ralph Ellison. Reprinted by permission of Random House, Inc.

THAT EVENING SUN: From *These Thirteen,* copyright 1931 by William Faulkner. Reprinted by permission of Random House, Inc.

AMERICA AND THE WHITE HOUSE: Both McKay poems are from *The Selected Poems of Claude McKay;* copyright 1953 by Bookman Associates, reprinted with permission of Twayne Publishers, Inc.

LETTER TO THE SALEM CONVENTION: This letter was written April 7, 1850. Text from *History of Woman Suffrage,* edited by Elizabeth Cady Stanton, Susan B. Anthony, and Matilda Josyln Gage, vol. I (1881).

CONFESSIONS OF AN EX-CHEERLEADER: Copyright 1973 by Louise Bernikow, reprinted by permission of Harold Matson Co., Inc.

WOUNDED KNEE: Chapter 19 from *Bury My Heart at Wounded Knee,* copyright 1970 by Dee Brown. Reprinted by permission of Holt, Rinehart and Winston, Inc.

THE CHICANOS: From *La Raza: The Mexican Americans* by Stan Steiner. Copyright 1969, 1970 by Stan Steiner. Reprinted by permission of Harper & Row, Publishers, Inc.

WAVES OF IMMIGRATION: Chapter 4 of *A Nation of Immigrants.* Revised and Enlarged Edition by John F. Kennedy. Copyright 1964 by Anti-Defamation League of B'nai B'rith. By permission of Harper and Row, Publishers, Inc.

EUROPE AND AMERICA: "Europe and America," copyright © 1948 by David Ignatow, Reprinted from *Figures of the Human* by David Ignatow, by permission of the publisher, Wesleyan University Press.

From **THE PROMISED LAND:** Chapter 9 from *The Promised Land,* Copyright © 1912, renewed 1940, by Mary Antin. Reprinted by permission of Houghton Mifflin Company.

THE SELF-MADE MAN IN AMERICA: From the Prologue and Chapter Two of *The Self-Made Man in America.* Copyright 1954 and reprinted by permission of The Trustees of Rutgers College in New Jersey.

PROPOSALS TO RICH MEN: From *Essays to Do Good.* Originally published in 1710, this is from an 1815 edition.

THE WAY TO WEALTH: From "The Way to Wealth," originally published as *The Preface to Poor Richard's Almanack* (1758).

FRANK IS OFFERED A POSITION: Chapter 33 of *The World Before Him,* serialized in *Golden Days* (1880).

RICHARD CORY: Reprinted by permission of Charles Scribners Sons from *The Children of the Night.*

BEWICK FINZER: Reprinted with permission of Macmillan Publishing Co., Inc., from *Collected Poems* by Edwin Arlington Robinson. Copyright 1916 by Edwin Arlington Robinson, renewed 1944 by Ruth Nivison.

NOBODY LOSES ALL THE TIME: Copyright 1926, by Horace Liveright; copyright, 1954, by E. E. Cummings. Reprinted from *Complete Poems 1913–1962* by E. E. Cummings. By permission of Harcourt Brace Jovanovich, Inc.

TRY, TRY AGAIN: *McGuffey's Newly Revised Eclectic Reader,* 1853.

O YOUTH AND BEAUTY!: From *The Housebreakers of Shady Hill and Other Stories* by John Cheever. Copyright 1953 by John Cheever. Originally appeared in *The New Yorker* and reprinted by permission of Harper and Row, Publishers, Inc.

THE INVISIBLE LAND: From Chapter 1. Reprinted with permission of Macmillan Publishing Co., Inc., from *The Other America,* revised edition by Michael Harrington. Copyright 1962, 1969 by Michael Harrington.

BUSINESS—A PROFESSION: An address delivered on Commencement Day at Brown University, 1912.

THE RISE OF THE STANDARD OIL COMPANY: From Chapter Two of *The History of the Standard Oil Company.* Published in 1904 by McClure, Phillips and Co.

THE STOCKYARDS: From Chapter 9 of *The Jungle.* First published in serial form in 1905, book form in 1906.

TIN LIZZIE: From *The Big Money* by John Dos Passos. Copyright 1936 by John Dos Passos, copyright renewed 1964, held by Elizabeth H. Dos Passos and reprinted with her permission.

JOE, THE VANISHING AMERICAN: Copyright © 1957, by Harvey Swados. From *On the Line* by Harvey Swados, by permission of Mrs. Harvey Swados.

THE FRAYING WHITE COLLAR: Judson Gooding, "The Fraying White Collar," FORTUNE, December 1970, Time Inc. Reprinted by permission of the author.

THE GIFT OUTRIGHT: From *The Poetry of Robert Frost* edited by Edward Connery Lathem. Copyright 1942 by Robert Frost. Copyright 1969 by Holt, Rinehart and Winston, Inc. Copyright 1970 by Lesley Frost Ballantine. Reprinted by permission of Holt, Rinehart and Winston, Inc.

BIRCHES: From *The Poetry of Robert Frost* edited by Edward Connery Lathem. Copyright 1916, copyright 1969 by Holt, Rinehart and Winston, Inc. Copyright 1944 by Robert Frost. Reprinted by permission of Holt, Rinehart and Winston, Inc.

SOLITUDE: From *Walden* (1854).

THE BOYS' AMBITION: Chapter 4 from *Life on the Mississippi*. The text is that of the first book edition, 1883.

SOPHISTICATION: From *Winesburg, Ohio* by Sherwood Anderson. Copyright 1919 by B. W. Huebsch, Inc. Copyright renewed 1947 by Eleanor Copenhaver Anderson. Reprinted by permission of The Viking Press, Inc.

From **THE GRAPES OF WRATH:** Chapter 25 of *The Grapes of Wrath*. Copyright 1939, copyright 1967 by John Steinbeck. Reprinted by permission of The Viking Press, Inc.

From **NORTH TOWARD HOME:** From *North Toward Home* by Willie Morris. Copyright 1967 by Willie Morris. Reprinted by permission of Houghton Mifflin Co.

THE SIGNIFICANCE OF THE FRONTIER IN AMERICAN HISTORY: This is from an address that he gave before The American Historical Association in 1893.

From **THE DEERSLAYER:** From Chapter 27 of *The Deerslayer* (1841).

PIONEERS! O PIONEERS!: From *Leaves of Grass* (1891 edition).

THE FRONTIER: Chapter 1 and from Chapter 4 of *The Oregon Trail: Sketches of Prairie and Rocky Mountain Life* (1849).

BARKIN' UP THE WRONG TREE: Chapter 1 from *Deadwood Dick on Deck or Calamity Jane, The Heroine of Whoop-Up*. Originally in Beadle's Pocket Library, February 11, 1885.

THE BRIDE COMES TO YELLOW SKY: The text is that of The University of Virginia Edition of *The Works of Stephen Crane*, edited by Fredson Bowers. Copyright 1970 by the Rector and Visitors of the University of Virginia Center for Editions of American Authors. Reprinted by permission.

UNDER THE LION'S PAW: This was written in 1889 and first included in *Main-Travelled Roads* (1891) from which this text is taken.

BUFFALO BILL'S: Copyright 1923, 1951 by E. E. Cummings. Reprinted from his volume, *Complete Poems 1913–1962*, by permission of Harcourt Brace Jovanovich, Inc.

MANNAHATTA: From *Leaves of Grass* (1891 edition).

CHICAGO and **SKYSCRAPER:** From *Chicago Poems* by Carl Sandburg, copyright 1916, by Holt, Rinehart and Winston, Inc.; copyright 1944, by Carl Sandburg. Reprinted by permission of Harcourt Brace Jovanovich, Inc.

MRS. MANSTEY'S VIEW: From *Scribner's Magazine* (July, 1891).

GOODBYE TO ALL THAT: In *Slouching Towards Bethlehem*, by Joan Didion. Copyright 1966 by Joan Didion. Reprinted with the permission of Farrar, Straus and Giroux, Inc.

THE END OF INNOCENCE: From *The End of the American Future*, copyright 1973 by Peter Schrag. Reprinted by permission of Simon and Schuster.

From **RABBIT REDUX:** From *Rabbit Redux* by John Updike, copyright 1971. By permission of Alfred A. Knopf, Inc.

THE MYTH OF SUBURBIA: Originally in the *Journal of Social Issues* 17, no. 1 (1961): 38-49. From *Looking for America*, by Bennett Berger, copyright 1971. Reprinted by permission of Prentice-Hall, Inc.

THE AMERICAN IMAGE: From Chapter 12, *The Waist-High Culture*, copyright 1959 by Thomas Griffith, reprinted by permission of Harper and Row, Inc.

AMERICA: From *Howl and Other Poems*, copyright 1956, 1959 by Allen Ginsburg. Reprinted by permission of City Lights Books.

THE PEOPLE WILL LIVE ON: From *The People, Yes* by Carl Sandburg. Copyright 1936 by Harcourt Brace Jovanovich, Inc.; renewed 1964 by Carl Sandburg. Reprinted by permission of the publisher.

FAREWELL ADDRESS: Delivered at the end of his Presidency (1961).

EISENHOWER'S VISIT TO FRANCO, 1959: From *The Branch Will Not Break,* copyright 1962 by James Wright. Reprinted by permission of Wesleyan University Press.

MILO: Chapter 24 from *Catch-22,* copyright 1955, 1961 by Joseph Heller. Reprinted by permission of Simon and Schuster, Inc.

From **THE PURSUIT OF LONELINESS:** From Chapter 1, *The Pursuit of Loneliness,* copyright 1970 by Philip E. Slater. Reprinted by permission of The Beacon Press.

THE CHANGING PLACE OF WOMEN IN AMERICA: Reprinted by permission of *Daedalus,* Journal of the American Academy of Arts and Sciences, Boston, Mass., Spring 1964, Vol. 93, No. 2, *The Woman in America.*

THE RESTORATION OF A RIVER: Copyright 1972 by Saturday Review Co. First appeared in *Saturday Review,* April 8, 1972. Reprinted by permission of the publisher and author.

CALIFORNIA 2001: Copyright, 1972, Los Angeles Times. Reprinted by permission.

THE TRADITION OF THE FUTURE: Copyright 1968 by Saturday Review Co. First appeared in *Saturday Review,* June 8, 1968. Used with permission of the publisher and Columbia University.

PURSUING
THE
AMERICAN
DREAM

INTRODUCTION

Two hundred years ago the Frenchman Hector St. Jean de Crèvecoeur asked a question which has fascinated us ever since: "What then is this new American?" The question seems especially significant during America's bicentennial, as we take stock of ourselves and examine the many influences on the American character throughout our history. As William Faulkner reminds us, the search is not for an outdated heritage, but for one which is continually shaping us: "The past is never dead. It's not even past."

The readings in this book, gathered from a variety of disciplines, have been chosen for the insights which they provide on what and where we have been, and on where we

continually "new Americans" are going. These different perspectives enable a reader to see interdisciplinary relationships between the literature of fact found in objective history and the literature of symbol developed through fictional modes.

The term "dreams," which can be defined as the hopes and ideals of a people, is applied extensively to the American experience and suggests an ongoing, active creation, a sense of possibility and hope. A recent immigrant from Turkey is delighted at Americans' freedom to criticize their government. A black man in an urban ghetto gets an engineering degree at night and now works on space satellites. A daughter of Italian immigrants becomes a college

1

professor. But what makes this sense of optimism, this ideal of opportunity, uniquely American? Certainly other countries have their own success stories, their own dreams. What seems to make the American dream unique is the coming together in one place of so many separate dreams: the search for freedom, the discovery and settlement of a vast wilderness, the exploitation of rich, natural resources. As Frederick I. Carpenter shows in his book, *American Literature and the Dream* (1955), the dream of the good life had previously always been attached to a country of the imagination, but America was the first real, physical place where either the ideals could be reached or progress toward them could be made.

But dreams sometime turn into mere illusions or even nightmares, and the nightmare of the corruption of ideals and failure of hopes reveals a very different America. Dissenters and other groups perceived as un-American have faced repression from the time of the Know-Nothing Party in the 1850s to the Palmer raids during the Red Scare following World War I, the Joseph McCarthy Communist witchhunt of the 1950s, and the recent conspiracy trials arising from Vietnam war protests. Immigrants often found barriers to opportunity: Irishmen seeking employment saw signs reading "No Irish Need Apply"; the West Coast had anti-Chinese riots in the 1870s. The settler on the frontier, looking for the New Eden of his dreams, often found only hardship and poverty.

At no time during America's two centuries have the dream and ideal excluded the illusion and nightmare, and conversely, at no time have the nightmare and illusion conquered the ideal and the dream; these two aspects of American life have always run concurrently. At the same time that the philosophical groundwork of the democratic ideal was being laid, the nightmare of slavery challenged and weakened that foundation. Historians point out this same contrast in the pursuit of success: at the end of the nineteenth century, when a few men were becoming huge financial successes, the mass of laborers worked in sweatshop conditions. Still with us is the duality of the dream: ecological abuses are everywhere; bureaucratic society threatens our privacy, and the pace of life has become too fast. Yet, hope persists in the lives of the average citizen: life expectancy has been extended; the work day has been shortened; wages and benefits have gone up; there is more than the chicken in every pot held out as a dream a half century ago; the educational level has increased; and social security, only forty years old, has given dignity to millions. The pursuit of the dream has been a real force in America's life for two hundred years, and it is the promise of the dream that will carry us into our future.

PART ONE

THE DEMOCRATIC IDEAL

DEMOCRATIC PHILOSOPHY

The philosophy of the democratic ideal is the cornerstone of the American dream, for from it come ideas of political and social equality, notions of individual freedom and independence, and the tradition of one nation out of many, of America as a melting pot of immigrants. We are all familiar with Thomas Jefferson's statement in *The Declaration of Independence* that all men are created equal; this statement, together with the guarantees of individual liberty in the *Bill of Rights,* forms the core of our democratic philosophy. Other early writers confirm these ideas as part of a new American creed. Hector St. Jean de Crèvecoeur, for example, sees America as a social paradise without an aristocracy, a true land of opportunity. Observing the independence and freedom of the citizens of the new nation, he describes America as a melting pot where individuals of all nations are blended into a harmonious whole. These ideals of equality and freedom became engraved in the American consciousness and are still held as tenets of faith.

Throughout the two hundred years of our history, many writers have responded to these ideals, commenting upon them from diverse perspectives of time, place, and personality. Some of the most profound and important responses are included among the selections in this section. Walt Whitman shows his enthusiastic acceptance of the ideals and praises America as a land of manifest destiny for the whole world. Henry David Thoreau reinterprets the ideals with an emphasis on the duty of each citizen to preserve freedom and equality in a democracy. Thoreau's advocacy of civil disobedience as a means to that end has become, for many concerned with civil rights, the Vietnam war, and other social problems, a part of our democratic philosophy. Meanwhile, Karl Shapiro reminds us how ideals can sometimes be perverted, by showing us the excesses of some early Americans who sought religious freedom, but whose zealous faith produced intolerance instead of brotherhood.

In this section, also, four contemporary essayists examine facets of democratic philosophy in the 1970s. Charles Kuralt explains why he still believes in the American dream. Jack Newfield proposes a political philosophy which, he feels, will meet the needs of the large majority of modern Americans who are no longer served by the present political system. Finally, Justice William O. Douglas examines the problems of civil rights for the white majority in an era of quota and rising minority representation in schools and jobs, and Henry Steele Commager assessses the impact of the Nixon presidency on the democratic process.

THE MINORITY EXPERIENCE

As Jefferson, de Crèvecoeur, and others were writing their expressions of the democratic ideal, black Americans lived lives that belied the promise of freedom, independence, equality, and opportunity; for them the American experience was nightmarish from the beginning. Ironically, Jefferson, the chief architect of the democratic ideal, owned slaves, though he felt this situation was morally reprehensible and

would change. Even after the Civil War, Supreme Court decisions like *Plessy* v. *Ferguson* (1896) separated the black person from other Americans in every aspect of daily life. Literary expressions of this nightmare experience range from narratives told by slaves or former slaves like Frederick Douglass to contemporary writers' attempts to assess the damage done by slavery and discrimination. In this anthology, Ralph Ellison portrays the confusion and humiliation faced by a black youth; William Faulkner shows the complex interrelationships between white people and black people in a southern town; and Claude McKay's poems describe the inner turmoil of a black person who does not want hate to destroy him.

Recent efforts to redress the grievances of black Americans, to end racial discrimination, are a tribute to the democratic dream. *Brown* v. *Board of Education* (1954) and the Civil Rights Acts of 1964 and 1965 are attempts to implement the dream, to make it work for all Americans. *Brown* states that the separate but equal doctrine of *Plessy* v. *Ferguson* is unconstitutional and that therefore segregated schools are unconstitutional. The Civil Rights Acts enforce the right to vote and the right to use public accommodations. Though twentieth-century America has not completely established the democratic idea for black Americans, it has not allowed the disheartening realities of the past to remain unchanged.

Other minority groups in America also found the democratic idea to be more dream than reality. Women were denied the right to vote or hold office, the right to speak in public to a mixed audience, and the right to hold property or conduct other business. Colleges would not admit women so the professions were closed to them. But conditions on the frontier, where men and women shared the hardships of settlement equally, helped alter people's attitudes toward women. The first baccalaureate colleges to admit them were Oberlin (1837) and Antioch (1853), both in Ohio, just behind the advancing frontier. And the territory of

Wyoming was the first to grant equal suffrage in 1869. The women's reform movement, another important force for change, began in 1837 as an antislavery crusade but quickly added women's rights to its list of needed humanitarian reforms. Elizabeth Cady Stanton, arguing for suffrage in her "Letter to the Salem Convention," was one of the movement's most articulate leaders. The feminist movement today has many spokeswomen; in this anthology, Louise Bernikow takes an irreverent look at growing up female in the 1950s.

The history of the American Indian is the most nightmarish of any minority group, for the Indians suffered almost total annihilation. Indians saw their lands crossed by railroads and fenced by settlers and the buffalo, upon which they depended for food, clothing, and covering for their tee-pees, exterminated. Although they fought an increasing number of desperate battles just before and after the Civil War, pitting as few as fifty braves against forces of two or three thousand soldiers, their bravery and fighting skill could not prevail against the combined pressure of the army, the settlers and gold seekers, and the loss of game. By the late nineteenth century, the remnants of most tribes were living in poverty on reservations. In 1890, one of the last bands of Sioux still at large, dispirited and led by an ailing chief, was wiped out at Wounded Knee, South Dakota, in a massacre described by Dee Brown.

Some minority groups with severe problems are almost invisible to the general populace. One group which has recently emerged from relative obscurity is the Chicanos. Though the plight of migrant workers and other Mexican-Americans has been acknowledged for years by social scientists like Oscar Lewis and novelists like John Steinbeck, it did not pierce the consciousness of most Americans until quite recently. East coast housewives had never heard of Chicanos until the campaigns to boycott grapes and lettuce in the late 1960s. Now Chicanos are becoming well organized and are receiving recognition; in "The Chicanos" Stan Steiner reports on their efforts to maintain dignity and identity.

Most Americans today may have forgotten the struggles of European immigrants, our largest minority group. Those of us of Irish, Italian, Scandinavian, German, Polish, or Jewish descent may not fully understand the barriers of language, culture, and prejudice our ancestors faced as immigrants. The historical background of each of the largest immigrant groups is discussed by John F. Kennedy who explains why the immigrants came, what problems they had, and what important contributions they made. Following his article, David Ignatow dramatizes the difference between the immigrant and his son, and Mary Antin vividly describes her own reactions to Boston as a newly arrived Russian-Jewish immigrant.

In his article Kennedy reminds us that over the years "established" Americans would say that the newer immigrants would never fit in and become good, worthwhile citizens, but they always did. The successful record of millions of immigrants of all nationalities is evidence that the American democratic ideal was a reality for many and provides hope that it will become a reality for all Americans.

DEMOCRATIC
PHILOSOPHY

Mark Tobey, **E Pluribus Unum** *(1942). Seattle Art Museum, gift of Mrs. Thomas D. Stimson.*

Hector St. Jean de Crèvecoeur

In this selection, Hector St. Jean de Crève-
coeur (1735–1813), born in France and na-
turalized as an American citizen, writes of
the new America with unbounded optimism.
For him America is the promised land where
new ideas will be born and new human re-
lationships formed. He is not blind, however,
to America's imperfections: in another of his
"Letters" (this is from his third), he attacks
slavery. Distrusted by many Americans for
his aristocratic background and conservative
political beliefs, de Crèvecoeur left America
in 1780, returning to New York in 1783 as
French consul and remaining until 1790. He
spent the last twenty-three years of his life in
France.

WHAT IS AN AMERICAN?

I wish I could be acquainted with the feelings and thoughts which must agitate the heart and present themselves to the mind of an enlightened Englishman, when he first lands on this continent. He must greatly rejoice that he lived at a time to see this fair country discovered and settled; he must necessarily feel a share of national pride, when he views the chain of settlements which embellishes these extended shores. When he says to himself, this is the work of my countrymen, who, when convulsed by factions, afflicted by a variety of miseries and wants, restless and impatient, took refuge here. They brought along with them their national genius, to which they principally owe what liberty they enjoy, and what substance they possess. Here he sees the industry of his native country dis-

played in a new manner, and traces in their works the embryos of all the arts, sciences, and ingenuity which flourish in Europe. Here he beholds fair cities, substantial villages, extensive fields, an immense country filled with decent houses, good roads, orchards, meadows, and bridges, where an hundred years ago all was wild, woody, and uncultivated! What a train of pleasing ideas this fair spectacle must suggest; it is a prospect which must inspire a good citizen with the most heartfelt pleasure. The difficulty consists in the manner of viewing so extensive a scene. He is arrived on a new continent; a modern society offers itself to his contemplation, different from what he had hitherto seen. It is not composed, as in Europe, of great lords who possess everything, and of a herd of people who have nothing. Here are no aristocratical families, no courts, no kings, no bishops, no ecclesiastical dominion, no invisible power giving to a few a very visible one; no great manufacturers employing thousands, no great refinements of luxury. The rich and the poor are not so far removed from each other as they are in Europe. Some few towns excepted, we are all tillers of the earth, from Nova Scotia to West Florida. We are a people of cultivators, scattered over an immense territory, communicating with each other by means of good roads and navigable rivers, united by the silken bands of mild government, all respecting the laws, without dreading their power, because they are equitable. We are all animated with the spirit of an industry which is unfettered and unrestrained, because each person works for himself. If he travels through our

7

rural districts he views not the hostile castle, and the haughty mansion, contrasted with the clay-built hut and miserable cabin, where cattle and men help to keep each other warm, and dwell in meanness, smoke, and indigence. A pleasing uniformity of decent competence appears throughout our habitations. The meanest of our log-houses is a dry and comfortable habitation. Lawyer or merchant are the fairest titles our towns afford; that of a farmer is the only appellation of the rural inhabitants of our country. It must take some time ere he can reconcile himself to our dictionary, which is but short in words of dignity, and names of honour. There, on a Sunday, he sees a congregation of respectable farmers and their wives, all clad in neat homespun, well mounted, or riding in their own humble waggons. There is not among them an esquire, saving the unlettered magistrate. There he sees a parson as simple as his flock, a farmer who does not riot on the labour of others. We have no princes, for whom we toil, starve, and bleed: we are the most perfect society now existing in the world. Here man is free as he ought to be; nor is this pleasing equality so transitory as many others are. Many ages will not see the shores of our great lakes replenished with inland nations, nor the unknown bounds of North America entirely peopled. Who can tell how far it extends? Who can tell the millions of men whom it will feed and contain? for no European foot has as yet travelled half the extent of this mighty continent!

The next wish of this traveller will be to know whence came all these people? they are a mixture of English, Scotch, Irish, French, Dutch, Germans, and Swedes. From this promiscuous breed, that race now called Americans have arisen. The eastern provinces must indeed be excepted, as being the unmixed descendants of Englishmen. I have heard many wish that they had been more intermixed also: for my part, I am no wisher, and think it much better as it

has happened. They exhibit a most conspicuous figure in this great and variegated picture; they too enter for a great share in the pleasing perspective displayed in these thirteen provinces. I know it is fashionable to reflect on them, but I respect them for what they have done; for the accuracy and wisdom with which they have settled their territory; for the decency of their manners; for their early love of letters; their ancient college, the first in this hemisphere; for their industry; which to me who am but a farmer, is the criterion of everything. There never was a people, situated as they are, who with so ungrateful a soil have done more in so short a time. Do you think that the monarchical ingredients which are more prevalent in other governments, have purged them from all foul stains? Their histories assert the contrary.

In this great American asylum, the poor of Europe have by some means met together, and in consequence of various causes; to what purpose should they ask one another what countrymen they are? Alas, two thirds of them had no country. Can a wretch who wanders about, who works and starves, whose life is a continual scene of sore affliction or pinching penury; can that man call England or any other kingdom his country? A country that had no bread for him, whose fields procured him no harvest, who met with nothing but the frowns of the rich, the severity of the laws, with jails and punishments; who owned not a single foot of the extensive surface of this planet? No! urged by a variety of motives, here they came. Every thing has tended to regenerate them; new laws, a new mode of living, a new social system; here they are become men: in Europe they were as so many useless plants, wanting vegetative mould, and refreshing showers; they withered, and were mowed down by want, hunger, and war; but now by the power of transplantation, like all other plants they have taken root and flourished! Formerly they were not numbered in any civil lists of their country, except in those of the poor; here they rank as citizens. By what invisible power has this surprising metamorphosis been performed? By that of the laws and that of their industry. The laws, the indulgent laws, protect them as they arrive, stamping on them the symbol of adoption; they receive ample rewards for their labours; these accumulated rewards procure them lands; those lands confer on them the title of freemen, and to that title every benefit is affixed which men can possibly require. This is the great operation daily performed by our laws. From whence proceed these laws? From our government. Whence the government? It is derived from the original genius and strong desire of the people ratified and confirmed by the crown. This is the great chain which links us all, this is the picture which every province exhibits, Nova Scotia excepted. There the crown has done all; either there were no people who had genius, or it was not much attended to: the consequence is, that the province is very thinly inhabited indeed; the power of the crown in conjunction with the musketos has prevented men from settling there. Yet some parts of it flourished once, and it contained a mild harmless set of people. But for the fault of a few leaders, the whole were banished. The greatest political error the crown ever committed in America, was to cut men from a country which wanted nothing but men!

What attachment can a poor European emigrant have for a country where he had nothing? The knowledge of the language, the love of a few kindred as poor as himself, were the only cords that tied him: his country is now that which gives him land, bread, protection, and consequence. *Ubi panis ibi patria*,[1] is the motto of all emigrants: What then is the American, this new man? He is either an European, or the descendant of an European, hence that strange mixture of blood, which you will find in no other

country. I could point out to you a family whose grandfather was an Englishman, whose wife was Dutch, whose son married a French woman, and whose present four sons have now four wives of different nations. *He* is an American, who, leaving behind him all his ancient prejudices and manners, receives new ones from the new mode of life he has embraced, the new government he obeys, and the new rank he holds. He becomes an American by being received in the broad lap of our great *Alma Mater*. Here individuals of all nations are melted into a new race of men, whose labours and posterity will one day cause great changes in the world. Americans are the western pilgrims, who are carrying along with them that great mass of arts, sciences, vigour, and industry which began long since in the east; they will finish the great circle. The Americans were once scattered all over Europe; here they are incorporated into one of the finest systems of population which has ever appeared, and which will hereafter become distinct by the power of the different climates they inhabit. The American ought therefore to love this country much better than that wherein either he or his forefathers were born. Here the rewards of his industry follow with equal steps the progress of his labour; his labour is founded on the basis of nature, *self-interest;* can it want a stronger allurement? Wives and children, who before in vain demanded of him a morsel of bread, now, fat and frolicsome, gladly help their father to clear those fields whence exuberant crops are to arise to feed and to clothe them all; without any part being claimed, either by a despotic prince, a rich abbot, or a mighty lord. Here religion demands but little of him; a small voluntary salary to the minister, and gratitude to God; can he refuse these? The American is a new man, who acts upon new principles; he must therefore entertain new ideas, and form new opinions. From involuntary idleness, servile dependence, penury, and useless labour, he

---

[1] Where there is bread, there is one's fatherland.

has passed to toils of a very different nature, rewarded by ample subsistence.—This is an American.

Thomas Jefferson

In a memorable tribute to Thomas Jefferson's (1743–July 4, 1826) abilities, President John Kennedy remarked to a group of intellectuals and artists dining at the White House that the last time such an array of talent had dined there was when Jefferson dined alone. Jefferson was probably the most influential mind of the early American republic: he was governor of Virginia, the first secretary of state, minister to France, vicepresident, and president; and he was actively involved in many fields of knowledge. In The Declaration of Independence, *which he wrote with the assistance of Benjamin Franklin and three others, Jefferson employs precise language and argument in attempting to convince the world of the rightness of revolution for the new country.*

THE DECLARATION OF INDEPENDENCE

In CONGRESS, July 4, 1776.

THE UNANIMOUS DECLARATION of the thirteen united STATES OF AMERICA.

When in the Course of human events, it becomes necessary for one people to dissolve the political bands which have connected them with another, and to assume among the powers of the earth, the separate and equal station to which the Laws of Nature and of Nature's God entitle them, a decent respect to the opinions of mankind requires that they should declare the causes which impel them to the separation.———We hold these truths to be self-evident, that all men are created equal, that they are endowed by their Creator with certain unalienable Rights, that among these are Life, Liberty and the pursuit of Happiness.—

That to secure these rights, Governments are instituted among Men, deriving their just powers from the consent of the governed,—That whenever any Form of Government becomes destructive of these ends, it is the Right of the People to alter or to abolish it, and to institute new Government, laying its foundation on such principles and organizing its powers in such form, as to them shall seem most likely to effect their Safety and Happiness. Prudence, indeed, will dictate that Governments long established should not be changed for light and transient causes; and accordingly all experience hath shewn, that mankind are more disposed to suffer, while evils are sufferable, than to right themselves by abolishing the forms to which they are accustomed. But when a long train of abuses and usurpations, pursuing invariably the same Object evinces a design to reduce them under absolute Despotism, it is their right, it is their duty, to throw off such Government, and to provide new Guards, for their future security.—Such has been the patient sufferance of these Colonies; and such is now the necessity which constrains them to alter their former Systems of Government. The history of the present King of Great Britain is a history of repeated injuries and usurpations, all having in direct object the establishment of an absolute Tyranny over these States. To prove this, let Facts be submitted to a candid world.———He has refused his Assent to Laws, the most wholesome and necessary for the public good.———He has forbidden his Governors to pass Laws of immediate and pressing importance, unless suspended in their operation till his Assent should be obtained; and when so suspended, he has utterly neglected to attend to them.———He has refused to pass other Laws for the accommodation of large districts of people, unless those people would relinquish the right of Representation in the Legislature, a right inestimable to them and formidable to tyrants only.———He has called together legislative bodies at places unusual, uncomfortable, and distant from the depository of their public Records, for the sole purpose of fatiguing them into compliance with his measures.——He has dissolved Representative Houses repeatedly, for opposing with manly firmness his invasions on the rights of the people.——He has refused for a long time, after such dissolutions, to cause others to be elected; whereby the Legislative powers, incapable of Annihilation, have returned to the People at large for their exercise; the State remaining in the mean time exposed to all the dangers of invasion from without, and convulsions within.——He has endeavoured to prevent the population of these States; for that purpose obstructing the Laws for Naturalization of Foreigners; refusing to pass others to encourage their migrations hither, and raising the conditions of new Appropriations of Lands.——He has obstructed the Administration of Justice, by refusing his Assent to Laws for establishing Judiciary powers.——He has made Judges dependent on his Will alone, for the tenure of their officers, and the amount and payment of their salaries.——He has erected a multitude of New Offices, and sent hither swarms of Officers to harass our people, and eat out their substance.——He has kept among us, in times of peace, Standing Armies without the Consent of our legislatures.——He has affected to render the Military independent of and superior to the Civil power.——He has combined with others to subject us to a jurisdiction foreign to our constitution, and unacknowledged by our laws; giving his Assent to their Acts of pretended Legislation:—For Quartering large bodies of armed troops among us:—For protecting them, by a mock Trial, from punishment for any Murders which they should commit on the Inhabitants of these States:—For cutting off our Trade with all parts of the world:—For imposing Taxes on us without our Consent:—For depriving us in many cases, of the benefits of Trial by Jury:— For transporting us beyond Seas to be tried for pretended offences:—For abolishing the free System of English Laws in a neighbouring Province, establishing therein an Arbitrary government, and enlarging its Boundaries so as to render it at once an example and fit instrument for introducing the same absolute rule into these Colonies:—For taking away our Charters, abolishing our most valuable Laws, and altering fundamentally the Forms of our Governments:—For suspending our own Legislatures, and declaring themselves invested with power to legislate for us in all cases whatsoever.—He has abdicated Government here, by declaring us out of his Protection and waging War against us:— He has plundered our seas, ravaged our Coasts, burnt our towns, and destroyed the lives of our people.—He is at this time transporting large Armies of foreign Mercenaries to compleat the works of death, desolation and tyranny, already begun with circumstances of Cruelty & perfidy scarcely paralleled in the most barbarous ages, and totally unworthy the Head of a civilized nation.—He has constrained our fellow Citizens taken Captive on the high Seas to bear Arms against their Country, to become the executioners of their friends and Brethren, or to fall themselves by their Hands.— He has excited domestic insurrections amongst us, and has endeavoured to bring on the inhabitants of our frontiers, the merciless Indian Savages, whose known rule of warfare, is an undistinguished destruction of all ages, sexes and conditions. In every stage of these Opressions We have Petitioned for Redress in the most humble terms: Our repeated Petitions have been answered only by repeated injury. A Prince, whose character is thus marked by every act which may define a Tyrant, is unfit to be the ruler of a free people. Nor have We been wanting in attentions to our British brethren. We have warned them from time to time of attempts by their legislature to extend an unwarrantable jurisdiction over us. We have reminded them of the circumstances of our emigration and settlement here. We have appealed to their native justice and magnanimity, and we have conjured them by the ties of our common kindred to disavow these usurpations, which, would inevitably interrupt our connections and correspondence. They too have been deaf to the voice of justice and of consanguinity. We must, therefore, acquiesce in the necessity, which denounces [1] our Separation, and hold them, as we hold the rest of mankind, Enemies in War, in Peace Friends.

WE, THEREFORE, the Representatives of the UNITED STATES OF AMERICA, in General Congress Assembled, appealing to the Supreme Judge of the world for the rectitude of our intentions, do, in the Name and by Authority of the good People of these Colonies, solemnly publish and declare, that these United Colonies are, and of Right ought to be FREE AND INDEPENDENT STATES; that they are Absolved from all Allegiance to the British Crown, and that all political connection between them and the State of Great Britain, is and ought to be totally dissolved; and that as Free and Independent States, they have full Power to levy War, conclude Peace, contract Alliances, establish Commerce, and to do all other Acts and Things which Independent States may of right do.——And for the support of this Declaration, with a firm reliance on the protection of divine Providence, we mutually pledge to each other our Lives, our Fortunes and our sacred Honor.

Karl Shapiro

Karl Shapiro (b. 1913), poet, editor, and teacher, has been Librarian of Congress and is the winner of a Pulitzer prize. In this poem he paints a vivid picture showing the character of the early Puritans, who were influential in shaping early American life and whose legacy survives to some extent in our society even today.

THE PURITAN

In tender May when the sweet laugh
  of Christ
Sounds in the fields, and bitter sorrows die,
Death wanes and lovers kill and everything
Made perfect dances in the earth and sky,
Then near the Maypole where the children
  sing
A shadow falls, the hand and the hoarse cry
Of one whom winter more than well
  sufficed.

He is the Puritan under whose tall hat
Evil is nested like an ugly toad,
And in his eye he holds the basilisk,
And in his weathered hand the knotted
  goad;
Brimstone is on his tongue, for he will risk
Hellfire to pleasure; sin is his abode,
A barn and Bible his best habitat.

He dwells in evil; beauty of the day,
Or drifting snows of spring or flowers wet
Or touch of woman's hand are not for him;
The flesh of pleasure which he must forget
Walks in his sleep, awakens him more grim;
Deeper he falls into the Devil's debt,
And harder must he rant and harder pray.

Till every stone that manifests a pose
Beckons him lewdly, binds him to the stake
Where the cold fires of suspicion burn,
And he would gladly die for his name's sake
And call it righteous; tortures he would
  learn
To teach that flesh must sting and bones
  must ache
And hell claim all that happiness bestows.

His is the heresy of gloom, to all
That's grace a sin, to God a
  stumbling-block,
And to himself damnation. Year by year
He sees the hypocrisy of nature mock
His steadfastness, and in old age his fear
Of beauty strikes him dead, becomes a rock
Fixed like a gargoyle on a cathedral wall.

---

[1] Proclaims.

Henry David Thoreau

Henry David Thoreau (1817–1862), far more famous today than during his lifetime, believed in the primacy of the individual over established order, and in Civil Disobedience *he argues for the concept of passive resistance against unjust governments. Thoreau was uninterested in working for money, and involved himself instead with many social issues such as abolition, taxes, and the United States's war with Mexico. Mahatma Gandhi and Martin Luther King were among those influenced by his writings.*

CIVIL DISOBEDIENCE

I heartily accept the motto,—"That government is best which governs least;" and I should like to see it acted up to more rapidly and systematically. Carried out, it finally amounts to this, which also I believe,—"That government is best which governs not at all;" and when men are prepared for it, that will be the kind of government which they will have. Government is at best but an expedient; but most governments are usually, and all governments are sometimes, inexpedient. The objections which have been brought against a standing army, and they are many and weighty, and deserve to prevail, may also at last be brought against a standing government. The standing army is only an arm of the standing government. The government itself, which is only the mode which the people have chosen to execute their will, is equally liable to be abused and perverted before the people can act through it. Witness the present Mexican war, the work of comparatively a few individuals using the standing government as their tool; for, in the outset, the people would not have consented to this measure.

This American government,—what is it but a tradition, though a recent one, endeavoring to transmit itself unimpaired to posterity, but each instant losing some of its integrity? It has not the vitality and force of a single living man; for a single man can bend it to his will. It is a sort of wooden gun to the people themselves. But it is not the less necessary for this; for the people must have some complicated machinery or other, and hear its din, to satisfy that idea of government which they have. Governments show thus how successfully men can be imposed on, even impose on themselves, for their own advantage. It is excellent, we must all allow. Yet this government never of itself furthered any enterprise, but by the alacrity with which it got out of its way. *It* does not keep the country free. *It* does not settle the West. *It* does not educate. The character inherent in the American people has done all that has been accomplished; and it would have done somewhat more, if the government had not sometimes got in its way. For government is an expedient by which men would fain succeed in letting one another alone; and, as has been said, when it is most expedient, the governed are most let alone by it. Trade and commerce, if they were not made of india-rubber, would never manage to bounce over the obstacles which legislators are continually putting in their way; and, if one were to judge these men wholly by the effects of their actions and not partly by their intentions, they would deserve to be classed and punished with those mischievous persons who put obstructions on the railroads.

But, to speak practically and as a citizen, unlike those who call themselves no-government men, I ask for, not at once no government, but *at once* a better government. Let every man make known what kind of government would command his respect, and that will be one step toward obtaining it.

After all, the practical reason why, when the power is once in the hands of the people, a majority are permitted, and for a long period continue, to rule is not because they are most likely to be in the right, nor because this seems fairest to the minority, but because they are physically the strongest. But a government in which the majority rule in all cases cannot be based on justice, even as far as men understand it. Can there not be a government in which majorities do not virtually decide right and wrong, but conscience? —in which majorities decide only those questions to which the rule of expediency is applicable? Must the citizen ever for a moment, or in the least degree, resign his conscience to the legislator? Why has every man a conscience, then? I think that we should be men first, and subjects afterward. It is not desirable to cultivate a respect for the law, so much as for the right. The only obligation which I have a right to assume is to do at any time what I think right. It is truly enough said that a corporation has no conscience; but a corporation of conscientious men is a corporation *with* a conscience. Law never made men a whit more just; and, by means of their respect for it, even the well-disposed are daily made the agents of injustice. A common and natural result of an undue respect for law is, that you may see a file of soldiers, colonel, captain, corporal, privates, powder-monkeys and all, marching in admirable order over hill and dale to the wars, against their wills, ay, against their common sense and consciences, which makes it very steep marching indeed, and produces a palpitation of the heart. They have no doubt that it is damnable business in which they are concerned; they are all peaceably inclined. Now, what are they? Men at all? or small movable forts and magazines, at the service of some unscrupulous man in power? Visit the Navy-Yard, and behold a marine, such a man as an American government can make, or such as it can make a man with its black arts,—a mere shadow and reminiscence of humanity, a man laid out alive and standing, and already, as one may say, buried under arms with funeral accompaniments, though it may be,—

"Not a drum was heard, not a funeral
  note,
 As his corse to the rampart we
  hurried;
Not a soldier discharged his farewell
  shot

O'er the grave where our hero we
  buried."

The mass of men serve the state thus, not as men mainly, but as machines, with their bodies. They are the standing army, and the militia, jailers, constables, *posse comitatus,* etc. In most cases there is no free exercise whatever of the judgment or of the moral sense; but they put themselves on a level with wood and earth and stones; and wooden men can perhaps be manufactured that will serve the purpose as well. Such command no more respect than men of straw or a lump of dirt. They have the same sort of worth only as horses and dogs. Yet such as these even are commonly esteemed good citizens. Others—as most legislators, politicians, lawyers, ministers, and officeholders—serve the state chiefly with their heads, and, as they rarely make any moral distinctions, they are as likely to serve the devil, without *intending* it, as God. A very few,—as heroes, patriots, martyrs, reformers in the great sense and *men*—serve the state with their consciences also, and so necessarily resist it for the most part; and they are commonly treated as enemies by it. A wise man will only be useful as a man, and will not submit to be "clay," and "stop a hole to keep the wind away," but leave that office to his dust at least:—

"I am too high-born to be propertied,
 To be a secondary at control,
 Or useful serving-man and instrument
 To any sovereign state throughout the
  world."

He who gives himself entirely to his fellow-men appears to them useless and selfish; but he who gives himself partially to them is pronounced a benefactor and philanthropist.

How does it become a man to behave toward this American government to-day? I answer, that he cannot without disgrace be associated with it. I cannot for an instant recognize that political organization as *my* government which is the *slave's* government also.

All men recognize the right of revolution; that is, the right to refuse allegiance to, and to resist, the government, when its tyranny or its inefficiency are great and unendurable. But almost all say that such is not the case now. But such was the case, they think, in the Revolution of '75. If one were to tell me that this was a bad government because it taxed certain foreign commodities brought to its ports, it is most probable that I should not make an ado about it, for I can do without them. All machines have their friction; and possibly this does enough good to counterbalance the evil. At any rate, it is a great evil to make a stir about it. But when the friction comes to have its machine, and oppression and robbery are organized, I say, let us not have such a machine any longer. In other words, when a sixth of the population of a nation which has undertaken to be the refuge of liberty are slaves, and a whole country is unjustly overrun and conquered by a foreign army, and subject to military law, I think that it is not too soon for honest men to rebel and revolutionize. What makes this duty the more urgent is the fact that the country so overrun is not our own, but ours is the invading army.

Paley, a common authority with many on moral questions, in his chapter on the "Duty of Submission to Civil Government," resolves all civil obligation into expediency; and he proceeds to say "that so long as the interest of the whole society requires it, that is, so long as the established government cannot be resisted or changed without public inconveniency, it is the will of God . . . that the established government be obeyed, —and no longer. This principle being admitted, the justice of every particular case of resistance is reduced to a computation of the quantity of the danger and grievance on the one side, and of the probability and expense of redressing it on the other." Of this, he says, every man shall judge for himself. But Paley appears never to have contemplated those cases to which the rule of expediency does not apply, in which a people, as well as an individual, must do justice, cost what it may. If I have unjustly wrested a plank from a drowning man, I must restore it to him though I drown myself. This, according to Paley, would be inconvenient. But he that would save his life, in such a case, shall lose it. This people must cease to hold slaves, and to make war on Mexico, though it cost them their existence as a people.

In their practice, nations agree with Paley; but does any one think that Massachusetts does exactly what is right at the present crisis?

"A drab of state, a cloth-o'-silver slut,
    To have her train borne up, and her soul
        trail in the dirt."

Practically speaking, the opponents to a reform in Massachusetts are not a hundred thousand politicians at the South, but a hundred thousand merchants and farmers here, who are more interested in commerce and agriculture than they are in humanity, and are not prepared to do justice to the slave and to Mexico, *cost what it may.* I quarrel not with far-off foes, but with those who, near at home, coöperate with, and do the bidding of, those far away, and without whom the latter would be harmless. We are accustomed to say, that the mass of men are unprepared; but improvement is slow, because the few are not materially wiser or better than the many. It is not so important that many should be as good as you, as that there be some absolute goodness somewhere; for that will leaven the whole lump. There are thousands who are *in opinion* opposed to slavery and to the war, who yet in effect do nothing to put an end to them; who, esteeming themselves children of Washington and Franklin, sit down with their hands in their pockets, and say that they know not what to do, and do nothing; who even postpone the question of freedom to the question of free trade, and quietly read the prices-current along with the latest advices from Mexico, after dinner, and, it may be, fall asleep over them both. What is the price-current of an honest man and patriot to-day? They hesitate, and they regret, and sometimes they petition; but they do nothing in earnest and with effect. They will wait, well disposed, for others to remedy the evil, that they may no longer have it to regret. At most, they give only a cheap vote, and a feeble countenance and God-speed, to the right, as it goes by them. There are nine hundred and ninety-nine patrons of virtue to one virtuous man. But it is easier to deal with the real possessor of a thing than with the temporary guardian of it. . . .

It is not a man's duty, as a matter of course, to devote himself to the eradication of any, even the most enormous, wrong; he may still properly have other concerns to engage him; but it is his duty, at least, to wash his hands of it, and, if he gives it no thought longer, not to give it practically his support. If I devote myself to other pursuits and contemplations, I must first see, at least, that I do not pursue them sitting upon another man's shoulders. I must get off him first, that he may pursue his contemplations too. See what gross inconsistency is tolerated. I have heard some of my townsmen say, "I should like to have them order me out to help put down an insurrection of the slaves, or to march to Mexico;—see if I would go;" and yet these very men have each, directly by their allegiance, and so indirectly, at least, by their money, furnished a substitute. The soldier is applauded who refuses to serve in an unjust war by those who do not refuse to sustain the unjust government which makes the war; is applauded by those whose own act and authority he disregards and sets at naught; as if the state were penitent to that degree that it hired one to scourge it while it sinned, but not to that degree that it left off sinning for a moment. Thus, under the name of Order and Civil Government, we are all made at last to pay homage to and support our own meanness. After the first blush of sin comes its indifference; and

from immoral it becomes, as it were, *un*moral and not quite unnecessary to that life which we have made. . . .

Unjust laws exist: shall we be content to obey them, or shall we endeavor to amend them, and obey them until we have succeeded, or shall we transgress them at once? Men generally, under such a government as this, think that they ought to wait until they have persuaded the majority to alter them. They think that, if they should resist, the remedy would be worse than the evil. But it is the fault of the government itself that the remedy *is* worse than the evil. *It* makes it worse. Why is it not more apt to anticipate and provide for reform? Why does it not cherish its wise minority? Why does it cry and resist before it is hurt? Why does it not encourage its citizens to be on the alert to point out its faults, and *do* better than it would have them? Why does it always crucify Christ, and excommunicate Copernicus and Luther, and pronounce Washington and Franklin rebels?

One would think, that a deliberate and practical denial of its authority was the only offense never contemplated by government; else, why has it not assigned its definite, its suitable and proportionate penalty? If a man who has no property refuses but once to earn nine shillings for the State, he is put in prison for a period unlimited by any law that I know, and determined only by the discretion of those who placed him there; but if he should steal ninety times nine shillings from the State, he is soon permitted to go at large again.

If the injustice is part of the necessary friction of the machine of government, let it go, let it go: perchance it will wear smooth,—certainly the machine will wear out. If the injustice has a spring, or a pulley, or a rope, or a crank, exclusively for itself, then perhaps you may consider whether the remedy will not be worse than the evil; but if it is of such a nature that it requires you to be the agent of injustice to another, then, I say, break the law. Let your life be a counter friction to stop the machine. What I have to do is to see, at any rate, that I do not lend myself to the wrong which I condemn.

As for adopting the ways which the State has provided for remedying the evil, I know not of such ways. They take too much time, and a man's life will be gone. I have other affairs to attend to. I came into this world, not chiefly to make this a good place to live in, but to live in it, be it good or bad. A man has not everything to do, but something; and because he cannot do *everything,* it is not necessary that he should do *something* wrong. . . .

I do not hesitate to say, that those who call themselves Abolitionists should at once effectually withdraw their support, both in person and property, from the government of Massachusetts, and not wait till they constitute a majority of one, before they suffer the right to prevail through them. I think that it is enough if they have God on their side, without waiting for that other one. Moreover, any man more right than his neighbors constitutes a majority of one already.

I meet this American government, or its representative, the State government, directly, and face to face, once a year—no more—in the person of its tax-gatherer; this is the only mode in which a man situated as I am necessarily meets it; and it then says distinctly, Recognize me; and the simplest, the most effectual, and, in the present posture of affairs, the indispensablest mode of treating with it on this head, of expressing your little satisfaction with and love for it, is to deny it then. My civil neighbor, the tax-gatherer, is the very man I have to deal with,—for it is, after all, with men and not with parchment that I quarrel,—and he has voluntarily chosen to be an agent of the government. How shall he ever know well what he is and does as an officer of the government, or as a man, until he is obliged to consider whether he shall treat me, his neighbor, for whom he has respect, as a neighbor and well-disposed man, or as a maniac and disturber of the peace,

and see if he can get over this obstruction to his neighborliness without a ruder and more impetuous thought or speech corresponding with his action. I know this well, that if one thousand, if one hundred, if ten men whom I could name,—if ten *honest* men only,—ay, if *one* HONEST man, in this State of Massachusetts, CEASING TO HOLD SLAVES, were actually to withdraw from this copartnership, and be locked up in the county jail therefor, it would be the abolition of slavery in America. For it matters not how small the beginning may seem to be: what is once well done is done forever. But we love better to talk about it: that we say is our mission. Reform keeps many scores of newspapers in its service, but not one man. If my esteemed neighbor, the State's ambassador,[1] who will devote his days to the settlement of the question of human rights in the Council Chamber, instead of being threatened with the prisons of Carolina, were to sit down the prisoner of Massachusetts, that State which is so anxious to foist the sin of slavery upon her sister,—though at present she can discover only an act of inhospitality to be the ground of a quarrel with her,—the Legislature would not wholly waive the subject the following winter.

Under a government which imprisons any unjustly, the true place for a just man is also a prison. The proper place to-day, the only place which Massachusetts has provided for her freer and less desponding spirits, is in her prisons, to be put out and locked out of the State by her own act, as they have already put themselves out by their principles. It is there that the fugitive slave, and the Mexican prisoner on parole, and the Indian come to plead the wrongs of his race should find them; on that separate, but more free and honorable ground,

---

[1] Thoreau is referring to a Concord congressman, Samuel Hoar, who journeyed to South Carolina to test that state's laws prohibiting black Massachusetts seamen from entering their ports. Hoar was expelled from the state by the South Carolina legislature.

where the State places those who are not *with* her, but *against* her,—the only house in a slave State in which a free man can abide with honor. If any think that their influence would be lost there, and their voices no longer afflict the ear of the State, that they would not be as an enemy within its walls, they do not know by how much truth is stronger than error, nor how much more eloquently and effectively he can combat injustice who has experienced a little in his own person. Cast your whole vote, not a strip of paper merely, but your whole influence. A minority is powerless while it conforms to the majority; it is not even a minority then; but it is irresistible when it clogs by its whole weight. If the alternative is to keep all just men in prison, or give up war and slavery, the State will not hesitate which to choose. If a thousand men were not to pay their tax-bills this year, that would not be a violent and bloody measure, as it would be to pay them, and enable the State to commit violence and shed innocent blood. This is, in fact, the definition of a peaceable revolution, if any such is possible. If the tax-gatherer, or any other public officer, asks me, as one has done, "But what shall I do?" my answer is, "If you really wish to do anything, resign your office." When the subject has refused allegiance, and the officer has resigned his office, then the revolution is accomplished. But even suppose blood should flow. Is there not a sort of blood shed when the conscience is wounded? Through this wound a man's real manhood and immortality flow out, and he bleeds to an everlasting death. I see this blood flowing now. . . .

The authority of government, even such as I am willing to submit to,—for I will cheerfully obey those who know and can do better than I, and in many things even those who neither know nor can do so well, —is still an impure one; to be strictly just, it must have the sanction and consent of the governed. It can have no pure right over my person and property but what I concede to it. The progress from an absolute to a limited monarchy, from a limited monarchy to a democracy, is a progress toward a true respect for the individual. Even the Chinese philosopher was wise enough to regard the individual as the basis of the empire. Is a democracy, such as we know it, the last improvement possible in government? Is it not possible to take a step further towards recognizing and organizing the rights of man? There will never be a really free and enlightened State until the State comes to recognize the individual as a higher and independent power, from which all its own power and authority are derived, and treats him accordingly. I please myself with imagining a State at last which can afford to be just to all men, and to treat the individual with respect as a neighbor; which even would not think it inconsistent with its own repose if a few were to live aloof from it, not meddling with it, nor embraced by it, who fulfilled all the duties of neighbors and fellow-men. A State which bore this kind of fruit, and suffered it to drop off as fast as it ripened, would prepare the way for a still more perfect and glorious State, which also I have imagined, but not yet anywhere seen.

Walt Whitman

Walt Whitman (1819–1892) produced a highly original, distinctly American poetry in subject matter and form. Responding to Ralph Waldo Emerson's call for a truly American literature in "The American Scholar", Whitman rejected standard English verse forms and adopted a freer verse which allowed him to express the vitality of a new land. He celebrates the American spirit, progress, and the worth of the common man more enthusiastically than any other American poet. Whitman knew and loved both rural and urban landscapes, having grown up on Long Island and in Brook-

lyn. *Until he settled into journalism as a career in 1841, he was an office boy, printer, country school teacher, and author. During the Civil War, he served as a volunteer nurse and wrote vivid war poems, which later appeared in* Drum Taps *(1865).* Leaves of Grass, *which first appeared in 1855 but was added to and revised many times throughout the rest of Whitman's life, was his greatest work, and though controversial, was a critical success. Whitman's influence on modern poets like Carl Sandburg and Allen Ginsberg is considerable.*

FOR YOU O DEMOCRACY

COME, I will make the continent
  indissoluble,
I will make the most splendid race the sun
  ever shone upon,
I will make divine magnetic lands,
    With the love of comrades,
      With the life-long love of
        comrades.

I will plant companionship thick as trees
    along all the rivers of America, and
    along the shores of the great lakes, and
    all over the prairies,
I will make inseparable cities with their
    arms about each other's necks,
    By the love of comrades,
      By the manly love of comrades.

For you these from me, O Democracy, to
  serve you ma femme!
For you, for you I am trilling these songs.

From PASSAGE TO INDIA

1

SINGING my days,
Singing the great achievements of the
  present,
Singing the strong light works of engineers,
Our modern wonders, (the antique
  ponderous Seven outvied,)

In the Old World the east the Suez canal,
The New by its mighty railroad spann'd,
The seas inlaid with eloquent gentle wires;
Yet first to sound, and ever sound, the cry
  with thee O soul,
The Past! the Past! the Past!

The Past—the dark unfathom'd retrospect!
The teeming gulf—the sleepers and the
  shadows!
The past—the infinite greatness of the past!
For what is the present after all but a
  growth out of the past?

(As a projectile form'd, impell'd, passing a
    certain line, still keeps on,
So the present, utterly form'd, impell'd by
    the past.)

2

Passage O soul to India!
Eclaircise the myths Asiatic, the primitive
  fables.
Not you alone proud truths of the world,
Nor you alone ye facts of modern science,
But myths and fables of eld, Asia's, Africa's
  fables,
The far-darting beams of the spirit, the
  unloos'd dreams,
The deep diving bibles and legends,
The daring plots of the poets, the elder
  religions;
O you temples fairer than lilies pour'd over
  by the rising sun!
O you fables spurning the known, eluding
  the hold of the known, mounting to
  heaven!
You lofty and dazzling towers, pinnacled,
  red as roses, burnish'd with gold!
Towers of fables immortal fashion'd from
  mortal dreams!
You too I welcome and fully the same as
  the rest!
You too with joy I sing.

Passage to India!
Lo, soul, seest thou not God's purpose from
  the first?

The earth to be spann'd, connected by
network,
The races, neighbors, to marry and be
given in marriage,
The oceans to be cross'd, the distant
brought near,
The lands to be welded together.

A worship new I sing,
You captains, voyagers, explorers, yours,
You engineers, you architects, machinists,
yours,
You, not for trade or transportation only,
But in God's name, and for thy sake O soul.

3

Passage to India!
Lo soul for thee of tableaus twain,
I see in one the Suez canal initiated,
open'd,
I see the procession of steamships,
the Empress Eugenie's leading the van,
I mark from on deck the strange landscape,
the pure sky, the level sand in the
distance,
I pass swiftly the picturesque groups, the
workmen gather'd,
The gigantic dredging machines.
In one again, different, (yet thine, all thine,
O soul, the same,)
I see over my own continent the Pacific
railroad surmounting every barrier,
I see continual trains of cars winding along
the Platte carrying freight and
passengers,
I hear the locomotives rushing and roaring,
and the shrill steamwhistle,
I hear the echoes reverberate through the
grandest scenery in the world,
I cross the Laramie plains, I note the rocks
in grotesque shapes, the buttes,
I see the plentiful larkspur and wild onions,
the barren, colorless, sage-deserts,
I see in glimpses afar or towering immediately above me the great mountains,
I see the Wind river and the Wahsatch
mountains,
I see the Monument mountain and the

Eagle's Nest, I pass the Promontory,
I ascend the Nevadas,
I scan the noble Elk mountain and wind
around its base,
I see the Humboldt range, I thread the
valley and cross the river,
I see the clear waters of lake Tahoe, I see
forests of majestic pines,
Or crossing the great desert, the alkaline
plains, I behold enchanting mirages of
waters and meadows,
Marking through these and after all, in
duplicate slender lines,
Bridging the three or four thousand miles
of land travel,
Tying the Eastern to the Western sea,
The road between Europe and Asia.

(Ah Genoese thy dream! thy dream!
Centuries after thou art laid in thy grave,
The shore thou foundest verifies thy
dream.)

4

Passage to India!
Struggles of many a captain, tales of many
a sailor dead,
Over my mood stealing and spreading they
come,
Like clouds and cloudlets in the unreach'd
sky.

Along all history, down the slopes,
As a rivulet running, sinking now, and now
again to the surface rising,
A ceaseless thought, a varied train—lo, soul,
to thee, thy sight, they rise,
The plans, the voyages again,
the expeditions;

Again Vasco de Gama sails forth,
Again the knowledge gain'd, the mariner's
compass,
Lands found and nations born, thou born
America,
For purpose vast, man's long probation
fill'd,
Thou rondure of the world at last
accomplish'd.

Charles Kuralt

Charles Kuralt (b. 1934) is best known for his "On the Road" features on CBS tele-vision's Evening News, *for which he travels around America capturing the diversity, com-plexity, and humanity of the American char-acter. Both in his television essays and in this selection, he shows an optimistic belief in the strength of people and the vitality of the democratic ideal.*

SOMETHING'S HAPPENING OUT THERE

Shed a tear for the passing of the dream. America has become computerized, plastic, impersonal. Americans have grown guilty, isolated, rootless. We are so accustomed to hearing those things about ourselves that we've come to believe them. Well, I don't believe them any more! For the last five years, I've been wandering through the great cities and down the back roads of the United States and, much to my surprise, I've come to know a country that's as sturdy as a New England fishing boat and as lively as a Georgia fiddle tune. Her brooding "silent majority" is not silent at all; it is talking all the time—questioning, debating with neighbors over the back fence and clamoring for attention on the radio tele-phone-talk shows. Her "alienated" youth are, in fact, far more deeply involved in the raucous give and take of the democratic system than any other youthful generation in our history. Her "oppressed" minorities, who still carry the unfair burden of cen-turies of discrimination and neglect, have felt that burden lightening perceptibly; few black Americans, or Mexican-Ameri-cans, or Puerto Ricans will ·tell you they see anything but hope in the turbulent events of recent years.

Of course, I know America has perplex-ing, knotty problems. I haven't been travel-ing the country with my eyes closed. Along the way, I've heard the ignorant words of

racial abuse. I've seen the cities' slums and the migrant workers' shacks. I've seen the scattered, ugly signs of financial greed, the hillsides skinned by strip miners, the forests ravished by clean-cutters, the grotesque billboard alleys some of our roadways have become. And in some café beside a highway some mornings, I've read the calamitous headlines about skyjacking and heroin ad-diction and war in distant places. What saves me from despair is that, after read-ing about these aberrations in our national life, I fold the morning paper and step outside the café into our national life itself.

The country of the headlines, which seems so insane and homicidal, gives way to the real country, where there are many strengths the headline writers have no space to describe. I look in vain for all the dis-affected people, poisoned by the networks, radicalized by the universities and dealing in narcotics on the side. What I find in-stead, at every hand, are people whose lives are lived in satisfying peace with their neighbors, who treat wayfaring strangers with openhanded friendliness and who re-main stubbornly hopeful about their coun-try. Most of them believe in America's es-sential fairness, and most of them are far from indifferent to America's many wounds. Lately, increasingly, I've found them will-ing to take a part, themselves, in binding up those wounds. Eric Sevareid told me once that there is such a thing as a national conscience in the United States, and that it can be felt more profoundly here than anywhere else in the world. I didn't know quite what he meant until I started travel-ing. Faces come back to me in close-up, a few of the people I've met on the road.

I remember the roughhewn face of Andy Spirer, bent over a desk in the Pilottown, Louisiana, public school, teaching first grader Kevin Nelson how to make the letter "M." Andy Spirer went to college on the G.I. Bill expressly for the purpose of teach-ing in Pilottown, which didn't have a teacher. It did have three pupils, and I found Andy Spirer teaching them, gently, lovingly, in a one-room school in a town without roads, isolated at the mouth of the Mississippi. He explained, "Sure, I get lonely here, but it's worth it. I try to give each child every bit of knowledge I've learned in the book world, in the social world, in the physical world. They have to go up the river to high school when they get old enough. Part of my pride goes with them, see, so that makes it worthwhile."

Without Andy Spirer, where would we be? But don't look for his name on the front pages.

The serene, aristocratic face of Frieda Klussman pops into my memory. She is riding a cable car in San Francisco, admiring her city from her alfresco perch. When city officials tried to replace the cable cars with buses, it was Mrs. Klussman who marched out of her hilltop mansion, rolled up her sleeves, organized her friends and went to war. "You can put a hundred people on a cable car and you have a feeling of camaraderie among them," she told me. "You hear laughter. Put these same people on a bus, and everybody is grouchy and grumpy. We *had* to save the cable cars!"

There's a rockbound guarantee in the City Charter of San Francisco that cable cars will go on forever. Frieda Klussman got it there, though hardly anyone who rides the cable cars today has any way of knowing that.

Here is the face of Fred Robards, squinting toward the sun. He is at the helm of a U.S. Fish and Wildlife boat off the coast of southeastern Alaska, looking for eagles. In spite of the opposition of lumber interests and the occasional indifference of his own employer, the U.S. Government, Fred Robards has an incredible purpose: To find every single eagle in Alaska and mark every eagle nest for preservation. Otherwise, he knows, the bald eagle, symbol of the nation, will vanish. If Fred Robards had not taken on this job, it's likely nobody else would have, either. If you ever

doubt what one man can accomplish in a big government, think of him.

Unselfish couple

And here is the dark, intense face of Rumel Fuentes and the contrasting, smiling face of Jo Fuentes at work on the neighborhood center in Eagle Pass, Texas. He's a young Mexican-American. She is his wife, a girl from Ohio who had never seen a Mexican-American until she came to Eagle Pass as a Vista Volunteer. When I met them, Jo, a Catholic, was running the Planned Parenthood Center, because *somebody* had to run the Planned Parenthood Center. In the afternoons, she worked as secretary at the Methodist Church. Saturdays, she had the Girl Scout troop. Rumel Fuentes got up before dawn each morning to ride 60 miles to the nearest college. Monday, Wednesday and Friday nights, he was teaching American citizenship classes. Tuesday, Thursday and Saturday nights, he was teaching high school classes for dropouts. Sundays, the Fuenteses worked on the neighborhood center, which was their idea, and which the people in the community were paying for with money from the sale of tamales and old clothes. The Fuenteses thought that some things were wrong in Eagle Pass, and that they could live better elsewhere, but they planned to stay.

I'm persuaded that there are more such faces in America than there were even a few short years ago. Writer George Orwell, who predicted a nation of robots, marching to the tick of a Big Government metronome, reckoned without the little surprises of which the American spirit is capable. Orwell could not have known that 12 years before 1984, many of the best young law school graduates would take to hanging out their shingles on ghetto storefronts, or that the *cum laude* products would begin questioning potential employers about their attitude toward the environment before agreeing to go to work.

I have the advantage over those who foresee that Americans will soon become robots—the advantage of looking into their faces.

I remember the stubborn rancher's face of Lloyd Tillett, who went to court against the government to prevent the destruction of a herd of wild horses near his land in the desert and badland country of Wyoming— just because he liked the sight of mustangs running free.

Created a park

And the pretty, dirt-smudged face of Pat Baker, a young, white mother of three who was told there was no money to turn a vacant lot in a black neighborhood of Reno, Nevada, into a park. So she organized a breathtaking community effort to do exactly that, and in 48 hours of one remarkable weekend, a park—with basketball courts, paved paths, benches, green grass and trees—came true.

And the gentle face of Paul Crews, county agent in Suwannee County, Florida, who perceived that what the poorest black farmers in the region needed were breeding stock and advice, which the most prosperous white farmers could give. So he sat them all down to have barbecue, beans and cole slaw together and, getting to know one another, white and black farmers in Suwannee County found themselves beginning to care about one another.

I remember the strong, black face of Larry Brooks, whose burglary career sent him to prison, and who, when he got out on parole, decided on a new career—parole officer. "See," he said, "parole officers don't know enough about what's going on in the head of the parolee, all the things he's worried about, his family, and finding a job, staying out of trouble. See, I *know*." Parole officials agreed Larry Brooks was one of the best they'd ever seen, good enough that he'd be getting off parole pretty soon himself.

I remember the face of old Walter Misenheimer, who worked for years after he retired at the age of 70 to convert a wasted, grown-over woodlot beside his house in Virginia into an exquisite 13-acre garden, just so tourists passing by would have a place to stretch their legs and enjoy the beauty of dogwood and azaleas.

As these faces of ordinary Americans have accumulated in my experience, the strident axioms about "guilty," "conformist," "materialistic" Americans that I used to half-accept as true have come to seem wildly inapplicable to the observable America before me. And those stronger words, "Fascist," "criminal" and "repressive," which are used by the most bitterly critical writers of the underground press to describe the country, I can only understand as a view from Oz, where words had no meaning. After all, Oz was also underground.

National problems being solved

Out in the light of day, Americans no longer seem mesmerized by their national problems. Somewhere in the course of our recent history, very many of them have shrugged off the hesitancy and doubt which characterized the country's mood and regained their old, jaunty certainty that for every problem, there is a solution. They are, as often before, well ahead of their leaders; the impetus for ending the Vietnam war, for revising the tax structure, for clearing up the environment, did not originate in the White House or Congress but out there among the people.

In Tarentum, Pennsylvania, this year, I remarked on the beauty of the riverbanks, and discovered it is an organization of the town's kids who keep them that way. In Dayton, Ohio, the kids took over an old gasoline station and made it into a city-wide recycling center. In Marin County, California, the kids reclaimed a marsh from beer cans and garbage and turned it into a school nature-study project. Hardly a town in the country is without a similar example of sensitivity to "ecology"—even though the word was unknown to all but a handful of worried specialists a few years ago.

A woman who is one of Somerset, Wisconsin's, leading citizens revealed herself to me recently as an ardent ally of the women's liberation movement. "I got tired of sitting around the house," she said. "I just saw there were some things I could do, and I've been doing them. And since this spring, I've even been *talking* about it!"

I can remember very well a time when *nobody* talked about improving the status of women. Now, they're talking about it in little towns in Wisconsin.

No doubt, the present openness of the American mind—and mouth—owes much to the likes of Martin Luther King and Ralph Nader and Cesar Chavez, who, though largely unknown, spoke up against injustices in a quieter time. Now, the country is abuzz with the issues they raised, and many others, too—on the farm no less than on the campus.

This spirited debate about every national issue from busing to big business is a wonderful thing, I think, a renewal of what used to be called "patriotism"—concern for one's country. It was Jefferson who said, "Enlighten the people generally, and tyranny and oppression of body and mind will vanish like evil spirits at the dawn of day." Rest easy, Mr. Jefferson. The people generally are busy enlightening one another.

I know some people fear we are being destroyed by all this clamor. I am of the opposite view. We're being revitalized by it. America's weaknesses and contradictions are out in the open for the world to see. Americans themselves have been the first to see them. Wherever I have gone, I have found Americans hard at work on their resolution.

Those faces keep coming back to me. They are all right, those faces. They are unsullied by false superiority, or hostility toward other people or any selfish motive, and they are numberless in my memory. They give me reason to hope that our country is growing, not just in size and wealth, but in wisdom and humanity too.

Jack Newfield

Jack Newfield (b. 1939) was involved with Robert Kennedy's presidential campaign and has written widely on politics both in books and magazine articles. In this selection he proposes a contemporary democratic philosophy based on an updating of old-style populism.

A POPULIST MANIFESTO: THE MAKING OF A NEW MAJORITY

I think of myself as neither a liberal nor a member of the current New Left. I think of myself as a populist, part of a political tradition that stretches back from Dr. Martin Luther King and Ralph Nader to Estes Kefauver, to the early CIO, to the muckrakers, to "prairie avenger" William Jennings Bryan, to Susan Anthony and Thomas Jefferson. I think of myself as part of a political school based on two old and simple goals: the more equal distribution of wealth and income and the decentralization of power to ensure more citizen participation in making decisions.

I guess I have been working toward a populist stance at least since we made "participatory democracy" the central idea of the *Port Huron Statement,* the founding manifesto of Students for a Democratic Society, drafted in 1962. I continued to think of myself as a populist as I followed Robert Kennedy through the steel mills of Gary, Indiana, in 1968, and watched those tough Wallace voters transfer their trust to an earthy enemy of hunger and war. I felt the effort to save 69 homes in Corona was a pure populist cause—working-class Italians against Lindsay's experts, the notion of community participation pitted against an abstract conception of progress.

Consensus liberals, the "problem solvers" like Humphrey, Brooke, Javits, Muskie, Tunney, Stevenson, and Rockefeller, seem to me fatally flawed by their lack of nerve and will, by their lingering faith in centralized bureaucracy, by their complicity in the Vietnam holocaust and in the perpetuation of the cold-warrior mentality, by their lack of original ideas, and by their failure to make important headway on any problems when last in power. On issues like the withdrawal of troops from Europe, conspiracy laws, and tax reform, liberalism has become indistinguishable from Nixonian conservatism.

The New Politics constituency appears limited to the white middle class, excessively preoccupied by nuances of style and personality, and uninterested in working-class discontents. They suffer from issue nymphomania, racing from gay liberation one week to fighting over an unimportant district leadership on the West Side of Manhattan the next. They shirk the hard labor of doing coherent institutional and economic analysis without which they cannot get to the root of things.

The New Left, in its Weathermen, Panther and Yippie incarnations, seems anti-democratic, terroristic, dogmatic, stoned on rhetoric and badly disconnected from everyday reality.

Of all the political traditions of redemption available to us, populism seems best to synthesize the root need to redistribute wealth and the commitment to broaden democratic participation, a synthesis that could unite the poor and almost-poor with the young into a new majority for justice.

So the thesis of this essay is that America is ripe for a new urban populist politic that daily life for millions of white workingmen has become a pain, and that contrary to Kevin Phillips and Richard Scammon,

they are now open to anti-establishment alternatives to Wallace and Procaccino.

Since 1952, since Adlai Stevenson's time, the Democratic Party has slowly abandoned the needs of the white working class, the factory worker, the small farmer, the sanitationman, the millions who earn between $6,000 and $10,000 a year with their hands and suffer the boredom of drudgery.

With the honorable exception of Estes Kefauver, who broke his heart trying to teach his party the economic facts of life in the U.S., Democratic politicians aspiring to be President during the 1950s broke with the tradition of Roosevelt and Truman and stopped making bread-and-butter issues —jobs, housing, corporate price-fixing, tax evasion by the rich—the point of their politics. At the same time, academics like professors Daniel Bell and Seymour M. Lipset authored popular obituaries for radicalism. Everything important was solved, they announced, and predicted an optimistic future in which the only dispute would be over means, not ends.

Satisfaction bordering on smugness became the mood of the liberal, middle-class world. The writers and thinkers turned away from the old economic concerns of the 1930s to take up essentially sociological and cultural questions like affluence, suburbia, status anxiety and the role of art in a mass culture. The best-selling books of this period were Daniel Bell's *The End of Ideology,* Vance Packard's *The Status Seekers,* David Riesman's *The Lonely Crowd* and William H. Whyte's *The Organization Man.*

Then came the revival of insurgent politics during the 1960s. But the power-liberals, the Bundys and McNamaras and the Rostows and the Moynihans, made two large errors. First, accepting the end-of-ideology theory of the fifties, they tended to see social problems in terms of efficient management, rather than as a function of unequal wealth. A technocrat elite from Harvard and RAND were recruited to Camelot as the new "problem solvers." Vietnam is their monument.

The second blunder of the sixties, which I did not fully understand at the time, was the misconception of the domestic crisis as one of color and not of class. Instead of fashioning agencies and programs that helped everyone, black and white, programs like national health insurance, or a $2.50 minimum wage law, or income guarantees, or tax reform that benefited blue-collar families, or creating more jobs . . . instead, the liberals put their energies into marginal programs aimed at blacks and paid for by the middle class; programs like school busing, and civilian review boards, and something LBJ called "an unconditional war to abolish poverty."

But it turned out to be something less. It turned out to be a patronage hustle for sociologists and consultants and a few black political operators. And it did not touch, much less fundamentally change, the lives of the black underclass.

But it did help generate what we would come to call the backlash, because there were no OEO programs in Corona or Bay Ridge, no storefronts offering legal services in Youngstown, no big grants to save decaying white neighborhoods in Hoboken or South Boston.

I cannot recall either Johnson in 1964 or Humphrey in 1968 campaigning on any positive or original ideas that might excite the almost-poor workers, whose votes they took for granted. I can remember LBJ warning that Goldwater would drag us into a war in Asia, and Humphrey talking tough about crime and trying to please everyone on Vietnam. In 1970, the Democrats ran against Herbert Hoover, which was progress.

In contrast, George Wallace recently has been sounding like William Jennings Bryan as he attacks concentrated wealth in his speeches. "The present tax laws," he said in May, "were written to protect the Rockefellers, the Fords, the Carnegies, and the Mellons. The tax-exempt foundations these families have set up are unfair . . . the average workingman is tired of the Internal Revenue Service snooping in every item of his business."

The Kerner Commission Report in 1968 declared "white racism" was the heart of the matter. At the same time the banks and *Fortune* magazine's 500 leading corporations and the utilities and the insurance companies and the oil and pharmaceutical industries continued to make generous profits. But white workers were finding themselves unemployed, laid-off, powerless, worried about crime, unable to pay the hospital bills, unable to send their children to college, breathing poisoned air, working in unsafe and unhealthy conditions in mines, factories and construction sites, and furious about taxes and inflation.

From 1960 to 1968 liberal Democrats governed the country. But nothing basic got done to make life decisively better for the white workingman. When he bitched about street crime, he was called a Goldwaterite by liberals who felt secure in the suburbs behind high fences and expensive locks. When he complained about his daughter being bused, he was called a racist by liberals who could afford to send their own children to private schools. Meanwhile, the liberal elite repeated their little Polish jokes at Yale and on the Vineyard, and they cheered when Eugene McCarthy reminded them in Oregon that the educated people voted for him and the uneducated people voted for Robert Kennedy.

Liberal hypocrisy created a lot of Wallace votes in 1968.

The current economic system in America can fairly be described as socialism for the rich and capitalism for the poor.

There are ample funds for highways, farm subsidies ($10 billion last year), Albany Malls, World Trade Centers, and $80 billion each year for the Pentagon, which, in turn, takes care of the RAND Corporation and the General Dynamics Corporation. There are oil depletion allowances, untaxed Swiss bank accounts, federal regulatory agencies dominated by the corporations they are supposed to watch, and tax-free foundations. Over 300 Americans with income of more than $200,000 paid no income tax at all for 1970, according to Congressman Henry Reuss of Wisconsin. Governor Ronald Reagan paid not one cent in state tax last year, although he drew from the state $76,500 in salary and perquisites. This year the Congress voted $200 million in subsidies to shipbuilders, while it refused to appropriate $5 million to prevent and treat lead poisoning in slum children.

Meanwhile, the myth of affluence fostered in the fifties has been shattered. More than 25 million American citizens are living in poverty, according to the Department of Labor's own statistics, and estimates by Michael Harrington and others run as high as 40 million. In New York City alone, more than a million people today live on welfare. More than 60 per cent of white families in New York City earn less than $9,400 a year.

On May 7 of this year the Census Bureau reported that the number of poor people in the nation increased last year for the first time in a decade. Two-thirds of the total are white. Another 7 million white families earn between $5,000 and $7,000 a year, just above the welfare level. And this is before taxes.

(It must be noted, however, that while one in ten whites lived in poverty, one out of every three blacks was below the poverty line of $4,000 a year for a family of four.)

Another recent Census Bureau study showed that the purchasing power of the typical American family did not increase last year, for the first time in a decade.

These two indexes, coupled with the inexorable rise in unemployment, suggest to me that populism is again on the agenda of domestic politics.

(The Harris Poll of July 1, 1971, revealed that 62 per cent of white people held the view that "the rich get richer, and the poor get poorer.")

What might a modern populist movement sound like? What would be its analysis and its priorities? Let's look at a half-dozen issues, six critical domestic problems, and consider specific programs and remedies.

I. Redistribution of wealth and income

First some boring obligatory data. According to Gus Tyler's excellent paper "The White Worker," the bottom fifth of the nation's families in 1968 received 5.7 per cent of the country's income; the top fifth received 40.6 per cent.

This maldistribution has been getting worse, not better. In 1949, Tyler says, the richest 1 per cent of the nation owned 21 per cent of the wealth. In 1956, this rose to 26 per cent. Today the top 1 per cent own more than 37 per cent of all the wealth.

So the first plank in my populist platform would be a demand for radical restructuring of all our tax laws. Currently, the poor and the middle class pay a higher percentage of their income in taxes than do the richest 1 per cent of the population. This system not only perpetuates the inequities, but helps make the white middle class conservative, since they are in fact paying more than their fair share of the bill for welfare, open admissions and other programs they oppose.

The super-rich manage to get richer through many complex exemptions, loopholes, and privileges written into the existing tax laws—capital gains, unreported dividends and interest, expense account gimmicks, sacred cow tax shelters for churches and other institutions, depletion allowances and import quotas. Most giant oil companies pay less than 6 per cent in taxes on their billions in profits, thanks to depletion allowances.

The remedies seem self-evident. Close the loopholes, tax church and foundation property and incomes, end the oil and gas depletion allowance, greatly increase the taxes of the superrich on inheritances, property, estates, stock transfers, bank and insurance company assets. Concentrations of wealth should not be passed along from generation to generation, to people who have never had to work for their millions, but scream about putting the "welfare chiseler" to work.

Again, let me stress I am talking about ending the monopoly the rich have on socialism. The wealthiest citizens, the biggest foundations and the most monopolistic corporations must be made to pay their share. I am in favor of lowering taxes on the policeman from Queens, and the dock worker from Brooklyn, because only on fairness can we build a new majority for justice.

II. Control of the giant corporations

The biggest corporations have become too powerful, too rich, and are not accountable to anyone. General Motors' annual revenues last year, $18.8 billion, were larger than the budgets of 100 countries in the world. Chase Manhattan Bank has $25 billion in assets. Standard Oil has $19 billion in assets.

The giant corporations help write the tax laws, dominate the regulatory agencies that are supposed to be the independent eyes of the consumers, and they elect senators and make Presidents. Between 1960 and 1970, corporate profits, after taxes, increased by 88 per cent.

These same corporations manufacture unsafe cars that kill people. They also pollute the air and water with carbon monoxide, mercury, lead, and other contaminants. They fix prices, manipulate our appetites, deceive us in their advertisements, put poisonous chemical additives in our foods, ignore antitrust laws with constant mergers that eliminate competition, and continue to sell us badly made and overpriced products. "Crime in the suites," Ralph Nader calls it.

There are various ways to rectify this situation, some sounding conservative, some sounding radical.

First, I would ban all mergers by any of the 500 largest corporations, break up all existing oligopolies, and actually start putting corporate executives in jail whose companies break antitrust laws and pollute the environment.

Second, I would re-invigorate the federal regulatory agencies. I would make Robert Townsend chairman of the SEC, Nicholas Johnson chairman of the FCC, Bess Myerson chairman of the FDA, journalist James Ridgeway chairman of the Federal Trade Commission, and Ralph Nader chief of the Justice Department's antitrust division. I would appoint Richard Ottinger and Pete Hamill to the state Public Service Commission. I'd also create a separate court to try business crimes committed in regulated industries.

Third, a good dose of workers' control is needed to democratize decision-making and make sure profits aren't the only corporate value. The staff of *Le Monde* in France and *Der Spiegel* in Germany now have a voice in editorial policy, and it has made for better publications. Worker councils in Yugoslavia seem to be successful. The only way to stop coal miners from dying of the black lung, and textile workers from suffering brown lung, is to empower them to allocate a certain amount of profit for the protection of their own safety and health.

And last, I would draft legislation to compel all corporations with Defense Department contracts to set aside 25 per cent of all profits for reconversion planning. There is no reason why Republic and Grumman can't build housing. And no reason why aerospace and electronic workers should face unemployment if we finally end the endless war.

III. A constructive effort to reduce crime

The right wing has grown fat on this issue. Careers have been made by politicians who act like they are running for sheriff of Tombstone.

This has happened partly because the liberals and the radicals have abdicated. The New Left has no program to combat crime. Students call cops "pigs" while they holler racist at anyone who calls a Vietnamese a "dink" or a "slope."

The liberals ignored the very real problems of street crime. They called it a euphemism for racism, until crime became a menace in their own middle-class neighborhoods. Some ambitious liberal politicians behaved shamelessly, joining the mindless search for scapegoats. Hubert Humphrey came out against strict gun control legislation. So did Frank Church and Eugene McCarthy. Senator Tydings of Maryland introduced a preventive detention bill. Adlai Stevenson II named Thomas Foran, the enthusiastic prosecutor of the Chicago Eight, to be honorary chairman of his Senate campaign. John Tunney praised the FBI and damned permissiveness, pot, and pornography in dozens of campaign speeches in California last autumn. Ed Muskie and Birch Bayh voted for a probably unconstitutional and definitely repressive anti-riot law.

But violent street crime continued to increase in the absence of any constructive legislation. In most places all that was done about crime by those in power was to add more policemen to the force. Policemen, however, do not actually prevent crime, as the "job action" by New York City's police earlier this year helped demonstrate. All they can do, most of the time, is make arrests, after the fact, which in turn only swamp the already inadequate courts and prisons which are underfunded by the law-and-order yahoos and are ignored by the press and reformers.

So the first step I would take to effectively reduce crime (short of eliminating poverty and heroin addiction) would be to give prison reform absolute priority. Eighty per cent of all crimes are committed by recidivists—by men and women who have been arrested before. Jails and penitentiaries are the places where we might actually rehabilitate the individual criminal. But our entire "correction" system is based on the Puritan concept of punishment rather than on rehabilitation. New York City last year spent less than 1 per cent of its $840-million criminal justice budget on rehabilitation programs. Corrections Commissioner George McGrath *requested* less money for rehabilitation this year ($3.2 million) than he asked for last year ($3.5 million). His new budget sought $2,000 for libraries, and $200,000 for consultant fees.

Only through vocational training classes, job training and placement, psychiatric care, halfway houses, reading and writing classes, better probation, parole and work-release programs can we possibly prevent last year's mugger from becoming next week's murderer. We must stop treating criminals like garbage to be dumped as far away as possible, and then forgotten.

IV. Democratize the concentrations of power in the mass media

This is a classic populist issue, but, as with crime, the left has abandoned it. Vice President Agnew seized on a legitimate injustice and distorted it, yet his essential point is correct: a handful of rich, white individuals do control all the mass media's outlets.

Among daily newspapers today, 1,483 cities have monopoly ownerships, and only 64 have competing ownerships. Only New York, Washington and Boston have three competing dailies. All news is transmitted through national monopolies, the telephone and telegraph systems. There are two centralized news services, and three television networks. In 90 cities, a single monopoly owns both the daily paper and the local television station.

Agnew delivered his fiercest attack on the *Times* and the *Washington Post* in Montgomery, Alabama, where there is a newspaper monopoly which he did not mention. He did not mention that the Newhouse chain owns dailies in Mobile and Huntsville, a television station, an FM station and an AM station in Birmingham, and a CATV franchise in Anniston (and 22 other papers around the country). Nor did Agnew refer to the conservative publishing empires of Hearst and Annenberg, or to the conservative media complex owned by the *Chicago Tribune* that includes the *Daily News* and WPIX in New York. And he neglected to mention Robert Wells, the owner of seven newspapers and four television stations, whom the President has just appointed to the FCC.

The usual liberal criticisms of television tend to concern content rather than access or ownership: less violence, less censorship, better children's programming, more muckraking specials like "The Selling of the Pentagon," fewer reruns, and equal time provisions that help the Democrats, but not George Wallace or Tom Hayden.

A populist program to redeem television would be based on the concept that the airwaves are owned by the people, not the corporate broadcasters or the corporate sponsors, and certainly not the government in power at the moment. NBC is just a trustee of the airwaves, GM just a renter of time.

First, we must decentralize ownership by using the antitrust laws to break up the conglomerates that dominate the media. RCA, a major Defense Department contractor, owns NBC, and owns Random House, which owns Pantheon and Knopf. CBS owns Holt, Rinehart and Winston, Columbia Records, Creative Playthings (toys) and the Yankees. The Times Mirror Company owns the *Los Angeles Times,* World Pub-

lishing Co., New American Library, *The Dallas Times Herald, Newsday* and some CATV franchises.

Citizens must have greater access to television. One way to do this would be to provide a free hour of prime television time every week to any organization of, say, 10,000 people. This would mean that the Fortune Society, block associations, women's groups, the PBA, Health-Pac and community organizations could prepare their own programs.

Other possible reforms: provide federal subsidies for community newspapers; give cable television franchises to indigenous community and civic groups, instead of to conglomerates backed by Time Inc. and Howard Hughes, as Lindsay has done in Manhattan; provide an hour of free air time each week for viewers to rebut or attack programming; require all television stations to make available free and equal time to all candidates during the election season, and refuse to sell time to candidates; develop a television equivalent of WBAI— a nonprofit, listener-owned channel; and perhaps most importantly, give television licenses to local stations owned by blacks, Indians, Eskimos, Polish-Americans, etc., since there are none operating today.

In short, create diversity through competition in programming and broad citizen participation.

V. Establish a system of national health insurance

Only the very rich can buy satisfactory health care. The poor can't afford doctors, and every working class family knows that one serious illness can wipe out its savings.

New York City has a segregated two-class hospital system: private hospitals with modern technology and excellent care for the affluent, and dirty, rundown municipal hospitals for the poor.

Life should not be for sale. Medicaid and Medicare have failed to remedy the inequities. They don't help the almost-poor, and they have inflated doctor and hospital costs. The chief beneficiaries of these programs have been the big pharmaceutical companies, the insurance companies like Blue Cross, and the hospital-supply companies—the medical-industrial complex. Last year, despite the economic chaos, the drug industry spent $800 million on public relations and advertising and still showed a 10 per cent increase in profits.

The shortrun answer is one class of medical care under national health insurance. A Harris poll in April showed that more than 60 per cent of the country wants it. And national health insurance would most directly help those families who are employed but don't qualify for Medicaid and can't afford private insurance.

Ted Kennedy has introduced, with fifteen co-sponsors, the 1971 Health Security Act (S3 and H.R. 22). This legislation would provide comprehensive protection for every citizen, including unlimited hospitalization, surgery, preventive and ambulatory care, unlimited nursing home care, comprehensive dental care for all children under fifteen, and cover the cost of all prescription drugs. These benefits would be financed under Social Security, with the employee contributing 1 per cent out of his salary, and the employer and the federal government each paying 3 per cent. (Nixon's proposals in the field would just amount to a windfall for the insurance industry.)

Until Kennedy's bill is enacted, the poor will get sick, the sick will get poor, and the medical-industrial complex will continue to get rich.

VI. Curb the power of the utilities

Con Edison is a monopoly. In exchange for this special privilege the company provides its consumers with blackouts, brownouts, power cutbacks during the summer and pollution of the air and water. (Con Ed is responsible for 40 per cent of the sulphur dioxide we inhale.) It also provides rate increases, exaggerated bills, and shuts off service if you complain.

The New York Telephone Company is also a monopoly. For that special status the company gives consumers no dial tones, wrong numbers, busy signals for information operators, pay phones that don't function and don't return your dime, and exaggerated bills. It also demands cash deposits from poor people, cooperates with the FBI in illegal taps on private citizens, spends millions each year for newspaper ads and public relations, doesn't answer letters of complaint, and bills customers for wrong numbers. The only stockholder in the New York Telephone Company is AT&T, one of the biggest Vietnam war contractors. Last year, despite deteriorating local service, the telephone company paid AT&T $202.7 million in dividends. In February of this year the telephone company asked the PSC to approve a new 29 per cent rate increase.

The usual consumer tactics—writing letters to legislators, trying to reform the PSC, not paying bills—have been ineffective.

So the answer, then, is to go to the root of the problem and end their monopoly status.

The most realistic way to accomplish this would be to municipalize them. This is the way it works in Los Angeles, and their utility rates are about half of New York's. City ownership would also pinpoint accountability. The mayor would feel compelled to improve service because the voters would hold him responsible. With a private monopoly, there is no accountability or retribution for ineptness.

The programs suggested here are not meant as a fixed blueprint. They merely try to suggest redistribution of wealth and power as the pivot of social change.

These ideas will not prevail without considerable social conflict. Their implementation will not be guaranteed merely by electing a Good Guy to the White House in 1972. They can triumph only as part of a larger movement that transcends party and personality and doesn't wait for national elections to energize itself.

The purest avatars of the movement I am talking about are organizers like Ralph Nader, Cesar Chavez, Jesse Jackson and Saul Alinsky. But there are also politicians who have advocated populist programs in the last three years, and who have won elections; Governor Gilligan in Ohio; Senators like McGovern, Harris, Kennedy, Proxmire and Hughes; Congressmen like Wright Patman (when the Republicans are in power), Dellums, Abzug, Reuss, Badillo, Drinan and Conyers; municipal figures like Abrams and Kretchmer.

All I argue is that these ideas are politically feasible, and if translated into policy, they would help a majority of people live a more humane life. That is all politics can do.

William O. Douglas

William O. Douglas (b. 1898), the longest-sitting Supreme Court Justice in history, is known for his eccentric personality, liberal court opinions, and concern for the environment. He has written many books on his two favorite subjects, including Of Men and Mountains *(1950),* My Wilderness: The Pacific West *(1961), and* A Living Bill of Rights *(1961). Douglas dissented in the 5–4 decision of the Court declaring the DeFunis case "moot," or of doubtful legal point.*

Marco DeFunis, a white student, sought admission to the University of Washington Law School in 1971. Refused admission (though accepted by several other law schools), he sued for admission on the basis that less qualified black students had been accepted. The case thus was significant in that it brought up the issue of using preferential quotas to ameliorate past racial discrimination. The Court chose to declare the case moot because DeFunis was, in fact, about to graduate from the University of Washington Law School, having been admitted by decree of a lower court.

DISSENTING OPINION, DEFUNIS V. ODEGAARD (1974)

MR. JUSTICE DOUGLAS, dissenting.

I agree with MR. JUSTICE BRENNAN that this case is not moot, and because of the significance of the issues raised I think it is important to reach the merits.

The University of Washington Law School received 1601 applications for admission to its first-year class beginning in September 1971. There were spaces available for only about 150 students, but in order to enroll this number the school eventually offered admission to 275 applicants. All applicants were put into two groups, one of which was considered under the minority admissions program. Thirty-seven of those offered admission had indicated on an optional question on their application that their "dominant" ethnic origin was either Black, Chicano, American Indian, or Filipino, the four groups included in the minority admissions program. Answers to this optional question were apparently the sole basis upon which eligibility for the program was determined. Eighteen of these 37 actually enrolled in the law school.

In general, the admissions process proceeded as follows: An index called the Predicted First Year Average (Average) was calculated for each applicant on the basis of a formula combining the applicant's score on the Law School Admission Test (LSAT) and his grades in his last two years in college.[1] On the basis of its experience with

---

[1] The grades are calculated on a conventional 4.0 scale, and the LSAT is scored on a scale ranging from 200 to 800. A Writing Test given on the same day as the LSAT and administered with it is also included in the formula; it is scored on a scale of 20 to 80. The Admissions Committee combines these scores into the Predicted First Year Average by calculating the sum of 51.3, 3.4751 $\times$ the grade point average, .0159 $\times$ LSAT score, and .0456 $\times$ the Writing Test score. Single Appendix, at 24. For a brief discussion of the use of the LSAT in combination with undergraduate grades to predict law

the previous years' applications, the admissions committee, consisting of faculty, administration, and students, concluded that the most outstanding applicants were those with averages above 77; the highest average of any applicant was 81. Applicants with averages above 77 were considered as their applications arrived by random distribution of their files to the members of the committee who would read them and report their recommendations back to the committee. As a result of the first three committee meetings in February, March, and April 1971, 78 applicants from this group were admitted, although virtually no other applicants were offered admission this early.[2] By the final conclusion of the admissions process in August 1971, 147 applicants with averages above 77 had been admitted, including all applicants with averages above 78, and 93 of 105 applicants with averages between 77 and 78.

Also beginning early in the admissions process was the culling out of applicants with averages below 74.5. These were reviewed by the Chairman of the Admissions Committee, who had the authority to reject them summarily without further consideration by the rest of the Committee. A small number of these applications were saved by the Chairman for committee considera-

school success, see Winterbottom. Comments on "A Study of the Criteria for Legal Education and Admission to the Bar: An Article by Dr. Thomas M. Goolsby, Jr.," 21 J. of Legal Education 75 (1968).

2 The only other substantial group admitted at this point were 19 "military" applicants. These were students who had previously been admitted to the school but who had either been unable to come, or forced to leave during their tenure, because of the draft. They were given preferential treatment upon reapplication after completing their military obligation. Since neither party has raised any issue concerning this group of applicants, the remaining discussion of the admissions procedure will not discuss them. Four minority applicants were also admitted at this time, although none apparently had scores above 77. Single Appendix, at 31. Their admission was presumably pursuant to the procedure for minority applicants described below.

tion on the basis of information in the file indicating greater promise than suggested by the Average. Finally during the early months the Committee accumulated the applications of those with averages between 74.5 and 77 to be considered at a later time when most of the applications had been received and thus could be compared with one another. Since DeFunis' average was 76.23, he was in this middle group.

Beginning in their May meeting the Committee considered this middle group of applicants, whose folders had been randomly distributed to committee members for their recommendations to the Committee. Also considered at this time were remaining applicants with averages below 74.5 who had not been summarily rejected, and some of those with averages above 77 who had not been summarily admitted, but instead held for further consideration. Each committee member would consider the applications competitively, following rough guidelines as to the proportion who could be offered admission. After the Committee had extended offers of admission to somewhat over 200 applicants, a waiting list was constructed in the same fashion, and was divided into four groups ranked by the Committee's assessment of their applications. DeFunis was on this waiting list, but was ranked in the lowest quarter. He was ultimately told in August 1971 that there would be no room for him.

Applicants who had indicated on their application forms that they were either Black, Chicano, American Indian, or Filipino were treated differently in several respects. Whatever their averages, none were given to the Committee Chairman for consideration of summary rejection, nor were they distributed randomly among committee members for consideration along with the other applications. Instead all applications of Black students were assigned separately to two particular committee members: a first-year Black law student on the Committee and a professor on the Committee who had worked the previous summer in a special program for disadvantaged college students considering application to law school.[3] Applications from among the other three minority groups were assigned to an assistant dean who was on the Committee. The minority applications, while considered competitively with one another, were never directly compared to the remaining applications, either by the subcommittee or by the full committee. As in the admissions process generally, the Committee sought to find "within the minority category, those persons who we thought had the highest probability of succeeding in law school." [4] In reviewing the minority applications, the Committee attached less weight to the Predicted First Year Average "in making a total judgmental evaluation as to the relative ability of the particular applicant to succeed in law school." In its publicly distributed Guide to Applicants, the Committee explained that "[a]n applicant's

racial or ethnic background was considered as one factor in our general attempt to convert formal credentials into realistic predictions."

Thirty-seven minority applicants were admitted under this procedure. Of these, 36 had Predicted First Year Averages below DeFunis' 76.23, and 30 had averages below 74.5, and thus would ordinarily have been summarily rejected by the Chairman. There were also 48 non-minority applicants admitted who had Predicted First Year Averages below DeFunis. Twenty-three of these were returning veterans . . . and 25 others presumably admitted because of other factors in their applications making them attractive candidates despite their relatively low averages.

It is reasonable to conclude from the above facts that while other factors were considered by the Committee, and were on occasion crucial, the Predicted First Year Average was for most applicants a heavily weighted factor, and was at the extremes virtually dispositive. A different balance was apparently struck, however, with regard to the minority applicants. Indeed, at oral argument, the law school advised us that were the minority applicants considered under the same procedure as was generally used, none of those who eventually enrolled at the law school would have been admitted.

The educational policy choices confronting a University Admissions Committee are not ordinarily a subject for judicial oversight; clearly it is not for us but for the law school to decide which tests to employ, how heavily to weigh recommendations from professors or undergraduate grades, and what level of achievement on the chosen criteria are sufficient to demonstrate that the candidate is qualified for admission. What places this case in a special category is the fact that the school did not choose one set of criteria but two, and then determined which to apply to a given applicant on the basis of his race. The Committee adopted this policy in order to achieve "a

---

[3] This was a Council on Legal Education Opportunities (CLEO) program, federally funded by OEO, and sponsored by the American Bar Association, the Association of American Law Schools, the National Bar Association, and the Law School Admissions Council.

[4] The Guide to Applicants explained:

"We gauged the potential for outstanding performance in law school not only from the existence of high test scores and grade point averages, but also from careful analysis of recommendations, the quality of the work in difficult analytical seminars, courses, and writing programs, the academic standards of the school attended by the applicant, the applicant's graduate work (if any) and the nature of the applicant's employment (if any) since graduation.

"An applicant's ability to make significant contributions to law school classes and the community at large was assessed from such factors as his extracurricular and community activities, employment, and general background.

"We gave no preference to, but did not discriminate against, either Washington residents or women in making our determinations. An applicant's racial or ethnic background was considered as one factor in our general attempt to convert formal credentials into realistic predictions."

reasonable representation" of minority groups in the law school. Although it may be speculated that the Committee sought to rectify what it perceived to be cultural or racial biases in the Law School Admissions Test or in the candidates undergraduate records, the record in this case is devoid of any evidence of such bias, and the school has not sought to justify its procedures on this basis.

Although testifying that "[w]e do not have quota . . ." the law school dean explained that "[w]e want a reasonable representation. We will go down to reach if we can," without "taking people who are unqualified in an absolute sense. . . ." By "unqualified in the absolute sense" the Dean meant candidates who "have no reasonable probable likelihood of having a chance at succeeding in the study of law. . . ." But the Dean conceded that in "reaching," the school does take "some minority students who at least, viewed as a group, have a less such likelihood than the majority student group taken as a whole.". . .

It thus appears that by the Committee's own assessment, it admitted minority students who, by the tests given, seemed less qualified than some white students who were not accepted, in order to achieve a "reasonable representation.". . .

But by whatever techniques, the law school must make choices. Neither party has challenged the validity of the Predicted First Year Average employed here as an admissions tool, and therefore consideration of its possible deficiencies is not presented as an issue. The law school presented no evidence to show that adjustments in the process employed were used in order validly to compare applicants of different races; instead it chose to avoid making such comparisons. Finally, although the Committee did consider other information in the files of all applicants, the law school has made no effort to show that it was because of these additional factors that it admitted minority applicants who would otherwise have been rejected. To the contrary, the school appears to have conceded that by its own assessment —taking all factors into account—it admitted minority applicants who would have been rejected had they been white. We have no choice but to evaluate the law school's case as it has made.

The Equal Protection Clause did not enact a requirement that Law Schools employ as the sole criterion for admissions a formula based upon the LSAT and undergraduate grades, nor does it proscribe law schools from evaluating an applicant's prior achievements in light of the barriers that he had to overcome. A Black applicant who pulled himself out of the ghetto into a junior college may thereby demonstrate a level of motivation, perseverance and ability that would lead a fairminded admissions committee to conclude that he shows more promise for law study than the son of a rich alumnus who achieved better grades at Harvard. That applicant would not be offered admission because he is Black, but because as an individual he has shown he has the potential, while the Harvard man may have taken less advantage of the vastly superior opportunities offered him. Because of the weight of the prior handicaps, that Black applicant may not realize his full potential in the first year of law school, or even in the full three years, but in the long pull of a legal career his achievements may far outstrip those of his classmates whose earlier records appeared superior by conventional criteria. There is currently no test available to the admissions committee that can predict such possibilities with assurance, but the committee may nevertheless seek to gauge it as best as it can, and weigh this factor in its decisions. Such a policy would not be limited to Blacks, or Chicanos or Filipinos or American Indians, although undoubtedly groups such as these may in practice be the principal beneficiaries of it. But a poor Appalachian white, or a second generation Chinese in San Francisco, or some other American whose lineage is so diverse as to defy ethnic labels, may demonstrate similar potential and thus be accorded favorable consideration by the committee.

The difference between such a policy and the one presented by this case is that the committee would be making decisions on the basis of individual attributes, rather than according a preference solely on the basis of race. To be sure, the racial preference here was not absolute—the committee did not admit all applicants from the four favored groups. But it did accord all such applicants a preference by applying, to an extent not precisely ascertainable from the record, different standards by which to judge their applications, with the result that the committee admitted minority applicants who, in the school's own judgment, were less promising than other applicants who were rejected. Furthermore, it is apparent that because the admissions committee compared minority applicants only with one another, it was necessary to reserve some proportion of the class for them, even if at the outset a precise number of places were not set aside. That proportion, apparently 15 to 20%, was chosen because the school determined it to be "reasonable," although no explanation is provided as to how that number rather than some other was found appropriate. Without becoming embroiled in a semantic debate over whether this practice constitutes a "quota," it is clear that given the limitation on the total number of applicants who could be accepted, this policy did reduce the total number of places for which DeFunis could compete—solely on account of his race. Thus, as the Washington Supreme Court concluded, whatever label one wishes to apply to it, "the minority admissions program is certainly not benign with respect to nonminority students who are displaced by it." A finding that the state school employed a racial classification in selecting its students subjects it to the strictest scrutiny under the Equal Protection Clause. . . .

The key to the problem is consideration of such applications *in a racially neutral way*. Abolition of the LSAT test would be a start. The invention of substitute tests might be made to get a measure of an applicant's cultural background, perception, ability to analyze, and his or her relation to groups. They are highly subjective, but unlike the LSAT they are not concealed but in the open. A law school is not bound by any legal principle to admit students by mechanical criteria which are insensitive to the potential of such an applicant which may be realized in a more hospitable environment. It will be necessary under such an approach to put more effort into assessing each individual than is required when LSAT scores and undergraduate grades dominate the selection process. Interviews with the applicant and others who know him is a time-honored test. Some schools currently run summer programs in which potential students who likely would be bypassed under conventional admissions criteria are given the opportunity to try their hand at law courses, and certainly their performance in such programs could be weighed heavily. There is, moreover, no bar to considering an individual's prior achievements in light of the racial discrimination that barred his way, as a factor in attempting to assess his true potential for a successful legal career. Nor is there any bar to considering on an individual basis, rather than according to racial classifications, the likelihood that a particular candidate will more likely employ his legal skills to service communities that are not now adequately represented than will competing candidates. Not every student benefited by such an expanded admissions program would fall into one of the four racial groups involved here, but it is no drawback that other deserving applicants will also get an opportunity they would otherwise have been denied. Certainly such a program would substantially fulfill the law school's interest in giving a more diverse group access to the legal profession. Such a program might be less convenient administratively than simply sorting students by race, but we have never held administrative convenience to justify racial discrimination. . . .

The Equal Protection Clause commands the elimination of racial barriers, not their creation in order to satisfy our theory as to how society ought to be organized. The purpose of the University of Washington cannot be to produce Black lawyers for Blacks, Polish lawyers for Poles, Jewish lawyers for Jews, Irish lawyers for the Irish. It should be to produce good lawyers for Americans and not to place First Amendment barriers against anyone. That is the point at the heart of all our school desegregation cases, from *Brown* v. *Board of Education,* 347 U.S. 483, through *Swann* v. *Charlotte-Mecklenburg Board of Educ.,* 402 U.S. 1. A segregated admissions process creates suggestions of stigma and caste no less than a segregated classroom, and in the end it may produce that result despite its contrary intentions. One other assumption must be clearly disapproved, that Blacks or Browns cannot make it on their individual merit. That is a stamp of inferiority that a State is not permitted to place on any lawyer.

If discrimination based on race is constitutionally permissible when those who hold the reins can come up with "compelling" reasons to justify it, then constitutional guarantees acquire an accordionlike quality. Speech is closely brigaded with action when it triggers a fight, *Chaplinsky* v. *New Hampshire,* 315 U.S. 568, as shouting "fire" in a crowded theatre triggers a riot. It may well be that racial strains, racial susceptibility to certain diseases, racial sensitiveness to environmental conditions that other races do not experience may in an extreme situation justify differences in racial treatment that no fairminded person would call "invidious" discrimination. Mental ability is not in the category. All races can compete fairly at all professional levels. So far as race is concerned, any state sponsored preference to one race over another in that competition is in my view "invidious" and violative of the Equal Protection Clause.

The problem tendered by this case is important and crucial to the operation of our constitutional system; and educators must be given leeway. It may well be that a whole congeries of applicants in the marginal group defy known methods of selection. Conceivably, an admissions committee might conclude that a selection by lot of say the last 20 seats is the only fair solution. Courts are not educators; their expertise is limited; and our task ends with the inquiry whether, judged by the main purpose of the Equal Protection Clause—the protection against racial discrimination—there has been an "invidious" discrimination. . . .

I cannot conclude that the admissions procedure of the Law School of the University of Washington that excluded DeFunis is violative of the Equal Protection Clause of the Fourteenth Amendment. The judgment of the Washington Supreme Court should be vacated and the case remanded for a new trial.

Henry Steele Commager

Henry Steele Commager (b. 1902) has had a long and distinguished career as lecturer and professor of history at several colleges and as editor and writer of over twenty books. Among the most important of these are The Growth of the American Republic, *coedited with Samuel Eliot Morison in 1931 and still in print,* The American Mind (1950), *and* The American Character (1970). *This essay, published three days after Richard Nixon resigned the presidency, places that event in a broad historical context, enumerates the abuses of Nixon's presidential power, and shows a faith in the democratic process.*

THE CONSTITUTION IS ALIVE AND WELL

ASPEN, Colo.—We have had constitutional crises before but, except for the Civil War and Reconstruction, none that had the dimensions of those precipitated by Richard M. Nixon. Never before have we had a crisis that challenged the basic assumptions of our constitutional system itself, and the basic processes and mechanisms through which it worked.

Alexander Hamilton, though he supported the Constitution, thought it "a frail and worthless fabric" and had no confidence that it would endure. And no wonder. It was, after all, without precedent or model in history. Never before had a people made a national Constitution; never before had they fabricated a Federal system; never before had they elected a national head of state; never before had they fixed effective limits on government by such devices as a genuine separation of powers, and bills of substantive rights, that had the force of law.

Almost miraculously the system worked. The "frail and worthless fabric" proved to be both tough and enduring and, what is more astonishing, proved wonderfully resilient. Under its auspices the United States grew from thirteen to fifty states; under its auspices it weathered one crisis after another, and that without suspending any of its great provisions, without impairing the authority and dignity of the Presidency, the power of the Congress or the independence of the judiciary.

In 1861 the South challenged the Constitution, and set up on its own; then it honored the document by transforming it, with only minor changes, into a constitution for the Confederacy.

The Constitution survived the First World War, the crisis of the great Depression and the challenge of the welfare state, and the unprecedented strains of the Second World War.

One reason the Constitution survived intact was that no President had ever attempted to subvert it, no politicians—with the exception of Aaron Burr—have even threatened it.

Notwithstanding the absence of any tradition of loyalty to the new Government, the United States, even in infancy, did not have a Cromwell, nor, in maturity, a Hitler.

Here—for perhaps the first time in modern history—it was not necessary to call upon loyalty to a king to preserve the commonwealth.

As Tom Paine put it, "Where then is the King of America? Know that in America the Constitution is King."

Or as Thomas Jefferson wrote, after he and Hamilton had frustrated Burr's attempt to steal the election of 1800:

"The tough sides of our Argosy had been thoroughly tried. Her strength has stood the waves into which she was steered, with a view to sink her. We shall put her on her republican tack and she will show by the beauty of her motion, the skill of her builders."

For the first time since 1861, an Administration, Mr. Nixon's, called into question both the beauty of her motion and the skill of her builders. For what is it that has been at stake for the last two years—what but the integrity and the vitality of the Constitution itself and of the principles it is designed to secure—a more perfect union, justice, domestic tranquillity, and the blessings of liberty, and the rule of law.

Let us be more specific.

First. The principle of a government of laws and not of men, a principle so precious that the Founding Fathers wrote it into many of the state constitutions. By countenancing burglary, wiretapping, *agents provocateurs,* the use of the Federal Bureau of Investigation, Central Intelligence Agency and even the Internal Revenue Service to punish "enemies," by endorsing the Huston Plan for the creation of a police state, and by resort to secrecy, duplicity and deception in the operations of Government, Mr. Nixon sought to substitute his own fiat for the law.

Second. The principle, vindicated by the United States Supreme Court in the great case of *ex parte* Milligan: "the Constitution is a law for rulers and people, equality in war and in peace, and covers with the shield of its protection all classes of men at all times and under all circumstances. No doctrine involving more pernicious consequences was ever invented by the wit of man than that any of its great provisions can be suspended during any of the great exigencies of government."

By creating sham "exigencies" involving "national security," Mr. Nixon sought to justify the violation of constitutional guarantees of due process and of the fundamental rights of citizens, and of the welfare of society, and authorized withholding of evidence essential to justice—in effect suspending vital provisions of the Constitution.

Third. The principle of the separation of powers, a principle established first by Americans as the most effective method of holding each branch of government within the framework of the Constitution.

By usurping Congressional power to declare war, making war on neutral Cambodia and concealing that war from the Congress and the American people; by shrouding much of the conduct of foreign affairs in a fog of secrecy, denying to the Congress information essential to the faithful performance of its constitutional duties; and by nullifying Congressional power over appropriations through the device of impounding funds duly voted by the Congress, Mr. Nixon undermined the integrity of this great principle.

Fourth. The principles of freedom and justice in the Bill of Rights. By attempting to impose, for the first time in our history, prior censorship of the press, by threatening hostile television stations with deprivation of their licenses, by directing the arrest without warrants of some 12,000 men and women gathered in the capital city to exercise their constitutional rights of assembly and petition, by flouting the constitutional prohibition against unreasonable search and seizure and the requirement of search warrants, by ignoring the provisions for due process of law in the endorsement of the Huston Plan and in the illegal use of the Central Intelligence Agency in domestic affairs, Mr. Nixon presented the most dangerous threat to the Bill of Rights in the whole of our history.

Fifth. The integrity and survival of democratic government in the United States.

By corrupting Presidential elections through the solicitation of illegal contributions, by a systematic campaign of mendacity, trickery and character assassination against opponents, by violating the integrity of the civil service and corrupting his closest subordinates, Mr. Nixon gravely endangered the integrity of our republican system of government.

Mr. Nixon's resignation is no voluntary act. It was not inspired by contrition or by a belated loyalty to the Constitution. It was forced on him by a ground swell of public outrage, by a popular ralliance to the Constitution comparable to that which swept the North at the time of Fort Sumter, and by a Congress that after long vacillation finally responded to the standards of duty and the obligations of the Constitution.

The long-drawn-out process of inquiry by committee, by the courts, by the Congress is a stunning vindication of our constitutional system, a vindication of the principle of separation of powers, of the independence of the courts and of the foresight of the framers.

The men who made our Constitution were familiar with the history of executive tyranny. They were steeped in the history of the ancient world and knew well the story of usurpation of power, revolution and assassination in the city-states of Greece and in Rome.

They knew, too, the tragic history of England and the fate of a Richard II, a Mary Queen of Scots and a Charles I; they had themselves just fought a war against what they thought to be the tyranny of George III. They were determined to write a new page in history, and did. They accepted the necessity of change in government and in leadership. They invented the great institution of the constitutional convention—a legal way to alter and abolish government and institute new government.

They took over the English practice of impeachment, applied it to their highest office, providing a legal and peaceful method of removing the President himself from office.

Thus, in the words of Alexander Hamilton, they "substituted the mild magistracy of the law for the terrible weapon of the sword."

Confronted, for the first time in our long history, with a chief magistrate who betrayed his oath of office, we have resorted to that "magistracy of the law" and vindicated once again the wisdom of the Founding Fathers. Thus, we have demonstrated to the world and, let us hope, to future generations that the Constitution is alive and well, that it can be adapted to the exigencies of governance, and that in an emergency an enlightened and determined democracy can protect and defend its principles, its honor, and its heritage.

When, on Sept. 17, 1787, members of the Federal Convention came forward to sign the Constitution that they had drafted during those long hot months in Philadelphia, the venerable Dr. Franklin arose and "looking toward the president's chair, at the back of which a rising sun happened to be painted, observed that painters had found it difficult to distinguish in their art between a rising and a setting sun. 'I have often and often,' said he, 'in the course of the session and the vicissitudes of my hopes and fears as to its issue looked at that behind the presidency, without being able to tell whether it was rising or setting. Now at length I have the happiness to know that it is a rising and not a setting sun.' "

THE MINORITY EXPERIENCE

Sitting Bull and W. F. Cody. Denver Public Library, Western History Department, photo by D. F. Barry.

Frederick Douglass

Frederick Douglass (1818–1895) was born into slavery in Maryland and experienced the incidents described here when he was sixteen years old. At twenty-one, he escaped to New York City, and by twenty-four he began his very active career of speaking, writing, and journal and newspaper editing. In this selection not only does he show the harshness of slavery, but he also makes significant insights into the psychology of slaveholders.

A SLAVE'S LIFE *

I left Master Thomas's house, and went to live with Mr. Covey, on the 1st of January, 1833. I was now, for the first time in my life, a field hand. In my new employment, I found myself even more awkward than a country boy appeared to be in a large city. I had been at my new home but one week before Mr. Covey gave me a very severe whipping, cutting my back, causing the blood to run, and raising ridges on my flesh as large as my little finger. The details of this affair are as follows: Mr. Covey sent me, very early in the morning of one of our coldest days in the month of January, to the woods, to get a load of wood. He gave me a team of unbroken oxen. He told me which was the in-hand ox, and which the off-hand one. He then tied the end of a large rope around the horns of the in-hand ox, and gave me the other end of it, and told me, if the oxen started to run, that I must hold on upon the rope. I had never driven oxen before,

* Editor's title.

and of course I was very awkward. I, however, succeeded in getting to the edge of the woods with little difficulty; but I had got a very few rods into the woods, when the oxen took fright, and started full tilt, carrying the cart against trees, and over stumps, in the most frightful manner. I expected every moment that my brains would be dashed out against the trees. After running thus for a considerable distance, they finally upset the cart, dashing it with great force against a tree, and threw themselves into a dense thicket. How I escaped death, I do not know. There I was, entirely alone, in a thick wood, in a place new to me. My cart was upset and shattered, my oxen were entangled among the young trees, and there was none to help me. After a long spell of effort, I succeeded in getting my cart righted, my oxen disentangled, and again yoked to the cart, I now proceeded with my team to the place where I had, the day before, been chopping wood, and loaded my cart pretty heavily, thinking in this way to tame my oxen. I then proceeded on my way home. I had now consumed one half of the day. I got out of the woods safely, and now felt out of danger. I stopped my oxen to open the woods gate; and just as I did so, before I could get hold of my ox-rope, the oxen again started, rushed through the gate, catching it between the wheel and the body of the cart, tearing it to pieces, and coming within a few inches of crushing me against the gate-post. Thus twice, in one short day, I escaped death by the merest chance. On my return, I told Mr. Covey what had happened, and how it happened. He ordered me to return to the woods again immediately. I did so, and he followed on after me. Just as I got into the woods, he came up and told me to stop my cart, and that he would teach me how to trifle away my time, and break gates. He then went to a large gum-tree, and with his axe cut three large switches, and, after trimming them up neatly with his pocket-knife, he ordered me to take off my clothes. I made him no answer, but stood with my clothes on. He repeated his order. I still made him no answer, nor did I move to strip myself. Upon this he rushed at me with the fierceness of a tiger, tore off my clothes, and lashed me till he had worn out his switches, cutting me so savagely as to leave the marks visible for a long time. This whipping was the first of a number just like it, and for similar offenses.

I lived with Mr. Covey one year. During the first six months, of that year, scarce a week passed without his whipping me. I was seldom free from a sore back. My awkwardness was almost always his excuse for whipping me. We were worked fully up to the point of endurance. Long before day we were up, our horses fed, and by the first approach of day we were off to the field with our hoes and ploughing teams. Mr. Covey gave us enough to eat, but scarce time to eat it. We were often less than five minutes taking our meals. We were often in the field from the first approach of day till its last lingering ray had left us; and at saving-fodder time, midnight often caught us in the field binding blades.

Covey would be out with us. The way he used to stand it, was this. He would spend the most of his afternoons in bed. He would then come out fresh in the evening, ready to urge us on with his words, example, and frequently with the whip. Mr. Covey was one of the few slaveholders who could and did work with his hands. He was a hard-working man. He knew by himself just what a man or a body could do. There was no deceiving him. His work went on in his absence almost as well as in his presence; and he had the faculty of making us feel that he was ever present with us. This he did by surprising us. He seldom approached the spot where we were at work openly, if he could do it secretly. He always aimed at taking us by surprise. Such was his cunning, that we used to call him, among ourselves, "the snake." When we were at work in the cornfield, he would sometimes crawl on his hands and knees to avoid detection, and all at once he would rise nearly in our midst, and scream out, "Ha, ha! Come, come! Dash on, dash on!" This being his mode of attack, it was never safe to stop a single minute. His comings were like a thief in the night. He appeared to us as being ever at hand. He was under every tree, behind every stump, in every bush, and at every window, on the plantation. He would sometimes mount his horse, as if bound to St. Michael's, a distance of seven miles, and in half an hour afterwards you would see him coiled up in the corner of the wood-fence, watching every motion of the slaves. He would, for this purpose, leave his horse tied up in the woods. Again, he would sometimes walk up to us, and give us orders as though he was upon the point of starting on a long journey, turn his back upon us, and make as though he was going to the house to get ready; and, before he would get half way thither, he would turn short and crawl into a fence-corner, or behind some tree, and there watch us till the going down of the sun.

Mr. Covey's *forte* consisted in his power to deceive. His life was devoted to planning and perpetrating the grossest deceptions. Every thing he possessed in the shape of learning or religion, he made conform to his disposition to deceive. He seemed to think himself equal to deceiving the Almighty. He would make a short prayer in the morning, and a long prayer at night; and, strange as it may seem, few men would at times appear more devotional than he. The exercises of his family devotions were always commenced with singing; and, as he was a very poor singer himself, the duty of raising the hymn generally came upon me.

He would read his hymn, and nod at me to commence. I would at times do so; at others, I would not. My noncompliance would almost always produce much confusion. To show himself independent of me, he would start and stagger through with his hymn in the most discordant manner. In this state of mind, he prayed with more than ordinary spirit. Poor man! such was his disposition, and success at deceiving, I do verily believe that he sometimes deceived himself into the solemn belief, that he was a sincere worshipper of the most high God; and this, too, at a time when he may be said to have been guilty of compelling his woman slave to commit the sin of adultery. The facts in the case are these: Mr. Covey was a poor man; he was just commencing in life; he was only able to buy one slave; and, shocking as is the fact, he bought her, as he said, for *a breeder*. This woman was named Caroline. Mr. Covey bought her from Mr. Thomas Lowe, about six miles from St. Michael's. She was a large, able-bodied woman, about twenty years old. She had already given birth to one child, which proved her to be just what he wanted. After buying her, he hired a married man of Mr. Samuel Harrison, to live with him one year; and him he used to fasten up with her every night! The result was, that, at the end of the year, the miserable woman gave birth to twins. At this result Mr. Covey seemed to be highly pleased, both with the man and the wretched woman. Such was his joy, and that of his wife, that nothing they could do for Caroline during her confinement was too good, or too hard, to be done. The children were regarded as being quite an addition to his wealth.

If at any one time of my life more than another, I was made to drink the bitterest dregs of slavery, that time was during the first six months of my stay with Mr. Covey. We were worked in all weathers. It was never too hot or too cold; it could never rain, blow, hail, or snow, too hard for us to work in the field. Work, work, work, was scarcely more the order of the day than of the night. The longest days were too short for him and the shortest nights too long for him. I was somewhat unmanageable when I first went there, but a few months of this discipline tamed me. Mr. Covey succeeded in breaking me. I was broken in body, soul, and spirit. My natural elasticity was crushed, my intellect languished, the disposition to read departed, the cheerful spark that lingered about my eye died; the dark night of slavery closed in upon me; and behold a man transformed into a brute!

Sunday was my only leisure time. I spent this in a sort of beast-like stupor, between sleep and wake, under some large tree. At times I would rise up, a flash of energetic freedom would dart through my soul, accompanied with a faint beam of hope, that flickered for a moment, and then vanished. I sank down again, mourning over my wretched condition. I was sometimes prompted to take my life, and that of Covey, but was prevented by a combination of hope and fear. My sufferings on this plantation seem now like a dream rather than a stern reality. . . .

My term of actual service to Mr. Edward Covey ended on Christmas day, 1833. The days between Christmas and New Year's day are allowed as holidays; and, accordingly, we were not required to perform any labor, more than to feed and take care of the stock. This time we regarded as our own, by the grace of our masters; and we therefore used or abused it nearly as we pleased. Those of us who had families at a distance, were generally allowed to spend the whole six days in their society. This time, however, was spent in various ways. The staid, sober, thinking and industrious ones of our number would employ themselves in making corn-brooms, mats, horse-collars, and baskets; and another class of us would spend the time in hunting opossums, hares, and coons. But by far the larger part engaged in such sports and merriments as playing ball, wrestling, running foot-races, fiddling, dancing, and drinking whisky; and this latter mode of spending the time was by far the most agreeable to the feelings of our masters. A slave who would work during the holidays was considered by our masters as scarcely deserving them. He was regarded as one who rejected the favor of his master. It was deemed a disgrace not to get drunk at Christmas; and he was regarded as lazy indeed, who had not provided himself with the necessary means, during the year, to get whisky enough to last him through Christmas.

From what I know of the effect of these holidays upon the slave, I believe them to be among the most effective means in the hands of the slaveholder in keeping down the spirit of insurrection. Were the slaveholders at once to abandon this practice, I have not the slightest doubt it would lead to an immediate insurrection among the slaves. These holidays serve as conductors, or safety-valves, to carry off the rebellious spirit of enslaved humanity. But for these, the slave would be forced up to the wildest desperation; and woe betide the slaveholder, the day he ventures to remove or hinder the operation of those conductors! I warn him that, in such an event, a spirit will go forth in their midst, more to be dreaded than the most appalling earthquake.

The holidays are part and parcel of the gross fraud, wrong, and inhumanity of slavery. They are professedly a custom established by the benevolence of the slaveholders; but I undertake to say, it is the result of selfishness, and one of the grossest frauds committed upon the down-trodden slave. They do not give the slaves this time because they would not like to have their work during its continuance, but because they know it would be unsafe to deprive them of it. This will be seen by the fact, that the slaveholders like to have their slaves spend those days just in such a manner as to make them as glad of their ending as of their beginning. Their object seems to be, to disgust their slaves with freedom,

by plunging them into the lowest depths of dissipation. For instance, the slaveholders not only like to see the slave drink of his own accord, but will adopt various plans to make him drunk. One plan is, to make bets on their slaves, as to who can drink the most whisky without getting drunk; and in this way they succeed in getting whole multitudes to drink to excess. Thus, when the slave asks for virtuous freedom, the cunning slaveholder, knowing his ignorance, cheats him with a dose of vicious dissipation, artfully labelled with the name of liberty. The most of us used to drink it down, and the result was just what might be supposed: many of us were led to think that there was little to choose between liberty and slavery. We felt, and very properly too, that we had almost as well be slaves to man as to rum. So, when the holidays ended, we staggered up from the filth of our wallowing, took a long breath, and marched to the field,—feeling, upon the whole, rather glad to go, from what our master had deceived us into a belief was freedom, back to the arms of slavery.

I have said that this mode of treatment is a part of the whole system of fraud and inhumanity of slavery. It is so. The mode here adopted to disgust the slave with freedom, by allowing him to see only the abuse of it, is carried out in other things. For instance, a slave loves molasses; he steals some. His master, in many cases, goes off to town, and buys a large quantity; he returns, takes his whip, and commands the slave to eat the molasses, until the poor fellow is made sick at the very mention of it. The same mode is sometimes adopted to make the slaves refrain from asking for more food than their regular allowance. A slave runs through his allowance, and applies for more. His master is enraged at him; but, not willing to send him off without food, gives him more than is necessary, and compels him to eat it within a given time. Then, if he complains that he cannot eat it, he is said to be satisfied neither full nor fasting, and is whipped for being hard to please! I have an abundance of such illustrations of the same principle, drawn from my own observation, but think the cases I have cited sufficient. The practice is a very common one.

On the first of January, 1834, I left Mr. Covey, and went to live with Mr. William Freeland, who lived about three miles from St. Michael's. I soon found Mr. Freeland a very different man from Mr. Covey. Though not rich, he was what would be called an educated southern gentleman. Mr. Covey, as I have shown, was a well-trained negro-breaker and slavedriver. The former (slaveholder though he was) seemed to possess some regard for honor, some reverence for justice, and some respect for humanity. The latter seemed totally insensible to all such sentiments. Mr. Freeland had many of the faults peculiar to slave-holders, such as being very passionate and fretful; but I must do him the justice to say, that he was exceedingly free from those degrading vices to which Mr. Covey was constantly addicted. The one was open and frank, and we always knew where to find him. The other was a most artful deceiver, and could be understood only by such as were skillful enough to detect his cunningly-devised frauds. Another advantage I gained in my new master was, he made no pretensions to, or profession of, religion; and this, in my opinion, was truly a great advantage. I assert most unhesitatingly, that the religion of the south is a mere covering for the most horrid crimes,—a justifier of the most appalling barbarity,—a sanctifier of the most hateful frauds,—and a dark shelter under, which the darkest, foulest, grossest, and most infernal deeds of slaveholders find the strongest protection. Were I to be again reduced to the chains of slavery, next to that enslavement, I should regard being the slave of a religious master the greatest calamity that could befall me. For of all slaveholders with whom I have ever met, religious slaveholders are the worst. I have ever found them the meanest and basest, the most cruel and cowardly, of all others. It was my unhappy lot not only to belong to a religious slave-holder, but to live in a community of such religionists. Very near Mr. Freeland lived the Rev. Daniel Weeden, and in the same neighborhood lived the Rev. Rigby Hopkins. These were members and ministers in the Reformed Methodist Church. Mr. Weeden owned, among others, a woman slave, whose name I have forgotten. This woman's back, for weeks, was kept literally raw, made so by the lash of this merciless, *religious* wretch. He used to hire hands. His maxim was, Behave well or behave ill, it is the duty of a master occasionally to whip a slave, to remind him of his master's authority. Such was his theory, and such his practice.

Mr. Hopkins was even worse than Mr. Weeden. His chief boast was his ability to manage slaves. The peculiar feature of his government was that of whipping slaves in advance of deserving it. He always managed to have one or more of his slaves to whip every Monday morning. He did this to alarm their fears, and strike terror into those who escaped. His plan was to whip for the smallest offenses, to prevent the commission of large ones. . . . And yet there was not a man any where round, who made higher professions of religion, or was more active in revivals,—more attentive to the class, love-feast, prayer and preaching meetings, or more devotional in his family, —that prayed earlier, later, louder, and longer,—than this same reverend slave-driver, Rigby Hopkins.

Ralph Ellison

Ralph Ellison (b. 1914), novelist and teacher, originally wrote the following as a short story, later incorporating it into his novel Invisible Man *as the first chapter. The narrator, who throughout the book has no name, traces the course of his life from his youth in the South to his adulthood in Harlem, powerfully describing the many forms of racism and hostility he encounters along the way. By the end of the book he has matured into a new consciousness which will permit him to establish a more positive relationship with whites. This chapter, however, vividly captures the nightmare of black-white relations as experienced by a sensitive black adolescent.*

BATTLE ROYAL

It goes a long way back, some twenty years. All my life I had been looking for something, and everywhere I turned someone tried to tell me what it was. I accepted their answers too, though they were often in contradiction and even self-contradictory. I was naïve. I was looking for myself and asking everyone except myself questions which I, and only I, could answer. It took me a long time and much painful boomeranging of my expectations to achieve a realization everyone else appears to have been born with: That I am nobody but myself. But first I had to discover that I am an invisible man!

And yet I am no freak of nature, nor of history. I was in the cards, other things having been equal (or unequal) eighty-five years ago. I am not ashamed of my grandparents for having been slaves. I am only ashamed of myself for having at one time been ashamed. About eighty-five years ago they were told that they were free, united with others of our country in everything pertaining to the common good, and, in everything social, separate like the fingers of the hand. And they believed it. They exulted in it. They stayed in their place, worked hard, and brought up my father to do the same. But my grandfather is the one. He was an odd old guy, my grandfather, and I am told I take after him. It was he who caused the trouble. On his deathbed he called my father to him and said, "Son, after I'm gone I want you to keep up the good fight. I never told you, but our life is a war and I have been a traitor all my born days, a spy in the enemy's country ever since I give up my gun back in the Reconstruction. Live with your head in the lion's mouth. I want you to overcome 'em with yeses, undermine 'em with grins, agree 'em to death and destruction, let 'em swoller you till they vomit or bust wide open." They thought the old man had gone out of his mind. He had been the meekest of men. The younger children were rushed from the room, the shades drawn and the flame of the lamp turned so low that it sputtered on the wick like the old man's breathing. "Learn it to the younguns," he whispered fiercely; then he died.

But my folks were more alarmed over his last words than over his dying. It was as though he had not died at all, his words caused so much anxiety. I was warned emphatically to forget what he had said and, indeed, this is the first time it has been mentioned outside the family circle. It had a tremendous effect upon me, however. I could never be sure of what he meant. Grandfather had been a quiet old man who never made any trouble, yet on his deathbed he had called himself a traitor and a spy, and he had spoken of his meekness as a dangerous activity. It became a constant puzzle which lay unanswered in the back of my mind. And whenever things went well for me I remembered my grandfather and felt guilty and uncomfortable. It was as though I was carrying out his advice in spite of myself. And to make it worse, everyone loved me for it. I was praised by the most lily-white men of the town. I was considered an example of desirable conduct—just as my grandfather had been. And what puzzled me was that the old man had defined it as *treachery*. When I was praised for my conduct I felt a guilt that in some way I was doing something that was really against the wishes of the white folks, that if they had understood they would have desired me to act just the opposite, that I should have been sulky and mean, and that that really would have been what they wanted, even though they were fooled and thought they wanted me to act as I did. It made me afraid that some day they would look upon me as a traitor and I would be lost. Still I was more afraid to act any other way because they didn't like that at all. The old man's words were like a curse. On my graduation day I believed an oration in which I showed that humility was the secret, indeed, the very essence of progress. (Not that I believed this—how could I, remembering my grandfather?—I only believed that it worked.) It was a great success. Everyone praised me and I was invited to give the speech at a gathering of the town's leading white citizens. It was a triumph for our whole community.

It was in the main ballroom of the leading hotel. When I got there I discovered that it was on the occasion of a smoker, and I was told that since I was to be there anyway I might as well take part in the battle royal to be fought by some of my schoolmates as part of the entertainment. The battle royal came first.

All of the town's big shots were there in their tuxedoes, wolfing down the buffet food, drinking beer and whiskey and smoking black cigars. It was a large room with a high ceiling. Chairs were arranged in neat rows around three sides of a portable boxing ring. The fourth side was clear, revealing a gleaming space of polished floor. I had some misgivings over the battle royal, by the way. Not from a distaste for fighting, but because I didn't care too much for the other fellows who were to take part. They were tough guys who seemed to have no grandfather's curse worrying their minds. No one could mistake their toughness. And besides, I suspected that fighting a battle royal might detract from the dignity of my speech. In those pre-invisible days I visualized myself as a potential Booker T. Washington. But the other fellows didn't care too much for me either, and there were nine of them. I felt superior to them in my way, and I didn't like the manner in which we were all crowded together into the servants'

elevator. Nor did they like my being there. In fact, as the warmly lighted floors flashed past the elevator we had words over the fact that I, by taking part in the fight, had knocked one of their friends out of a night's work.

We were led out of the elevator through a rococo hall into an anteroom and told to get into our fighting togs. Each of us was issued a pair of boxing gloves and ushered out into the big mirrored hall, which we entered looking cautiously about us and whispering, lest we might accidentally be heard above the noise of the room. It was foggy with cigar smoke. And already the whiskey was taking effect. I was shocked to see some of the most important men of the town quite tipsy. They were all there—bankers, lawyers, judges, doctors, fire chiefs, teachers, merchants. Even one of the more fashionable pastors. Something we could not see was going on up front. A clarinet was vibrating sensuously and the men were standing up and moving eagerly forward. We were a small tight group, clustered together, our bare upper bodies touching and shining with anticipatory sweat; while up front the big shots were becoming increasingly excited over something we still could not see. Suddenly I heard the school superintendent, who had told me to come, yell, "Bring up the shines, gentlemen! Bring up the little shines!"

We were rushed up to the front of the ballroom, where it smelled even more strongly of tobacco and whiskey. Then we were pushed into place. I almost wet my pants. A sea of faces, some hostile, some amused, ringed around us, and in the center, facing us, stood a magnificent blonde—stark naked. There was dead silence. I felt a blast of cold air chill me. I tried to back away, but they were behind me and around me. Some of the boys stood with lowered heads, trembling. I felt a wave of irrational guilt and fear. My teeth chattered, my skin turned to goose flesh, my knees knocked. Yet I was strongly attracted and looked in spite of myself. Had the price of looking been blindness, I would have looked. The hair was yellow like that of a circus kewpie doll, the face heavily powdered and rouged, as though to form an abstract mask, the eyes hollow and smeared a cool blue, the color of a baboon's butt. I felt a desire to spit upon her as my eyes brushed slowly over her body. Her breasts were firm and round as the domes of East Indian temples, and I stood so close as to see the fine skin texture and beads of pearly perspiration glistening like dew around the pink and erected buds of her nipples. I wanted at one and the same time to run from the room, to sink through the floor, or go to her and cover her from my eyes and the eyes of the others with my body; to feel the soft thighs, to caress her and destroy her, to love her and murder her, to hide from her, and yet to stroke where below the small American flag tattooed upon her belly her thighs formed a capital V. I had a notion that of all in the room she saw only me with her impersonal eyes.

And then she began to dance, a slow sensuous movement; the smoke of a hundred cigars clinging to her like the thinnest of veils. She seemed like a fair bird-girl girdled in veils calling to me from the angry surface of some gray and threatening sea. I was transported. Then I became aware of the clarinet playing and the big shots yelling at us. Some threatened us if we looked and others if we did not. On my right I saw one boy faint. And now a man grabbed a silver pitcher from a table and stepped close as he dashed ice water upon him and stood him up and forced two of us to support him as his head hung and moans issued from his thick bluish lips. Another boy began to plead to go home. He was the largest of the group, wearing dark red fighting trunks much too small to conceal the erection which projected from him as though in answer to the insinuating low-registered moaning of the clarinet. He tried to hide himself with his boxing gloves.

And all the while the blonde continued dancing, smiling faintly at the big shots who watched her with fascination, and faintly smiling at our fear. I noticed a certain merchant who followed her hungrily, his lips loose and drooling. He was a large man who wore diamond studs in a shirtfront which swelled with the ample paunch underneath, and each time the blonde swayed her undulating hips he ran his hand through the thin hair of his bald head and, with his arms upheld, his posture clumsy like that of an intoxicated panda, wound his belly in a slow and obscene grind. This creature was completely hypnotized. The music had quickened. As the dancer flung herself about with a detached expression on her face, the men began reaching out to touch her. I could see their beefy fingers sink into the soft flesh. Some of the others tried to stop them and she began to move around the floor in graceful circles, as they gave chase, slipping and sliding over the polished floor. It was mad. Chairs went crashing, drinks were spilt, as they ran laughing and howling after her. They caught her just as she reached a door, raised her from the floor, and tossed her as college boys are tossed at a hazing, and above her red, fixed-smiling lips I saw the terror and disgust in her eyes, almost like my own terror and that which I saw in some of the other boys. As I watched, they tossed her twice and her soft breasts seemed to flatten against the air and her legs flung wildly as she spun. Some of the more sober ones helped her to escape. And I started off the floor, heading for the anteroom with the rest of the boys.

Some were still crying and in hysteria. But as we tried to leave we were stopped and ordered to get into the ring. There was nothing to do but what we were told. All ten of us climbed under the ropes and allowed ourselves to be blindfolded with broad bands of white cloth. One of the men seemed to feel a bit sympathetic and tried to cheer us up as we stood with our backs against the ropes. Some of us tried to grin. "See that boy over there?" one of the men said. "I want you to run across at the bell and give it to him right in the belly. If you don't get him, I'm going to get you. I don't like his looks." Each of us was told the same. The blindfolds were put on. Yet even then I had been going over my speech. In my mind each word was as bright as flame. I felt the cloth pressed into place, and frowned so that it would be loosened when I relaxed.

But now I felt a sudden fit of blind terror. I was unused to darkness. It was as though I had suddenly found myself in a dark room filled with poisonous cotton-mouths. I could hear the bleary voices yelling insistently for the battle royal to begin.

"Get going in there!"

"Let me at that big nigger!"

I strained to pick up the school superintendent's voice, as though to squeeze some security out of that slightly more familiar sound.

"Let me at those black sonsabitches!" someone yelled.

"No, Jackson, no!" another voice yelled. "Here, somebody, help me hold Jack."

"I want to get at that ginger-colored nigger. Tear him limb from limb," the first voice yelled.

I stood against the ropes trembling. For in those days I was what they called ginger-colored, and he sounded as though he might crunch me between his teeth like a crisp ginger cookie.

Quite a struggle was going on. Chairs were being kicked about and I could hear voices grunting as with a terrific effort. I wanted to see, to see more desperately than ever before. But the blindfold was as tight as a thick skin-puckering scab and when I raised my gloved hands to push the layers of white aside a voice yelled, "Oh, no you don't, black bastard! Leave that alone!"

"Ring the bell before Jackson kills him a coon!" someone boomed in the sudden silence. And I heard the bell clang and the sound of the feet scuffling forward.

A glove smacked against my head. I pivoted, striking out stiffly as someone went past, and felt the jar ripple along the length of my arm to my shoulder. Then it seemed as though all nine of the boys had turned upon me at once. Blows pounded me from all sides while I struck out as best I could. So many blows landed upon me that I wondered if I were not the only blindfolded fighter in the ring, or if the man called Jackson hadn't succeeded in getting me after all.

Blindfolded, I could no longer control my motions. I had no dignity. I stumbled about like a baby or a drunken man. The smoke had become thicker and with each new blow it seemed to scar and further restrict my lungs. My saliva became like hot bitter glue. A glove connected with my head, filling my mouth with warm blood. It was everywhere. I could not tell if the moisture I felt upon my body was sweat or blood. A blow landed hard against the nape of my neck. I felt myself going over, my head hitting the floor. Streaks of blue light filled the black world behind the blindfold. I lay prone, pretending that I was knocked out, but felt myself seized by hands and yanked to my feet. "Get going, black boy! Mix it up!" My arms were like lead, my head smarting from blows. I managed to feel my way to the ropes and held on, trying to catch my breath. A glove landed in my mid-section and I went over again, feeling as though the smoke had become a knife jabbed into my guts. Pushed this way and that by the legs milling around me, I finally pulled erect and discovered that I could see the black, sweat-washed forms weaving in the smoky-blue atmosphere like drunken dancers weaving to the rapid drum-like thuds of blows.

Everyone fought hysterically. It was complete anarchy. Everybody fought everybody else. No group fought together for long. Two, three, four, fought one, then turned to fight each other, were themselves attacked. Blows landed below the belt and in the kidney, with the gloves open as well as closed, and with my eyes partly opened now there was not so much terror. I moved carefully, avoiding blows, although not too many to attract attention, fighting from group to group. The boys groped about like blind, cautious crabs crouching to protect their mid-sections, their heads pulled in short against their shoulders, their arms stretched nervously before them, with their fists testing the smoke-filled air like the knobbed feelers of hypersensitive snails. In one corner I glimpsed a boy violently punching the air and heard him scream in pain as he smashed his hand against a ring post. For a second I saw him bent over holding his hand, then going down as a blow caught his unprotected head. I played one group against the other, slipping in and throwing a punch then stepping out of range while pushing the others into the melee to take the blows blindly aimed at me. The smoke was agonizing and there were no rounds, no bells at three minute intervals to relieve our exhaustion. The room spun round me, a swirl of lights, smoke, sweating bodies surrounded by tense white faces. I bled from both nose and mouth, the blood spattering upon my chest.

The men kept yelling, "Slug him, black boy! Knock his guts out!"

"Uppercut him! Kill him! Kill that big boy!"

Taking a fake fall, I saw a boy going down heavily beside me as though we were felled by a single blow, saw a sneaker-clad foot shoot into his groin as the two who had knocked him down stumbled upon him. I rolled out of range, feeling a twinge of nausea.

The harder we fought the more threatening the men became. And yet, I had began to worry about my speech again. How would it go? Would they recognize my ability? What would they give me?

I was fighting automatically when suddenly I noticed that one after another of the boys was leaving the ring. I was surprised, filled with panic, as though I had been left alone with an unknown danger. Then I understood. The boys had arranged it among themselves. It was the custom for

the two men left in the ring to slug it out for the winner's prize. I discovered this too late. When the bell sounded two men in tuxedoes leaped into the ring and removed the blindfold. I found myself facing Tatlock, the biggest of the gang. I felt sick at my stomach. Hardly had the bell stopped ringing in my ears than it clanged again and I saw him moving swiftly toward me. Thinking of nothing else to do I hit him smash on the nose. He kept coming, bringing the rank sharp violence of stale sweat. His face was a black blank of a face, only his eyes alive—with hate of me and aglow with a feverish terror from what had happened to us all. I became anxious. I wanted to deliver my speech and he came at me as though he meant to beat it out of me. I smashed him again and again, taking his blows as they came. Then on a sudden impulse I struck him lightly and as we clinched, I whispered, "Fake like I knocked you out, you can have the prize."

"I'll break your behind," he whispered hoarsely.

"For *them?*"

"For *me,* sonofabitch!"

They were yelling for us to break it up and Tatlock spun me half around with a blow, and as a joggled camera sweeps in a reeling scene, I saw the howling red faces crouching tense beneath the cloud of blue-gray smoke. For a moment the world wavered, unraveled, flowed, then my head cleared and Tatlock bounced before me. That fluttering shadow before my eyes was his jabbing left hand. Then falling forward, my head against his damp shoulder, I whispered.

"I'll make it five dollars more."

"Go to hell!"

But his muscles relaxed a trifle beneath my pressure and I breathed, "Seven?"

"Give it to your ma," he said, ripping me beneath the heart.

And while I still held him I butted him and moved away. I felt myself bombarded with punches. I fought back with hopeless desperation. I wanted to deliver my speech more than anything else in the world, because I felt that only these men could judge truly my ability, and now this stupid clown was ruining my chances. I began fighting carefully now, moving in to punch him and out again with my greater speed. A lucky blow to his chin and I had him going too —until I heard a loud voice yell, "I got my money on the big boy."

Hearing this, I almost dropped my guard. I was confused: Should I try to win against the voice out there? Would not this go against my speech, and was not this a moment for humility, for nonresistance? A blow to my head as I danced about sent my right eye popping like a jack-in-the-box and settled my dilemma. The room went red as I fell. It was a dream fall, my body languid and fastidious as to where to land, until the floor became impatient and smashed up to meet me. A moment later I came to. An hypnotic voice said FIVE emphatically. And I lay there, hazily watching a dark red spot of my own blood shaping itself into a butterfly, glistening and soaking into the soiled gray world of the canvas.

When the voice drawled TEN I was lifted up and dragged to a chair. I sat dazed. My eye pained and swelled with each throb of my pounding heart and I wondered if now I would be allowed to speak. I was wringing wet, my mouth still bleeding. We were grouped along the wall now. The other boys ignored me as they congratulated Tatlock and speculated as to how much they would be paid. One boy whimpered over his smashed hand. Looking up front, I saw attendants in white jackets rolling the portable ring away and placing a small square rug in the vacant space surrounded by chairs. Perhaps, I thought, I will stand on the rug to deliver my speech.

Then the M.C. called to us, "Come on up here boys and get your money."

We ran forward to where the men laughed and talked in their chairs, waiting. Everyone seemed friendly now.

"There it is on the rug," the man said. I saw the rug covered with coins of all dimensions and a few crumpled bills. But what excited me, scattered here and there, were the gold pieces.

"Boys, it's all yours," the man said. "You get all you grab."

"That's right, Sambo," a blond man said, winking at me confidentially.

I trembled with excitement, forgetting my pain. I would get the gold and the bills, I thought. I would use both hands. I would throw my body against the boys nearest me to block them from the gold.

"Get down around the rug now," the man commanded, "and don't anyone touch it until I give the signal."

"This ought to be good," I heard.

As told, we got around the square rug on our knees. Slowly the man raised his freckled hand as we followed it upward with our eyes.

I heard, "These niggers look like they're about to pray-"

Then, "Ready," the man said, "Go!"

I lunged for a yellow coin lying on the blue design of the carpet, touching it and sending a surprised shriek to join those rising around me. I tried frantically to remove my hand but could not let go. A hot, violent force tore through my body, shaking me like a wet rat. The rug was electrified. The hair bristled up on my head as I shook myself free. My muscles jumped, my nerves jangled, writhed. But I saw that this was not stopping the other boys. Laughing in fear and embarrassment, some were holding back and scooping up the coins knocked off by the painful contortions of the others. The men roared above us as we struggled.

"Pick it up, goddammit, pick it up!" someone called like a bass-voiced parrot. "Go on, get it!"

I crawled rapidly around the floor, picking up the coins, trying to avoid the coppers and to get greenbacks and the gold. Ignoring the shock by laughing, as I brushed the coins off quickly, I discovered that I could contain the electricity—a contradiction, but it works. Then the men began to push us onto the rug. Laughing embarrassedly, we struggled out of their hands and kept after the coins. We were all wet and slippery and hard to hold. Suddenly I saw a boy lifted into the air, glistening with sweat like a circus seal, and dropped, his wet back landing flush upon the charged rug, heard him yell and saw him literally dance upon his back, his elbows beating a frenzied tattoo upon the floor, his muscles twitching like the flesh of a horse stung by many flies. When he finally rolled off, his face was gray and no one stopped him when he ran from the floor amid booming laughter.

"Get the money," the M.C. called. "That's good hard American cash!"

And we snatched and grabbed, snatched and grabbed. I was careful not to come too close to the rug now, and when I felt the hot whiskey breath descend upon me like a cloud of foul air I reached out and grabbed the leg of a chair. It was occupied and I held on desperately.

"Leggo, nigger! Leggo!"

The huge face wavered down to mine as he tried to push me free. But my body was slippery and he was too drunk. It was Mr. Colcord, who owned a chain of movie houses and "entertainment palaces." Each time he grabbed me I slipped out of his hands. It became a real struggle. I feared the rug more than I did the drunk, so I held on, surprising myself for a moment by trying to topple *him* upon the rug. It was such an enormous idea that I found myself actually carrying it out. I tried not to be obvious, yet when I grabbed his leg, trying to tumble him out of the chair, he raised up roaring with laughter, and, looking at me with soberness dead in the eye, kicked me viciously in the chest. The chair leg flew out of my hand and I felt myself going and rolled. It was as though I had rolled through a bed of hot coals. It seemed a whole century would pass before I would roll free, a century in which I was seared through the deepest level of my body to the fearful breath within me and the breath seared

and heated to the point of explosion. It'll all be over in a flash, I thought as I rolled clear. It'll all be over in a flash.

But not yet, the men on the other side were waiting, red faces swollen as though from apoplexy as they bent forward in their chairs. Seeing their fingers coming toward me I rolled away as a fumbled football rolls off the receiver's fingertips, back into the coals. That time I jerkily sent the rug sliding out of place and heard the coins ringing against the floor and the boys scuffling to pick them up and the M.C. calling, "All right, boys, that's all. Go get dressed and get your money."

I was limp as a dish rag. My back felt as though it had been beaten with wires.

When we had dressed the M.C. came in and gave us each five dollars, except Tatlock, who got ten for being last in the ring. Then he told us to leave. I was not to get a chance to deliver my speech, I thought. I was going out into the dim alley in despair when I was stopped and told to go back. I returned to the ballroom, where the men were pushing back their chairs and gathering in groups to talk.

The M.C. knocked on a table for quiet. "Gentlemen," he said, "we almost forgot an important part of the program. A most serious part, gentlemen. This boy was brought here to deliver a speech which he made at his graduation yesterday . . ."

"Bravo!"

"I'm told that he is the smartest boy we've got out there in Greenwood. I'm told that he knows more big words than a pocket-sized dictionary."

Much applause and laughter.

"So now, gentlemen, I want you to give him your attention."

There was still laughter as I faced them, my mouth dry, my eye throbbing. I began slowly, but evidently my throat was tense, because they began shouting, "Louder! Louder!"

"We of the younger generation extol the wisdom of that great leader and educator," I shouted, "who first spoke these flaming words of wisdom: 'A ship lost at sea for many days suddenly sighted a friendly vessel. From the mast of the unfortunate vessel was seen a signal: "Water, water, we die of thirst!" The answer from the friendly vessel came back: "Cast down your bucket where you are." The captain of the distressed vessel, at last heeding the injunction, cast down his bucket, and it came up full of fresh sparkling water from the mouth of the Amazon River.' And like him I say, and in his words, 'To those of my race who depend upon bettering their condition in a foreign land, or who underestimate the importance of cultivating friendly relations with the Southern white man, who is his next-door neighbor, I would say: "Cast down your bucket where you are"—cast it down in making friends in every manly way of the people of all races by whom we are surrounded . . .' "

I spoke automatically and with such fervor that I did not realize that the men were still talking and laughing until my dry mouth, filling up with blood from the cut, almost strangled me. I coughed, wanting to stop and go to one of the tall brass, sand-filled spittoons to relieve myself, but a few of the men, especially the superintendent, were listening and I was afraid. So I gulped it down, blood, saliva and all, and continued. (What powers of endurance I had during those days! What enthusiasm! What a belief in the rightness of things!) I spoke even louder in spite of the pain. But still they talked and still they laughed, as though deaf with cotton in dirty ears. So I spoke with greater emotional emphasis. I closed my ears and swallowed blood until I was nauseated. The speech seemed a hundred times as long as before, but I could not leave out a single word. All had to be said, each memorized nuance considered, rendered. Nor was that all. Whenever I uttered a word of three or more syllables a group of voices would yell for me to repeat it. I used the phrase "social responsibility" and they yelled:

"What's that word you say, boy?"

"Social responsibility," I said.

"What?"

"Social . . ."

"Louder."

". . . responsibility."

"More!"

"Respon—"

"Repeat!"

"—sibility."

The room filled with the uproar of laughter until, no doubt, distracted by having to gulp down my blood, I made a mistake and yelled a phrase I had often seen denounced in newspaper editorials, heard debated in private.

"Social . . ."

"What?" they yelled.

". . . equality—"

The laughter hung smokelike in the sudden stillness. I opened my eyes, puzzled. Sounds of displeasure filled the room. The M.C. rushed forward. They shouted hostile phrases at me. But I did not understand.

A small dry mustached man in the front row blared out, "Say that slowly, son!"

"What sir?"

"What you just said!"

"Social responsibility, sir," I said.

"You weren't being smart, were you, boy?" he said, not unkindly.

"No, sir!"

"You sure that about 'equality' was a mistake?"

"Oh, yes, sir," I said. "I was swallowing blood."

"Well, you had better speak more slowly so we can understand. We mean to do right by you, but you've got to know your place at all times. All right, now, go on with your speech."

I was afraid. I wanted to leave but I wanted also to speak and I was afraid they'd snatch me down.

"Thank you, sir," I said, beginning where I had left off, and having them ignore me as before.

Yet when I finished there was a thunderous applause. I was surprised to see the superintendent come forth with a package wrapped in white tissue paper, and, gesturing for quiet, address the men.

"Gentlemen, you see that I did not overpraise this boy. He makes a good speech and some day he'll lead his people in the proper paths. And I don't have to tell you that that is important in these days and times. This is a good, smart boy, and so to encourage him in the right direction, in the name of the Board of Education I wish to present him a prize in the form of this . . ."

He paused, removing the tissue paper and revealing a gleaming calfskin brief case.

". . . in the form of this first-class article from Shad Whitmore's shop."

"Boy," he said, addressing me, "take this prize and keep it well. Consider it a badge of office. Prize it. Keep developing as you are and some day it will be filled with important papers that will help shape the destiny of your people."

I was so moved that I could hardly express my thanks. A rope of bloody saliva forming a shape like an undiscovered continent drooled upon the leather and I wiped it quickly away. I felt an importance that I had never dreamed.

"Open it and see what's inside," I was told.

My fingers a-tremble, I complied, smelling the fresh leather and finding an official-looking document inside. It was a scholarship to the state college for Negroes. My eyes filled with tears and I ran awkwardly off the floor.

I was overjoyed; I did not even mind when I discovered that the gold pieces I had scrambled for were brass pocket tokens advertising a certain make of automobile.

When I reached home everyone was excited. Next day the neighbors came to congratulate me. I even felt safe from grandfather, whose deathbed curse usually spoiled my triumphs. I stood beneath his photograph with my brief case in hand and smiled triumphantly into his stolid black peasant's face. It was a face that fascinated me. The eyes seemed to follow everywhere I went.

That night I dreamed I was at a circus with him and that he refused to laugh at the clowns no matter what they did. Then later he told me to open my brief case and read what was inside and I did, finding an official envelope stamped with the state seal; and inside the envelope I found another, endlessly, and I thought I would fall of weariness. "Them's years," he said. "Now open that one." And I did and in it I found an engraved document containing a short message in letters of gold. "Read it," my grandfather said. "Out loud."

"To Whom It May Concern," I intoned. "Keep This Nigger-boy Running."

I awoke with the old man's laughter in my ears.

(It was a dream I was to remember and dream again for many years after. But at that time I had no insight into its meaning. First I had to attend college.)

William Faulkner

William Faulkner (1897–1962), Nobel Prize winner and probably the finest twentieth century American novelist, whose works include The Sound and the Fury *(1929) and* Light in August *(1932) among his sixteen novels and seven volumes of short stories, came from an aristocratic Mississippi family. Most of Faulkner's works concern the old families and their descendants in the fictional town of Jefferson, Mississippi, and the surrounding Yoknapatawpha County, who have suffered the sin and guilt of slavery and who have seen their land destroyed by dissipation caused by guilt and frustration. In chronicling their stories and those of the black people and Indians who also inhabit the county, Faulkner writes in a rich style which is often earthy, humorous, and direct, and just as often extremely complex, shifting chronology and point of view while establishing the symbolic and mythic values of the incidents and characters. "That Evening Sun" shows the relationship between the Compson family and other white townspeople and the black servant woman Nancy in turn-of-the-century Jefferson.*

THAT EVENING SUN

Monday is no different from any other weekday in Jefferson now. The streets are paved now, and the telephone and electric companies are cutting down more and more of the shade trees—the water oaks, the maples and locusts and elms—to make room for iron poles bearing clusters of bloated and ghostly and bloodless grapes, and we have a city laundry which makes the rounds on Monday morning, gathering the bundles of clothes into bright-colored, specially-made motor cars: the soiled wearing of a whole week now flees apparitionlike behind alert and irritable electric horns, with a long diminishing noise of rubber and asphalt like tearing silk, and even the Negro women who still take in white people's washing after the old custom, fetch and deliver it in automobiles.

But fifteen years ago, on Monday morning the quiet, dusty, shady streets would be full of Negro women with, balanced on their steady, turbaned heads, bundles of clothes tied up in sheets, almost as large as cotton bales, carried so without touch of hand between the kitchen door of the white house and the blackened washpot beside a cabin door in Negro Hollow.

Nancy would see her bundle on the top of her head, then upon the bundle in turn she would set the black straw sailor hat which she wore winter and summer. She was tall, with a high, sad face sunken a little where her teeth were missing. Sometimes we would go a part of the way down the lane and across the pasture with her, to watch the balanced bundle and the hat that never bobbed nor wavered, even when she walked down into the ditch and up the other side and stooped through the fence. She would go down on her hands and knees and crawl through the gap, her head rigid, uptilted, the bundle steady as a rock or a balloon, and rise to her feet again and go on.

Sometimes the husbands of the washing women would fetch and deliver the clothes, but Jesus never did that for Nancy, even before father told him to stay away from our house, even when Dilsey was sick and Nancy would come to cook for us.

And then about half the time we'd have to go down the lane to Nancy's cabin and tell her to come on and cook breakfast. We would stop at the ditch, because father told us not to have anything to do with Jesus—he was a short black man, with a razor scar down his face—and we would throw rocks at Nancy's house until she came to the door, leaning her head around it without any clothes on.

"What yawl mean, chunking my house?" Nancy said. "What you little devils mean?"

"Father says for you to come on and get breakfast," Caddy said. "Father says it's over a half an hour now, and you've got to come this minute."

"I aint studying no breakfast," Nancy said. "I going to get my sleep out."

"I bet you're drunk," Jason said. "Father says you're drunk. Are you drunk, Nancy?"

"Who says I is?" Nancy said. "I got to get my sleep out. I aint studying no breakfast."

So after a while we quit chunking the cabin and went back home. When she finally came, it was too late for me to go to school. So we thought it was whisky until that day they arrested her again and they were taking her to jail and they passed Mr Stovall. He was the cashier in the bank and a deacon in the Baptist church, and Nancy began to say:

"When you going to pay me, white man? When you going to pay me, white man? It's been three times now since you paid me a cent—" Mr Stovall knocked her down, but she kept on saying, "When you going to pay me, white man? It's been three times now since—" until Mr Stovall kicked her in the mouth with his heel and the marshal caught Mr Stovall back, and Nancy lying in the street, laughing. She turned her head and spat out some blood and teeth and said,

"It's been three times now since he paid me a cent."

That was how she lost her teeth, and all that day they told about Nancy and Mr Stovall, and all that night the ones that passed the jail could hear Nancy singing and yelling. They could see her hands holding to the window bars, and a lot of them stopped along the fence, listening to her and to the jailer trying to make her stop. She didn't shut up until almost daylight, when the jailer began to hear a bumping and scraping upstairs and he went up there and found Nancy hanging from the window bar. He said that it was cocaine and not whisky, because no nigger would try to commit suicide unless he was full of cocaine, because a nigger full of cocaine wasn't a nigger any longer.

The jailer cut her down and revived her; then he beat her, whipped her. She had hung herself with her dress. She had fixed it all right, but when they arrested her she didn't have on anything except a dress and so she didn't have anything to tie her hands with and she couldn't make her hands let go of the window ledge. So the jailer heard the noise and ran up there and found Nancy hanging from the window, stark naked, her belly already swelling out a little, like a little balloon.

When Dilsey was sick in her cabin and Nancy was cooking for us, we could see her apron swelling out; that was before father told Jesus to stay away from the house. Jesus was in the kitchen, sitting behind the stove, with his razor scar on his black face like a piece of dirty string. He said it was a watermelon that Nancy had under her dress.

"It never come off of your vine, though," Nancy said.

"Off of what vine?" Caddy said.

"I can cut down the vine it did come off of," Jesus said.

"What makes you want to talk like that before these chillen?" Nancy said. "Whyn't you go on to work? You done et. You want

Mr. Jason to catch you hanging around his kitchen, talking that way before these chillen?"

"Talking what way?" Caddy said. "What vine?"

"I cant hang around white man's kitchen," Jesus said. "But white man can hang around mine. White man come in my house, but I cant stop him. When white man want to come in my house, I aint got no house. I cant stop him, but he cant kick me outen it. He cant do that."

Dilsey was still sick in her cabin. Father told Jesus to stay off our place. Dilsey was still sick. It was a long time. We were in the library after supper.

"Isn't Nancy through in the kitchen yet?" mother said. "It seems to me that she has had plenty of time to have finished the dishes."

"Let Quentin go and see," father said. "Go and see if Nancy is through, Quentin. Tell her she can go on home."

I went to the kitchen. Nancy was through. The dishes were put away and the fire was out. Nancy was sitting in a chair, close to the cold stove. She looked at me.

"Mother wants to know if you are through," I said.

"Yes," Nancy said. She looked at me. "I done finished." She looked at me.

"What is it?" I said. "What is it?"

"I aint nothing but a nigger," Nancy said. "It aint none of my fault."

She looked at me, sitting in the chair before the cold stove, the sailor hat on her head. I went through to the library. It was the cold stove and all, when you think of a kitchen being warm and busy and cheerful. And with a cold stove and the dishes all put away, and nobody wanting to eat at that hour.

"Is she through?" mother said.

"Yessum," I said.

"What is she doing?" mother said.

"She's not doing anything. She's through."

"I'll go and see," father said.

"Maybe she's waiting for Jesus to come and take her home," Caddy said.

"Jesus is gone," I said. Nancy told us how one morning she woke up and Jesus was gone.

"He quit me," Nancy said. "Done gone to Memphis, I reckon. Dodging them city *po*-lice for a while, I reckon."

"And a good riddance," father said. "I hope he stays there."

"Nancy's scaired of the dark," Jason said.

"So are you," Caddy said.

"I'm not," Jason said.

"Scairy cat," Caddy said.

"I'm not," Jason said.

"You, Candace!" mother said. Father came back.

"I am going to walk down the lane with Nancy," he said. "She says that Jesus is back."

"Has she seen him?" mother said.

"No. Some Negro sent her word that he was back in town. I wont be long."

"You'll leave me alone, to take Nancy home?" mother said. "Is her safety more precious to you than mine?"

"I wont be long," father said.

"You'll leave these children unprotected, with that Negro about?"

"I'm going too," Caddy said. "Let me go, Father."

"What would he do with them, if he were unfortunate enough to have them?" father said.

"I want to go, too," Jason said.

"Jason!" mother said. She was speaking to father. You could tell that by the way she said the name. Like she believed that all day father had been trying to think of doing the thing she wouldn't like the most, and that she knew all the time that after a while he would think of it. I stayed quiet, because father and I both knew that mother would want him to make me stay with her if she just thought of it in time. So father didn't look at me. I was the oldest. I was nine and Caddy was seven and Jason was five.

"Nonsense," father said. "We wont be long."

Nancy had her hat on. We came to the lane. "Jesus always been good to me," Nancy said. "Whenever he had two dollars, one of them was mine." We walked in the lane. "If I can just get through the lane," Nancy said, "I be all right then."

The lane was always dark. "This is where Jason got scared on Hallowe'en," Caddy said.

"I didn't," Jason said.

"Cant Aunt Rachel do anything with him?" father said. Aunt Rachel was old. She lived in a cabin beyond Nancy's, by herself. She had white hair and she smoked a pipe in the door, all day long; she didn't work any more. They said she was Jesus' mother. Sometimes she said she was and sometimes she said she wasn't any kin to Jesus.

"Yes, you did," Caddy said. "You were scairder than Frony. You were scairder than T.P. even. Scairder than niggers."

"Cant nobody do nothing with him," Nancy said. "He say I done woke up the devil in him and aint but one thing going to lay it down again."

"Well, he's gone now," father said. "There's nothing for you to be afraid of now. And if you'd just let white men alone."

"Let what white men alone?" Caddy said. "How let them alone?"

"He aint gone nowhere," Nancy said. "I can feel him. I can feel him now, in this lane. He hearing us talk, every word, hid somewhere, waiting. I aint seen him, and I aint going to see him again but once more, with that razor in his mouth. That razor on that string down his back, inside his shirt. And then I aint going to be even surprised."

"I wasn't scaired," Jason said.

"If you'd behave yourself, you'd have kept out of this," father said. "But it's all right now. He's probably in St. Louis now. Probably got another wife by now and forgot all about you."

"If he has, I better not find out about it," Nancy said. "I'd stand there right over them, and every time he wropped her, I'd cut that arm off. I'd cut his head off and I'd slit her belly and I'd shove—"

"Hush," father said.

"Slit whose belly, Nancy?" Caddy said.

"I wasn't scaired," Jason said. "I'd walk right down this lane by myself."

"Yah," Caddy said. "You wouldn't dare to put your foot down in it if we were not here too."

II

Dilsey was still sick, so we took Nancy home every night until mother said, "How much longer is this going on? I to be left alone in this big house while you take home a frightened Negro?"

We fixed a pallet in the kitchen for Nancy. One night we waked up, hearing the sound. It was not singing and it was not crying, coming up the dark stairs. There was a light in mother's room and we heard father going down the hall, down the back stairs, and Caddy and I went into the hall. The floor was cold. Our toes curled away from it while we listened to the sound. It was like singing and it wasn't like singing, like the sounds that Negroes make.

Then it stopped and we heard father going down the back stairs, and we went to the head of the stairs. Then the sound began again, in the stairway, not loud, and we could see Nancy's eyes halfway up the stairs, against the wall. They looked like cat's eyes do, like a big cat against the wall, watching us. When we came down the steps to where she was, she quit making the sound again, and we stood there until father came back up from the kitchen, with his pistol in his hand. He went back down with Nancy and they came back with Nancy's pallet.

We spread the pallet in our room. After the light in mother's room went off, we could see Nancy's eyes again. "Nancy," Caddy whispered, "are you asleep, Nancy?"

Nancy whispered something. It was oh or no, I dont know which. Like nobody had made it, like it came from nowhere and went nowhere, until it was like Nancy was not there at all; that I had looked so hard at her eyes on the stairs that they had got printed on my eyeballs, like the sun does

when you have closed your eyes and there is no sun. "Jesus," Nancy whispered, "Jesus."

"Was it Jesus?" Caddy said. "Did he try to come into the kitchen?"

"Jesus," Nancy said. Like this: Jeeeeeeee-eeeeeeeesus, until the sound went out, like a match or a candle does.

"It's the other Jesus she means," I said.

"Can you see us, Nancy?" Caddy whispered. "Can you see our eyes too?"

"I aint nothing but a nigger," Nancy said. "God knows. God knows."

"What did you see down there in the kitchen?" Caddy whispered. "What tried to get in?"

"God knows," Nancy said. We could see her eyes. "God knows."

Dilsey got well. She cooked dinner. "You'd better stay in bed a day or two longer," father said.

"What for?" Dilsey said. "If I had been a day later, this place would be to rack and ruin. Get out of here now, and let me get my kitchen straight again."

Dilsey cooked supper too. And that night, just before dark, Nancy came into the kitchen.

"How do you know he's back?" Dilsey said. "You aint seen him."

"Jesus is a nigger," Jason said.

"I can feel him," Nancy said. "I can feel him laying yonder in the ditch."

"Tonight?" Dilsey said. "Is he there tonight?"

"Dilsey's a nigger too," Jason said.

"You try to eat something," Dilsey said.

"I dont want nothing," Nancy said.

"I aint a nigger," Jason said.

"Drink some coffee," Dilsey said. She poured a cup of coffee for Nancy. "Do you know he's out there tonight? How come you know it's tonight?"

"I know," Nancy said. "He's there, waiting. I know. I done lived with him too long. I know what he is fixing to do fore he know it himself."

"Drink some coffee," Dilsey said. Nancy held the cup to her mouth and blew into the cup. Her mouth pursed out like a spreading adder's, like a rubber mouth, like she had blown all the color out of her lips with blowing the coffee.

"I aint a nigger," Jason said. "Are you a nigger, Nancy?"

"I hellborn, child," Nancy said. "I wont be nothing soon. I going back where I come from soon."

III

She began to drink the coffee. While she was drinking, holding the cup in both hands, she began to make the sound again. She made the sound into the cup and the coffee sploshed out onto her hands and her dress. Her eyes looked at us and she sat there, her elbows on her knees, holding the cup in both hands, looking at us across the wet cup, making the sound. "Look at Nancy," Jason said. "Nancy cant cook for us now. Dilsey's got well now."

"You hush up," Dilsey said. Nancy held the cup in both hands, looking at us, making the sound, like there were two of them: one looking at us and the other making the sound. "Whyn't you let Mr Jason telefoam the marshal?" Dilsey said. Nancy stopped then, holding the cup in her long brown hands. She tried to drink some coffee again, but it sploshed out of the cup, onto her hands and her dress, and she put the cup down. Jason watched her.

"I cant swallow it," Nancy said. "I swallows but it wont go down me."

"You go down to the cabin," Dilsey said. "Frony will fix you a pallet and I'll be there soon."

"Wont no nigger stop him," Nancy said.

"I aint a nigger," Jason said. "Am I, Dilsey?"

"I reckon not," Dilsey said. She looked at Nancy. "I dont reckon so. What you going to do, then?"

Nancy looked at us. Her eyes went fast, like she was afraid there wasn't time to look, without hardly moving at all. She looked at us, at all three of us at one time. "You member that night I stayed in yawls' room?" she

said. She told about how we waked up early the next morning, and played. We had to play quiet, on her pallet, until father woke up and it was time to get breakfast. "Go and ask your maw to let me stay here tonight," Nancy said. "I wont need no pallet. We can play some more."

Caddy asked mother. Jason went too. "I cant have Negroes sleeping in the bedrooms," mother said. Jason cried. He cried until mother said he couldn't have any dessert for three days if he didn't stop. Then Jason said he would stop if Dilsey would make a chocolate cake. Father was there.

"Why dont you do something about it?" mother said. "What do we have officers for?"

"Why is Nancy afraid of Jesus?" Caddy said. "Are you afraid of father, mother?"

"What could the officers do?" father said. "If Nancy hasn't seen him, how could the officers find him?"

"Then why is she afraid?" mother said.

"She says he is there. She says she knows he is there tonight."

"Yet we pay taxes," mother said. "I must wait here alone in this big house while you take a Negro woman home."

"You know that I am not lying outside with a razor," father said.

"I'll stop if Dilsey will make a chocolate cake," Jason said. Mother told us to go out and father said he didn't know if Jason would get a chocolate cake or not, but he knew what Jason was going to get in about a minute. We went back to the kitchen and told Nancy.

"Father said for you to go home and lock the door, and you'll be all right," Caddy said. "All right from what, Nancy?" Is Jesus mad at you?" Nancy was holding the coffee cup in her hands again, her elbows on her knees and her hands holding the cup between her knees. She was looking into the cup. "What have you done that made Jesus mad?" Caddy said. Nancy let the cup go. It didn't break on the floor, but the coffee spilled out, and Nancy sat there with her hands still making the shape of the cup. She began to make the sound again, not loud. Not singing and not unsinging. We watched her.

"Here," Dilsey said. "You quit that, now. You get aholt of yourself. You wait here. I going to get Versh to walk home with you." Dilsey went out.

We looked at Nancy. Her shoulders kept shaking, but she quit making the sound. We watched her. "What's Jesus going to do to you?" Caddy said. "He went away."

Nancy looked at us. "We had fun that night I stayed in yawls' room, didn't we?"

"I didn't," Jason said. "I didn't have any fun."

"You were asleep in mother's room," Caddy said. "You were not there."

"Let's go down to my house and have some more fun," Nancy said.

"Mother wont let us," I said. "It's too late now."

"Dont bother her," Nancy said. "We can tell her in the morning. She wont mind."

"She wouldn't let us," I said.

"Dont ask her now," Nancy said. "Dont bother her now."

"She didn't say we couldn't go," Caddy said.

"We didn't ask," I said.

"If you go, I'll tell," Jason said.

"We'll have fun," Nancy said. "They won't mind, just to my house. I been working for yawl a long time. They won't mind."

"I'm not afraid to go," Caddy said. "Jason is the one that's afraid. He'll tell."

"I'm not," Jason said.

"Yes, you are," Caddy said. "You'll tell."

"I won't tell," Jason said. "I'm not afraid."

"Jason ain't afraid to go with me," Nancy said. "Is you, Jason?"

"Jason is going to tell," Caddy said. The lane was dark. We passed the pasture gate. "I bet if something was to jump out from behind that gate, Jason would holler."

"I wouldn't," Jason said. We walked down the lane. Nancy was talking loud.

"What are you talking so loud, for, Nancy?" Caddy said.

"Who; me?" Nancy said. "Listen at Quentin and Caddy and Jason saying I'm talking loud."

"You talk like there was five of us here," Caddy said. "You talk like father was here too."

"Who; me talking loud, Mr Jason?" Nancy said.

"Nancy called Jason 'Mister,'" Caddy said.

"Listen how Caddy and Quentin and Jason talk," Nancy said.

"We're not talking loud," Caddy said. "You're the one that's talking like father—"

"Hush," Nancy said; "hush, Mr Jason."

"Nancy called Jason 'Mister' aguh—"

"Hush," Nancy said. She was talking loud when we crossed the ditch and stooped through the fence where she used to stoop through with the clothes on her head. Then we came to her house. We were going fast then. She opened the door. The smell of the house was like the lamp and the smell of Nancy was like the wick, like they were waiting for one another to begin to smell. She lit the lamp and closed the door and put the bar up. Then she quit talking loud, looking at us.

"What're we going to do?" Caddy said.

"What do yawl want to do?" Nancy said.

"You said we would have some fun," Caddy said.

There was something about Nancy's house; something you could smell besides Nancy and the house. Jason smelled it, even. "I don't want to stay here," he said. "I want to go home."

"Go home, then," Caddy said.

"I don't want to go by myself," Jason said.

"We're going to have some fun," Nancy said.

"How?" Caddy said.

Nancy stood by the door. She was looking at us, only it was like she had emptied her eyes, like she had quit using them. "What do you want to do?" she said.

"Tell us a story," Caddy said. "Can you tell a story?"

"Yes," Nancy said.

"Tell it," Caddy said. We looked at Nancy. "You don't know any stories."

"Yes," Nancy said. "Yes, I do."

She came and sat in a chair before the hearth. There was a little fire there. Nancy built it up, when it was already hot inside. She built a good blaze. She told a story. She talked like her eyes looked, like her eyes watching us and her voice talking to us did not belong to her. Like she was living somewhere else, waiting somewhere else. She was outside the cabin. Her voice was inside and the shape of her, the Nancy that could stoop under a barbed wire fence with a bundle of clothes balanced on her head as though without weight, like a balloon, was there. But that was all. "And so this here queen come walking up to the ditch, where that bad man was hiding. She was walking up to the ditch, and she say, 'If I can just get past this here ditch,' was what she say . . ."

"What ditch?" Caddy said. "A ditch like the one out there? Why did a queen want to go into a ditch?"

"To get to her house," Nancy said. She looked at us. "She had to cross the ditch to get into her house quick and bar the door."

"Why did she want to go home and bar the door?" Caddy said.

IV

Nancy looked at us. She quit talking. She looked at us. Jason's legs stuck straight out of his pants where he sat on Nancy's lap. "I don't think that's a good story," he said. "I want to go home."

"Maybe we had better," Caddy said. She got up from the floor. "I bet they are looking for us right now." She went toward the door.

"No," Nancy said. "Don't open it." She got up quick and passed Caddy. She didn't touch the door, the wooden bar.

"Why not," Caddy said.

"Come back to the lamp," Nancy said. "We'll have fun. You don't have to go."

"We ought to go," Caddy said. "Unless we have a lot of fun." She and Nancy came back to the fire, the lamp.

"I want to go home," Jason said. "I'm going to tell."

"I know another story," Nancy said. She stood close to the lamp. She looked at Caddy, like when your eyes look up at a stick balanced on your nose. She had to look down to see Caddy, but her eyes looked like that, like when you are balancing a stick.

"I won't listen to it," Jason said. "I'll bang on the floor."

"It's a good one," Nancy said. "It's better than the other one."

"What's it about?" Caddy said. Nancy was standing by the lamp. Her hand was on the lamp, against the light, long and brown.

"Your hand is on that hot globe," Caddy said. "Don't it feel hot to your hand?"

Nancy looked at her hand on the lamp chimney. She took her hand away, slow. She stood there, looking at Caddy, wringing her long hand as though it were tied to her wrist with a string.

"Let's do something else," Caddy said.

"I want to go home," Jason said.

"I got some popcorn," Nancy said. She looked at Caddy and then at Jason and then at me and then at Caddy again. "I got some popcorn."

"I don't like popcorn," Jason said. "I'd rather have candy."

Nancy looked at Jason. "You can hold the popper." She was still wringing her hand; it was long and limp and brown.

"All right," Jason said. "I'll stay a while if I can do that. Caddy can't hold it. I'll want to go home again if Caddy holds the popper."

Nancy built up the fire. "Look at Nancy putting her hands in the fire," Caddy said. "What's the matter with you, Nancy?"

"I got popcorn," Nancy said. "I got some." She took the popper from under the bed. It was broken. Jason began to cry.

"Now we can't have any popcorn," he said.

"We ought to go home, anyway," Caddy said, "Come on, Quentin."

"Wait," Nancy said; "wait. I can fix it. Don't you want to help me fix it?"

"I don't think I want any," Caddy said. "It's too late now."

"You help me, Jason," Nancy said. "Don't you want to help me?"

"No," Jason said. "I want to go home."

"Hush," Nancy said; "hush. Watch. Watch me. I can fix it so Jason can hold it and pop the corn." She got a piece of wire and fixed the popper.

"It won't hold good," Caddy said.

"Yes, it will," Nancy said. "Yawl watch. Yawl help me shell some corn."

The popcorn was under the bed too. We shelled it into the popper and Nancy helped Jason hold the popper over the fire.

"It's not popping," Jason said. "I want to go home."

"You wait," Nancy said. "It'll begin to pop. We'll have fun then." She was sitting close to the fire. The lamp was turned up so high it was beginning to smoke.

"Why don't you turn it down some?" I said.

"It's all right," Nancy said. "I'll clean it. Yawl wait. The popcorn will start in a minute."

"I don't believe it's going to start," Caddy said. "We ought to start home, anyway. They'll be worried."

"No," Nancy said. "It's going to pop. Dilsey will tell um yawl with me. I been working for yawl long time. They won't mind if yawl at my house. You wait, now. It'll start popping any minute now."

Then Jason got some smoke in his eyes and he began to cry. He dropped the popper into the fire. Nancy got a wet rag and wiped Jason's face, but he didn't stop crying.

"Hush," she said. "Hush." But he didn't hush. Caddy took the popper out of the fire.

"It's burned up," she said. "You'll have to get some more popcorn, Nancy."

"Did you put all of it in?" Nancy asked.

"Yes," Caddy said. Nancy looked at Caddy. Then she took the popper and opened it and poured the cinders into her apron and began to sort the grains, her hands long and brown, and we watching her.

"Haven't you got any more?" Caddy said.

"Yes," Nancy said; "yes. Look. This here ain't burnt. All we need to do is—"

"I want to go home," Jason said. "I'm going to tell."

"Hush," Caddy said. We all listened. Nancy's head was already turned toward the barred door, her eyes filled with red lamplight. "Somebody is coming," Caddy said.

Then Nancy began to make that sound again, not loud, sitting there above the fire, her long hands dangling between her knees; all of a sudden water began to come out of her face in big drops, running down her face, carrying in each one a little turning ball of firelight like a spark until it dropped off her chin. "She's not crying," I said.

"I ain't crying," Nancy said. Her eyes were closed. "I aint crying. Who is it?"

"I don't know," Caddy said. She went to the door and looked out. "We've got to go now," she said. "Here comes father."

"I'm going to tell," Jason said. "Yawl made me come."

The water still ran down Nancy's face. She turned in her chair. "Listen. Tell him. Tell him we going to have fun. Tell him I take good care of yawl until in the morning. Tell him to let me come home with yawl and sleep on the floor. Tell him I won't need no pallet. We'll have fun. You member last time how we had so much fun?"

"I didn't have any fun," Jason said. "You hurt me. You put smoke in my eyes. I'm going to tell."

V

Father came in. He looked at us. Nancy did not get up.

"Tell him," she said.

"Caddy made us come down here," Jason said. "I didn't want to."

Father came to the fire. Nancy looked up at him. "Can't you go to Aunt Rachel's and stay?" he said. Nancy looked up at father, her hands between her knees. "He's not here," father said. "I would have seen him. There's not a soul in sight."

"He in the ditch," Nancy said. "He waiting in the ditch yonder."

"Nonsense," father said. He looked at Nancy. "Do you know he's there?"

"I got the sign," Nancy said.

"What sign?"

"I got it. It was on the table when I come in. It was a hogbone, with blood meat still on it, laying by the lamp. He's out there. When yawl walk out that door, I gone."

"Gone where, Nancy?" Caddy said.

"I'm not a tattletale," Jason said.

"Nonsense," father said.

"He out there," Nancy said. "He looking through that window this minute, waiting for yawl to go. Then I gone."

"Nonsense," father said. "Lock up your house and we'll take you on to Aunt Rachel's."

" 'Twont do no good," Nancy said. She didn't look at father now, but he looked down at her, at her long, limp, moving hands. "Putting it off wont do no good."

"Then what do you want to do?" father said.

"I don't know," Nancy said. "I can't do nothing. Just put it off. And that don't do no good. I reckon it belong to me. I reckon what I going to get ain't no more than mine."

"Get what?" Caddy said. "What's yours?"

"Nothing," father said. "You all must get to bed."

"Caddy made me come," Jason said.

"Go on to Aunt Rachel's," father said.

"It won't do no good," Nancy said. She sat before the fire, her elbows on her knees, her long hands between her knees. "When even your own kitchen wouldn't do no good. When even if I was sleeping on the floor in the room with your chillen, and the next morning there I am, and blood—"

"Hush," father said. "Lock the door and put out the lamp and go to bed."

"I scared of the dark," Nancy said. "I scared for it to happen in the dark."

"You mean you're going to sit right here with the lamp lighted?" father said. Then Nancy began to make the sound again, sitting before the fire, her long hands between her knees. "Ah, damnation," father said. "Come along, chillen. It's past bedtime."

"When yawl go home, I gone," Nancy said. She talked quieter now, and her face looked quiet, like her hands. "Anyway, I got my coffin money saved up with Mr. Lovelady." Mr. Lovelady was a short, dirty man who collected the Negro insurance, coming around to the cabins or the kitchens every Saturday morning, to collect fifteen cents. He and his wife lived at the hotel. One morning his wife committed suicide. They had a child, a little girl. He and the child went away. After a week or two he came back alone. We would see him going along the lanes and the back streets on Saturday mornings.

"Nonsense," father said. "You'll be the first thing I'll see in the kitchen tomorrow morning."

"You'll see what you'll see, I reckon," Nancy said. "But it will take the Lord to say what that will be."

VI

We left her sitting before the fire.

"Come and put the bar up," father said. But she didn't move. She didn't look at us again, sitting quietly there between the lamp and the fire. From some distance down the lane we could look back and see her through the open door.

"What, Father?" Caddy said. "What's going to happen?"

"Nothing," father said. Jason was on father's back, so Jason was the tallest of all of us. We went down into the ditch. I looked at it, quiet. I couldn't see much where the moonlight and the shadows tangled.

"If Jesus is hid here, he can see us, cant he?" Caddy said.

"He's not there," father said. "He went away a long time ago."

"You made me come," Jason said, high; against the sky it looked like father had two heads, a little one and a big one. "I didn't want to."

We went up out of the ditch. We could

still see Nancy's house and the open door, but we couldn't see Nancy now, sitting before the fire with the door open, because she was tired. "I just done got tired," she said. "I just a nigger. It ain't no fault of mine."

But we could hear her, because she began just after we came up out of the ditch, the sound that was not singing and not unsinging. "Who will do our washing now, Father?" I said.

"I'm not a nigger," Jason said, high and close above father's head.

"You're worse," Caddy said, "you are a tattletale. If something was to jump out, you'd be scairder than a nigger."

"I wouldn't," Jason said.

"You'd cry," Caddy said.

"Caddy," father said.

"I wouldn't!" Jason said.

"Scairy cat," Caddy said.

"Candace!" father said.

Claude McKay

Claude McKay (1890–1948), was born and raised in Jamaica, coming to the United States when he was twenty-two. He lived both here and abroad, publishing poetic protests against the status of black people. These two poems show his anger at the nightmare of the black minority experience.

AMERICA

Although she feeds me bread of bitterness,
And sinks into my throat her tiger's tooth,
Stealing my breath of life, I will confess
I love this cultured hell that tests my youth!
Her vigor flows like tides into my blood,
Giving me strength erect against her hate.
Her bigness sweeps my being like a flood.
Yet as a rebel fronts a king in state,
I stand within her walls with not a shred
Of terror, malice, not a word of jeer.
Darkly I gaze into the days ahead,

And see her might and granite wonders there,
Beneath the touch of Time's unerring hand,
Like priceless treasures sinking in the sand.

THE WHITE HOUSE

Your door is shut against my tightened face,
And I am sharp as steel with discontent;
But I possess the courage and the grace
To bear my anger proudly and unbent.
The pavement slabs burn loose beneath my feet,
A chafing savage, down the decent street;
And passion rends my vitals as I pass,
Where boldly shines your shuttered door of glass.
Oh, I must search for wisdom every hour,
Deep in my wrathful bosom sore and raw,
And find in it the superhuman power
To hold me to the letter of your law!
Oh, I must keep my heart inviolate
Against the potent poison of your hate.

Elizabeth Cady Stanton

Elizabeth Cady Stanton (1815–1902) was a founder and influential leader of the women's suffrage movement. She graduated from Emma Willard in 1832 and for a time studied law in her father's office. She married Henry Brewster Stanton, journalist, lawyer, and abolitionist, in 1840 (there was no promise to "obey" in the ceremony) and worked for abolition and temperance in addition to women's rights. Her major accomplishments were the passage of women's property bills in the New York State legislature, the sponsorship of the Seneca Falls Convention in 1848 which officially began the women's rights movement, and the writing of several books, including the first three volumes of The History of Woman Suffrage 1881–1886 with Susan B. Anthony and Matilda Gage. This letter offers ringing arguments for women's right to vote; many of her statements sound quite contemporary and are echoed today.

LETTER TO THE SALEM CONVENTION

DEAR MARIANA:—How rejoiced I am to hear that the women of Ohio have called a Convention preparatory to the remodeling of their State Constitution. The remodeling of a Constitution, in the nineteenth century, speaks of progress, of greater freedom, and of more enlarged views of human rights and duties. It is fitting that, at such a time, woman, who has so long been the victim of ignorance and injustice, should at length throw off the trammels of a false education, stand upright, and with dignity and earnestness manifest a deep and serious interest in the laws which are to govern her and her country. It needs no argument to teach woman that she is interested in the laws which govern her. Suffering has taught her this already. It is important now that a change is proposed, that she speak, and loudly too. Having decided to petition for a redress of grievances, the question is, *for what shall you first petition?* For the exercise of your right to the elective franchise—nothing short of this. The grant to you of this right will secure all others; and the granting of every other right, whilst this is denied, is a mockery. For instance: What is the right to property without the right to protect it? The enjoyment of that right to-day is no security that it will be continued to-morrow, so long as it is granted to us as a favor, and not claimed by us as a right. Woman must exercise her right to the elective franchise, and have her own representatives in our National councils, for two good reasons:

1st. Men can not represent us. They are so thoroughly educated into the belief that woman's nature is altogether different from their own, that they have no idea that she can be governed by the same laws of mind as themselves. So far from viewing us like themselves, they seem, from their legislation, to consider us their moral and intellectual antipodes; for whatever law they find good for themselves, they forthwith pass its opposite for us, and express the most profound astonishment if we manifest the least dissatisfaction. For example, our forefathers, *full of righteous indignation,* pitched King George, his authority, and his tea-chests, all into the sea, and because, forsooth, they were forced to pay taxes without being represented in the British Government. "Taxation without representation," was the text for many a hot debate in the forests of the New World, and for many an eloquent oration in the Parliament of the Old. Yet, in forming our new Government, they have taken from us the very rights which they fought and bled and died to secure to themselves. They not only tax us, but in many cases they strip us of all we inherit, the wages we earn, the children of our love; and for such grievances we have no redress in any court of justice this side of Heaven. They tax our property to build colleges, then pass a special law prohibiting any woman to enter there. A married woman has no legal existence; she has no more absolute rights than a slave on a Southern plantation. She takes the name of her master, holds nothing, owns nothing, can bring no action in her own name; and the principle in which she and the slave is educated is the same. The slave is taught what is considered best for him to know—which is nothing; the woman is taught what is best for her to know—which is little more than nothing, man being the umpire in both cases. A woman can not follow out the impulses of her own mind in her sphere, any more than the slave can in his sphere. Civilly, socially, and religiously, she is what man chooses her to be, nothing more or less, and such is the slave. It is impossible for us to convince man that we think and feel exactly as he does; that we have the same sense of right and justice, the same love of freedom and independence. Some men regard us as devils, and some as angels; hence, one class would shut us up in a certain sphere for fear of the evil we might do, and the other for fear of the evil that *might be done to us;* thus, except for the sentiment of the thing, for all the good that it does us, we might as well be thought the one as the other. But we ourselves have to do with what *we are* and what *we shall be.*

2d. Men can not legislate for us. Our statute books and all past experience teach us this fact. His laws, where we are concerned, have been, without one exception, unjust, cruel, and aggressive. Having denied our identity with himself, he has no data to go upon in judging of our wants and interests. If we are alike in our mental structure, then there is no reason why we should not have a voice in making the laws which govern us; but if we are not alike, most certainly we must make laws for ourselves, for who else can understand what we need and desire? If it be admitted in this Government that all men and women are free and equal, then must we claim a place in our Senate Chamber and House of Representatives. But if, after all, it be found that even here we have classes and caste, not "Lords and Commons," but lords and women, then must we claim a lower House, where our Representatives can watch the passage of all bills affecting our own welfare, or the good of our country. Had the women of this country had a voice in the Government, think you our national escutcheon would have been stained with the guilt of aggressive warfare upon such weak, defenceless nations as the Seminoles and Mexicans? Think you we should cherish and defend, in the heart of our nation, such a wholesale system of piracy, cruelty, licentiousness, and ignorance as our slavery? Think you that relic of barbarism, the gallows, by which the wretched murderer is sent with blood upon his soul, uncalled for, into the presence of his God, would be sustained by law? Verily, no, or I mistake woman's heart, her instinctive love of justice, and mercy, and truth!

Who questions woman's right to vote? We can show our credentials to the right of self-government; we get ours just where man got his; they are all Heaven-descended, God-given. It is our duty to assert and re-assert this right, to agitate, discuss, and peti-tion, until our political equality be fully recognized. Depend upon it, this is the point to attack, the stronghold of the fortress— *the one* woman will find most difficult to take, *the one* man will most reluctantly give up; therefore let us encamp right under its shadow; there spend all our time, strength, and *moral* ammunition, year after year, with perseverance, courage, and decision. Let no sallies of wit or ridicule at our expense; no soft nonsense of woman's beauty, delicacy, and refinement; no promise of gold and silver, bank stock, road stock, or landed estate, seduce us from our position until that one stronghold totters to the ground. This done, the rest they will surrender *at discretion.* Then comes equality in Church and State, in the family circle, and in all our social relations.

The cause of woman is onward. For our encouragement, let us take a review of what has occurred during the last few years. Not two years since the women of New York held several Conventions. Their meetings were well attended by both men and women, and the question of woman's true position was fully and freely discussed. The proceedings of those meetings and the Declaration of Sentiments were all published and scattered far and near. Before that time, the newspapers said but little on that subject. Immediately after, there was scarcely a newspaper in the Union that did not notice these Conventions, and generally in a tone of ridicule. Now you seldom take up a paper that has not something about woman; but the tone is changing—ridicule is giving way to reason. Our papers begin to see that this is no subject for mirth, but one for serious consideration. Our literature is also assuming a different tone. . . . The women of Massachusetts, ever first in all moral movements, have sent, but a few weeks since, to their Legislature, a petition demanding their right to vote and hold office in their State. Woman seems to be preparing herself for a higher and holier destiny. That same love of liberty which burned in the hearts of our sires, is now being kindled anew in the daughters of this proud Republic. From the present state of public sentiment, we have every reason to look hopefully into the future. I see a brighter, happier day yet to come; but woman must say how soon the dawn shall be, and whether the light shall first shine in the East or the West. By her own efforts the change must come. She must carve out her future destiny with her own right hand. If she have not the energy to secure for herself her true position, neither would she have the force or stability to maintain it, if placed there by another. Farewell!

Yours sincerely,
E. C. STANTON.

Louise Bernikow

Louise Bernikow is a feminist journalist and poet who has written a critical anthology of women's poetry. This article, originally appearing in Ms. Magazine, *is a section of her memoirs. In this reminiscence of her high school days, Ms. Bernikow reveals the stereotype of the "ideal American girl" growing up in the 1950s and the effects that stereotype had on her and her classmates.*

CONFESSIONS OF AN EX-CHEERLEADER

The trick is to be up in the air with a big Ipana smile on your face, touching the heels of your saddle shoes to the back of your head, bending your elbows as close as you can get them behind you. This makes your short red dress rise, revealing a quick glimpse of thigh and underpants. It also makes your 16-year-old tits, aided and abetted by stuffings of cotton or the professional padding of Maidenform, stick far out.

I am doing this of my own free will on a spring afternoon in Madison Square Garden. The year is 1957, halfway between my sixteenth and seventeenth birthdays. I have aimed at, plotted and waited for this moment. It is living up to my expectations. The Garden is crowded. This is the play-off game for the New York City championships: Forest Hills against Boys High.

The old Madison Square Garden smells like a locker room, which is what makes it such a triumph that I find myself the center of attention in it. I am a star at last on male turf. There are 10 of us at halftime in the middle of the wooden floor with all the lights out except for the spotlight shining on us. I turn my face upward into the smell of sweat, into the applause and whistles dropping like confetti from the tiers of spectator seats above me.

Tip of my head to Maidenform padding to saddle-shoed toes, dizzy with ecstasy, I go into the first cheer.

WE GOT THE T-E-A-M

I shake my shoulders and wiggle my ass.

IT'S ON THE B-E-A-M

I do some chorus-girl high-kicking, wiggle and shake a little faster, and smile my smile a little bigger.

COME ON, FOREST HILLS, SKIN 'EM ALIVE!

Up in the air, head back, back arched, trembling all over. I hit the ground squarely on my feet and run off to the sound of thunderous applause. The team emerges for the second half.

I am a cheerleader.

Forest Hills is defeated. I am sitting in the ladies' room, having changed the short red dress for a gray flannel skirt and button-down pinstripe shirt. The Garden is dark and silent. The cheerleaders are dark and silent, too. We are all quietly weeping. When we leave the ladies' room to meet the team in the corridor, each of us embraces each of them. I move from one boy to another, despondently hugging. No funeral has brought more grief.

On the way home, I see the *Daily News* centerfold photograph of the Forest Hills cheerleaders. We are lined up like chorus girls, grinning, shoulders back. I feel as though I am looking at faded glory. When

I get home, the telephone is ringing. My mother answers and says it is for me. I can tell from her face that she does not recognize the voice, and she hovers near my shoulder, monitoring me.

"Hello?"

There is no sound on the other end, then there is heavy breathing, then faster huffing and puffing. I am terrified. I hang up.

"Who was that?"

"No one."

And not until 16 years later do I understand the connection: obscene phone calls are the other side of cheerleader glory.

Glory. I was hell-bent on glory when I started high school. On my awkward first day, I saw that cheerleaders were the queens of the school, and I determined to become one.

Forest Hills was a "rich" neighborhood, but not everyone at the high school was rich. I wasn't. In fact, I didn't live in Forest Hills at all, but in Kew Gardens Hills, on the other side of the tracks. I always felt like an outsider. When I became a cheerleader, every time I put on that red dress and went out there to jump and shout, every time I looked at the gold megaphone on my charm bracelet, and every time I walked through the corridors of the school knowing freshmen and sophomores were whispering and pointing with envy, I thought that I had managed, by hook and by crook, to wiggle my way into the ruling class.

Methodical, ruthless, ambitious, and manipulative, I studied the way "in" and discovered that, since cheerleaders chose their replacements, I had to learn how to charm women. Everything else in my life had depended on charming men and I, the original all-time Daddy's Little Girl, had that one down pat; but women?

Sororities were the key. Although they were officially outlawed, sororities ran things. The school cafeteria had special tables by custom for each sorority. As a sophomore, I would walk by those tables on my way to the nonspecial area where nobodies like me downed egg salad and Oreo cookies. I studied the sorority girls.

At night, I stood before the mirror "doing" my hair as I had seen it on the girls at those tables. I studied *Mademoiselle* and *Glamour,* full of girls who looked like cheerleaders, and there I discovered that fuzzy hair was my problem. Fuzzy Jewish hair. The girls in *Mademoiselle* had sleek blonde hair. Not me. The most popular cheerleaders at Forest Hills had sleek blonde hair. Not me.

I pin-curled as per instructions, every night, half going left and half going right. Still, in the morning, I combed it out to find kinks and fuzz. Somehow, in spite of it, I was "rushed" by sororities and, in blue serge Bermuda shorts and pink knee socks, was accepted.

I discovered how you charm women: you imitate them.

From Nora I picked up the names of painters and "acquired culture"; from Ellen I got my taste in plaid pleated skirts; from Arlene I saw how to bite my lower lip cutely. I was a sorority girl. I felt myself on shaky ground, always, but I hung in there, selling bananas on the streets of Manhattan as a "pledge," making the carfare back to Forest Hills where I joined my "sisters" who had dumped me off without a penny. We had an initiation ceremony; the fraternity boys came over afterward.

Two sorority sisters were cheerleaders. When "tryouts" time came, they taught the cheers to those of us who were going to try. We practiced all the time. I did cheers in my sleep and on the bus and in the shower. My family went nuts from the "Yea, Team" thundering from my bedroom.

"I wanna use the bathroom," my brother pounded at the door.

"Forest Hills—Forest Hills—THAT'S WHO!" I screamed from within, my teeth all freshly Ipana white.

If I made cheerleaders, my mother would stop clicking the hall light off and on when I came home from a date and "lingered" in the hall.

If I made cheerleaders, boys would arrive in rows and rows bearing tennis rackets, basketballs, baseball gloves, and fencing masks to lay in tribute at my feet.

If I made cheerleaders, Jimmy Dean and Marlon Brando would fall in love with me.

If I made cheerleaders, my hair would be straight.

Many tried; few were chosen. A jury of gym teachers and cheerleaders watched as we, with numbers on our backs, went through the cheers. I was Number Five. Something of the Miss America pageant in all this and something of the dance marathon. Girls were tapped on the shoulder and asked to leave the floor.

What were the criteria? I have gone over the old photographs in vain. They do not say. It was not "looks," for even by fifties standards, the cheerleaders were not the best-looking girls. My own photograph shows an ordinary middle-class Jewish girl. Her hair is short and flipped-up, with bangs. Her large nose has a bump on it. (I resisted the nose-job binge my friends went on. I have no idea where I got the courage.) She is wearing dark-red lipstick and her eyebrows are heavily lined. She looks older in the high school yearbook than she does now.

It wasn't looks that made a cheerleader, but "personality" or a certain kind of energy. Something called aggressiveness. Or bitchiness. Or pep.

Pep is what happened in American history before *vigah*, but it only applied to females. Pep was cheerfulness. It mysteriously resided in the Ipana smile. "Weird" or "eccentric" girls, moody girls or troublemaking girls did not have pep. We who had it became cheerleaders, committing ourselves to a season of steady pep, bouncy activity, and good clean dispositions.

I do.

We played some humid swimming meets in Far Rockaway and Flushing, tottering at the edge of the pool and getting our hair all fuzzy, but basketball was the main attraction. (There was no football. Rumor said a boy had once been killed on the field and the sport discontinued.) Cheerleaders as a group were married to the basketball team as a group. We played wife.

Our job was to support the team. We were the decorative touches in the gyms they played. We had some "prestige" in the city because the team was good that year. They had a little of our prestige rub off on them, too, for Forest Hills was known for the good-looking stuck-up bitches there. We learned to cater to the boys' moods, not to talk to Gary after he had a bad game (he would glower and shake us off), and yet to *be* there when he or Stanley or Steve came out of the locker room all showered and handsome. We were there for them always, peppy and smiling. Boys had acceptable temper tantrums on the court, but cheerleaders never did. We were expected to be consistently "happy," like the Rockettes at Radio City Music Hall.

We were the best athletic supporters that ever lived.

We paired off, cheerleader and basketball player, like a socialite wife and corporation executive, leading lady and leading man. My social life was defined by my "status." I only went out with jocks. "Who's *he?*" or "What a creep!" applied to boys who wore desert boots or girls who were "brains." We knew kids "like us" in other middle-class ghettos in the city, and we stayed away from the Greek and Italian kids in our school, from "rocks" like Howie and Dominic who played cards and drank and "laid girls," and from girls like Carole and Anita whom we called "hitter chicks" and who, we whispered, went all the way.

Cheerleaders had a reputation for chastity. No one ever said it, but we all understood it. On top of the general fifties hangups about sex, cheerleaders had a special role to play. Vestal virgins in the rites of puberty. Jewish madonnas.

Half the time, in real "civilian" life, I had to keep pulling those gray flannel skirts down, making sure "nothing showed," keeping my legs crossed. I would have been incarcerated on the spot by my mother if, one morning, I refused to layer the top of my body with a bra and all its padding followed by a slip followed by a blouse. Even if I were to evade Mother, my peers would have condemned me as a "slut" if I appeared less dressed.

The other half the time, as a cheerleader, I dropped a skimpy red costume over only bra and panties and got out there in the middle of a gym full of screaming spectators to wiggle my hips all over the place.

What does it do to the mind of a 16-year-old girl to be Marilyn Monroe one moment and Little Goody Two-Shoes the next? I don't know, but it sure wasn't sane.

For weeks before we went, the word was whispered from ear to ear among us: *Jamaica.*

Jamaica High School was the first "away" game we went to in my senior year. The word was full of terror. Jamaica had black kids. Forest Hills High School had been redistricted every year and there were *no* blacks in the school. Aside from the rocks and hitter chicks, nearly everyone was white, middle class, and Jewish. We held mirrors up to each other and told each other we were very heavenly and the whole world was like us, except we never really believed it. We called Manhattan "New York" or "The City." It was as far away and glamorous to us as it was to Clarence in Peoria or Pat in Kansas. Our mothers wouldn't let us go there.

I confess: when I left the Forest Hills ghetto for the first "away" game, I, Princess of the Pom-Poms, Our Lady of the Saddle Shoes, Culture Queen, carried with me, hidden in my purse, a menacing kitchen knife. For protection.

Every time I say "sure" when I mean "no," every time I smile brightly when I'm exploding with rage, every time I imagine my man's achievement is my own, I know the cheerleader never really died. I feel her shaking her ass inside me and I hear her breathless, girlish voice mutter "T-E-A-M, Yea, Team."

God knows, I tried hard to kill her. For-

est Hills had a history of sending its red-skirted stars bouncing off for the big league at Cornell, and it looked for a few months just before I turned 17 as though I might follow their saddle-shoed footsteps, but something happened. I went to Barnard College instead.

Barnard was another kind of game, requiring a different kind of coin to play. No points there for having been a cheerleader. It was no longer a high-priced commodity, but now a social deficit. I, alert to the winds of change and being a good mimic, buried my cheerleader past. Fast.

"What did you do in high school?"

"I wrote poetry."

"I was in the theater."

"I listened to jazz."

And the cheerleader stayed buried until recently, when I had a series of strange revelations:

Beautiful, exotic Janet, painter-poet, was a cheerleader in Connecticut.

Acid-freak Nina, unwed hippie mother, was a cheerleader in Ohio.

Elegant Susan, theatrical and literary, was a cheerleader in Philadelphia.

Shaggy Bob, radical lawyer, was a basketball player at Midwood.

Junk dealer Joe was on the Bayside team.

I am not alone.

It *was* the only game in town for middle-class kids in the American fifties.

The world is full of us.

T-E-A-M.

Yea, Team!

Dee Brown

Dee Brown (b. 1908), writer of several books about the Western frontier, researcher, and librarian, traces in Bury My Heart at Wounded Knee *the history of the American Indian. This, the last chapter in that book, shows the physical and spiritual destruction of a people.*

WOUNDED KNEE

There was no hope on earth, and God seemed to have forgotten us. Some said they saw the Son of God; others did not see Him. If He had come, He would do some great things as He had done before. We doubted it because we had seen neither Him nor His works.

The people did not know; they did not care. They snatched at the hope. They screamed like crazy men to Him for mercy. They caught at the promise they heard He had made.

The white men were frightened and called for soldiers. We had begged for life, and the white men thought we wanted theirs. We heard that soldiers were coming. We did not fear. We hoped that we could tell them our troubles and get help. A white man said the soldiers meant to kill us. We did not believe it, but some were frightened and ran away to the Badlands.

—RED CLOUD

Had it not been for the sustaining force of the Ghost Dance religion, the Sioux in their grief and anger over the assassination of Sitting Bull might have risen up against the guns of the soldiers. So prevalent was their belief that the white men would soon disappear and that with the next greening of the grass their dead relatives and friends would return, they made no retaliations. By the hundreds, however, the leaderless Hunkpapas fled from Standing Rock, seeking refuge in one of the Ghost Dance camps or with the last of the great chiefs, Red Cloud, at Pine Ridge. In the Moon When the Deer Shed Their Horns (December 17) about a hundred of these fleeing Hunkpapas reached Big Foot's Minneconjou camp near Cherry Creek. That same day the War Department issued orders for the arrest and imprisonment of Big Foot. He was on the list of "fomenters of disturbances."

As soon as Big Foot learned that Sitting Bull had been killed, he started his people toward Pine Ridge, hoping that Red Cloud could protect them from the soldiers. En route, he fell ill of pneumonia, and when hemorrhaging began, he had to travel in a wagon. On December 28, as they neared Porcupine Creek, the Minneconjous sighted four troops of cavalry approaching. Big Foot immediately ordered a white flag run up over his wagon. About two o'clock in the afternoon he raised up from his blankets to greet Major Samuel Whitside, Seventh U.S. Cavalry. Big Foot's blankets were stained with blood from his lungs, and as he talked in a hoarse whisper with Whitside, red drops fell from his nose and froze in the bitter cold.

Whitside told Big Foot that he had orders to take him to a cavalry camp on Wounded Knee Creek. The Minneconjou chief replied that he was going in that direction; he was taking his people to Pine Ridge for safety.

Turning to his half-breed scout, John Shangreau, Major Whitside ordered him to begin disarming Big Foot's band.

"Look here, Major," Shangreau replied, "if you do that, there is liable to be a fight here; and if there is, you will kill all those women and children and the men will get away from you."

Whitside insisted that his orders were to capture Big Foot's Indians and disarm and dismount them.

"We better take them to camp and then take their horses from them and their guns," Shangreau declared.

"All right," Whitside agreed. "You tell Big Foot to move down to camp at Wounded Knee."

The major glanced at the ailing chief, and then gave an order for his Army ambulance to be brought forward. The ambulance would be warmer and would give Big Foot an easier ride than the jolting springless wagon. After the chief was transferred to the ambulance, Whitside formed a column for the march to Wounded Knee

Creek. Two troops of cavalry took the lead, the ambulance and wagons following, the Indians herded into a compact group behind them, with the other two cavalry troops and a battery of two Hotchkiss guns bringing up the rear.

Twilight was falling when the column crawled over the last rise in the land and began descending the slope toward Chankpe Opi Wakpala, the creek called Wounded Knee. The wintry dusk and the tiny crystals of ice dancing in the dying light added a supernatural quality to the somber landscape. Somewhere along this frozen stream the heart of Crazy Horse lay in a secret place, and the Ghost Dancers believed that his disembodied spirit was waiting impatiently for the new earth that would surely come with the first green grass of spring.

At the cavalry tent camp on Wounded Knee Creek, the Indians were halted and carefully counted. There were 120 men and 230 women and children. Because of the gathering darkness, Major Whitside decided to wait until morning before disarming his prisoners. He assigned them a camping area immediately to the south of the military camp, issued them rations, and as there was a shortage of tepee covers, he furnished them several tents. Whitside ordered a stove placed in Big Foot's tent and sent a regimental surgeon to administer to the sick chief. To make certain that none of his prisoners escaped, the major stationed two troops of cavalry as sentinels around the Sioux tepees, and then posted his two Hotchkiss guns on top of a rise overlooking the camp. The barrels of these rifled guns, which could hurl explosive charges for more than two miles, were positioned to rake the length of the Indian lodges.

Later in the darkness of that December night the remainder of the Seventh Regiment marched in from the east and quietly bivouacked north of Major Whitside's troops. Colonel James W. Forsyth, commanding Custer's former regiment, now took charge of operations. He informed Whitside that he had received orders to take Big Foot's band to the Union Pacific Railroad for shipment to a military prison in Omaha.

After placing two more Hotchkiss guns on the slope beside the others, Forsyth and his officers settled down for the evening with a keg of whiskey to celebrate the capture of Big Foot.

The chief lay in his tent, too ill to sleep, barely able to breathe. Even with their protective Ghost Shirts and their belief in the prophecies of the new Messiah, his people were fearful of the pony soldiers camped all around them. Fourteen years before, on the Little Bighorn, some of these warriors had helped defeat some of these soldier chiefs—Moylan, Varnum, Wallace, Godfrey, Edgerly—and the Indians wondered if revenge could still be in their hearts.

"The following morning there was a bugle call," said Wasumaza, one of Big Foot's warriors who years afterward was to change his name to Dewey Beard. "Then I saw the soldiers mounting their horses and surrounding us. It was announced that all men should come to the center for a talk and that after the talk they were to move on to Pine Ridge agency. Big Foot was brought out of his tepee and sat in front of his tent and the older men were gathered around him and sitting right near him in the center."

After issuing hardtack for breakfast rations, Colonel Forsyth informed the Indians that they were now to be disarmed. "They called for guns and arms," White Lance said, "so all of us gave the guns and they were stacked up in the center." The soldier chiefs were not satisfied with the number of weapons surrendered, and so they sent details of troopers to search the tepees. "They would go right into the tents and come out with bundles and tear them open," Dog Chief said. "They brought our axes, knives, and tent stakes and piled them near the guns."

Still not satisfied, the soldier chiefs ordered the warriors to remove their blankets and submit to searches for weapons. The Indians' faces showed their anger, but only the medicine man, Yellow Bird, made any overt protest. He danced a few Ghost Dance steps, and chanted one of the holy songs, assuring the warriors that the soldiers' bullets could not penetrate their sacred garments. "The bullets will not go toward you," he chanted in Sioux. "The prairie is large and the bullets will not go toward you."

The troopers found only two rifles, one of them a new Winchester belonging to a young Minneconjou named Black Coyote. Black Coyote raised the Winchester above his head, shouting that he paid much money for the rifle and that it belonged to him. Some years afterward Dewey Beard recalled that Black Coyote was deaf. "If they had left him alone he was going to put his gun down where he should. They grabbed him and spinned him in the east direction. He was still unconcerned even then. He hadn't his gun pointed at anyone. His intention was to put that gun down. They came on and grabbed the gun that he was going to put down. Right after they spun him around there was the report of a gun, was quite loud. I couldn't say that anybody was shot, but following that was a crash."

"It sounded much like the sound of tearing canvas, that was the crash," Rough Feather said. Afraid-of-the-Enemy described it as a "lightning crash."

Turning Hawk said that Black Coyote "was a crazy man, a young man of very bad influence and in fact a nobody." He said that Black Coyote fired his gun and that "immediately the soldiers returned fire and indiscriminate killing followed."

In the first seconds of violence, the firing of carbines was deafening, filling the air with powder smoke. Among the dying who lay sprawled on the frozen ground was Big Foot. Then there was a brief lull in the rattle of arms, with small groups of Indians and soldiers grappling at close quarters,

using knives, clubs, and pistols. As few of the Indians had arms, they soon had to flee, and then the big Hotchkiss guns on the hill opened up on them, firing almost a shell a second, raking the Indian camp, shredding the tepees with flying shrapnel, killing men, women, and children.

"We tried to run," Louise Weasel Bear said, "but they shot us like we were a buffalo. I know there are some good white people, but the soldiers must be mean to shoot children and women. Indian soldiers would not do that to white children."

"I was running away from the place and followed those who were running away," said Hakiktawin, another of the young women. "My grandfather and grandmother and brother were killed as we crossed the ravine, and then I was shot on the right hip clear through and on my right wrist where I did not go any further as I was not able to walk, and after the soldier picked me up where a little girl came to me and crawled into the blanket."

When the madness ended, Big Foot and more than half of his people were dead or seriously wounded; 153 were known dead, but many of the wounded crawled away to die afterward. One estimate placed the final total of dead at very nearly three hundred of the original 350 men, women, and children. The soldiers lost twenty-five dead and thirty-nine wounded, most of them struck by their own bullets or shrapnel.

After the wounded cavalrymen were started for the agency at Pine Ridge, a detail of soldiers went over the Wounded Knee battlefield, gathering up Indians who were still alive and loading them into wagons. As it was apparent by the end of the day that a blizzard was approaching, the dead Indians were left lying where they had fallen. (After the blizzard, when a burial party returned to Wounded Knee, they found the bodies, including Big Foot's, frozen into grotesque shapes.)

The wagonloads of wounded Sioux (four men and forty-seven women and children) reached Pine Ridge after dark. Because all available barracks were filled with soldiers, they were left lying in the open wagons in the bitter cold while an inept Army officer searched for shelter. Finally the Episcopal mission was opened, the benches taken out, and hay scattered over the rough flooring.

It was the fourth day after Christmas in the Year of Our Lord 1890. When the first torn and bleeding bodies were carried into the candlelit church, those who were conscious could see Christmas greenery hanging from the open rafters. Across the chancel front above the pulpit was strung a crudely lettered banner: PEACE ON EARTH, GOOD WILL TO MEN.

I did not know then how much was ended. When I look back now from this high hill of my old age, I can still see the butchered women and children lying heaped and scattered all along the crooked gulch as plain as when I saw them with eyes still young. And I can see that something else died there in the bloody mud, and was buried in the blizzard. A people's dream died there. It was a beautiful dream . . . the nation's hoop is broken and scattered. There is no center any longer, and the sacred tree is dead.

—BLACK ELK

Stan Steiner

This selection describes the conditions of the "barrio" or ghetto and the various ways Chicanos adapt to these conditions. Steiner sees the use of gangs and of more socially committed groups like United Mexican American Students as ways that Chicanos achieve pride in their racial and cultural heritage.

THE CHICANOS

The girl was thirteen when she tried to kill herself. She was "tired of working." But she was too inexperienced with death to die, and she lived through her death. To escape her loneliness she married, at fifteen. Her child was born that year, but her husband was sent to prison. "I got a car. The car broke down. I couldn't pay for it. They wanted to sue me. So I forged a check." In the barrios of Denver to be left with a baby, without a husband, at fifteen, was to be lonelier than death. She became a prostitute.

"I worked the town. They call it hustling. I wouldn't go for less than thirty dollars. Because I needed the money. I got it too. All you have to do is be nice," the young girl said. "But to go out and hustle I had to be under the influence of narcotics."

Diana Perea told her own life story to the National Conference on Poverty in the Southwest, held in January, 1965, to launch the War on Poverty. In the winter sun of Tucson, Arizona, the nearly two hundred delegates who had gathered under the auspices of the Choate Foundation, to hear Vice President Hubert Humphrey, were as overwhelmed by the frail and frightened girl as she was by the presidential emissary. "Go back and tell them [your people] that the war against unemployment, discrimination, disease, and ignorance has begun. Tell them to get out and fight!" the Vice President said. "The wonderful thing about the War on Poverty is that we have the means to win it. We cannot fail." He reminded his listeners, "Fifteen minutes from where we sit tonight there is abject poverty."

In the audience was Diana Perea. A few weeks later she succeeded in killing herself.

Her death was due to an overdose of narcotics, the autopsy report declared. There were some nonmedical causes. On the frontispiece of the Summary Report of the National Conference on Poverty in the Southwest there was a black border of mourning around these simple words:

DIANA PEREA
1946–1965
VICTIM OF POVERTY

Death is an ordinary thing. No one

would have heard of the young girl from the streets of Denver's barrio if she had not happened to share a microphone with the Vice President of the United States.

In the streets misery is said to be so common no one notices. Life in the barrios is cruel—to outsiders, for the sons and daughters of the poor, it is said, are too hardened and brutalized to be able to do anything but fight to survive.

A young girl cries of a brown child dying of hunger in the barrios of San Antonio:

> in the land of the free
> and the home of the brave,
> He is dying of hunger,
> he cannot be saved;
> Come brothers and sisters
> and weep by his grave.
> This is our child—

The ordeal of these youths is bemoaned by sympathetic writers. Not by the youth. Diana Perea did not weep. The Chicana was matter of fact: this is the way it is. Life in the barrio streets is just a way of life—happy, unhappy, ordinary, exciting, boring, deadly. The streets are not dangerous, they are only treacherous. It doesn't frighten youth. Seldom do they curse the barrio. They curse themselves for their inability to survive. It is not the barrio that the Chicano fears but the lonely and hostile world outside.

Loneliness, the coldness of urban life, is what depresses the Chicano. In his family there is a warmth and gregarious love voiced with passion, uninhibited honesty, and gusto. The city frustrates and mutes this love. Faced with a society that he feels is hostile, the barrio youth becomes lost. He tries to defend himself by forming a gang, not just to fight for his manhood, his *macho,* but for his right to be a Chicano.

"The most brutal method of birth control is the one we practice on ourselves," a young man writes in *La Raza.*

To *La Raza Chicana,* a young girl writes a bitter note: "I wish to compliment brother Perfecto Vallego and his friends for doing

with Caterino B. Heredia. Keep up the good work, Baby, you and the cops [can] get together on the Chicano Annual School. Your game is as bad as the racist cop who goes after Chicano's who fail to halt. You dudes don't have to kill your brothers; Uncle Sam is doing that for you in Viet Nam. You are shooting the wrong guy. *No sean tan pende-jos.* If you have enough *huevos* [testicles] to shoot your brother you should be able to take on a racist cop."

The street gangs of the barrios are different from those in most ghettos. In a sense they are born not solely of poverty, but also of cultural pride. Like street-corner chambers of commerce the gangs of barrio youth defend the spirit of La Raza with bravado and youthful boisterousness.

Of the many barrio gangs the oldest and best known is that of the legendary Pachucos, who have become a heroic myth. They were born in blood that was real enough, and they not only are remembered but are imitated with awe. They began on a day in August, 1942. In the tensions of World War II, the racial hatreds of Los Angeles were about to erupt in what was to be known as the "Zoot Suit Riots." Two groups of Chicanos had a boyish fight over a pretty girl and hurt pride, in a gravel pit on the outskirts of the city. In the morning the body of young José Díaz was found on a dirt road nearby, dead. Bored newspapermen, seeking local color, dubbed the gravel pit the "Sleepy Lagoon" (it had a mud puddle in it), and an orgy of sensational headlines celebrated the boy's death.

Not one but twenty-four Mexican boys were arrested; nine were convicted of second-degree murder. All were freed later, two years later, when the Court of Appeals reversed the sentences unanimously for "lack of evidence."

The "Sleepy Lagoon" case is still remembered bitterly in the barrios, much as the Dreyfus case in France, or that of the Scottsboro Boys in the Deep South.

Amid headlines of hysteria—"Zoot Suit Hoodlums" and "Pachuco Gangsters"—the

Los Angeles police raided the barrios, blockaded the main streets, searched every passing car and passer-by. Six hundred Chicanos were taken into custody in a two-day sweep that Police Captain Joseph Reed called "a drive on Mexican gangs." The Los Angeles sheriff's "Bureau of *Foreign* Relations" justified the dragnet by officially philosophizing that the Chicanos' "desire to kill, or at least let blood" was an "inborn characteristic."

The next summer the tensions exploded. When a fist fight broke out on a downtown street between a gang of Chicano boys and U.S. Navy men in June, 1943, fourteen off-duty policemen led by a lieutenant of the Detective Squad set up an impromptu group of vigilantes they named the "Vengeance Squad" and set out "to clean up" the Mexicans.

Night after night hundreds of restless and beached sailors of the U.S. Navy, bored and frustrated by their inaction in the war against Japan, seized upon the nearest available dark-skinned enemies—the young Chicanos—and beat them up. The white rioters toured the barrios in convoys of taxi cabs, attacking every brown boy they found on the streets, in bars and restaurants and movie houses, by the dozens, by the hundreds, while the Los Angeles police looked the other way. No sailor was arrested. Inspired by the inflammatory news stories about "zoot suit roughnecks," the white rioters sought out these most of all—zoot suits were an early Humphrey Bogart style Mexicanized by Chicano boys and lately revived in its classic form by *Bonnie and Clyde.*

It was a long, hot summer week. When the white rioters exhausted their racial fervor, the riots—known not as the "U.S. Navy Riots" but oddly as the "Zoot Suit Riots"—had left hundreds of injured and a residue of race hatred in Los Angeles.

The zoot-suit boys were Pachucos. Where the name came from is vague, but it may have been taken from the city of Pachuco in Mexico, known for its brilliantly hued costumes. In the riots, these gangs of Pachucos were not the aggressors but the defenders of the barrios. They were an early self-defense group. Youths who never knew the Pachucos remember them not as victims but as resistance fighters of the streets, the Minutemen of *machismo,* who fought to defend the reputation of La Raza. Wherever the barrio youth organize, the spirit of the Pachucos is evoked and revived.

"I hope you tell the story of the Pachucos," a Brown Beret says to me. "We have to learn about our heroes."

One of many Pachuco-type gangs is the Vatos. It is a fictitious name of a small gang in the San Fernando Valley of Los Angeles whose "territory" ranges from Laurel Canyon Boulevard to O'Melveny Street. The Vatos hang out mostly in the dark alleys near Acala Avenue, a poorly lit thoroughfare.

A member of the Vatos talks of his gang:

"This is the story of life in a Mexican barrio. The barrio is called 'San Fer.' The kids, so-called Pachucos, run this barrio. Life in this barrio is rough, harsh. The boys learned early to carry can openers and knives. As soon as they got a little older they graduated to switchblades, lengths of chain, and guns, if they could get hold of them.

"Boys joined together to form street gangs, and some of them sported the Pachuco brand between the thumb and forefinger of their left hand," the Vato says. "This gang is the stuff of life, as the Pachuco knows it."

The gang member has to prove his manhood and his ability to survive. "He will undertake the most fantastic stunts to prove a great deal. He will risk his life and his freedom to maintain his growing reputation as a tough fighter, a rugged guy." These rituals are not merely rites of initiation, or idle bravado. The gang youth has to demonstrate not only that he can fight in the streets, but that he has the strength to withstand the hostility of society, to stand up to the *placa,* the police, and if he is courageous enough, to become visible to the outsider, by wearing a Brown Beret. "That is real *macho*," a Los Angeles community leader says.

It is a new kind of political and urban *pachuquismo*. The society outside the barrio is defined by the gang. Consciously the rituals of brotherhood enforce the laws and culture of the barrio. Inside the gang the Chicano is insulated from his own conflicts. The Chicanos "find conflicts so perplexing and so full of both cultures—that of their parents and that of America—that [they] create their own world of *pachuquismo*," says the Vato.

The Vato goes on: "The Vatos have created their own language, Pachucano, their own style of dress, their own folklore, and their own behavior patterns. The Vatos have developed a barrio group spirit. The Vatos in this area are better organized and a little tighter, due to the fact that it is a smaller group; and therefore all the Vatos participate in the activities planned by them.

"They formed a closely knit group that regarded the Anglos as their natural enemies."

In every barrio the social clubs and folk religious societies have always existed in semisecrecy, with their own rules and symbols, hidden from the world outside. Chicano gangs are the progeny of that invisible heritage—to outsiders—by which the barrio has protected itself. They re-create in their own youthful way, the society and culture of their forefathers; yet they are urban.

Eliezer Risco, the editor of *La Raza*, describes these methods of barrio organizations as "our own survival techniques. It is difficult for the culture of a minority to survive in the larger society. If we can utilize them for social action, now that we are stronger, we will surprise the country," he says. "The country won't know where our strength is coming from or how we organize."

In the dark alleyways and gregarious streets, the Brown Berets began. They have developed a political *pachuquismo*. A generation ago they would have been a street gang, nothing more. Less obvious are the barrio origins of the youthful leaders of the La Raza movements that have gained national prominence and importance. Cesar Chavez, Rodolfo "Corky" Gonzales, Reies Tijerina: these men learned their organizing techniques on the back streets of the barrio.

"They say the La Raza movements come from the universities. I disagree," says "José," the "Field Marshal" of the Brown Berets. "I say they come from the streets."

So few youths in the barrios graduated from high school in the past or entered college, that those who achieved that miraculous feat feared to look down from their pinnacle of anxiety. If they did, the barrios beneath them seemed a bottomless arroyo. And yet, in the wholly anglicized realms of higher education they were also strangers.

"You see a Chicano [university] student is alienated from his language; he is deculturized and finally dehumanized so as to be able to function in a white, middle-class, protestant bag," the *Chicano Student News* reports. "It is damn obvious to the Chicano in college that education means one of two things: either accept the system—study, receive a diploma, accept the cubicle and the IBM machine in some lousy bank or factory, and move out of the barrio—or reject the system. . . ."

Youths who made it to the university clung to their privileged and precarious achievements: non-Mexican name and anglicized accent, an Ivy League suit, a blond wife, and a disdain for the "dumb Mexicans" left behind: "THE PURPLE TIO TOMAS" (Uncle Tom), *El Gallo* has dubbed these high achievers. "This is the middle class Tomás. He isn't a Tomás because he lives on the other side of town, but because the Purple Tomás believes he is better than other Chicanos. Purple is the Royal Color!" The would-be intellectual *patróns*—"the new conservatives," Corky Gonzales calls them.

Now the university students have begun to climb down from their lonely success to the streets of the barrios and the fields of the campesinos. They come as on a pilgrimage, seeking an identity. Los Angeles community leader Eduardo Pérez says, "I find that many Mexicans-turned-Spanish are coming back into the fold and are being identified for what they are: Mexicans." They have a "pride in being Mexican."

In the vineyards of Delano, when the striking grape pickers gathered their banners and walked north on the highway in their 250-mile pilgrimage to Sacramento to see the Governor, the university Chicanos who walked with the *huelguistas* were wide-eyed with wonder. Not only were these young people from the universities, but they were the children of the barrios who had at last escaped, had "made it." Some even had blond hair.

Here were "farm workers with dark faces, aged prematurely by the California sun, marching side by side with students with youthful faces," wrote Daniel de los Reyes in the union newspaper *El Malcriado,* the "farm workers with black hair and a determined look, by the side of blond and red-haired students with brilliant, sparkling eyes." It was "a spectacle to see, these thousands and thousands of young people" who had come "because the Farm Workers Organizing Committee had agreed to join side by side with their brothers, the students." There was a tone of wonder in the union newspaper story. It seemed unbelievable, this "brotherhood against ignorance and poverty." These were "the same students we have seen so many times on the picketlines at the vineyards of DiGiorgio, the same youth working so tirelessly on the boycotts," declared *El Malcriado.*

Still it was not to be believed. The university students respected, listened to, and obeyed the campesinos of the fields; that was what was so strange. It was as though they who were illiterate were the teachers of the university students.

The experience of the *huelga* was a strange and exhilarating one for the students as well, for it profoundly affected the lives of many who had come. Luis Valdez, who went on to found El Centro Cultural Campesino, and Eliezer Risco, who became editor of *La Raza,* were but two of dozens of student leaders whose lives were changed by their pilgrimage to the vineyards of Delano.

"I was writing my thesis," Risco recalls. "I came thinking, well, it's a way of doing my research. But it was my Graduate School."

Venustiano Olguin was a brilliant student in a graduate school of the University of California at Los Angeles and was studying for his Ph.D. The son of a bracero who had grown up in the migrant barrios of the Coachella Valley, he had worked his way to first place in his high school class and graduated with honors from the University of Redlands.

"I'd been very successful with the system." But he had begun to have the uneasy feeling he was becoming a "Tío Tomás," an Uncle Tom. "At UCLA I knew that somewhere along the line I had been betraying something." He did not know what.

One summer the young man and some of his fellow students in the United Mexican American Students (UMAS) had a meeting with Cesar Chavez. Olguin went to Delano—not to stay, just to look around and help the farm workers if he could. He decided to join *La Huelga.* He has abandoned the honors of higher education that he says were anglicizing him, indoctrinating him with materialistic values, and forcing him to reject his Mexican heritage. He lives on $5 a week strike pay. "Some people think I am crazy. But I think my life is very rich." In the campesinos he feels he has found "a special kind of courage," of manhood. "I've learned more than in all the time I was in graduate school."

University communities of Chicanos were affected as strongly. In San Antonio, Texas, a leader of the Mexican American Youth Organization recalls how the campesinos of the Rio Grande Valley became godfathers of his group. "The strike of the farm workers got everyone excited. St. Mary's University students got together to see what they could do," says William Vazquez. "And that is how we began."

Luis Valdez, whose life was changed by Delano, feels it is a necessary school for students. "In advance of their people, the Chicano leader in the cities and universities must go through the whole bourgeois scene, find it distasteful, and then strike out in new directions. This is what happened with Corky Gonzales and Cesar Chavez. Divorcing themselves from the petty aims of success, they see the middle class for what it is. Then they can see the lower class plain.

"In short, they discover there is a world out there," Valdez says.

Out of the upheaval have come dozens of new barrio and university clubs. In the last few years there has been more youth organizing than in the entire history of the Chicanos. University students have been especially outspoken and active. The United Mexican American Students (UMAS) in California and the National Organization of Mexican American Students (NOMAS, literally "No More") in Texas are but two of more than thirty groups on the campuses alone.

The university and barrio youth are talking and walking together. David Sanchez, the prime minister of the Brown Berets, talks to students at UCLA, while the students of UMAS walk not only on the picket lines of the campesinos of Delano but also beside the Brown Berets protesting school conditions in East Los Angeles. The *Chicano Student News* reports: "UMAS is an organization of Chicano college students which is bringing the business of education back into the Chicano community"; and the headline says, "UMAS COMES HOME!"

"Old hatreds and quarrels are being put aside," *La Raza* writes, for *"Todos son Chicanos"*—"We are all Chicanos."

Several dozen Chicanos gathered at a dude ranch near Santa Barbara on the California seacoast for one of the many conferences of students and barrio youths. Eduardo Pérez, who helped run the conference, describes the occasion:

"Nowadays the young lions and lionesses have their own cars, buy their own clothes, work their way through college, and are very much on their own. Their whole thinking and outlook on life is as different from ours as night is from day.

"These Mexican American 'world leaders of tomorrow' are an exceptional breed. They can put on a *charro* [the real cowboy Mexican] costume and be proud of it. They can even put on American clothes and feel at ease. They can eat enchiladas and hamburgers on the same plate, tacos and pizza in one sitting, and possibly drink tequila with beer as a chaser and feel right at home. They have become anglicized, but only to the point that there is no excuse for them not being accepted. They take pride in being of Mexican ancestry and do not deny being what they are. These kids don't change their names just to become Spanish or European heirs. . . ."

In spite of the ease with which they seemed to go from one culture to another, the young Chicanos suffered an inner paralysis. They doubted not their emotions or their thoughts, but to create one culture out of two so different. Pérez had written of another youth conference, "The Mexican Americans attending (most of them) did not really understand themselves . . . and how they happened to be in the mess they're in."

The university and barrio youth had this in common too.

"I stand naked in the world, lost in

angry solitude," the Chicano poet Benjamin Luna writes in *La Raza*. The loneliness of the urban society—impersonal, cold, efficient, foreign to his heart—evokes the feeling of a hostile world. The futility the Chicano feels is not fatalism, but a rage of frustration.

Soy Indio con alma hambrienta,
  traigo en la sangre coraje,
  rojo coraje en la sangre.

I am Indian with a hungry soul,
  tragic in the passionate blood,
  red passion in the blood.

I stand naked in the world,
  hungry
  homeless
  despised. . . .

In the barrios, brotherhood is in the blood, the blood of La Raza. "One boy will bring beer, while others will bring *rifa;* still others bring money for the use of activities, or gas in a member's car. This is a thing that goes on every night with something different every night that can be called a 'dead kick.'" At best, their inner brotherhood is limited by the outer world of their "natural enemy," and at worst is defined by it.

A Brown Beret laments, "We are not what we were when we started out. All those TV cameras and news reporters took over our image and changed us into their image of us."

"Who am I?" asks a young woman in a suburban church of Los Angeles. "I have been afraid to speak up for my rights. Rights? What rights do we have? So many of our youth plead guilty in court when they know they are not guilty of anything. Anything but being a Mexican."

"Soul searching," Dr. Ernesto Galarza calls it. The scholar, a sparse man of wiry thoughts and whitening hair, who talks with hard, dry words, is recognized by many of the Chicano youth leaders as the dean of the La Raza movement; perhaps the dean emeritus. "There is an incredible amount of soul searching going on among this generation. Of questioning. Of seeking," he says one midnight over coffee in a motel in Santa Barbara, where he has gone to teach a youth workshop.

"Many of these youth have been propelled into crises of considerable tension. There have been tragic losses, where some of them have been torn asunder by the conflicts, internal and external, within themselves. There has been a loss of much potential. The youth are resilient, however.

"I believe there are few phoneys in this generation. Anyone who believes this is a time for the promotion of Uncle Toms, of acquiescence, among the younger generation of Mexicans, is mistaken. Unquestionably this generation is confronted with some crippling problems. But *that* is not one of them," says the scholar.

Dr. Galarza's weary eyes light up when he talks of these youths. "I am delighted by the happenstance of the last ten years. There has been the growth of quite a small army of young men, a phalanx of potential leaders who are searching for a breakthrough. The younger generation holds much promise.

"It is too early to foresee where these movements will lead. There is little unity of thought. There is precious little cohesion. Every movement is its own little stirring of activity. In five or ten years, there may be a reckoning; a culmination.

"We will wait," the scholar says, "and we will see."

Of course, the youth will not wait. They want action now, ideology later. Having had a small glimpse of their cultural identity, they want the rest; and having had a foretaste of Chicano power, they yearn for more: "Mañana is here!" says Maclovio Barraza, leader of the Arizona miners.

"Who the hell are we? What are we? Where do we belong? Study it! Announce it to the world!" Joe Benitos, a Chicano leader in Arizona, exclaims impatiently. "Let's end this hangup about identity. We know who we are. In order to survive we have learned survival skills. Sure, but let's not confuse our survival skills in Anglo society with our culture. We have a parallel culture. We have to keep it. I say we can do it. We don't have to be one of *them!*"

His impatience with the talk of the "identity crisis" is typical of the young Chicano. Benitos feels the problem of identity is perpetuated by university study projects, "so that they will have something to study"; he has worked with several of these projects. "I've been there," he says. "And that's not where it's at.

"Yes, having two cultures creates problems. Why emphasize the problems? Why not emphasize the opportunities it gives the Chicano in the new world scene?

"There is a Chicano wave coming in," says Benitos. "I see it as part of the worldwide scene. As the world shrinks everyone will have to learn more than one language, one culture. Everyone will have to be bilingual and trilingual. It will put us in a fantastic position, if we can keep our languages and cultures.

"Our experience will be a lesson for the whole world," he says.

"Chicano" is a new word, not yet in the dictionary. La Raza writers cannot yet define it except by what it is not; the Chicano is not, they say, half-Mexican, half-American, who blends two cultures in his being. He is not just one more second- and third-generation city-bred descendant of a rural villager who has learned to drive a car like a wild horse and pay for it on the installment plan. La Raza is a new people with a new culture and the Chicano is its youngest offspring. He has inherited many things from Mexico and the United States, but he imitates neither. The Chicano is a new man.

In the La Raza newspapers there appears a "Definition of the Word Chicano" by Benito Rodríguez. He is a member of MANO (Hand), a group of Chicano ex-con-

victs in San Antonio, Texas. Rodríguez's words, even more than his ideas, the way he writes, the style, the language he uses, give some of the feeling of being a Chicano in the barrio of a modern city. Even in the pale English translation the strong flavor of that life comes through, although it is stronger in the Spanish. He writes:

"Many designations have been used to refer to us, the descendants of Mexicans. Every ten or fifteen years, or so, we feel like searching for a new image of ourselves. First, in the time of the 'Wild West' we were 'Mexican bandits,' then 'greasers,' then 'Mescins,' and now we are 'Spanish Americans,' 'Mexican Americans,' 'Americans,' etc.

"The migrant Mexicans, workers in the field, call themselves Chicapatas (short legs), or Raza (race, as in Raza del Sol, People of the Sun). City workers use the term Chicano a little more. The phrase Mexican-American is really used by the middle-class Mexicans. What is truly Mexican is covered by a layer, Chicano, to satisfy all the conditions in which we find ourselves. How shall we describe ourselves tomorrow, or the day after?

"Now they want to make us half Mexicans and half Americans, as if they were talking about geography. Well, we already know who we are. Why do we come on like a chicken with its head cut off? Why do we let them make fakes, if we are Chicanos down to the phlegm in our mouths? If you don't like the taste you'll swallow it anyway.

"Just because we've seen their marvelous technology doesn't mean we believe that those who exploit us are gods."

Benito Rodríguez concludes with a curse that is pure Chicano: "A poor man who thinks he lives in heaven is gonna get fucked, coming and going."

John F. Kennedy

WAVES OF IMMIGRATION

John F. Kennedy (1917–1963) was the first Roman Catholic elected President of the United States (1961–1963). In this article Kennedy, a fourth generation Irish American, examines the contributions to America of the major immigrant groups.

American independence, the spreading westward of the new nations, the beginnings of economic diversification and industrialization, all these factors gave immigration in the nineteenth century a new context and a new role. The gates were now flung open, and men and women in search of a new life came to these shores in ever-increasing numbers—150,000 in the 1820's, 1.7 million in the 1840's, 2.8 million in the 1870's, 5.2 million in the 1880's, 8.8 million in the first decade of the twentieth century. And, as the numbers increased, the sources changed. As the English had predominated in the seventeenth and eighteenth centuries, so the Irish and Germans predominated in the first half of the nineteenth and the Italians and East Europeans in the last part of the nineteenth and the early part of the twentieth centuries. Each new wave of immigration helped meet the needs of American development and made its distinctive contribution to the American character.

The Irish

The Irish were in the vanguard of the great waves of immigration to arrive during the nineteenth century. By 1850, after the potato famine, they had replaced England as the chief source of new settlers, making up 44 percent of the foreign-born in the United States. In the century between 1820 and 1920, some four and a quarter million people left Ireland to come to the United States.

They were mostly country folk, small farmers, cottagers, and farm laborers. Yet they congregated mainly in cities along the Eastern seaboard, for they did not have the money to travel after reaching shore. Few could read or write; some spoke only Gaelic.

The Irish were the first to endure the scorn and discrimination later to be inflicted, to some degree at least, on each successive wave of immigrants by already settled "Americans." In speech and dress they seemed foreign; they were poor and unskilled; and they were arriving in overwhelming numbers. The Irish are perhaps the only people in our history with the distinction of having a political party, the Know-Nothings, formed against them. Their religion was later also the target of the American Protective Association and, in this century, the Ku Klux Klan.

The Irish found many doors closed to them, both socially and economically. Advertisements for jobs specified: "No Irish need apply." But there was manual labor to be done, and the Irish were ready to do it. They went to work as longshoremen, as ditch-diggers or as construction workers. When their earnings were not enough to support their families, their wives and daughters obtained employment as servants.

Contractors usually met them at the dock. The Erie Canal, linking New York with the Great Lakes in 1825, and other canals in Massachusetts, New Jersey, Pennsylvania and Maryland were largely built by Irish labor. But the canals soon became obsolete, and the frenzied building of railroads followed. In the three decades from 1830 to 1860, a network of thirty thousand miles of rails was laid across the middle part of the country. Again Irish labor furnished the muscle. When railroad construction was pushed westward in the latter part of the century, the Irish again figured prominently, by now often as foremen and section bosses. They also provided, at the same time, a supply of cheap labor for the mills of Rhode Island and Massachusetts and the coal mines of Pennsylvania.

But as the years passed and new generations were born, things began to change. Gradually, rung by rung, the Irish climbed up the economic and social ladder. Some settled on farms, especially along the canals they had dug. But it was in the cities that they found their principal outlet, in areas in which they could demonstrate their abilities of self-expression, of administration and organization. They gravitated first into law and from that into politics and government. Having experienced for themselves the handicaps of illiteracy, they were determined that their children would have the advantages of education. To that end, they not only started parochial schools, but founded such institutions of higher learning as Notre Dame, Fordham, Holy Cross, Villanova, St. Louis University, Catholic University and Georgetown. They became teachers, writers, journalists, labor organizers, orators and priests. As an expanding society offered more opportunities, they swelled not only the civil service rosters, but the ranks of clerical and administrative workers in industry.

The Irish eased the way for other immigrant groups and speeded their assimilation in several ways. They firmly established the Catholic Church, originally French on this continent, as an English-speaking institution. The schools they founded offered educational opportunities to children of later immigrants of other tongues. The Irish had their own press, their own fraternal orders and their own charitable organizations.

Irish labor leaders fought for the rights of other groups as well as their own. Workers of Irish descent helped organize the Knights of Labor, the first big national union, which was a forerunner of the American Federation of Labor.

The Germans

Between 1830 and 1930, the period of the greatest migration from Europe to the United States, Germany sent six million people to the United States—more than any other nation. Their migrations, increasing in numbers after 1850, overlapped the Irish, whose immigration declined.

The Germans were unique among immigrant groups in their wide dispersal, both geographically and occupationally. This was due, at least in part, to the fact that most of them came with some resources, and were not forced to cluster along the Eastern seaboard. Attracted to the United States by cheap public and railroad lands, and later by free homesteads, the German farmer helped to farm the New West and to cultivate the Mississippi Valley. German artisans, much sought after because of their skills, became an important factor in industrial expansion.

Almost every state in the Union profited from their intellectual and material contributions. Hard-working and knowledgeable about agricultural methods, the Germans became propagators of scientific farming, crop rotation, soil conservation. They share with the Scandinavians the credit for turning millions of acres of wilderness into productive farm land.

The urban settlers lent a distinctive German flavor to many of our cities. Cincinnati, then known as "Queen City" of the West, Baltimore, St. Louis, Minneapolis and Milwaukee, all had substantial German populations. Milwaukee has perhaps retained its distinctive German character longer than any of the others.

In these urban centers Germans entered the fields of education, science, engineering and the arts. German immigrants founded and developed industrial enterprises in the fields of lumbering, food-processing, brewing, steel-making, electrical engineering, piano-making, railroading and printing.

A small but significant part of the German immigration consisted of political refugees. Reaction in Germany against the reform ideas of the French Revolution had caused heavy suppression of liberal thought. There was strict censorship of the press, of public meetings and of the schools and universities. Nevertheless, a liberal movement had emerged, nurtured in the universities by young intellectuals. This movement led to unsuccessful revolutions in 1830 and 1848. The United States welcomed a large number of veterans of 1848 —men of education, substance and social standing, like Carl Schurz, the statesman and reformer, and General Franz Sigel. In addition, some of the German religious groups established utopian communities in parts of Pennsylvania, Ohio, Indiana, Texas and Oregon.

German immigration reflected all the chaotic conditions of Central Europe after Napoleon: the population growth, the widespread hunger, the religious dissension and oppression. The Germans included Lutherans, Jews and Catholics, as well as freethinkers. Their talents, training and background greatly enriched the burgeoning nation.

To the influence of the German immigrants in particular—although all minority groups contributed—we owe the mellowing of the austere Puritan imprint on our daily lives. The Puritans observed the Sabbath as a day of silence and solemnity. The Germans clung to their concept of the "Continental Sunday" as a day, not only of churchgoing, but also of relaxation, of picnics, of visiting, of quiet drinking in beer gardens while listening to the music of a band.

The Christmas ritual of religious services combined with exchanging gifts around the Christmas tree is of German origin. So, too, is the celebration of the New Year.

The fact that today almost every large American city has its symphony orchestra can be traced to the influence of the German migration. Leopold Damrosch and his son, Walter, helped build the famous New York Philharmonic. Originally composed mainly of German immigrant musicians and called the Germania Orchestra, it became the seed bed of similar organizations all over the country. This tradition was carried to the Midwest by Frederick Stock and to Boston by Carl Zerrahn. Others

spread this form of cultural expression to additional urban centers throughout the land.

Community singing and glee clubs owe much to the German immigrant, who remembered his singing societies. The first *Männerchor* was founded in Philadelphia in 1835; the first *Liederkranz* was organized in Baltimore in 1836. Their counterparts have been a feature of the German-American community everywhere.

The ideas of German immigrants helped to shape our educational system. They introduced the kindergarten, or "children's play school." They also promoted the concept of the state-endowed university, patterned after the German university. The University of Michigan, founded in 1837, was the first such school to add to the philosophy of general liberal arts education an emphasis upon vocational training. The colonial concept of a university as a place to prepare gentlemen for a life of leisured culture was modified to include training in specialized skills.

The program of physical education in the schools had its roots in the *Turnverein,* or German gymnastic society. It was adopted and introduced to the American public by the YMCA.

German immigrant influence has been pervasive, in our language, in our mores, in our customs and in our basic philosophy. Even the hamburger, the frankfurter and the delicatessen, that omnipresent neighborhood institution, came to us via the German immigrants.

Although they were mostly Democrats prior to 1850, the Germans broke party lines in the decade before the Civil War and played a prominent part in the formation of the Republican party. They were most united on two issues. They opposed the Blue Laws, and they vigorously fought the extension of slavery into new territories. Indeed, the first protest against Negro slavery came from Germantown settlers, led by Franz Pastorius, in 1688.

During the Civil War they fought on

both sides. Following the Civil War, Germans infused the faltering American labor movement with new strength by organizing craft unions for printers, watchmakers, carpenters, ironworkers, locksmiths, butchers and bakers.

Adjusting with relative ease, they did not feel the sting of ethnic discrimination until the outbreak of the First World War, when they became targets of wartime hysteria. This hysteria even caused overardent "patriots" to call sauerkraut "Liberty cabbage" and hamburger "Salisbury steak." Nonetheless, when the United States entered the war in 1917, men of German ancestry entered the armed forces of the United States and served with distinction.

As the Second World War drew near, Americans of German descent faced another test. Only a few joined the pro-Nazi German-American Bund, and many of those left as soon as they discovered its real nature. More "older Americans" than those of German descent could be counted in the ranks of America-Firsters. Again, after the U.S. was attacked, descendants of German immigrants fought with valor in our armed services.

The Scandinavians

Scandinavian immigrants left their homelands for economic rather than political or religious reasons. In America they found a political and social climate wholly compatible with their prior experience. Democratic institutions and a homogeneous society were already developing in Scandinavia, in an atmosphere of comparative tranquillity.

The seemingly limitless availability of farm land in America was an attractive prospect to land-hungry people.

The tide of Scandinavian immigration overlapped the tide of German immigration just as the Germans overlapped the Irish. The Swedes came first. They started coming about 1840, reaching their crest after 1860. Between 1840 and 1930, about 1.3 million Swedes came to the United States. In the 1880's migrations of other Scandinavians—Danes, Finns, Icelanders and principally the Norwegians—also reached their peak.

Following the Erie Canal and the Great Lakes, the Swedes pushed westward until they found a familiar landscape in the prairie states of the upper Mississippi Valley. There they settled.

The first colony of these Swedes settled at a place they named Pine Lakes (now New Upsala), in Wisconsin, in 1841. Later colonists showed a preference for a broad belt of land extending westward from Michigan, through Illinois, Wisconsin, Minnesota, Nebraska, Iowa and Kansas.

Other Scandinavian migrations followed more or less the same geographical pattern, except for the Norwegians. Although not so large numerically as other immigrant groups, Norwegian immigration in proportion to their population at home was second only to the Irish. Some of the Norwegians drove far west to the Dakotas, Oregon and Washington. Norwegian immigration to the United States is estimated at 840,000; Danes at 350,000. Most Scandinavians settled in rural areas, except for the Finns, some of whom went to work in the copper mines of Michigan or the iron mines of Minnesota.

Physically hardy, conditioned by the rigors of life at home to withstand the hardships of the frontier, the Scandinavians made ideal pioneers. Ole Rölvaag, the Norwegian-American novelist, movingly chronicled their struggles in *Giants in the Earth*.

Often they started their homesteading in sod huts, some of which were no more than holes in a hillside shored up with logs, with greased-paper windows. They looked forward to the day they could live in a log cabin or in a house. Then began the struggle with the unrelenting forces of nature: hailstorms, droughts, blizzards, plagues of grasshoppers and locusts. But they endured.

America was an expanding continent in urgent need of housing. It was the Swedes, familiar with the ax and the saw—called "the Swedish fiddle"—who went into the forests across the Northern United States, felled the logs, slid them into the streams and sent them on their way to the mills, where they were cut into boards to provide shelter for millions of other immigrants. Norwegians and Finns were also among the loggers. On the West Coast the Norwegians tended to become fishermen.

The Swedes did many other things too. In the long nights of the Swedish winter, they had learned to fashion things with their hands and had become skilled craftsmen and artisans. The "do-it-yourself" hobbyist of today is an avocational descendant of the Swedes. Manual training in our own public school system is derived from a basic course in Swedish schools.

The Scandinavians were avid supporters of the public school system. And they contributed to the school system and to education generally in a variety of ways. The home economics courses of our public schools were introduced by Scandinavians. They also helped launch adult education programs. The 4-H Clubs, now an international as well as a national institution, were originated at a farm school in Minnesota by Americans of Scandinavian descent. A number of colleges today stand as monuments to the early efforts of Norwegians and Swedes to make higher learning available. Among these are Augustana College in Illinois, Gustavus Adolphus in Minnesota, Bethany College in Kansas and Luther College in Nebraska. All were founded by Swedish immigrants. Luther College in Iowa and St. Olaf College in Minnesota were founded by the Norwegians. They have added to our cultural life with their choral groups and singing societies.

With their background, it was inevitable that the Swedes would develop many engineers, scientists and inventors. One of the most famous was John Ericsson, who not only designed the *Monitor,* one of the first armor-clad ships, but also perfected the screw propeller.

The Danes, who had an intimate knowledge of animal husbandry, laid the foundations of our dairy industry and early creamery cooperatives. Together with the Germans and the Swiss, they developed cheese-making into an American industry.

Since the Danes were primarily agriculturists, it is curious that the one who made the most distinctive individual contribution was a city boy, Jacob Riis. As a crusading journalist and documentary photographer, he exposed the conditions under which other immigrants lived and worked in New York, and was instrumental in bringing about major social reforms.

Politically, Scandinavians cannot be classified into a single mold. At times they have been conservative. At times they have provided support for such liberal movements as the Farmer-Labor party, Senator Robert M. La Follette's Progressive party and the Non-Partisan League. Both major parties have benefited from Scandinavian political thought, and both major parties have had Scandinavians in both state and federal office.

Other immigrant groups

Toward the end of the nineteenth century, emigration to America underwent a significant change. Large numbers of Italians, Russians, Poles, Czechs, Hungarians, Rumanians, Bulgarians, Austrians and Greeks began to arrive. Their coming created new problems and gave rise to new tensions.

For these people the language barrier was even greater than it had been for earlier groups and the gap between the world they had left behind and the one to which they came was wider. For the most part, these were people of the land and, for the most part, too, they were forced to settle in the cities when they reached America. Most large cities had well-defined "Little Italys" or "Little Polands" by 1910. In the 1960 census, New York City had more people of Italian birth or parentage than did Rome.

The history of cities shows that when conditions become overcrowded, when people are poor and when living conditions are bad, tensions run high. This is a situation that feeds on itself; poverty and crime in one group breed fear and hostility in others. This, in turn, impedes the acceptance and progress of the first group, thus prolonging its depressed condition. This was the dismal situation that faced many of the Southern and Eastern European immigrants just as it had faced some of the earlier waves of immigrants. One New York newspaper had these intemperate words for the newly arrived Italians: "The flood gates are open. The bars are down. The sally-ports are unguarded. The dam is washed away. The sewer is choked . . . the scum of immigration is viscerating upon our shores. The horde of $9.60 steerage slime is being siphoned upon us from Continental mud tanks."

Italy has contributed more immigrants to the United States than any country except Germany. Over five million Italians came to this country between 1820 and 1963. Large-scale immigration began in 1880, and almost four million Italian immigrants arrived in the present century.

The first Italians were farmers and artisans from northern Italy. Some planted vineyards in Vineland, New Jersey, in the Finger Lakes region of New York State and in California, where they inaugurated our domestic wine industry. Others settled on the periphery of cities, where they started truck gardens.

But most Italians were peasants from the south. They came because of neither religious persecution nor political repression, but simply in search of a brighter future. Population in Italy was straining the limits of the country's resources and more and more people had to eke out a living from small plots of land, held in many instances by oppressive landlords.

In many ways the experience of the later Italian immigrants parallels the story of the Irish. Mostly farmers, their lack of financial resources kept them from reaching the rural areas of the United States. Instead, they crowded into cities along the Eastern seaboard, often segregating themselves by province, even by village, in a density as high as four thousand to the city block.

Untrained in special skills and unfamiliar with the language, they had to rely on unskilled labor jobs to earn a living. Italians thus filled the gap left by earlier immigrant groups who had now moved up the economic ladder. As bricklayers, masons, stonecutters, ditchdiggers and hod carriers, they helped build our cities, subways and skyscrapers. They worked on the railroads and the dams, went into the coal mines, iron mines and factories. Some found a place in urban life as small storekeepers, peddlers, shoemakers, barbers and tailors. Wages were small and families were large. In the old country everyone worked. Here everyone worked too. Wives went into the needle trades. Boys picked up what pennies they could as news vendors, bootblacks and errand-runners. Through these difficult years of poverty, toil and bewilderment, the Italians were bolstered by their adherence to the church, the strength of their family ties, Italian-language newspapers and their fraternal orders. But they overcame obstacles of prejudice and misunderstanding quickly, and they have found places of importance in almost every phase of American life. Citizens of Italian descent are among our leading bankers, contractors, food importers, educators, labor leaders and government officials. Italians have made special contributions to the emergence of American culture, enriching our music, art and architecture.

An Italian, Filippo Traetta (Philip Trajetta), founded the American Conservatory in Boston in 1800, and another in Philadelphia shortly thereafter. Another Italian, Lorenzo da Ponte, brought the first Italian opera troupe to New York in 1832, where it developed into a permanent institution. Italians have founded and supported the opera as an institution in New York, Chicago, San Francisco and other large cities, providing from their ranks many impresarios and singers. Italian-born music teachers and bandmasters are numerous. Arturo Toscanini, for many years leader of the New York Philharmonic, and our most distinguished conductor of recent years, was Italian-born.

Italians have also been among our most prominent sculptors, architects and artists. A West Indian and a Frenchman designed our nation's Capitol. An Italian beautified it. Constantino Brumidi painted the historical frieze in the rotunda of the Capitol building. Other Italian painters and sculptors depicted our history in paintings, murals, friezes and statues. Historical monuments and statues up and down the country have been wrought by Italian-American sculptors. On a humbler scale, the taste and skill of Italian-American landscape gardeners and architects have placed our homes and communities in beautiful settings.

About the time the Italians began coming, other great tides of immigration from the countries of Eastern and Southeastern Europe also began arriving in the United States. In the years between 1820 and 1963 these areas, Italy included, sent over fifteen million immigrants to our shores.

They came for all manner of reasons: political upheavals, religious persecution, hopes for economic betterment. They comprised a wide ethnic variety, from Lithuanians and Latvians on the Baltic to Greeks, Turks and Armenians on the eastern Mediterranean. They brought with them a bewildering variety of language, dress, custom, ideology and religious belief. To many Americans already here who had grown accustomed to a common way of life, they presented a dismaying bedlam, difficult to understand and more difficult to respond to. Indeed, because of the many changes in national boundaries and prior migrations of races within that area of Europe, there is no way of accurately reporting on them statistically.

The largest number from any of these countries of Eastern Europe were Poles, who for 125 years had been under the domina-

tion of Russia, Germany and Austria-Hungary. Some followed the pattern of the Germans and Scandinavians, settling on individual farms or forming small rural communities which still bear Polish place names. But most gravitated to the cities. Four-fifths were Roman Catholic. Longer than most immigrant groups they kept their language, their customs and their dances. At first, like other immigrants, they lived under substandard conditions. Gradually they, too, improved their status. They aspired to own their own homes and their own plots of land. In Hamtramck, Michigan, an almost wholly Polish community, three-quarters of the residents own their own homes.

By 1963, almost 130,000 Czechs had migrated to this country. They tended to gravitate to the farming communities. It is one of these homesteads that is portrayed by novelist Willa Cather in *My Antonia.* They also formed enclaves in cities, principally in Chicago, Cleveland and New York.

A potent force in the development of Czech life in this country has been the *Sokol,* a traditional cultural, social and gymnastic society. These societies stressed high standards of physical fitness and an interest in singing, music and literature.

The immigrants from Old Russia are estimated at almost three and a half million. Most of this wave of immigration went into the mines and factories. However, there were also many Russian intellectuals, scientists, scholars, musicians, writers and artists, who came here usually during periods of political oppression.

Most students of the history of immigration to America make special mention of the Jews. Although they appeared as part of several of the waves of immigration, they warrant separate discussion because of their religion, culture and historical background.

In colonial times most Jews in America were of Spanish-Portuguese origin. Throughout the nineteenth century most came from Germany. Beginning at the end of the nineteenth century they began to come in large numbers from Russia, Poland, Austria-Hungary, Rumania and, in smaller numbers from almost every European nation. The American Jewish population today numbers approximately six million.

The Jews who came during the early nineteenth century were often peddlers, wandering throughout the land with their packs and their carts or settling down to open small stores. They prospered in this era of opportunity and expansion, for from these humble beginnings have grown many of our large department stores and mercantile establishments.

The exodus from Germany after 1848 brought Jewish intellectuals, philosophers, educators, political leaders and social reformers. These shared much the same experiences as the other immigrants. "Like the Scandinavian Lutherans and the Irish Catholics," says Oscar Handlin, "they appeared merely to maintain their distinctive heritage while sharing the rights and obligations of other Americans within a free society."

At the turn of the century the Jews fleeing persecution in Russia came in such numbers that they could not be so readily absorbed into the mainstream of life as the earlier comers. They clustered in Jewish communities within the large cities, like New York.

Like the Irish and the Italians before them, they had to work at whatever they could find. Most found an outlet for their skills in the needle trades, as garment workers, hatmakers and furriers. Often they worked in sweatshops. In an effort to improve working conditions (which involved child labor and other forms of exploitation), they joined with other immigrant workers to form, in 1900, the International Ladies' Garment Workers Union. In time, they developed the clothing industry as we know it today, centered in New York but reaching into every small town and rural area. The experience and tradition of these pioneers produced many effective leaders in the labor movement, such as Morris Hillquit, Sidney

Hillman, Jacob Potofsky and David Dubinsky.

Jewish immigrants have also made immense contributions to thought: as scholars, as educators, as scientists, as judges and lawyers, as journalists, as literary figures. Refugee scientists such as Albert Einstein and Edward Teller brought great scientific knowledge to this country.

Immigration from the Orient in the latter part of the nineteenth century was confined chiefly to California and the West Coast. Our behavior toward these groups of newcomers represented a shameful episode in our relationships to those seeking the hospitality of our shores. They were often mobbed and stoned by native Americans. The Chinese suffered and were barred from our shores as far back as the Chinese Exclusion Act of 1882. After the Japanese attack on Pearl Harbor many Japanese-Americans were victimized by prejudice and unreasoning discrimination. They were arbitrarily shipped to relocation camps. It took the extraordinary battlefield accomplishments of the nisei, Americans of Japanese descent, fighting in the U.S. Army in Europe, to help restore our perspective. While our attitude toward these citizens has been greatly improved over the years, many inequities in the law regarding Oriental immigration must still be redressed.

Today many of our newcomers are from Mexico and Puerto Rico. We sometimes forget that Puerto Ricans are U.S. citizens by birth and therefore cannot be considered immigrants. Nonetheless, they often receive the same discriminatory treatment and opprobrium that were faced by other waves of newcomers. The same things are said today of Puerto Ricans and Mexicans that were once said of Irish, Italians, Germans and Jews: "They'll never adjust; they can't learn the language; they won't be absorbed."

Perhaps our brightest hope for the future lies in the lessons of the past. The people who have come to this country have made America, in the words of one perceptive writer, "a heterogeneous race but a homogeneous nation."

In sum, then, we can see that as each new wave of immigration has reached America it has been faced with problems, not only the problems that come with making new homes and learning new jobs, but, more important, the problems of getting along with people of different backgrounds and habits.

Each new group was met by the groups already in America, and adjustment was often difficult and painful. The early English settlers had to find ways to get along with the Indians; the Irish who followed were met by these "Yankees"; German immigrants faced both Yankee and Irish; and so it has gone down to the latest group of Hungarian refugees. Somehow, the difficult adjustments are made and people get down to the tasks of earning a living, raising a family, living with their new neighbors and, in the process, building a nation.

David Ignatow

David Ignatow (b. 1914), Brooklyn-born poet, is on the faculty of Columbia University and has edited books on William Carlos Williams and Walt Whitman. His own poetry has been published in several volumes including Figures of the Human (1964) and Rescue the Dead (1968). A realistic poet, Ignatow shows in this poem the differing visions that an immigrant and his offspring have of the dream of America.

EUROPE AND AMERICA

My father brought the emigrant bundle
of desperation and worn threads,
that in anxiety as he stumbles
tumble out distractedly;
while I am bedded upon soft green money
that grows like grass. Thus,
between my father who lives on a bed of
  anguish

for his daily bread, and I who tear money
at leisure by the roots,
where I lie in sun or shade,
a vast continent of breezes, storms to him,
shadows, darkness to him, small lakes,
difficult channels to him, and hills,
mountains to him, lie between us.

My father comes of a hell
where bread and man have been kneaded
and baked together. You have heard the
  scream
as the knife fell; while I have slept
as guns pounded on the shore.

Mary Antin

Mary Antin (1881–1949), a native of Russia, immigrated to the United States in 1894. She was educated at Columbia University and Barnard College. The Promised Land, in which she describes the immigrant dream of opportunity in America, first appeared in The Atlantic Monthly *and won such wide acclaim that Antin traveled as a lecturer throughout the country.*

THE PROMISED LAND

Having made such good time across the ocean, I ought to be able to proceed no less rapidly on *terra firma,* where, after all, I am more at home. And yet here is where I falter. Not that I hesitated, even for the space of a breath, in my first steps in America. There was no time to hesitate. The most ignorant immigrant, on landing, proceeds to give and receive greetings, to eat, sleep, and rise, after the manner of his own country; wherein he is corrected, admonished, and laughed at, whether by interested friends or the most indifferent strangers; and his American experience is thus begun. The process is spontaneous on all sides, like the education of the child by the family circle. But while the most stupid nursery maid is able to contribute her part toward the result, we do not expect an analysis of the process to be furnished by any member of the family, least of all by the engaging infant. The philosophical maiden aunt alone, or some other witness equally psychological and aloof, is able to trace the myriad efforts by which the little Johnnie or Nellie acquires a secure hold on the disjointed parts of the huge plaything, life.

Now I was not exactly an infant when I was set down, on a May day some fifteen years ago, in this pleasant nursery of America. I had long since acquired the use of my faculties, and had collected some bits of experience, practical and emotional, and had even learned to give an account of them. Still, I had very little perspective, and my observations and comparisons were superficial. I was too much carried away to analyze the forces that were moving me. My Polotzk I knew well before I began to judge it and experiment with it. America was bewilderingly strange, unimaginably complex, delightfully unexplored. I rushed impetuously out of the cage of my provincialism and looked eagerly about the brilliant universe. My question was, What have we here?—not, What does this mean? That query came much later. When I now become retrospectively introspective, I fall into the predicament of the centipede in the rhyme, who got along very smoothly until he was asked which leg came after which, whereupon he became so rattled that he couldn't take a step. I know I have come on a thousand feet, on wings, winds, and American machines,—I have leaped and run and climbed and crawled,—but to tell which step came after which I find a puzzling matter. Plenty of maiden aunts were present during my second infancy, in the guise of immigrant officials, school-teachers, settlement workers, and sundry other unprejudiced and critical observers. Their statistics I might properly borrow to fill the gaps in my recollections, but I am prevented by my sense of harmony. The individual, we know, is a creature unknown to the statistician,

whereas I undertook to give the personal view of everything. So I am bound to unravel, as well as I can, the tangle of events, outer and inner, which made up the first breathless years of my American life.

During his three years of probation, my father had made a number of false starts in business. His history for that period is the history of thousands who come to America, like him, with pockets empty, hands untrained to the use of tools, minds cramped by centuries of repression in their native land. Dozens of these men pass under your eyes every day, my American friend, too absorbed in their honest affairs to notice the looks of suspicion which you cast at them, the repugnance with which you shrink from their touch. You see them shuffle from door to door with a basket of spools and buttons, or bending over the sizzling irons in a basement tailor shop, or rummaging in your ash can, or moving a pushcart from curb to curb, at the command of the burly policeman. "The Jew peddler!" you say, and dismiss him from your premises and from your thoughts, never dreaming that the sordid drama of his days may have a moral that concerns you. What if the creature with the untidy beard carries in his bosom his citizenship papers? What if the cross-legged tailor is supporting a boy in college who is one day going to mend your state constitution for you? What if the ragpicker's daughters are hastening over the ocean to teach your children in the public schools? Think, every time you pass the greasy alien on the street, that he was born thousands of years before the oldest native American; and he may have something to communicate to you, when you two shall have learned a common language. Remember that his very physiognomy is a cipher the key to which it behooves you to search for most diligently.

By the time we joined my father, he had surveyed many avenues of approach toward the coveted citadel of fortune. One of these, heretofore untried, he now proposed to essay, armed with new courage, and cheered on by the presence of his family. In partnership with an energetic little man who had an English chapter in his history, he prepared to set up a refreshment booth on Crescent Beach. But while he was completing arrangements at the beach we remained in town, where we enjoyed the educational advantages of a thickly populated neighborhood; namely, Wall Street, in the West End of Boston.

Anybody who knows Boston knows that the West and North Ends are the wrong ends of that city. They form the tenement district, or, in the newer phrase, the slums of Boston. Anybody who is acquainted with the slums of any American metropolis knows that that is the quarter where poor immigrants foregather, to live, for the most part, as unkempt, half-washed, toiling, unaspiring foreigners; pitiful in the eyes of social missionaries, the despair of boards of health, the hope of ward politicians, the touchstone of American democracy. The well-versed metropolitan knows the slums as a sort of house of detention for poor aliens, where they live on probation till they can show a certificate of good citizenship.

He may know all this and yet not guess how Wall Street, in the West End, appears in the eyes of a little immigrant from Polotzk. What would the sophisticated sightseer say about Union Place, off Wall Street, where my new home waited for me? He would say that it is no place at all, but a short box of an alley. Two rows of three-story tenements are its sides, a stingy strip of sky is its lid, a littered pavement is the floor, and a narrow mouth its exit.

But I saw a very different picture on my introduction to Union Place. I saw two imposing rows of brick buildings, loftier than any dwelling I had ever lived in. Brick was even on the ground for me to tread on, instead of common earth or boards. Many friendly windows stood open, filled with uncovered heads of women and children. I thought the people were interested in us, which was very neighborly. I looked up to the topmost row of windows, and my eyes were filled with the May blue of an American sky!

In our days of affluence in Russia we had been accustomed to upholstered parlors, embroidered linen, silver spoons and candlesticks, goblets of gold, kitchen shelves shining with copper and brass. We had featherbeds heaped halfway to the ceiling; we had clothes presses dusky with velvet and silk and fine woollen. The three small rooms into which my father now ushered us, up one flight of stairs, contained only the necessary beds, with lean mattresses; a few wooden chairs; a table or two; a mysterious iron structure, which later turned out to be a stove; a couple of unornamental kerosene lamps; and a scanty array of cooking-utensils and crockery. And yet we were all impressed with our new home and its furniture. It was not only because we had just passed through our seven lean years, cooking in earthen vessels, eating black bread on holidays and wearing cotton; it was chiefly because these wooden chairs and tin pans were American chairs and pans that they shone glorious in our eyes. And if there was anything lacking for comfort or decoration we expected it to be presently supplied—at least, we children did. Perhaps my mother alone, of us newcomers, appreciated the shabbiness of the little apartment, and realized that for her there was as yet no laying down of the burden of poverty.

Our initiation into American ways began with the first step on the new soil. My father found occasion to instruct or correct us even on the way from the pier to Wall Street, which journey we made crowded together in a rickety cab. He told us not to lean out of the windows, not to point, and explained the word "greenhorn." We did not want to be "greenhorns," and gave the strictest attention to my father's instructions. I do not know when my parents found opportunity to review together the history of Polotzk in the three years past, for we children had no patience with the subject; my mother's narrative was constantly interrupted by irrelevant questions, interjections, and explanations.

The first meal was an object lesson of much variety. My father produced several kinds of food, ready to eat, without any cooking, from little tin cans that had printing all over them. He attempted to introduce us to a queer, slippery kind of fruit, which he called "banana," but had to give it up for the time being. After the meal, he had better luck with a curious piece of furniture on runners, which he called "rocking-chair." There were five of us newcomers, and we found five different ways of getting into the American machine of perpetual motion, and as many ways of getting out of it. One born and bred to the use of a rocking-chair cannot imagine how ludicrous people can make themselves when attempting to use it for the first time. We laughed immoderately over our various experiments with the novelty, which was a wholesome way of letting off steam after the unusual excitement of the day.

In our flat we did not think of such a thing as storing the coal in the bathtub. There was no bathtub. So in the evening of the first day my father conducted us to the public baths. As we moved along in a little procession, I was delighted with the illumination of the streets. So many lamps, and they burned until morning, my father said, and so people did not need to carry lanterns. In America, then, everything was free, as we had heard in Russia. Light was free; the streets were as bright as a synagogue on a holy day. Music was free; we had been serenaded, to our gaping delight, by a brass band of many pieces, soon after our installation on Union Place.

Education was free. That subject my father had written about repeatedly, as comprising his chief hope for us children, the essence of American opportunity, the treasure that no thief could touch, not even misfortune or poverty. It was the one thing that he was able to promise us when he sent for us; surer, safer than bread or shelter. On our second day I was thrilled with the realization of what this freedom of education meant. A little girl from across the alley came and offered to conduct us to school. My father was out, but we five between us had a few words of English by this time. We knew the word school. We understood. This child, who had never seen us till yesterday, who could not pronounce our names, who was not much better dressed than we, was able to offer us the freedom of the schools of Boston! No application made, no questions asked, no examinations, rulings, exclusions; no machinations, no fees. The doors stood open for every one of us. The smallest child could show us the way.

This incident impressed me more than anything I had heard in advance of the freedom of education in America. It was a concrete proof—almost the thing itself. One had to experience it to understand it.

It was a great disappointment to be told by my father that we were not to enter upon our school career at once. It was too near the end of the term, he said, and we were going to move to Crescent Beach in a week or so. We had to wait until the opening of the schools in September. What a loss of precious time—from May till September!

Not that the time was really lost. Even the interval on Union Place was crowded with lessons and experiences. We had to visit the stores and be dressed from head to foot in American clothing; we had to learn the mysteries of the iron stove, the washboard, and the speaking-tube; we had to learn to trade with the fruit peddler through the window, and not to be afraid of the policeman; and, above all, we had to learn English.

The kind people who assisted us in these important matters form a group by themselves in the gallery of my friends. If I had never seen them from those early days till now, I should still have remembered them with gratitude. When I enumerate the long list of my American teachers, I must begin with those who came to us on Wall Street and taught us our first steps. To my mother, in her perplexity over the cookstove, the woman who showed her how to make the fire was an angel of deliverance. A fairy godmother to us children was she who led us to a wonderful country called "uptown," where, in a dazzlingly beautiful palace called a "department store," we exchanged our hateful homemade European costumes, which pointed us out as "greenhorns" to the children on the street, for real American machine-made garments, and issued forth glorified in each other's eyes.

With our despised immigrant clothing we shed also our impossible Hebrew names. A committee of our friends, several years ahead of us in American experience, put their heads together and concocted American names for us all. Those of our real names that had no pleasing American equivalents they ruthlessly discarded, content if they retained the initials. My mother, possessing a name that was not easily translatable, was punished with the undignified nickname of Annie. Fetchke, Joseph, and Deborah issued as Frieda, Joseph, and Dora, respectively. As for poor me, I was simply cheated. The name they gave me was hardly new. My Hebrew name being Maryashe in full, Mashke for short, Russianized into Marya (*Mar-ya*), my friends said that it would hold good in English as *Mary*; which was very disappointing, as I longed to possess a strange-sounding American name like the others.

I am forgetting the consolation I had, in this matter of names, from the use of my surname, which I have had no occasion to mention until now. I found on my arrival that my father was "Mr. Antin" on the slightest provocation, and not, as in Polotzk, on state occasions alone. And so I was "Mary Antin," and I felt very important to answer to such a dignified title. It was just like America that even plain people should wear their surnames on week days.

As a family we were so diligent under instruction, so adaptable, and so clever in hiding our deficiencies, that when we made

the journey to Crescent Beach, in the wake of our small wagon-load of household goods, my father had very little occasion to admonish us on the way, and I am sure he was not ashamed of us. So much we had achieved toward our Americanization during the two weeks since our landing.

Crescent Beach is a name that is printed in very small type on the maps of the environs of Boston, but a life-size strip of sand curves from Winthrop to Lynn; and that is historic ground in the annals of my family. The place is now a popular resort for holiday crowds, and is famous under the name of Revere Beach. When the reunited Antins made their stand there, however, there were no boulevards, no stately bath-houses, no hotels, no gaudy amusement places, no illuminations, no showmen, no tawdry rabble. There was only the bright clean sweep of sand, the summer sea, and the summer sky. At high tide the whole Atlantic rushed in, tossing the seaweeds in his mane; at low tide he rushed out, growling and gnashing his granite teeth. Between tides a baby might play on the beach, digging with pebbles and shells, till it lay asleep on the sand. The whole sun shone by day, troops of stars by night, and the great moon in its season.

Into this grand cycle of the seaside day I came to live and learn and play. A few people came with me, as I have already intimated; but the main thing was that *I* came to live on the edge of the sea—I, who had spent my life inland, believing that the great waters of the world were spread out before me in the Dvina. My idea of the human world had grown enormously during the long journey; my idea of the earth had expanded with every day at sea; my idea of the world outside the earth now budded and swelled during my prolonged experience of the wide and unobstructed heavens.

Not that I got any inkling of the conception of a multiple world. I had had no lessons in cosmogony, and I had no spontaneous revelation of the true position of the earth in the universe. For me, as for my fathers, the sun set and rose, and I did not feel the earth rushing through space. But I lay stretched out in the sun, my eyes level with the sea, till I seemed to be absorbed bodily by the very materials of the world around me; till I could not feel my hand as separate from the warm sand in which it was buried. Or I crouched on the beach at full moon, wondering, wondering, between the two splendors of the sky and the sea. Or I ran out to meet the incoming storm, my face full in the wind, my being a-tingle with an awesome delight to the tips of my fog-matted locks flying behind; and stood clinging to some stake or upturned boat, shaken by the roar and rumble of the waves. So clinging, I pretended that I was in danger, and was deliciously frightened; I held on with both hands, and shook my head, exulting in the tumult around me, equally ready to laugh or sob. Or else I sat, on the stillest days, with my back to the sea, not looking at all, but just listening to the rustle of the waves on the sand; not thinking at all, but just breathing with the sea.

Thus courting the influence of sea and sky and variable weather, I was bound to have dreams, hints, imaginings. It was no more than this, perhaps: that the world as I knew it was not large enough to contain all that I saw and felt; that the thoughts that flashed through my mind, not half understood, unrelated to my utterable thoughts, concerned something for which I had as yet no name. Every imaginative growing child has these flashes of intuition, especially one that becomes intimate with some one aspect of nature. With me it was the growing time, that idle summer by the sea, and I grew all the faster because I had been so cramped before. My mind, too, had so recently been worked upon by the impressive experience of a change of country that I was more than commonly alive to impressions, which are the seeds of ideas.

Let no one suppose that I spent my time

entirely, or even chiefly, in inspired solitude. By far the best part of my day was spent in play—frank, hearty, boisterous play, such as comes natural to American children. In Polotzk I had already begun to be considered too old for play, excepting set games or organized frolics. Here I found myself included with children who still played, and I willingly returned to childhood. There were plenty of playfellows. My father's energetic little partner had a little wife and a large family. He kept them in the little cottage next to ours; and that the shanty survived the tumultuous presence of that brood is a wonder to me to-day. The young Wilners included an assortment of boys, girls, and twins, of every possible variety of age, size, disposition, and sex. They swarmed in and out of the cottage all day long, wearing the door-sill hollow, and trampling the ground to powder. They swung out of windows like monkeys, slid up the roof like flies, and shot out of trees like fowls. Even a small person like me couldn't go anywhere without being run over by a Wilner; and I could never tell which Wilner it was because none of them ever stood still long enough to be identified; and also because I suspected that they were in the habit of interchanging conspicuous articles of clothing, which was very confusing.

You would suppose that the little mother must have been utterly lost, bewildered, trodden down in this horde of urchins; but you are mistaken. Mrs. Wilner was a positively majestic little person. She ruled her brood with the utmost coolness and strictness. She had even the biggest boy under her thumb, frequently under her palm. If they enjoyed the wildest freedom outdoors, indoors the young Wilners lived by the clock. And so at five o'clock in the evening, on seven days in the week, my father's partner's children could be seen in two long rows around the supper table. You could tell them apart on this occasion, because they all had their faces washed. And this is the time to count them: there are twelve little Wilners at table.

I managed to retain my identity in this multitude somehow, and while I was very much impressed with their numbers, I even dared to pick and choose my friends among the Wilners. One or two of the smaller boys I liked best of all, for a game of hide-and-seek or a frolic on the beach. We played in the water like ducks, never taking the trouble to get dry. One day I waded out with one of the boys, to see which of us dared go farthest. The tide was extremely low, and we had not wet our knees when we began to look back to see if familiar objects were still in sight. I thought we had been wading for hours, and still the water was so shallow and quiet. My companion was marching straight ahead, so I did the same. Suddenly a swell lifted us almost off our feet, and we clutched at each other simultaneously. There was a lesser swell, and little waves began to run, and a sigh went up from the sea. The tide was turning —perhaps a storm was on the way—and we were miles, dreadful miles from dry land.

Boy and girl turned without a word, four determined bare legs ploughing through the water, four scared eyes straining toward the land. Through an eternity of toil and fear they kept dumbly on, death at their heels, pride still in their hearts. At last they reach high-water mark—six hours before full tide.

Each has seen the other afraid, and each rejoices in the knowledge. But only the boy is sure of his tongue.

"You was scared, war n't you?" he taunts.

The girl understands so much, and is able to reply:—

"You can schwimmen, I not."

"Betcher life I can schwimmen," the other mocks.

And the girl walks off, angry and hurt.

"An' I can walk on my hands," the tormentor calls after her. "Say, you greenhorn, why don'tcher look?"

The girl keeps straight on, vowing that she would never walk with that rude boy again, neither by land nor sea, not even though the waters should part at his bidding.

I am forgetting the more serious business which had brought us to Crescent Beach. While we children disported ourselves like mermaids and mermen in the surf, our respective fathers dispensed cold lemonade, hot peanuts, and pink popcorn, and piled up our respective fortunes, nickel by nickel, penny by penny. I was very proud of my connection with the public life of the beach. I admired greatly our shining soda fountain, the rows of sparkling glasses, the pyramids of oranges, the sausage chains, the neat white counter, and the bright array of tin spoons. It seemed to me that none of the other refreshment stands on the beach—there were a few—were half so attractive as ours. I thought my father looked very well in a long white apron and shirt sleeves. He dished out ice cream with enthusiasm, so I supposed he was getting rich. It never occurred to me to compare his present occupation with the position for which he had been originally destined; or if I thought about it, I was just as well content, for by this time I had by heart my father's saying, "America is not Polotzk." All occupations were respectable, all men were equal, in America.

DISCUSSION QUESTIONS

"What Is an American?"

1. What uniquely American characteristics of the people and government does de Crèvecoeur note?

2. How does he explain the classlessness of Americans?

3. What criticisms of Europe does he make?

4. What evidence is there that de Crève-

coeur believed in the land and frontier as creators of equality?

5. De Crèvecoeur said, "Here individuals of all nations are melted into a new race of men. . . ." Based on your reading in this section, do you think his statement is valid? Explain.

"The Declaration of Independence"

1. The list of King George's "injuries and usurpations" is often ignored in a reading of the *Declaration*. Why did Jefferson include such a long list?

2. What were the Crown's major offenses? Which ones would we consider to be equally harmful? What protection do we have against our government's committing these same offenses? Note the provisions in the *Constitution* and *Bill of Rights* which are directly related to preventing these offenses from occurring again.

3. Jefferson shows great concern over the control of the military. Compare Eisenhower's *Farewell Address* on the subject of military influence.

4. What does Jefferson say about revolution? Compare his ideas with Thoreau's. Can you see any possible justification for revolution today?

"The Puritan"

1. What picture of the Puritan do you get from this poem? How accurate is this picture?

2. How does nature "mock" the Puritan?

3. Could the poem apply to others besides Puritans? If so, what is Shapiro's fundamental idea?

4. What connection does this poem have with the reality of the democratic ideal?

"Civil Disobedience"

1. How does Thoreau view government? What is his view of the Mexican War? Revolution? Taxes? The duty of the individual?

2. How would Thoreau's ideas apply to the problems of the 1960s? To today's concerns?

3. What premises and relationships today would have to change for Thoreau's statement "That government is best which governs not at all" to be valid?

4. What does he see as the relationship between minorities and the majority in a government?

5. Is his suggestion that men serve the state as machines, not as human beings, supported by contemporary events?

"For You O Democracy" and *"A Passage to India"*

1. What does Whitman feel is the unifying force in America? Do you agree? Can you think of other forces which unify?

2. How does he show his love for the land? Compare his exuberance of spirit with de Crèvecoeur's.

3. Where does Whitman show his belief in the "melting pot"?

4. What does America mean to the world in Whitman's view?

5. Who was the "Genoese" and what was his dream? Who was Vasco de Gama? What is the meaning of a passage to India?

"Something's Happening Out There"

1. What point does Kuralt make about the media and our national image? Is his criticism valid?

2. From your own observations, do you agree with Kuralt that Americans are working on their problems?

3. He defines patriotism as "concern for one's country" and sees a rebirth of this spirit in the debate over national issues. When do some people think that the debating of issues is unpatriotic? Is the democratic philosophy still believed, in your opinion?

"A Populist Manifesto"

1. What is a "populist," according to Newfield? How does a "populist" differ from a "consensus liberal," an advocate of the New Politics, or a member of the New Left?

2. What are Newfield's stated goals? Do all his suggested reforms meet these goals?

3. He gives us an extensive outline of programs and legislation which he favors. Choose any *one* area (crime, national health insurance, control of giant corporations) and discuss whether his suggestions are desirable and practical.

4. If Newfield got all his programs passed, what would living in the United States be like for the average citizen?

"Dissenting Opinion, DeFunis v. Odegaard (1974)"

1. What problems does Justice Douglas see with "reverse discrimination" in the DeFunis case? What area of democratic philosophy is crucial to this case?

2. What area of the Constitution is at issue here? Why is it ironic that a white student would sue a school using this section of the Constitution as a basis for the suit?

3. The Court as a whole did not decide the case, declaring it moot. Can you think of a reason for the Court's so deciding?

4. What possible remedies does Justice Douglas suggest in order to admit members of minorities without discriminating against the majority? What are your reactions to admissions standards for various groups? What about job quotas?

"The Constitution Is Alive and Well"

1. What specific constitutional principles does Commager say were violated by the Nixon administration? Do you agree that the actions were in violation of our Constitution?

2. What forces brought about Nixon's resignation? In what ways can this episode in our history be seen as "a stunning vindication of our constitutional system"?

3. In what areas does the Constitution seem to be "alive" and functioning well today? In what areas is there a need for reform in order to reestablish constitutional safeguards?

4. Commager says that this recent crisis was more serious than any other event since the Civil War. After reading his brief list of other challenges (the First World War, the Depression, the Second World War) and the charges laid against Mr. Nixon, do you agree with Commager?

"A Slave's Life"

1. How do the facts of slave life, according to Frederick Douglass, produce the stereotype of the lazy, crafty slave?

2. How did the "Christmas vacation" period reinforce the whites' attitudes towards their slaves? How was this period more a necessity for the owners than the slaves?

3. What is Douglass's opinion of religious masters? What reason does he give for this opinion? Compare his opinion to the views of the Puritan in Karl Shapiro's poem.

"Battle Royal"

1. How is the sense of nightmare developed in this story? Do you believe the story is factually probable? Is it meant to be realistic or symbolic?

2. What does the youth mean when he says he was "invisible"?

3. Was the youth's grandfather an "Uncle Tom"? Could the slaves have used his advice? Why should a free person?

4. In what ways do the following details suggest black-white relationships: blindfolds; the naked girl; the electric rug; the

"gold" coins? Why does Tatlock want to continue fighting even though he is offered the prize?

5. What is the meaning of the dream the youth has at the end of the chapter?

"That Evening Sun"

1. When was Nancy "invisible" and when was she visible? Compare Harrington's views on the invisibility of the poor with the invisibility of black people in Ellison's and Faulkner's stories.

2. What implicit black-white relationships does Faulkner suggest? What is Nancy's relationship with the children?

3. What is the significance of the measures that Nancy takes to ward off the violence that she feels may occur? What do you think will happen to Nancy? Does Faulkner provide any clues?

4. What is the importance of the title?

5. Compare the varying degrees of freedom allowed to black people as portrayed by Douglass, Ellison, and Faulkner.

"America" and "The White House"

1. What, according to McKay, lies in America's future?

2. Why does the poet resist hating those who oppress him? Does his advice shed any light on the grandfather's advice in "Battle Royal"?

3. The title "The White House" is said to be symbolic, not necessarily referring to the President's house. What do you think the title means after reading the poem?

"Letter to the Salem Convention"

1. How does Elizabeth Cady Stanton deal with the argument that men and women do not think alike?

2. What similarities does she see between the condition of women and slaves? Is the analogy valid?

3. What argument of Ms. Stanton's seems most modern?

4. Why does she emphasize that women's own efforts must be the force for changing their condition? Should this idea apply to other minority groups? Explain.

"Confessions of an Ex-Cheerleader"

1. What was the ideal female image that Louise Bernikow describes? What image would a high school girl today admire?

2. How has being a cheerleader affected her as an adult? What point is the author making about both her male and female college classmates and their relationship to basketball?

3. What attitudes toward outsiders (blacks, "rocks," "hitter chicks") does she reveal? Why did the cheerleaders have those attitudes? In what ways was the author herself an outsider? What groups were "in" or "out" in your high school? Why?

4. What similarity is there between Ms. Bernikow's statement about imagining "my man's achievement is my own" and Elizabeth Cady Stanton's argument for women's right to govern themselves?

5. What is the price of one's success as a high school cheerleader?

"Wounded Knee"

1. What part did the Ghost Dance religion play in the incident?

2. What was the condition of the Sioux prior to encampment at Wounded Knee?

3. From the conflicting reports, can you tell what precipitated the firing of the soldiers?

4. Why is Black Elk's speech appropriate for the end of this episode and the end of Brown's history?

"The Chicanos"

1. What does the Chicano fear in urban life?

2. Who are the "Pachucos" and what misunderstandings have arisen about them?

3. In what ways have Chicano university students joined with street leaders?

4. What evidence does Steiner present that Chicano youth are becoming proud of their ethnic heritage? What identity problems still exist?

"Waves of Immigration"

1. What evidence does Kennedy use to show that crime in city slums is more a result of the conditions there than it is a result of which ethnic group lives there?

2. What unique contributions has each group made to America? What barriers to opportunity did white European immigrants face?

3. Why do many more established immigrants oppose the succeeding waves of immigration?

4. Does Kennedy believe in the "melting pot"? Compare his ideas to de Crèvecoeur's. What point does Kennedy make about more recent arrivals like the Mexicans and Puerto Ricans?

5. What do you think American policy should be on immigration?

"Europe and America"

1. What are the differences between the father and the son in David Ignatow's poem?

2. What do these differences suggest about the process of assimilation?

"The Promised Land"

1. What is the difference between the way the established city dweller looks at the slums and the way the recently arrived foreigner sees them? How can she call the slums the "touchstone of American democracy"?

2. Miss Antin describes the process of being "melted" or assimilated into the

American way of life. What specific things did she and her family change upon coming to America? What is her attitude towards this assimilation? Do you think her attitude would be different today?

3. What opportunities particularly amazed the fifteen-year-old girl?

4. What evidence of some prejudice against immigrants does she note?

SUGGESTED READINGS

BALDWIN, JAMES. *Notes of a Native Son.* Boston, 1955.

BALTZELL, E. DIGBY. *The Protestant Establishment: Aristocracy and Caste in America.* New York, 1964.

BARAKA, IMAMU. *Dutchman* and *The Slave.* New York, 1964.

BROWN, CLAUDE. *Manchild in the Promised Land.* New York, 1965.

HALEY, ALEX and MALCOLM X. *The Autobiography of Malcolm X.* New York, 1964.

HAMILTON, ALEXANDER, JAMES MADISON, and JOHN JAY. *The Federalist Papers,* 1787–1788.

HANDLIN, OSCAR. *The Uprooted.* Boston, 1951.

HUGHES, LANGSTON. *The Langston Hughes Reader.* New York, 1958.

JAMES, HENRY. *The Ambassadors.* 1903.

———. *The American.* 1877.

JONES, M. A. *American Immigration.* Chicago, 1960.

KOPIT, ARTHUR. *Indians.* New York, 1969.

KRADITOR, AILEEN S., ed. *Up from the Pedestal: Selected Readings in the History of American Feminism.* Chicago, 1968.

LIEBOW, ELLIOT. *Tally's Corner.* Boston, 1967.

MAILER, NORMAN. *An American Dream.* New York, 1965.

MILLER, ARTHUR. *The Crucible.* New York, 1953.

MYRDAL, GUNNAR. *An American Dilemma.* New York, 1944.

OSOFSKY, GILBERT, ed. *Puttin' on Ole Massa.* New York, 1969.

PAINE, THOMAS. *Common Sense.* 1776.

———. *The Rights of Man,* Parts I and II. 1791–1792.

SACKLER, HOWARD. *The Great White Hope.* New York, 1968.

SILBERMAN, CHARLES. *Crisis in Black and White.* New York, 1964.

TOCQUEVILLE, ALEXIS DE. *Democracy in America.* 1835–1840.

WARREN, ROBERT PENN. *All the King's Men.* New York, 1946.

WRIGHT, RICHARD. *Black Boy: A Record of Childhood and Youth.* New York, 1945.

———. *Native Son.* New York, 1940.

PART TWO

THE PURSUIT
OF SUCCESS

THE SUCCESS ETHIC

William James's famous statement, "The exclusive worship of the bitch-goddess SUCCESS . . . is our national disease," emphasizes the paradox in the dream of success. Throughout America's history there has been the dream of the individual succeeding "big," but there has also been a concurrent feeling that this very success is what destroys the successful person. Cotton Mather in his sermon warns rich men of the dangers of success and urges them not to devote their wealth to "appetites of the flesh" but to repay God for his confidence and beneficence by doing good works. And Edwin Arlington Robinson's poem "Rich-ard Cory" subtly handles the paradox of success. Cory, who has everything, is a walking dream to his workers, yet he has nothing of any real value, as his suicide proves. The workers, however, do not perceive Cory's failure to buy happiness with his wealth, and because they themselves have no success, they still envy the dead Cory.

The dichotomy between success and failure, between dream and illusion, persists in many of our self-images. The prototype of the successful man in America is Benjamin Franklin: he was the self-made man, in Irvin Wyllie's phrase, true to the democratic ideal and opposed to the inherited wealth of European aristocracy, who after achieving success, made his methods into a gospel

103

for those wishing to follow. Thomas Mellon, the financier, was so inspired by Franklin that he had his statue erected in front of his Pittsburgh bank and passed out copies of *The Way to Wealth* to young men needing advice. The Franklin ideal persisted throughout the nineteenth century: Horatio Alger, Jr., who molded himself in Franklin's image, wrote a series of novels which dealt with the realities of poverty and the subsequent realization of success, his books echoing Franklin's idea that "Diligence is the Mother of Good Luck." By the end of the nineteenth century, there were real-life models for Alger's fiction; Andrew Carnegie, a poor boy from Scotland, amassed a fortune of $400 million in steel, an achievement not unlike the rise of Rockefeller in oil or Harriman in railroads. Many found a contradiction inherent in Franklin's dream, though. John Cheever in "O Youth and Beauty!" shows that success can mean many things—youth, physical attractiveness, popularity, athletic grace, love, as well as money—but that all are extremely fragile. Millions found that success was not as common as Alger and others like the McGuffey Reader claimed it to be, for in the twentieth century fewer and fewer rich men emerged from the ranks of the working class. Many, of course, like E. E. Cummings's Uncle Sol, never succeeded at all. Michael Harrington's book *The Other America* details the conditions existing among the often invisible poor in contemporary America, showing that failure is still the dark side of the dream of success.

THE BUSINESS OF AMERICA

The conduct of business in America shows both the positive and negative aspects of the success ethic. Progressive businessmen like the Filenes of Boston, according to Justice Brandeis, provided good working conditions for their employees, adequate wages, and a voice in the operation of the company. And dozens of enterprising businessmen made American life richer, safer, and more comfortable. Gail Borden invented condensed milk, a healthy, safe product in a time (1859) when fresh milk was often dangerous; Willis Carrier named his 1902 invention "air conditioning"; Clarence Birdseye discovered frozen foods; and Aaron Montgomery Ward brought the department store to the most isolated farm through the innovation of the mail order catalogue.

However, unethical businessmen have tarnished the image of American business throughout our history. Business practices which badly needed reform included stock and credit manipulation, the formation of monopolies and trusts, and the exploitation of the worker through long hours, hazardous working conditions, poor wages, and the use of child labor. Just as reform movements helped right the wrongs done to minority groups, so the labor unions, muckrakers, and some legislators began to correct business abuses. Ida Tarbell, a famous muckraking journalist, exposed the monopolistic practices of Standard Oil, and Upton Sinclair's novel *The Jungle* (in particular the passage here called "The Stockyards") stirred the Congress to pass The Pure Food and Drug Act.

The effect of business on those involved in it—both owners and workers—has attracted the attention of many writers. John Dos Passos, writing about the 1920s in *The Big Money,* includes a highly individual and experimental biography of Henry Ford, called "Tin Lizzie." Examining life at the other end of the automobile industry, Harvey Swados looks at a young worker facing the monotony and frustration of the auto assembly line in his short story "Joe, the Vanishing American." In the final article in this section, Judson Gooding discusses such problems as automation, the impersonality of the huge corporation, and alienation of workers from their work, pointing out the efforts some companies have made to solve these problems for white-collar workers.

THE SUCCESS ETHIC

The American Way. M. Bourke-White, Time-Life Picture Agency.

Irvin G. Wyllie

Irvin G. Wyllie (b. 1920), professor of history, has written an extensive analysis of the American success ethic. In this selection, Wyllie defines success and discusses those individual qualities which were said to lead to success.

THE SELF-MADE MAN IN AMERICA

Men who search for meaning in history know that it is difficult to divine the central tendency of an age or discover the ruling spirit of a people. Tendencies and spirits are as varied as men themselves, and the records which embody them are confused, faulty, and fragmentary. Occasionally, however, the record is very clear. Thirty years ago a perceptive American writer, Claude C. Washburn, suggested that the record of the American people would eventually be found in the ephemeral books and magazines preserved in the Library of Congress. He also predicted that these volumes would reveal that the principal American aspiration could be expressed by the single word Success. Indeed the gospel of success has been a noisy one through all our history, and thousands of evangelists have been enlisted in its service. The pulpit, the platform, and the press have overflowed with its catchwords, its aphorisms, and its instances. Across the land from Benjamin Franklin's day to our own, young men have sought direction and inspiration in its glittering lore.

But what is success? Americans have defined it in various ways. Politicians equate it with power, publicists with fame. Teachers and moralists rate themselves successful when they have influenced the minds and characters of others. Men of creative instinct strive for self-realization. Humanitarians identify success with service, reformers with the alteration of the social order. To the devout, success is salvation, and to thousands of plain people it is nothing more than contentment and a sense of happiness. Each of these definitions embodies worthy ideals, and all have their champions. But no one of these concepts enjoys such universal favor in America as that which equates success with making money. "Every one knows that success with the great masses spells money," said John C. Van Dyke in 1908 in his book *The Money God*. "It is money that the new generation expects to win, and it is money that the parents want them to win. The boy will make it, and the girl, if she is not a goose, will marry it. They will get it in one way or another."

Strangers to our shores have often commented on this our ruling passion—sometimes with distaste, occasionally with appreciation, always with wonder. In the 1830s that friendly critic of democracy, Alexis de Tocqueville, asserted that he knew of no other country where the love of money had a stronger hold in the affections of the people, or where wealth circulated so rapidly from generation to generation. Some years later the Englishman James Bryce reported that the most remarkable phenomenon of the preceding half century had been the rise of the American millionaire, a man whose triumphs nourished ambition, emulation, and envy. "The pursuit of wealth is nowhere so eager as in America," he observed, "the opportunities for acquiring it are nowhere so numerous." To Europeans our possessions were our principal glory, and worship of them, our principal fault. No American characteristic excited so much unfavorable comment as devotion to the dollar. Even today our boasting about material possessions tends to isolate us from other less fortunate peoples. In 1949, when the Common Council for American Unity sponsored a study of European beliefs regarding the United States, investigators discovered that Europeans still cling to the idea that Americans are too materialistic. This conviction breeds suspicions which stand in the way of better foreign understanding of the United States.

Europeans who share these misgivings assume that Americans value money for its own sake, that their interests do not extend beyond gold. Such assumptions have some basis in fact. Greedy men have often sacrificed virtue and justice upon the altar of Mammon, and valued lucre above learning, or religion, or love of country. It is a mistake, however, to deduce the motives of an entire people from the careers of a few representatives, for though some Americans look upon wealth as an end in itself, and sacrifice everything to its acquisition, many more view it only as an instrumentality. The view of the majority squares with that central precept of the folklore of success which says that money has no value except in relation to its uses. Even when foreign critics acknowledge the principle of utility they complain that we devote our substance to material ends. Who can deny it? We have used money to promote physical progress, but the crucial fact is that we have not continued it to this sphere. Can the story of American education be told apart from the story of wealth? or the story of our advancing aesthetic interests? or even the story of religion? It would be foolish to pretend that moneymakers sought wealth simply to build churches, finance art galleries, or endow universities; business motivation cannot be reduced to such simple, idealistic terms. But it is equally unrealistic to ignore the fact that the quest for money has often had consequences beyond the realm of the material.

Nor is the assertion that the American measures success by the yardstick of wealth anything more than a half truth. If success consists simply of power and fame, wealth will buy both, but when we find elements of creativeness and self-realization in the careers of men who conquer fortune, such a definition becomes hopelessly inadequate. Does our yardstick of success exclude such elements as "doing good to others," the attainment of happiness, and the winning of salvation? The American does not believe so, and he will argue that a man can accomplish more good with money than without it, that money is practically a prerequisite for happiness, and that he has heard clergymen say that no man is more pleasing unto God than the morally upright millionaire. He may even feel a trace of patriotic pride in his material success. Where but in America is there such an abundance of opportunity? Where, except under our institutions, is the individual so free to work out his economic destiny? Where has the nobody so often become somebody on the strength of his personal powers?

The legendary hero of America is the self-made man. He has been active in every field from politics to the arts, but nowhere has he been more active, or more acclaimed, than in business. To most Americans he is the office boy who has become the head of a great concern, making millions in the process. He represents our most cherished conceptions of success, and particularly our belief that any man can achieve fortune through the practice of industry, frugality, and sobriety. . . .

What makes the man? Is he shaped by conditions that surround him, or by forces inherent in himself? Through the long history of American thinking on the subject of success no questions have been more central, and none have been answered more confidently. To the generation that sired Andrew Carnegie and John D. Rockefeller the relation of a favorable economic environment to personal fortune should have been obvious. And sometimes it was. P. T. Barnum, for example, admitted that "In a new country, where we have more land than people, it is not at all difficult for persons in good health to make money." But most prophets of success refused to tell their tales in terms of the favorable ratio of men to resources, preferring instead to talk about how character could triumph over circumstance. "The things which are really essential for a successful life are not circumstances, but qualities," one spokesman said, "not the things which surround a man, but the things which are in him; not the adjuncts of his position, but the attributes of his character." This had to be the emphasis, of course, for otherwise there could be no such social being as a self-made man.

In minimizing the role of the economic environment advocates of self-help did not, however, dismiss it entirely. They simply insisted that American opportunities were so plentiful, and so open to all, that each and every man could make as much of himself as he desired. "The road to fortune, like the public turnpike, is open alike to the children of the beggar, and the descendant of kings," one adviser declared. "There are tolls to be paid by all, yet all have rights, and it only remains for us to avail ourselves of these." It was a matter of common agreement that never in the history of the world had chances for success been greater than in post–Civil-War America. As Horace Greeley told an audience of young hopefuls at the Cooper Union in 1867, "There is in this land of ours larger opportunities, more just and well grounded hopes, than any other land whereon the sun ever shone." In less fortunate lands men might behold success from afar and worship it, but few could dream of achieving it. Here on the other hand the attainment of fame and fortune was a common expectation.

How could this be? In America was there not inequality in the land, and more poverty than wealth? True, the apostles of self-help admitted, but this condition forced the young to struggle against adversity and thus furnished the very means by which they might develop the qualities necessary for success. "It is the struggle which develops," said an authority on self-help, "—the effort to redeem one's self from iron surroundings;—which calls out manhood and unfolds womanhood to the highest possibilities." In the religion of success poverty became the equivalent of sin in Calvinist theology, an evil to be struggled against and overcome. The greater the poverty out of which a man climbed, the greater the testimony to the force of his character. According to this reasoning, those who would be least likely to succeed would be the children of the rich, for without struggle against adversity they would be deprived of the means of developing the necessary strength of character. This was what Henry Ward Beecher tried to convey to the wealthy merchants of Brooklyn's Plymouth Church when he told them that their financial losses might be their children's gain. "How blessed, then, is the stroke of disaster which sets the children free, and gives them over to the hard but kind bosom of Poverty, who says to them, 'Work!' and, working, makes them men."

Among business enterprisers the stoutest defender of the advantages of poverty was Andrew Carnegie, who insisted that practically all the titans of his generation has been trained in poverty's stern but efficient school. "They appear upon the stage, athletes trained for the contest, with sinews braced, indomitable wills, resolved to do or die. Such boys always have marched, and always will march, straight to the front and lead the world; they are the epochmakers." Society could ill afford to be without poverty, Carnegie argued, for without poverty there would be no extraordinary men, and without extraordinary men there could be no social progress. "Abolish luxury, if you please," he said, "but leave us the soil, upon which alone the virtues and all that is precious in human character grow; poverty—honest poverty."

In defending poverty Carnegie was not simply justifying maldistribution of wealth under a capitalist economy. He was also romanticizing the circumstances which had surrounded his own childhood and that of many other business leaders of his generation. Just how many of these wealthy men of the nineteenth century actually did rise from poverty we shall probably never know, but there have been some informed guesses. In his study of deceased American millionaires, mostly men of the last century, Pitirim Sorokin, for example, discovered that 38.8 percent of them started life poor. Another statistical study of the American business elite showed that 43 percent of those leaders who came to maturity around the year 1870 originated in the lower classes; they encountered fewer difficulties on their road from rags to riches than earlier or later generations. From a strictly statistical point of view, around 1835 appears to have been the most propitious birth year for a poor boy who hoped to rise into the business elite. Carnegie hit it right on the mark, for he was born in 1835 and came to his business maturity after the Civil War. With the evidence around him, it is not surprising that he should have sensed that in his generation, more than ever before, poor boys were on the march. And what was more natural than his attempts and those of other self-made men to discover in the poverty of their youth the source of their later strength?

II

Along with the glorification of poverty in the success cult's ideology went the glorification of rural childhood. Throughout the last century self-help propagandists insisted that rural origins foretold success and urban origins failure. It is not difficult to understand the basis for such assertions for it is an historic fact that the great cities of the nineteenth century were built up, in part at least, by migrations from rural areas, and that the country boy sometimes did rise into the ranks of the urban business elite. Philip D. Armour, James J. Hill, Collis P. Huntington, Cornelius Vanderbilt, Daniel Drew, and Jay Gould all came from the farm. Self-help publicists needed only a hasty glance at the rolls of wealth to convince themselves that there must be some cause and effect relationship between country origins and the qualities that enabled a man to conquer fortune. As Orison Marden noted, "The sturdy, vigorous, hardy qualities, the stamina, the brawn, the grit which characterize men who do great things in this world, are, as a rule, country bred."

One of the favorite migrations of ambitious country boys was from New England to the urban centers of New York and Pennsylvania. Because of its accessibility New York City was especially attractive to boys from back-country New England. In the years after 1820 they swarmed into the rising metropolis, captured it, and dominated its business life until after the Civil War. "All do not succeed," a contemporary reported, "but some do, and this is quite sufficient to keep the ambition to get a clerkship in New York alive." Joseph A. Scoville, who knew as much as any man about the New York business community at mid-century, thought there was no mystery about the country boy's rise to positions of leadership. "He needs but a foothold," said Scoville. "He asks no more . . . wherever this boy strikes, he fastens." According to Scoville New York merchants preferred to hire country boys, on the theory that they worked harder, and were more resolute, obedient, and cheerful than native New Yorkers. Too often city boys objected to menial tasks, complaining that they were intended for better things. Nothing, not even the blackening of the employer's boots, was beneath the dignity of the New Englander. Presumably this attitude went far towards explaining his rapid rise.

It would be difficult to say how many farmers' sons thus won fame and fortune but there is little doubt that contemporaries exaggerated their number. In 1883 a Brooklyn clergyman, Wilbur F. Crafts, published the results of his investigations of the lives of five hundred successful Americans representing all lines of endeavor. According to his data 57 percent of the successful men of his day were born in the country, and only 17 percent in the city. "The first conclusion from these facts," said Crafts, "is that a man who wishes to succeed should select a country farm for his birthplace. . . ." Another study, published in 1909, showed that out of 47 railroad presidents who answered questions about their origins, 55.4 percent came from farms or villages. Three more recent surveys, however, point toward the opposite direction. Farm boys accounted for only 24.6 percent of the deceased American millionaires investigated by Sorokin; only 23.8 percent of the elite businessmen whose origins were checked by C. Wright Mills; and only 12 percent of the twentieth-century leaders studied by William Miller. Even so, as a group farmers' sons ranked second only to the sons of businessmen in the achievement of outstanding success. This and the fact that farm boys started with fewer advantages made them the favorite candidates for heroes in the cult of the self-made man.

The alleged advantages of rural beginnings concerned mostly health and morals. Fresh air and good food kept the country boy in good physical condition, and his daily round of work left him little time for the mischief that distracted his less busy city cousin. Whereas city boys wasted their lives and their substance in saloons, gambling dens, and houses of prostitution, country boys supposedly led a Spartan life that prepared them for the hard struggle of the business world. "Our successful men did not feed themselves on boyhood cigarettes and late suppers, with loafing as their only labor, and midnight parties for their regular evening dissipation," a clergyman declared in 1883. "Such city-trained bodies often give out when the strain comes in business, while

the sound body and mind and morals of the man from the country hold on and hold out." In 1909 President Louis W. Hill of the Great Northern Railway testified that, despite the personal inconvenience involved, he had chosen to live on a farm rather than in the city in order to give his three boys the best possible start in life. "I believe," said Hill, "there is no end of arguments that living on the farm gives the best chance for a growing boy."

In only one respect, and that a crucial one, did philosophers of success concede that cities offered advantages which rural villages could not match. Opportunities for making money, they agreed, were better in the city. If the farm boy expected to become a millionaire he had to migrate to a metropolis. Even the most insensitive observers seemed to understand that the road to fortune must pass through the city. Many self-help handbooks therefore encouraged farm boys to leave home. "A boy at home seldom has a chance," said one blunt adviser. "Nobody believes in him,—least of all his relations." Out of deference to parents most writers tried to be more subtle; instead of telling boys to leave home they advised them indirectly to do so by talking about the importance of setting up in the right location. "No man can expect to become distinguished in any sphere unless he has the amplest field for the exercise of his powers," one handbook declared. "A. T. Stewart located anywhere out of New York City, would not be what he is, and many a clergyman or lawyer, fixed in a small village, would not have reached the eminence which the world freely accords them." It was sad, but true, that if a country boy desired fortune he had to leave home to achieve it. If there was any consolation in this uprooting, it was in the conviction that his chance of failure was slight so long as he remained faithful to the virtues that formed his country character.

Cotton Mather

Cotton Mather (1663–1728) was a deeply religious Puritan who developed a pragmatic philosophy for doing good works, a philosophy known to have influenced Benjamin Franklin. Mather's fanatical spirit (he wrote tracts defending the existence of witches which set off the hysteria leading to the infamous Salem witch trials) and his labored style have typed him as a dull, narrow Puritan. However, Mather did help to found Yale University, was the first American to belong to the Royal Society of Science, and supported smallpox inoculation, even though people threatened his life for his advocacy.

PROPOSALS TO RICH MEN

"I will get me unto the *rich men,* and will speak unto them," for they will know the ways to "do good," and will think what they shall be able to say when they come into the judgment of their God. A person of quality, quoting that passage, "the desire of a man is his kindness," invited me so to read it, "the only desirable thing in a man is his goodness." How happy would the world be, if every person of quality were to become of this persuasion! It is an article in my commission, "charge them that are rich in this world, that they do good that they be rich in good works, ready to distribute, willing to communicate." In pursuance thereof, I will remind rich men of the opportunities to "do good," with which God, who gives power to get wealth, has favored and enriched them. It is a very good account that has been sometimes given of a good man; "as to the wealth of this world, he knew no good in it, but the doing of good with it." Yea, those men who have had very little goodness in them, yet in describing "the manners of the age," in which perhaps they themselves have had too deep a share, have seen occasion to subscribe and publish this prime dictate of reason: "we are none the better for any thing, barely for the propriety's sake; but it is the application of it that gives every thing its value. Whoever buries his talent, betrays a sacred trust, and defrauds those who stand in need of it." Sirs, you cannot but acknowledge that it is the sovereign God who has bestowed upon you the riches which distinguish you. A devil himself, when he saw a rich man, could not but make this acknowledgment to the God of heaven: "thou hast blessed the work of his hands, and his substance is increased in the land." It is also to be hoped, that you are not unmindful that the riches in your possession are some of the talents of which you must give an account to the glorious Lord who has entrusted you with them; and that you will give your account with grief, and not with joy, if it should be found that all your property has been laid out to gratify the appetites of the flesh, and little or nothing of it consecrated to the service of God, and of his kingdom in the world. It was said to the priests of old, when the servants were assigned them; "unto you they are given as a gift for the Lord." This may be said of all our estates: what God gives us is not given us for ourselves, but "for the Lord." "When God's gifts to us are multiplied, our obligations to give are multiplied." Indeed there is hardly any professor of christianity so vicious that he will not confess that all his property is to be used for honest purposes, and part of it for pious ones. If any plead their poverty to excuse and exempt them from doing any thing this way: O thou poor widow with thy two mites, eternised in the history of the gospel, thou shalt "rise up in the judgment with this generation, and shall condemn it;" and let them also know, that they take a course to condemn and confine themselves to eternal *poverty.* . . .

I now renew my appeal to the light of nature: to nature thou shalt go! It is very certain that the Pagans used to *decimate* for sacred uses. Pliny tells us, that the Arabians did so. Xenophon informs us, that the Grecians had the same practice. You find the custom to be as ancient as the pen of Herodotus can make it. It is confirmed by Pausanias and Diodorus Siculus, and a whole army of authors besides Doughty, have related and asserted it. I will only introduce Festus to speak for them all: "the ancients offered to their gods the tenth of every thing." Christian, wilt thou do less for thy God than the poor perishing Pagans did for theirs? "O tell it not"—but this I will tell; that they who have conscientiously employed their tenths in pious uses, have usually been remarkably blessed in their estates, by the providence of God. The blessing has been sometimes delayed, with some trial of their patience: Not for any injustice in their hands; their prayer has been "pure." And their belief of the future state has been sometimes tried, by their meeting with losses and disappointments. But then, their *little* has been so blessed as to be still a *competency;* and God has so favored them with contentment, that it has yielded more than the abundance of many others. Very frequently too, they have been rewarded with remarkable success in their affairs, and increase of their property; and even in this world have seen the fulfilment of those promises; "cast thy grain into the moist ground, and thou shalt find it after many days." "Honor the Lord with thy substance; so shall thy barns be filled with plenty." History has given us many delightful examples of those who have had their *decimations* followed and rewarded by a surprising prosperity of their affairs. Obscure mechanics and husbandmen have risen to estates, of which once they had not the most distant expectation. The excellent Gouge, in his treatise, entitled, "the surest and safest way of thriving," has collected some such examples. The Jewish proverb, "decima, ut dives fias—tithe, and be rich," would be oftener verified, if more frequently practised. "Prove me now herewith, saith the Lord of hosts, if I will not pour out a blessing upon you." . . .

The Christian emperor Tiberius II. was famous for his religious bounties: his empress thought him even profuse in them. But he told her that he should never want

money so long as, in obedience to a glorious Christ, he should supply the necessities of the poor, and abound in religious benevolence. Once, immediately after he had made a liberal distribution, he unexpectedly found a mighty treasure, and at the same time tidings were brought to him of the death of a very rich man who had bequeathed to him all his wealth. And men in far humbler stations can relate very many and interesting anecdotes of this nature, even from their own happy experience. I cannot forbear transcribing some lines of my honored Gouge on this occasion:

"I am verily persuaded that there is scarcely any man who gives to the poor proportionably to what God has bestowed on him; but, if he observe the dealings of God's providence towards him will find the same doubled and redoubled upon him in temporal blessings. I dare challenge all the world to produce one instance, (or at least any considerable number of instances) of a merciful man, whose charity has undone him. On the contrary, as the more living wells are exhausted, the more freely they spring and flow; so the substance of charitable men frequently multiplies in the very distribution: even as the five loaves and few fishes multiplied, while being broken and distributed, and as the widow's oil increased by being poured out."

I will add a consideration which, methinks, will act as a powerful motive upon the common feelings of human nature. Let rich men, who are not "rich towards God," especially such as have no children of their own to make their heirs, consider the vile ingratitude with which their successors will treat them. Sirs, they will hardly allow you a tombstone; but, wallowing in the wealth you have left them, and complaining that you left it no sooner, they will insult your memory and ridicule your economy and parsimony. How much wiser would it be for you to do good with your estates while you live, and at your death to dispose of them in a manner which may embalm your names to posterity, and be for your advantage in the world to which you are going? That your souls may enjoy the good of paradisaical reflections, at the same time that others are inheriting what you have left to them.

I will only annex the compliment of a certain person to his friend, upon his accession to an estate; "much good may it do you; that is, much good may you do with it."

I hope we are now ready for *proposals;* and that we shall set ourselves to "devise liberal things."

Gentlemen! To relieve the necessities of the poor is a thing acceptable to the compassionate God, who has given to you what he might have given to them, and has given it to you that you might have the honor and pleasure of imparting it to them; and who has said, "he that hath pity upon the poor, lendeth unto the Lord." The more you regard the command and example of a glorious Christ in what you do this way, the more assurance you have that in the day of God you shall joyfully hear him saying, "you have done it unto me." And the more humble, silent, reserved modesty you express, concealing even from the left hand what is done with the right, the more you are assured of a great reward in the heavenly world. Such liberal men, it is observed, are generally long-lived men; ("gathering the fruit relieves the tree") and at last they pass from this into everlasting life.

Benjamin Franklin

Benjamin Franklin (1706–1790) was truly an amazing man. His accomplishments are probably unequalled: a self-made man, he became a public benefactor who helped draft The Declaration of Independence, *founded the first lending library, first fire company, and first police department in America, as well as a hospital and a university, was a scientist who invented bifocal lenses, and served as postmaster-general of the colonies. He became a successful businessman through relentless perseverance; renowned as a printer, he simultaneously sold lottery tickets, sherry, rags, and a family recipe patent medicine. He founded his firm in 1728 and retired twenty years later to devote himself to public life. "The Way to Wealth" was written four years after he retired. Franklin's writing is especially interesting because of the complex relationship between the materialistic, pragmatic, and spiritual in his philosophy.*

THE WAY TO WEALTH

COURTEOUS READER,

I have heard that nothing gives an Author so great Pleasure, as to find his Works respectfully quoted by other learned Authors. This Pleasure I have seldom enjoyed; for tho' I have been, if I may say it without Vanity, an *eminent Author* of Almanacks annually now a full Quarter of a Century, my Brother Authors in the same Way, for what Reason I know not, have ever been very sparing in their Applauses; and no other Author has taken the least Notice of me, so that did not my Writings produce me some *solid Pudding,* the great Deficiency of *Praise* would have quite discouraged me.

I concluded at length, that the People were the best Judges of my Merit; for they buy my Works; and besides, in my Rambles, where I am not personally known, I have frequently heard one or other of my Adages repeated, with, *as Poor Richard says,* at the End on't; this gave me some Satisfaction, as it showed not only that my Instructions were regarded, but discovered likewise some Respect for my Authority; and I own, that to encourage the Practice of remembering and repeating those wise Sentences, I have sometimes *quoted* myself with great Gravity.

Judge then how much I must have been gratified by an Incident I am going to relate to you. I stopt my Horse lately where a great Number of People were collected at a Vendue of Merchant Goods. The Hour of Sale not being come, they were conversing on the Badness of the Times, and one of the Company call'd to a plain clean old Man, with white Locks, *Pray, Father* Abraham, *what think you of the Times? Won't these heavy Taxes quite ruin the Country? How shall we ever be able to pay them? What would you advise us to?*— Father *Abraham* stood up, and reply'd, If you'd have my Advice, I'll give it you in short, for a *Word to the Wise is enough,* and *many Words won't fill a Bushel,* as *Poor Richard* says. They join'd in desiring him to speak his Mind, and gathering round him, he proceeded as follows;

"Friends, says he, and Neighbours, the Taxes are indeed very heavy, and if those laid on by the Government were the only Ones we had to pay, we might more easily discharge them; but we have many others, and much more grievous to some of us. We are taxed twice as much by our *Idleness,* three times as much by our *Pride,* and four times as much by our *Folly,* and from these Taxes the Commissioners cannot ease or deliver us by allowing an Abatement. However let us hearken to good Advice, and something may be done for us; *God helps them that help themselves,* as *Poor Richard* says, in his Almanack of 1733.

It would be thought a hard Government that should tax its People one tenth Part of their *Time,* to be employed in its Service. But *Idleness* taxes many of us much more, if we reckon all that is spent in absolute *Sloth,* or doing of nothing, with that which is spent in idle Employments or Amusements, that amount to nothing. *Sloth,* by bringing on Diseases, absolutely shortens Life. *Sloth, like Rust, consumes faster than Labour wears, while the used Key is always bright,* as *Poor Richard* says. But *dost thou love Life, then do not squander Time, for that's the Stuff Life is made of,* as *Poor Richard* says.—How much more than is necessary do we spend in Sleep! forgetting that *The sleeping Fox catches no Poultry,* and that *there will be sleeping enough in the Grave,* as *Poor Richard* says. If Time be of all Things the most precious, *wasting*

Time must be, as *Poor Richard* says, *the greatest Prodigality,* since, as he elsewhere tells us, *Lost Time is never found again;* and what we call *Time-enough, always proves little enough:* Let us then up and be doing, and doing to the Purpose; so by Diligence shall we do more with less Perplexity. *Sloth makes all Things difficult, but Industry all easy,* as *Poor Richard* says; and *He that riseth late, must trot all Day, and shall scarce overtake his Business at Night.* While *Laziness travels so slowly, that Poverty soon overtakes him, as we* read in *Poor Richard,* who adds, *Drive thy Business, let not that drive thee;* and *Early to Bed, and early to rise, makes a Man healthy, wealthy and wise.*

So what signifies *wishing* and *hoping* for better Times. We may make these Times better if we bestir ourselves. *Industry need not wish,* as *Poor Richard* says, and *He that lives upon Hope will die fasting. There are no Gains, without Pains;* then *Help Hands, for I have no Lands,* or if I have, they are smartly taxed. And, as *Poor Richard* likewise observes, *He that hath a Trade hath an Estate,* and *He that hath a Calling, hath an Office of Profit and Honour;* but then the *Trade* must be worked at, and the *Calling* well followed, or neither the *Estate,* nor the *Office,* will enable us to pay our Taxes.—If we are industrious we shall never starve; for, as *Poor Richard* says, *At the working Man's House Hunger looks in, but dares not enter.* Nor will the Bailiff or the Constable enter, for *Industry pays Debts, while Despair encreaseth them,* says *Poor Richard.*—What though you have found no Treasure, nor has any rich Relation left you a Legacy, *Diligence is the Mother of Good luck,* as *Poor Richard* says, *and God gives all Things to Industry.* Then *plough deep, while Sluggards sleep, and you shall have Corn to sell and to keep,* says *Poor Dick.* Work while it is called To-day, for you know not how much you may be hindered To-morrow, which makes *Poor Richard* say, *One To-day is worth two To-morrow;* and farther, *Have you somewhat to do To-mor-row, do it To-day*. If you were a Servant, would you not be ashamed that a good Master should catch you idle? Are you then your own Master, *be ashamed to catch yourself idle,* as *Poor Dick* says. When there is so much to be done for yourself, your Family, your Country, and your gracious King, be up by Peep of Day; *Let not the Sun look down and say, Inglorious here he lies.* Handle your Tools without Mittens; remember that *the Cat in Gloves catches no Mice,* as *Poor Richard* says. 'Tis true there is much to be done, and perhaps you are weak handed, but stick to it steadily, and you will see great Effects for *constant Dropping wears away Stones,* and by *Diligence and Patience the Mouse ate in two the Cable;* and *little Strokes fell great Oaks,* as *Poor Richard* says in his Almanack, the Year I cannot just now remember.

Methinks I hear some of you say, *Must a Man afford himself no Leisure?*—I will tell thee, my Friend, what *Poor Richard* says, *Employ thy Times well if thou meanest to gain Leisure;* and *since thou art not sure of a Minute, throw not away an Hour.* Leisure, is Time for doing something useful; this Leisure the diligent Man will obtain, but the lazy Man never; so that, as *Poor Richard* says, a *Life of Leisure and a Life of Laziness are two Things.* Do you imagine that Sloth will afford you more Comfort than Labour? No, for as *Poor Richard* says, *Trouble springs from Idleness, and grievous Toil from needless Ease. Many without Labour, would live by their* WITS *only, but they break for want of Stock.* Whereas Industry gives Comfort, and Plenty, and Respect: *Fly Pleasures, and they'll follow you. The diligent Spinner has a large Shift;* and *now I have a Sheep and a Cow, every Body bids me Good morrow;* all which is well said by *Poor Richard.*

But with our Industry, we must likewise be *steady, settled* and *careful,* and oversee our own Affairs *with our own Eyes,* and not trust too much to others; for, as *Poor Richard* says,

I never saw an oft removed Tree,
Nor yet an oft removed Family,
That throve so well as those that settled be.

And again, *Three Removes is as bad as a Fire;* and again, *Keep thy Shop, and thy Shop will keep thee;* and again, *if you would have your Business done, go; If not, send.* And again,

He that by the Plough would thrive,
Himself must either hold or drive.

And again, *The Eye of a Master will do more Work than both His Hands;* and again, *Want of Care does us more Damage than Want of Knowledge;* and again, *Not to oversee Workmen, is to leave them your Purse open.* Trusting too much to others Care is the Ruin of many; for, as the *Almanack* says, *In the Affairs of this World, Men are saved, not by Faith, but by the Want of it;* but a Man's own Care is profitable; for, saith *Poor Dick, Learning is to the Studious,* and *Riches to the Careful,* as well as *Power to the Bold,* and *Heaven to the Virtuous.* And farther, *If you would have a faithful Servant, and one that you like, serve yourself.* And again, he adviseth to Circumspection and Care, even in the smallest Matters, because sometimes *a little Neglect may breed great Mischief;* adding, *For want of a Nail the Shoe was lost; for want of a Shoe the Horse was lost; and for want of a Horse the Rider was lost,* being overtaken and slain by the Enemy, all for want of Care about a Horse shoe Nail.

So much for Industry, my Friends, and Attention to one's own Business; but to these we must add *Frugality,* if we would make our *Industry* more certainly successful. A Man may, if he knows not how to save as he gets, *keep his Nose all his Life to the Grindstone,* and die not worth a *Groat* at last. *A fat Kitchen makes a lean Will,* as *Poor Richard* says; and,

Many Estates are spent in the Getting,
Since Women for Tea forsook Spinning and Knitting,

And Men for Punch forsook Hewing and Splitting.

If you would be wealthy, says he, in another Almanack, *think of Saving as well as of Getting: The* Indies *have not made* Spain *rich, because her* Outgoes *are greater than her* Incomes: Away then with your expensive Follies, and you will not have so much Cause to complain of hard Times, heavy Taxes, and chargeable Families; for, as *Poor Dick* says,

Women and Wine, Game and Deceit,
Make the Wealth small, and the Wants great.

And farther, *What maintains one Vice, would bring up two Children.* You may think perhaps, That a *little Tea,* or a *little* Punch now and then, Diet a *little* more costly, Clothes a *little* finer, and a *little* Entertainment now and then, can be no *great* Matter; but remember what *Poor Richard* says, *Many a* Little *makes a Mickle;* and farther, *Beware of* little *Expences; a small Leak will sink a great Ship;* and again, *Who Dainties love, shall Beggars prove;* and moreover, *Fools make Feasts, and wise Men eat them.*

Horatio Alger, Jr.

FRANK IS OFFERED A POSITION

Horatio Alger, Jr. (1843–1899) was the most successful writer of boys' books in America, his books being read by over fifty million readers. He wrote over one hundred works, in series entitled Ragged Dick, Tattered Tom, *or* Luck and Pluck, *and did biographies of famous self-made men. Although he made much money, he spent it carelessly, gave much of it away to real-life equivalents of the heroes in his novels, and died poor.*

That the "rags to riches" theme of the success ethic may have some contemporary basis in fact is supported by the lives of two suc-

cessful Americans. Ray Kroc, owner of McDonald's Hamburgers, in the 1930s was only an average travelling salesman, but he had a desire to succeed and a willingness to experiment. His belief in quality standards and uniformity of product led him to a fortune estimated at $500 million in 1974. One of the fastest financial successes ever is H. Ross Perot. In 1962, dissatisfied with his career as a salesman with IBM, where he had reached his yearly sales quota limit by mid-January, he founded Electronic Data Systems with $1,000 on his thirty-second birthday. By late 1969 his personal wealth, based on stock holdings, was estimated at over $1 billion.

Before this chapter begins, Frank Courtney, wealthy before his mother died, was cheated out of his inheritance by his stepfather. On his first day in New York seeking work, Frank foils a robber's attempts to sell stolen bonds. Later, he pays the streetcar fare for a woman and her son who had lost their money. Both of these acts lead him, in Chapter 33, to the door of Henry Percival, who rewards him.

Mr. Percival engaged Frank in conversation on general topics while Mrs. Gordon was out of the room. His young visitor had been an extensive reader, and displayed a good deal of general information. Moreover, he expressed himself intelligently and modestly, and deepened the favorable impression which he had already succeeded in making.

When Mrs. Gordon returned, she placed in Frank's hands a small sum of money, saying:

"Allow me to repay my debt, with many thanks."

"You are quite welcome," answered our hero.

He had too much tact to refuse the money, but quietly put it into his pocket.

"Helen," said Mr. Percival, "I would like a word with you. We will leave our young friend here alone for five minutes."

"Certainly, father."

The two went into an adjoining room, and Mr. Percival commenced by asking:

"How do you like this boy, Helen?"

"Very much. He seems to have been brought up as a gentleman."

"He has. Till a short time since he supposed himself the heir to a fortune."

"Indeed!" said Mrs. Gordon, with curiosity.

Briefly, Mr. Percival rehearsed the story which Frank had told him.

"What a shame!" exclaimed Mrs. Gordon, indignantly. "His stepfather ought to be punished."

"That may come in time. Wickedness does not always prosper. But as regards our young friend, I have a plan in view."

"What is it, father?"

"I find he has an excellent education, having been nearly ready for college when the crisis in his fortunes came. I have been thinking whether we could not find a place for him in this house. My eyes, you know, are so weak that they are often strained by attention to my correspondence and reading. I have an idea of engaging Frank Courtney as a sort of private secretary, upon whom I can call at any time. Of course he would have his home in the house."

"There will be no difficulty about that. Our family is small, and we have plenty of vacant rooms. But, father, will he be qualified to undertake the duties you have designed for him? He is very young."

"That is true, my dear; but he is remarkably well educated. I have tested his capacity by dictating a letter for him to copy."

"Did he do the work satisfactorily?"

"Without a single mistake."

"Then, father, I would not hesitate to engage him. Freddie likes him, and will be delighted to have him in the house."

"Another idea, Helen. It is time Freddie began to study. Suppose we make him Freddie's private tutor—say for an hour daily?"

"That is really an excellent idea, father," said Mrs. Gordon, in a tone of satisfaction. "It will please and benefit Freddie, and be a relief to me. Do you think Frank will have patience enough?"

"I watched him with the little fellow, and I could see that he liked children. I am sure he will succeed in this as well as in the duties which he will undertake for me."

"I suppose he will have no objection to the plan?"

"I think he will accept gladly. He has had a hard struggle thus far in maintaining himself, and I can relieve him from all anxiety on that score. I am indebted to him for helping me to recover my bonds, and this will be an excuse for offering him a larger salary than the services of so young a secretary could be expected to command."

"Very well, father. Your plan pleases me very much, and I shall be glad to have Frank commence to-morrow, if he chooses. Now let us return to the library."

While father and daughter were absent Frank had taken from the table a volume of "Macaulay's History," and had become interested in it.

He laid it down upon their return.

Mr. Percival resumed his easy chair, and said, with a smile:

"My daughter and I have been consulting about you."

Frank bowed, and his hopes rose.

"I suppose you are open to an offer of employment?"

"I am not only open to it, Mr. Percival, but I shall be grateful for it."

He could not help wondering what sort of employment Mr. Percival was about to offer him. He concluded that it might be a place in some business house.

"The fact is," said the old gentleman, "I have a great mind to offer you a situation as my private secretary."

Frank was astonished. This was something he had not thought of.

"Do you think I am qualified to fill such a position, Mr. Percival?" he asked.

"The duties would not be difficult," was the reply. "Though not in active business, the care of my property, and looking after my scattered investments, involves me in considerable correspondence. My eyes are not as strong as they once were, and I find them at times taxed by letter-writing, not to mention reading. You can relieve me very materially."

"I shall be very glad to do so, sir. The duties would be very agreeable to me."

"But that is not all. My daughter proposes to employ you as private tutor for Freddie."

Frank smiled.

"I think my scholarship would be sufficient for that," he said.

"Freddie likes you," said Mrs. Gordon, "and if you think you would have patience enough—"

"I think I should," assured Frank. "I was always fond of children, and Freddie is a very attractive boy."

"I believe he has an equally favorable opinion of you," said Mrs. Gordon, smiling.

"We are very good friends, I think," said Frank.

"Then I am to understand that you will not object to this double position?" asked Mr. Percival.

"I shall be very glad to accept," replied Frank, quickly.

"Of course you will need to make your home with us," continued the old gentleman. "My daughter will assign you a room, and you may move in as soon as you like."

"That will be to-morrow, sir."

"I like your promptness. There remains one thing to be considered. We have not settled about the amount of your salary."

Salary sounded well, and Frank began to feel himself a young man.

"I will leave that entirely to you, sir," he said.

"Will fifty dollars a month satisfy you?" asked Mr. Percival, with a benevolent smile.

"Fifty dollars a month, besides my board?" ejaculated Frank.

"Yes."

"But I am sure I cannot earn so much," said Frank, candidly.

"It is, I am aware, more than would usually be offered to a boy of your age; but I owe you something for the service you rendered me, in helping me to recover my bonds. I have not offered you any pecuniary recompense, thinking you would prefer employment."

"You judged rightly, sir, and I feel very grateful to you."

"I did not think, this morning," said Mrs. Gordon, laughing, "that I should find a tutor for Freddie before night."

"It is rather a surprise to me," said Frank, "but a very agreeable one. I feel very much indebted to you both for the confidence you feel in me, and I will now bid you good-evening!"

"One minute, Frank," said Mr. Percival. "Would it be convenient for you to receive a month's salary in advance?"

"I shall not need the whole of it, sir; but if you will let me have twenty dollars, I can easily wait for the balance till the end of the month."

Mr. Percival drew from his pocketbook twenty dollars in bills and placed them in the hands of his young visitor. Frank thanked him earnestly.

"We shall expect to see you to-morrow," said Mr. Percival. "Goodnight!"

Frank left the house in high spirits. He had found strong friends, and secured a position and a salary beyond his highest expectations. He determined to do his best to satisfy his employer.

The next day Frank transferred his residence to Madison Avenue. He was assigned a pleasant room, decidedly superior, it need hardly be said, to his room at Clinton Place. It seemed agreeable to him once more to enjoy the comforts of a liberal home.

Frank had had some doubts as to how he would satisfy Mr. Percival in his capacity of private secretary.

He was determined to do his best, but thought it possible that the old gentleman might require more than he could do well. He looked forward, therefore, with some apprehension to his first morning's work.

Mr. Percival, though not engaged in active business, was a wealthy man, and his capital was invested in a great variety of enterprises. Naturally, therefore, he received a large number of business letters, which required to be answered.

The first day he dictated several replies, which Frank put upon paper. He wished, however, to put Frank's ability to a severe test.

"Here are two letters," he said, "which you may answer. I have noted on each instructions which you will follow. The wording of the letters I leave to you."

"I will try to satisfy you, sir," said Frank.

Our hero was a good writer for his age. Moreover he had been well trained at school, and did not shrink from the task assigned him.

He read carefully the instructions of his employer, and composed the letters in strict accordance with them.

Mr. Percival awaited with some interest the result of his experiment. If Frank proved competent to the task assigned him, his own daily labor would be considerably abridged.

"Here are the letters, sir," said Frank, passing the drafts to Mr. Percival.

The old gentleman examined them carefully. As he did so, his face expressed his satisfaction. "Upon my word, Frank," he said, familiarly, "you have done your work exceedingly well. They are brief, concise and yet comprehensive. I feared that you would use too many words."

"I am glad you are pleased, sir. Doctor Brush trained us to write letters, and he cut down our essays when they were too diffuse."

"Then I feel indebted to Doctor Brush for providing me with so competent a young secretary. You will be able to assist me even more than I anticipated. I shall, of course, read over your letters before they are sent, to make sure that you have fully comprehended and carried out my instructions, but don't expect they will need much correction."

Frank was much gratified by these words. This was the only point on which he had felt at all doubtful as to his ability to please his employer.

Sometimes, when his eyes pained him more than usual, Mr. Percival also employed him to read to him from the daily papers, or from some book in which he was interested, but this did not occur regularly.

Every day, however, Frank was occupied with Freddie. The little boy knew the alphabet, but nothing more, so that his young teacher had to begin with him at the beginning of the primer.

He succeeded in interesting his little pupil, and did not protract his term of study so as to weary him.

Finding that the little fellow was fond of hearing stories, he read to him every day a story or two from Hans Christian Andersen, or from a collection of German fairy stories, and sometimes went out to walk with him.

Freddie was delighted with his teacher, and freely expressed his approval to his mother and grandfather.

"Really, Frank," said Mrs. Gordon, "I shall begin to be jealous of your hold upon Freddie. I am not sure but he likes your company better than mine."

"I don't think Freddie will prefer any one to his mother," said Frank "but I am glad he likes to be with me."

"You have certainly proved very successful as a private tutor, Frank," said Mrs. Gordon, "and my father tells me you succeed equally well as a secretary."

"It is partly because you both treat me so indulgently," answered Frank, gracefully.

This answer pleased Mr. Percival and Mrs. Gordon, who more than ever congratulated themselves upon the lucky chance that had thrown Frank in their way.

Assuredly he made himself very useful

in the small household, contributing to the comfort and pleasure of Freddie, his mother and grandfather, in nearly equal measure.

While Frank's monthly salary was of great value and importance to him, it was nothing to Mr. Percival in comparison with the pleasure and relief afforded by his presence in the house.

It must not be supposed, however, that Frank's time was wholly occupied by the duties of his two positions. Usually he had several hours daily at his disposal, and these he was allowed to spend as he pleased.

Part of this he occupied in visiting different localities of the city and points of interest in the neighborhood, and part in reading and study.

Mr. Percival had a large and well-selected library, which, to a boy of Frank's studious tastes, was a great attraction.

He entered upon a course of solid reading, embracing some of the standard histories, and devoted some hours every week to keeping up his acquaintance with the Greek and Latin authors which he had read at school.

In this way his time was well and usefully employed, and the weeks slipped by till almost before he was aware six months had passed. The next chapter will record a meeting with some old acquaintances.

Edwin Arlington Robinson

Edwin Arlington Robinson (1869–1935) felt himself a failure who was outdistanced as a material success by his brothers. Tragedy struck his family when his father died when Robinson was twenty-four; his mother soon became seriously ill; and his brothers died at an early age. An expected sizeable inheritance was greatly reduced by his father's stock market losses, and Robinson had to work in several confining jobs until Theodore Roosevelt, who was interested in his poetry, found him a sinecure in the New York Customs House in 1905. As a result of this background, a view of the fast-changing nature of fortune is prominent in his poetry.

RICHARD CORY

Whenever Richard Cory went down town,
We people on the pavement looked at him:
He was a gentleman from sole to crown,
Clean favored, and imperially slim.

And he was always quietly arrayed,
And he was always human when he talked;
But still he fluttered pulses when he said,
'Good-morning,' and he glittered when he
   walked.

And he was rich—yes, richer than a king—
And admirably schooled in every grace:
In fine, we thought that he was everything
To make us wish that we were in his place.

So on we worked, and waited for the light,
And went without the meat, and cursed
   the bread;
And Richard Cory, one calm summer night,
Went home and put a bullet through his
   head.

BEWICK FINZER

Time was when his half million drew
   The breath of six per cent;
But soon the worm of what-was-not
   Fed hard on his content;
And something crumbled in his brain
   When his half million went.

Time passed, and filled along with his
   The place of many more;
Time came, and hardly one of us
   Had credence to restore,
From what appeared one day, the man
   Whom we had known before.

The broken voice, the withered neck,
   The coat worn out with care,
The cleanliness of indigence,
   The brilliance of despair,
The fond imponderable dreams
   Of affluence,—all were there.

Poor Finzer, with his dreams and schemes,
   Fares hard now in the race,

With heart and eye that have a task
 When he looks in the face
Of one who might so easily
 Have been in Finzer's place.

He comes unfailing for the loan
 We give and then forget;
He comes, and probably for years
 Will he be coming yet,—
Familiar as an old mistake,
 And futile as regret.

E. E. Cummings

E. E. Cummings (1894–1962), famed for his idiosyncratic typography and his poetic innovation, has a distinct simplicity and directness in his poetry. He attacks ignorance wherever he finds it, whether in a person or an idea. His poems are lyrics or satires, often involving a memorable character. The following is a humorous comment on the inevitability of success for one who tries long enough.

nobody loses all the time

nobody loses all the time

i had an uncle named
Sol who was a born failure and
nearly everybody said he should have gone
into vaudeville perhaps because my Uncle
 Sol could
sing McCann He Was A Diver on Xmas
 Eve like Hell itself which
may or may not account for the fact that
 my Uncle

Sol indulged in that possibly most in-
 excusable
of all to use a highfalootin phrase
luxuries that is or to
wit farming and be
it needlessly
added

my Uncle Sol's farm
failed because the chickens
ate the vegetables so

my Uncle Sol had a
chicken farm till the
skunks ate the chickens when

my Uncle Sol
had a skunk farm but
the skunks caught cold and
died and so
my Uncle Sol imitated the
skunks in a subtle manner

or by drowning himself in the watertank
but somebody who'd given my Uncle Sol a
 Victor
Victrola and records while he lived
 presented to
him upon the auspicious occasion of his
 decease a
scrumptious not to mention splendiferous
 funeral with
tall boys in black gloves and flowers and
 everything and

i remember we all cried like the Missouri
when my Uncle Sol's coffin lurched because
somebody pressed a button
(and down went
my Uncle
Sol

and started a worm farm)

The McGuffey's Reader

William Holmes McGuffey (1800–1873), an Ohio schoolmaster, probably influenced more schoolchildren in the nineteenth century than any other single writer. His McGuffey's Readers first began in 1836 and have sold over one hundred and twenty million copies since then. Editions can still be found today. The readers were moral texts filled with maxims on character-building and success.

TRY, TRY AGAIN

Once or twice though you should fail,
 Try, Try Again;

If you would, at last, prevail,
    Try, Try Again;
If we strive, 'tis no disgrace,
Though we may not win the race;
What should you do in that case?
    Try, Try Again.
If you find your task is hard,
    Try, Try Again;
Time will bring you your reward,
    Try, Try Again;
All that other folks can do,
Why, with patience, should not you:
Only keep this rule in view;
    Try, Try Again.

John Cheever

John Cheever (b. 1912), is the author of three novels, including The Wapshot Chronicle, *which won a National Book Award, and five collections of short stories. He writes mostly about middle-class suburbia, which he views ambivalently, both defending and satirizing its inhabitants. This story shows some hazards in the pursuit of success.*

O YOUTH AND BEAUTY!

At the tag end of nearly every long, large Saturday-night party in the suburb of Shady Hill, when almost everybody who was going to play golf or tennis in the morning had gone home hours ago and the ten or twelve people remaining seemed powerless to bring the evening to an end although the gin and whiskey were running low, and here and there a woman who was sitting out her husband would have begun to drink milk; when everybody had lost track of time, and the baby sitters who were waiting at home for these diehards would have long since stretched out on the sofa and fallen into a deep sleep, to dream about cooking-contest prizes, ocean voyages, and romance; when the bellicose drunk, the crapshooter, the pianist, and the woman faced with the ex-

piration of her hopes had all expressed themselves; when every proposal—to go to the Farquarsons' for breakfast, to go swimming, to go and wake up the Townsends, to go here and go there—died as soon as it was made, then Trace Bearden would begin to chide Cash Bentley about his age and thinning hair. The chiding was preliminary to moving the living-room furniture. Trace and Cash moved the tables and the chairs, the sofas and the fire screen, the woodbox and the footstool; and when they had finished, you wouldn't know the place. Then if the host had a revolver, he would be asked to produce it. Cash would take off his shoes and assume a starting crouch behind a sofa. Trace would fire the weapon out of an open window, and if you were new to the community and had not understood what the preparations were about, you would then realize that you were watching a hurdle race. Over the sofa went Cash, over the tables, over the fire screen and the woodbox. It was not exactly a race, since Cash ran it alone, but it was extraordinary to see this man of forty surmount so many obstacles so gracefully. There was not a piece of furniture in Shady Hill that Cash could not take in his stride. The race ended with cheers, and presently the party would break up.

Cash was, of course, an old track star, but he was never aggressive or tiresome about his brilliant past. The college where he had spent his youth had offered him a paying job on the alumni council, but he had refused it, realizing that that part of his life was ended. Cash and his wife, Louise, had two children, and they lived in a medium-cost ranchhouse on Alewives Lane. They belonged to the country club, although they could not afford it, but in the case of the Bentleys nobody ever pointed this out, and Cash was one of the best-liked men in Shady Hill. He was still slender—he was careful about his weight—and he walked to the train in the morning with a light and vigorous step that marked him as an athlete. His hair was thin, and there were mornings when his eyes looked bloodshot, but this did not detract much from a charming quality of stubborn youthfulness.

In business Cash had suffered reverses and disappointments, and the Bentleys had many money worries. They were always late with their tax payments and their mortgage payments, and the drawer of the hall table was stuffed with unpaid bills; it was always touch and go with the Bentleys and the bank. Louise looked pretty enough on Saturday night, but her life was exacting and monotonous. In the pockets of her suits, coats, and dresses there were little wads and scraps of paper on which was written: "Oleomargarine, frozen spinach, Kleenex, dog biscuit, hamburger, pepper, lard . . ." When she was still half awake in the morning, she was putting on the water for coffee and diluting the frozen orange juice. Then she would be wanted by the children. She would crawl under the bureau on her hands and knees to find a sock for Toby. She would lie flat on her belly and wriggle under the bed (getting dust up her nose) to find a shoe for Rachel. Then there were the housework, the laundry, and the cooking, as well as the demands of the children. There always seemed to be shoes to put on and shoes to take off, snowsuits to be zipped and unzipped, bottoms to be wiped, tears to be dried, and when the sun went down (she saw it set from the kitchen window) there was the supper to be cooked, the baths, the bedtime story, and the Lord's Prayer. With the sonorous words of the Our Father in a darkened room the children's day was over, but the day was far from over for Louise Bentley. There were the darning, the mending, and some ironing to do, and after sixteen years of housework she did not seem able to escape her chores even while she slept. Snowsuits, shoes, baths, and groceries seemed to have permeated her subconscious. Now and then she would speak in her sleep—so loudly that she woke her husband. "I can't *afford* veal cutlets," she said one night. Then she sighed uneasily and was quiet again.

By the standards of Shady Hill, the Bentleys were a happily married couple, but they had their ups and downs. Cash could be very touchy at times. When he came home after a bad day at the office and found that Louise, for some good reason, had not started supper, he would be ugly. "Oh, for Christ sake!" he would say, and go into the kitchen and heat up some frozen food. He drank some whiskey to relax himself during this ordeal, but it never seemed to relax him, and he usually burned the bottom out of a pan, and when they sat down for supper the dining space would be full of smoke. It was only a question of time before they were plunged into a bitter quarrel. Louise would run upstairs, throw herself onto the bed, and sob. Cash would grab the whiskey bottle and dose himself. These rows, in spite of the vigor with which Cash and Louise entered into them, were the source of a great deal of pain for both of them. Cash would sleep downstairs on the sofa, but sleep never repaired the damage, once the trouble had begun, and if they met in the morning, they would be at one another's throats in a second. Then Cash would leave for the train, and, as soon as the children had been taken to nursery school, Louise would put on her coat and cross the grass to the Beardens' house. She would cry into a cup of warmed-up coffee and tell Lucy Bearden her troubles. What was the meaning of marriage? What was the meaning of love? Lucy always suggested that Louise get a job. It would give her emotional and financial independence, and that, Lucy said, was what she needed.

The next night, things would get worse. Cash would not come home for dinner at all, but would stumble in at about eleven, and the whole sordid wrangle would be repeated, with Louise going to bed in tears upstairs and Cash again stretching out on the living-room sofa. After a few days and nights of this, Louise would decide that she was at the end of her rope. She would decide to go and stay with her married sister in Mamaroneck. She usually chose a Saturday, when Cash would be at home, for her departure. She would pack a suitcase and get her War Bonds from the desk. Then she would take a bath and put on her best slip. Cash, passing the bedroom door, would see her. Her slip was transparent, and suddenly he was all repentance, tenderness, charm, wisdom, and love. "Oh, my darling!" he would groan, and when they went downstairs to get a bite to eat about an hour later, they would be sighing and making cow eyes at one another; they would be the happiest married couple in the whole Eastern United States. It was usually at about this time that Lucy Bearden turned up with the good news that she had found a job for Louise. Lucy would ring the doorbell, and Cash, wearing a bathrobe, would let her in. She would be brief with Cash, naturally, and hurry into the dining room to tell poor Louise the good news. "Well that's very nice of you to have looked," Louise would say wanly, "but I don't think that I want a job any more. I don't think that Cash wants me to work, do you, sweetheart?" Then she would turn her big dark eyes on Cash, and you could practically smell smoke. Lucy would excuse herself hurriedly from this scene of depravity, but she never left with any hard feelings, because she had been married for nineteen years herself and she knew that every union has its ups and downs. She didn't seem to leave any wiser, either; the next time the Bentleys quarreled, she would be just as intent as ever on getting Louise a job. But these quarrels and reunions, like the hurdle race, didn't seem to lose their interest through repetition.

On a Saturday night in the spring, the Farquarsons gave the Bentleys an anniversary party. It was their seventeenth anniversary. Saturday afternoon, Louise Bentley put herself through preparations nearly as arduous as the Monday wash. She rested for an hour, by the clock, with her feet high in the air, her chin in a sling, and her eyes bathed in some astringent solution. The clay packs, the too tight girdle, and the plucking and curling and painting that went on were all aimed at rejuvenation. Feeling in the end that she had not been entirely successful, she tied a piece of veiling over her eyes—but she was a lovely woman, and all the cosmetics that she had struggled with seemed, like her veil, to be drawn transparently over a face where mature beauty and a capacity for wit and passion were undisguisable. The Farquarsons' party was nifty, and the Bentleys had a wonderful time. The only person who drank too much was Trace Bearden. Late in the party, he began to chide Cash about his thinning hair and Cash good-naturedly began to move the furniture around. Harry Farquarson had a pistol, and Trace went out onto the terrace to fire it up at the sky. Over the sofa went Cash, over the end table, over the arms of the wing chair and the fire screen. It was a piece of carving on a chest that brought him down, and down he came like a ton of bricks.

Louise screamed and ran to where he lay. He had cut a gash in his forehead, and someone made a bandage to stop the flow of blood. When he tried to get up, he stumbled and fell again, and his face turned a terrible green. Harry telephoned Dr. Parminter, Dr. Hopewell, Dr. Altman, and Dr. Barnstable, but it was two in the morning and none of them answered. Finally, a Dr. Yerkes—a total stranger—agreed to come. Yerkes was a young man—he did not seem old enough to be a doctor—and he looked around at the disordered room and the anxious company as if there was something weird about the scene. He got off on the wrong foot with Cash. "What seems to be the matter, old-timer?" he asked.

Cash's leg was broken. The doctor put a splint on it, and Harry and Trace carried the injured man out to the doctor's car. Louise followed them in her own car to the hospital, where Cash was bedded down in a ward. The doctor gave Cash a sedative, and Louise kissed him and drove home in the dawn.

Cash was in the hospital for two weeks, and when he came home he walked with a crutch and his broken leg was in a heavy cast. It was another ten days before he could limp to the morning train. "I won't be able to run the hurdle race any more, sweetheart," he told Louise sadly. She said that it didn't matter, but while it didn't matter to her, it seemed to matter to Cash. He had lost weight in the hospital. His spirits were low. He seemed discontented. He did not himself understand what had happened. He, or everything around him, seemed subtly to have changed for the worse. Even his senses seemed to conspire to damage the ingenuous world that he had enjoyed for so many years. He went into the kitchen late one night to make himself a sandwich, and when he opened the icebox door he noticed a rank smell. He dumped the spoiled meat into the garbage, but the smell clung to his nostrils. A few days later he was in the attic, looking for his old varsity sweater. There were no windows in the attic and his flashlight was dim. Kneeling on the floor to unlock a trunk, he broke a spider web with his lips. The frail web covered his mouth as if a hand had been put over it. He wiped it impatiently, but also with the feeling of having been gagged. A few nights later, he was walking down a New York side street in the rain and saw an old whore standing in a doorway. She was so sluttish and ugly that she looked like a cartoon of Death, but before he could appraise her— the instant his eyes took an impression of her crooked figure—his lips swelled, his breathing quickened, and he experienced all the other symptoms of erotic excitement. A few nights later, while he was reading *Time* in the living room, he noticed that the faded roses Louise had brought in from the garden smelled more of earth than of anything else. It was a putrid, compelling smell. He dropped the roses into a waste-basket, but not before they had reminded him of the spoiled meat, the whore, and the spider web.

He had started going to parties again, but without the hurdle race to run, the parties of his friends and neighbors seemed to him interminable and stale. He listened to their dirty jokes with an irritability that was hard for him to conceal. Even their countenances discouraged him, and, slumped in a chair, he would regard their skin and their teeth narrowly, as if he were himself a much younger man. The brunt of his irritability fell on Louise, and it seemed to her that Cash, in losing the hurdle race, had lost the thing that had preserved his equilibrium. He was rude to his friends when they stopped in for a drink. He was rude and gloomy when he and Louise went out. When Louise asked him what was the matter, he only murmured, "Nothing, nothing, nothing," and poured himself some bourbon. May and June passed, and then the first part of July, without his showing any improvement.

Then it is a summer night, a wonderful summer night. The passengers on the eight-fifteen see Shady Hill—if they notice it at all —in a bath of placid golden light. The noise of the train is muffled in the heavy foliage, and the long car windows look like a string of lighted aquarium tanks before they flicker out of sight. Up on the hill, the ladies say to one another, "Smell the grass! Smell the trees!" The Farquarsons are giving another party, and Harry has hung a sign, WHISKEY GULCH, from the rose arbor, and is wearing a chef's white hat and an apron. His guests are still drinking, and the smoke from his meat fires rises, on this windless evening, straight up into the trees.

In the clubhouse on the hill, the first of the formal dances for the young people begins around nine. On Alewives Lane sprinklers continue to play after dark. You can smell the water. The air seems as fragrant as it is dark—it is a delicious element to walk through—and most of the windows on Alewives Lane are open to it. You can see Mr. and Mrs. Bearden, as you pass, looking at their television. Joe Lockwood, the young lawyer who lives on the corner, is practicing a speech to the jury before his wife. "I intend to show you," he says, "that a man of probity, a man whose reputation for honesty and reliability . . ." He waves his bare arms as he speaks. His wife goes on knitting. Mrs. Carver—Harry Farquarson's mother-in-law—glances up at the sky and asks, "*Where did all the stars come from?*" She is old and foolish, and yet she is right: Last night's stars seem to have drawn to themselves a new range of galaxies, and the night sky is not dark at all, except where there is a tear in the membrane of light. In the unsold house lots near the track a hermit thrush is singing.

The Bentleys are at home. Poor Cash has been so rude and gloomy that the Farquarsons have not asked him to their party. He sits on the sofa beside Louise, who is sewing elastic into the children's underpants. Through the open window he can hear the pleasant sounds of the summer night. There is another party, in the Rogerses' garden, behind the Bentleys'. The music from the dance drifts down the hill. The band is sketchy—saxophone, drums, and piano—and all the selections are twenty years old. The band plays "Valencia," and Cash looks tenderly toward Louise, but Louise, tonight, is a discouraging figure. The lamp picks out the gray in her hair. Her apron is stained. Her face seems colorless and drawn. Suddenly, Cash begins frenziedly to beat his feet in time to the music. He sings some gibberish—Jabajabajabajaba—to the distant saxophone. He sighs and goes into the kitchen.

Here a faint, stale smell of cooking clings to the dark. From the kitchen window Cash can see the lights and figures of the Rogerses' party. It is a young people's party. The Rogers girl has asked some friends in for dinner before the dance, and now they seem to be leaving. Cars are driving away.

"I'm covered with grass stains," a girl says. "I hope the old man remembered to buy gasoline," a boys says, and a girl laughs. There is nothing on their minds but the passing summer night. Taxes and the elastic in underpants—all the unbeautiful facts of life that threaten to crush the breath out of Cash—have not touched a single figure in this garden. Then jealousy seizes him—such savage and bitter jealousy that he feels ill.

He does not understand what separates him from these children in the garden next door. He has been a young man. He has been a hero. He has been adored and happy and full of animal spirits, and now he stands in a dark kitchen, deprived of his athletic prowess, his impetuousness, his good looks—of everything that means anything to him. He feels as if the figures in the next yard are the specters from some party in that past where all his tastes and desires lie, and from which he has been cruelly removed. He feels like a ghost of the summer evening. He is sick with longing. Then he hears voices in the front of the house. Louise turns on the kitchen light. "Oh, here you are," she says. "The Beardens stopped in. I think they'd like a drink."

Cash went to the front of the house to greet the Beardens. They wanted to go up to the club, for one dance. They saw, at a glance, that Cash was at loose ends, and they urged the Bentleys to come. Louise got someone to stay with the children and then went upstairs to change.

When they got to the club, they found a few friends of their age hanging around the bar, but Cash did not stay in the bar. He seemed restless and perhaps drunk. He banged into a table on his way through the lounge to the ballroom. He cut in on a young girl. He seized her too vehemently and jigged her off in an ancient two-step. She signaled openly for help to a boy in the stag line, and Cash was cut out. He walked angrily off the dance floor onto the terrace. Some young couples there withdrew from one another's arms as he pushed open the screen door. He walked to the end of the terrace, where he hoped to be alone, but here he surprised another young couple, who got up from the lawn, where they seemed to have been lying, and walked off in the dark toward the pool.

Louise remained in the bar with the Beardens. "Poor Cash is tight," she said. And then, "He told me this afternoon that he was going to paint the storm windows," she said. "Well, he mixed the paint and washed the brushes and put on some old fatigues and went into the cellar. There was a telephone call for him at around five, and when I went down to tell him, do you know what he was doing? He was just sitting there in the dark with a cocktail shaker. He hadn't touched the storm windows. He was just sitting there in the dark, drinking Martinis."

"Poor Cash," Trace said.

"You ought to get a job," Lucy said. "That would give you emotional and financial independence." As she spoke, they all heard the noise of furniture being moved around in the lounge.

"Oh, my God!" Louise said. "He's going to run the race. Stop him, Trace, stop him! He'll hurt himself. He'll kill himself!"

They all went to the door of the lounge. Louise again asked Trace to interfere, but she could see by Cash's face that he was way beyond remonstrating with. A few couples left the dance floor and stood watching the preparations. Trace didn't try to stop Cash—he helped him. There was no pistol, so he slammed a couple of books together for the start.

Over the sofa went Cash, over the coffee table, the lamp table, the fire screen, and the hassock. All his grace and strength seemed to have returned to him. He cleared the big sofa at the end of the room and instead of stopping there, he turned and started back over the course. His face was strained. His mouth hung open. The tendons of his neck protruded hideously. He made the hassock, the fire screen, the lamp

table, and the coffee table. People held their breath when he approached the final sofa, but he cleared it and landed on his feet. There was some applause. Then he groaned and fell. Louise ran to his side. His clothes were soaked with sweat and he gasped for breath. She knelt down beside him and took his head in her lap and stroked his thin hair.

Cash had a terrible hangover on Sunday, and Louise let him sleep until it was nearly time for church. The family went off to Christ Church together at eleven, as they always did. Cash sang, prayed, and got to his knees, but the most he ever felt in church was that he stood outside the realm of God's infinite mercy, and, to tell the truth, he no more believed in the Father, the Son, and the Holy Ghost than does my bull terrier. They returned home at one to eat the overcooked meat and stony potatoes that were their customary Sunday lunch. At around five, the Parminters called up and asked them over for a drink. Louise didn't want to go, so Cash went alone. (Oh, those suburban Sunday nights, those Sunday-night blues! Those departing weekend guests, those stale cocktails, those half-dead flowers, those trips to Harmon to catch the Century, those post-mortems and pickup suppers!) It was sultry and overcast. The dog days were beginning. He drank gin with the Parminters for an hour or two and then went over to the Townsends' for a drink. The Farquarsons called up the Townsends and asked them to come over and bring Cash with them, and at the Farquarsons' they had some more drinks and ate the leftover party food. The Farquarsons were glad to see that Cash seemed like himself again. It was half past ten or eleven when he got home. Louise was upstairs, cutting out of the current copy of *Life* those scenes of mayhem, disaster, and violent death that she felt might corrupt her children. She always did this. Cash came upstairs and spoke to her and then went down again. In a little while, she heard him moving the living-room furniture around. Then he called to her, and when she went down, he was standing at the foot of the stairs in his stocking feet, holding the pistol out to her. She had never fired it before, and the directions he gave her were not much help.

"Hurry up," he said. "I can't wait all night."

He had forgotten to tell her about the safety, and when she pulled the trigger nothing happened.

"It's that little lever," he said. "Press that little lever." Then, in his impatience, he hurdled the sofa anyhow.

The pistol went off and Louise got him in midair. She shot him dead.

Michael Harrington

Michael Harrington (b. 1928), a former welfare worker in St. Louis, helped inspire Lyndon Johnson's War on Poverty. Harrington's book The Other America *brought home to many the paradox of poverty existing in a land of affluence, where those who fail often become "invisible."*

THE INVISIBLE LAND

There is a familiar America. It is celebrated in speeches and advertised on television and in the magazines. It has the highest mass standard of living the world has ever known.

In the 1950's this America worried about itself, yet even its anxieties were products of abundance. The title of a brilliant book was widely misinterpreted, and the familiar America began to call itself 'the affluent society.' There was introspection about Madison Avenue and tail fins; there was discussion of the emotional suffering taking place in the suburbs. In all this, there was an implicit assumption that the basic grinding economic problems had been solved in the United States. In this theory the nation's

problems were no longer a matter of basic human needs, of food, shelter, and clothing. Now they were seen as qualitative, a question of learning to live decently amid luxury.

While this discussion was carried on, there existed another America. In it dwelt somewhere between 40,000,000 and 50,-000,000 citizens of this land. They were poor. They still are.

To be sure, the other America is not impoverished in the same sense as those poor nations where millions cling to hunger as a defense against starvation. This country has escaped such extremes. That does not change the fact that tens of millions of Americans are, at this very moment, maimed in body and spirit, existing at levels beneath those necessary for human decency. If these people are not starving, they are hungry, and sometimes fat with hunger, for that is what cheap foods do. They are without adequate housing and education and medical care. . . .

The millions who are poor in the United States tend to become increasingly invisible. Here is a great mass of people, yet it takes an effort of the intellect and will even to see them.

I discovered this personally in a curious way. After I wrote my first article on poverty in America, I had all the statistics down on paper. I had proved to my satisfaction that there were around 50,000,000 poor in this country. Yet, I realized I did not believe my own figures. The poor existed in the Government reports; they were percentages and numbers in long, close columns, but they were not part of my experience. I could prove that the other America existed, but I had never been there.

My response was not accidental. It was typical of what is happening to an entire society, and it reflects profound social changes in this nation. The other America, the America of poverty, is hidden today in a way that it never was before. Its millions are socially invisible to the rest of us. No wonder that so many misinterpreted Galbraith's title and assumed that 'the affluent society' meant that everyone had a decent standard of life. The misinterpretation was true as far as the actual day-to-day lives of two-thirds of the nation were concerned. Thus, one must begin a description of the other America by understanding why we do not see it.

There are perennial reasons that make the other America an invisible land.

Poverty is often off the beaten track. It always has been. The ordinary tourist never left the main highway, and today he rides interstate turnpikes. He does not go into the valleys of Pennsylvania where the towns look like movie sets of Wales in the thirties. He does not see the company houses in rows, the rutted roads (the poor always have bad roads whether they live in the city, in towns, or on farms), and everything is black and dirty. And even if he were to pass through such a place by accident, the tourist would not meet the unemployed men in the bar or the women coming home from a runaway sweatshop.

Then, too, beauty and myths are perennial masks of poverty. The traveler comes to the Appalachians in the lovely season. He sees the hills, the streams, the foliage—but not the poor. Or perhaps he looks at a run-down mountain house and, remembering Rousseau rather than seeing with his eyes, decides that 'those people' are truly fortunate to be living the way they are and that they are lucky to be exempt from the strains and tensions of the middle class. The only problem is that 'those people,' the quaint inhabitants of those hills, are undereducated, underprivileged, lack medical care, and are in the process of being forced from the land into a life in the cities, where they are misfits.

These are normal and obvious causes of the invisibility of the poor. They operated a generation ago; they will be functioning a generation hence. It is more important to understand that the very development of American society is creating a new kind of

blindness about poverty. The poor are increasingly slipping out of the very experience of consciousness of the nation.

If the middle class never did like ugliness and poverty, it was at least aware of them. 'Across the tracks' was not a very long way to go. There were forays into the slums at Christmas time; there were charitable organizations that brought contact with the poor. Occasionally, almost everyone passed through the Negro ghetto or the blocks of tenements, if only to get downtown to work or to entertainment.

Now the American city has been transformed. The poor still inhabit the miserable housing in the central area, but they are increasingly isolated from contact with, or sight of, anybody else. Middle-class women coming in from Suburbia on a rare trip may catch the merest glimpse of the other America on the way to an evening at the theater, but their children are segregated in suburban schools. The business or professional man may drive along the fringes of slums in a car or bus, but it is not an important experience to him. The failures, the unskilled, the disabled, the aged, and the minorities are right there, across the tracks, where they have always been. But hardly anyone else is.

In short, the very development of the American city has removed poverty from the living, emotional experience of millions upon millions of middle-class Americans. Living out in the suburbs, it is easy to assume that ours is, indeed, an affluent society.

This new segregation of poverty is compounded by a well-meaning ignorance. A good many concerned and sympathetic Americans are aware that there is much discussion of urban renewal. Suddenly, driving through the city, they notice that a familiar slum has been torn down and that there are towering, modern buildings where once there had been tenements or hovels. There is a warm feeling of satisfaction, of pride in the way things are working out: the poor, it is obvious, are being taken care of.

The irony in this . . . is that the truth is nearly the exact opposite to the impression. The total impact of the various housing programs in postwar America has been to squeeze more and more people into existing slums. More often than not, the modern apartment in a towering building rents at $40 a room or more. For, during the past decade and a half, there has been more subsidization of middle- and upper-income housing than there has been for the poor.

Clothes make the poor invisible too: America has the best-dressed poverty the world has ever known. For a variety of reasons, the benefits of mass production have been spread much more evenly in this area than in many others. It is much easier in the United States to be decently dressed than it is to be decently housed, fed, or doctored. Even people with terribly depressed incomes can look prosperous.

This is an extremely important factor in defining our emotional and existential ignorance of poverty. In Detroit the existence of social classes became much more difficult to discern the day the companies put lockers in the plants. From that moment on, one did not see men in work clothes on the way to the factory, but citizens in slacks and white shirts. This process has been magnified with the poor throughout the country. There are tens of thousands of Americans in the big cities who are wearing shoes, perhaps even a stylishly cut suit or dress, and yet are hungry. It is not a matter of planning, though it almost seems as if the affluent society had given out costumes to the poor so that they would not offend the rest of society with the sight of rags.

Then, many of the poor are the wrong age to be seen. A good number of them (over 8,000,000) are sixty-five years of age or better; an even larger number are under eighteen. The aged members of the other America are often sick, and they cannot move. Another group of them live out their lives in loneliness and frustration: they sit in rented rooms, or else they stay close to a house in a neighborhood that has completely changed from the old days. Indeed, one of the worst aspects of poverty among the aged is that these people are out of sight and out of mind, and alone.

The young are somewhat more visible, yet they too stay close to their neighborhoods. Sometimes they advertise their poverty through a lurid tabloid story about a gang killing. But generally they do not disturb the quiet streets of the middle class.

And finally, the poor are politically invisible. It is one of the cruelest ironies of social life in advanced countries that the dispossessed at the bottom of society are unable to speak for themselves. The people of the other America do not, by far and large, belong to unions, to fraternal organizations, or to political parties. They are without lobbies of their own; they put forward no legislative program. As a group, they are atomized. They have no face; they have no voice.

Thus, there is not even a cynical political motive for caring about the poor, as in the old days. Because the slums are no longer centers of powerful political organizations, the politicians need not really care about their inhabitants. The slums are no longer visible to the middle class, so much of the idealistic urge to fight for those who need help is gone. Only the social agencies have a really direct involvement with the other America, and they are without any great political power. . . .

Forty to 50,000,000 people are becoming increasingly invisible. That is a shocking fact. But there is a second basic irony of poverty that is equally important: if one is to make the mistake of being born poor, he should choose a time when the majority of the people are miserable too.

J. K. Galbraith develops this idea in *The Affluent Society,* and in doing so defines the 'newness' of the kind of poverty in contemporary America. The old poverty, Galbraith notes, was general. It was the condition of life of an entire society, or at least of that huge majority who were without special skills or the luck of birth. When the entire economy advanced, a good many of these people gained higher standards of living. Unlike the poor today, the majority poor of a generation ago were an immediate (if cynical) concern of political leaders. The old slums of the immigrants had the votes; they provided the basis for labor organizations; their very numbers could be a powerful force in political conflict. At the same time the new technology required higher skills, more education, and stimulated an upward movement for millions.

Perhaps the most dramatic case of the power of the majority poor took place in the 1930's. The Congress of Industrial Organizations literally organized millions in a matter of years. A labor movement that had been declining and confined to a thin stratum of the highly skilled suddenly embraced masses of men and women in basic industry. At the same time this acted as a pressure upon the Government, and the New Deal codified some of the social gains in laws like the Wagner Act. The result was not a basic transformation of the American system, but it did transform the lives of an entire section of the population.

In the thirties one of the reasons for these advances was that misery was general. There was no need then to write books about unemployment and poverty. That was the decisive social experience of the entire society, and the apple sellers even invaded Wall Street. There was political sympathy from middle-class reformers; there were an élan and spirit that grew of a deep crisis.

Some of those who advanced in the thirties did so because they had unique and individual personal talents. But for the great mass, it was a question of being at the right point in the economy at the right time in history, and utilizing that position for common struggle. Some of those who failed did so because they did not have the will to take advantage of new opportunities. But for the most part the poor who were left behind had been at the wrong place in the economy at the wrong moment in history.

These were the people in the unorganizable jobs, in the South, in the minority groups, in the fly-by-night factories that were low on capital and high on labor. When some of them did break into the economic mainstream—when, for instance, the CIO opened up the way for some Negroes to find good industrial jobs—they proved to be as resourceful as anyone else. As a group, the other Americans who stayed behind were not originally composed primarily of individual failures. Rather, they were victims of an impersonal process that selected some for progress and discriminated against others.

Out of the thirties came the welfare state. Its creation had been stimulated by mass impoverishment and misery, yet it helped the poor least of all. Laws like unemployment compensation, the Wagner Act, the various farm programs, all these were designed for the middle third in the cities, for the organized workers, and for the upper third in the country, for the big market farmers. If a man works in an extremely low-paying job, he may not even be covered by social security or other welfare programs. If he receives unemployment compensation, the payment is scaled down according to his low earnings. . . .

Today's poor, in short, missed the political and social gains of the thirties. They are, as Galbraith rightly points out, the first minority poor in history, the first poor not to be seen, the first poor whom the politicians could leave alone.

The first step toward the new poverty was taken when millions of people proved immune to progress. When that happened, the failure was not individual and personal, but a social product. But once the historic accident takes place, it begins to become a personal fate.

The new poor of the other America saw the rest of society move ahead. They went on living in depressed areas, and often they tended to become depressed human beings. In some of the West Virginia towns, for instance, an entire community will become shabby and defeated. The young and the adventurous go to the city, leaving behind those who cannot move and those who lack the will to do so. The entire area becomes permeated with failure, and that is one more reason the big corporations shy away.

Indeed, one of the most important things about the new poverty is that it cannot be defined in simple, statistical terms. Throughout this book a crucial term is used: aspiration. If a group has internal vitality, a will—if it has aspiration—it may live in dilapidated housing, it may eat an inadequate diet, and it may suffer poverty, but it is not impoverished. So it was in those ethnic slums of the immigrants that played such a dramatic role in the unfolding of the American dream. The people found themselves in slums, but they were not slum dwellers.

But the new poverty is constructed so as to destroy aspiration; it is a system designed to be impervious to hope. The other America does not contain the adventurous seeking a new life and land. It is populated by the failures, by those driven from the land and bewildered by the city, by old people suddenly confronted with the torments of loneliness and poverty, and by minorities facing a wall of prejudice. . . .

Finally, one might summarize the newness of contemporary poverty by saying: These are the people who are immune to progress. But then the facts are even more cruel. The other Americans are the victims of the very inventions and machines that have provided a higher living standard for the rest of the society. They are upside-down in the economy, and for them greater productivity often means worse jobs; agricultural advance becomes hunger.

In the optimistic theory, technology is an undisguised blessing. A general increase in productivity, the argument goes, generates a higher standard of living for the whole people. And indeed, this has been true for the middle and upper thirds of American society, the people who made such striking gains in the last two decades. It tends to overstate the automatic character of the process, to omit the role of human struggle. (The CIO was organized by men in conflict, not by economic trends.) Yet it states a certain truth—for those who are lucky enough to participate in it.

But the poor, if they were given to theory, might argue the exact opposite. They might say: Progress is misery.

As the society became more technological, more skilled, those who learn to work the machines, who get the expanding education, move up. Those who miss out at the very start find themselves at a new disadvantage. A generation ago in American life, the majority of the working people did not have high-school educations. But at that time industry was organized on a lower level of skill and competence. And there was a sort of continuum in the shop: the youth who left school at sixteen could begin as a laborer, and gradually pick up skill as he went along.

Today the situation is quite different. The good jobs require much more academic preparation, much more skill from the very outset. Those who lack a high-school education tend to be condemned to the economic underworld—to low-paying service industries, to backward factories, to sweeping and janitorial duties. If the fathers and mothers of the contemporary poor were penalized a generation ago for their lack of schooling, their children will suffer all the more. The very rise in productivity that created more money and better working conditions for the rest of the society can be a menace to the poor.

But then this technological revolution might have an even more disastrous consequence: it could increase the ranks of the poor as well as intensify the disabilities of poverty. At this point it is too early to make any final judgment, yet there are obvious danger signals. There are millions of Americans who live just the other side of poverty. When a recession comes, they are pushed onto the relief rolls. (Welfare payments in New York respond almost immediately to any economic decline.) If automation continues to inflict more and more penalties on the unskilled and the semi-skilled, it could have the impact of permanently increasing the population of the other America.

Even more explosive is the possibility that people who participated in the gains of the thirties and the forties will be pulled back down into poverty. Today the mass-production industries where unionization made such a difference are contracting. Jobs are being destroyed. In the process, workers who had achieved a certain level of wages, who had won working conditions in the shop, are suddenly confronted with impoverishment. This is particularly true for anyone over forty years of age and for members of minority groups. Once their job is abolished, their chances of ever getting similar work are very slim.

It is too early to say whether or not this phenomenon is temporary, or whether it represents a massive retrogression that will swell the numbers of the poor. To a large extent, the answer to this question will be determined by the political response of the United States in the sixties.

THE BUSINESS
OF AMERICA

Louis D. Brandeis

Louis Brandeis (1856–1941), Supreme Court Justice 1916–1939, delivered the following address at Brown University on Commencement Day in 1912. In it he shows an optimism toward American business and the businessman, whose potential accomplishments he felt should rank with those of the doctor and the lawyer.

BUSINESS—A PROFESSION

Each commencement season we are told by the college reports the number of graduates who have selected the professions as their occupation and the number of those who will enter business. The time has come for abandoning such a classification. Business should be, and to some extent already is, one of the professions. The once meagre list of the learned professions is being constantly enlarged. Engineering in its many branches already takes rank beside law, medicine, and theology. Forestry and scientific agriculture are securing places of honor. The new professions of manufacturing, of merchandising, of transportation, and of finance must soon gain recognition. The establishment of business schools in our universities is a manifestation of the modern conception of business.

The peculiar characteristics of a profession as distinguished from other occupations, I take to be these:

First. A profession is an occupation for which the necessary preliminary training is intellectual in character, involving knowledge and to some extent learning, as distinguished from mere skill.

Second. It is an occupation which is pursued largely for others and not merely for one's self.

Third. It is an occupation in which the amount of financial return is not the accepted measure of success.

Is not each of these characteristics found today in business worthily pursued?

The field of knowledge requisite to the more successful conduct of business has been greatly widened by the application to industry not only of chemical, mechanical and electrical science, but also the new science of management; by the increasing difficulties involved in adjusting the relations of labor to capital; by the necessary intertwining of social with industrial problems; by the ever extending scope of state and federal regulation of business. Indeed, mere size and territorial expansion have compelled the business man to enter upon new and broader fields of knowledge in order to match his achievements with his opportunities.

This new development is tending to make business an applied science. Through this development the relative value in business of the trading instinct and of mere shrewdness have, as compared with other faculties, largely diminished. The conception of trade itself has changed. The old idea of a good bargain was a transaction in which one man got the better of another. The new idea of a good contract is a transaction which is good for both parties to it.

Under these new conditions, success in business must mean something very different from mere money-making. In business the able man ordinarily earns a larger income than one less able. So does the able man in the recognized professions—in law, medicine, or engineering; and even in those professions more remote from money-making, like the ministry, teaching, or social work. The world's demand for efficiency is so great and the supply so small, that the price of efficiency is high in every field of human activity.

The recognized professions, however, definitely reject the size of the financial return as the measure of success. They select as their test, excellence of performance in the broadest sense—and include, among other things, advance in the particular occupation and service to the community. These are the basis of all worthy reputations in the recognized professions. In them a large income is the ordinary incident of success; but he who exaggerates the value of the incident is apt to fail of real success.

To the business of to-day a similar test must be applied. True, in business the earning of profit is something more than an incident of success. It is an essential condition of success; because the continued absence of profit itself spells failure. But while loss spells failure, large profits do not connote success. Success must be sought in business also in excellence of performance; and in business, excellence of performance manifests itself among other things, in the advancing of methods and processes; in the improvement of products; in more perfect organization, eliminating friction as well as waste; in bettering the condition of the workingmen, developing their faculties and promoting their happiness; and in the establishment of right relations with customers and with the community.

In the field of modern business, so rich in opportunity for the exercise of man's finest and most varied mental faculties and moral qualities, mere money-making cannot be regarded as the legitimate end. Neither can mere growth in bulk or power be admitted as a worthy ambition. Nor can a man nobly mindful of his serious responsibilities to society, view business as a game; since with the conduct of business human hap-

piness or misery is inextricably interwoven.

Real success in business is to be found in achievements comparable rather with those of the artist or the scientist, of the inventor or the statesman. And the joys sought in the profession of business must be like their joys and not the mere vulgar satisfaction which is experienced in the acquisition of money, in the exercise of power, or in the frivolous pleasure of mere winning.

It was such a real success, comparable with the scientist's, the inventor's, the statesman's, which marked the career of William H. McElwain of Boston, who died in 1908 at the age of forty-one. He had been in business on his own account but thirteen years. Starting without means, he left a fortune, all of which had been earned in the competitive business of shoe manufacturing, without the aid of either patent or trademark. That shows McElwain did not lack the money-making faculty. His company's sales grew from $75,957 in 1895 to $8,691,-274 in 1908. He thus became one of the largest shoe manufacturers in the world. That shows he did not lack either ambition or organizing ability. The working capital required for this rapidly growing business was obtained by him without surrendering to outside investors or to bankers any share in the profits of business: all the stock in his company being owned either by himself or his active associates. That shows he did not lack financial skill.

But this money-making faculty, organizing ability, and financial skill were with him servants, not masters. He worked for nobler ends than mere accumulation or lust of power. In those thirteen years McElwain made so many advances in the methods and practices of the long-established and prosperous branch of industry in which he was engaged, that he may be said to have revolutionized shoe manufacturing. He found it a trade; he left it an applied science.

This is the kind of thing he did: In 1902 the irregularity in the employment of the shoe worker was brought to his attention. He became greatly impressed with its economic waste, with the misery to the workers and the demoralization which attended it. Irregularity of employment is the worst and most extended of industrial evils. Even in fairly prosperous times the workingmen of America are subjected to enforced idleness and loss of earnings, on the average, probably ten to twenty percent of their working time. The irregularity of employment was no greater in the McElwain factories than in other shoe factories. The condition was not so bad in shoe manufacturing as in many other branches of industry. But it was bad enough; for shoe manufacturing was a seasonal industry. Most manufacturers closed their factories twice a year. Some manufacturers had two additional slack periods.

This irregularity had been accepted by the trade—by manufacturers and workingmen alike—as inevitable. It had been bowed to as if it were a law of nature—a cross to be borne with resignation. But with McElwain an evil recognized was a condition to be remedied; and he set his great mind to solving the problem of irregularity of employment in his own factories; just as Wilbur Wright applied his mind to the aeroplane, as Bell, his mind to the telephone, and as Edison, his mind to the problems of electric light. Within a few years irregularity of employment had ceased in the McElwain factories; and before his death every one of his many thousand employees could find work three hundred and five days in the year.

Closely allied with the establishment of regularity of employment was the advance made by McElwain in introducing punctual delivery of goods manufactured by his company. Shoes are manufactured mainly upon orders; and the orders are taken on samples submitted. The samples are made nearly a year before the goods are sold to the consumer. Samples for the shoes which will be bought in the spring and summer of 1913 were made in the early summer of 1912. The solicitation of orders on these samples began in the late summer. The manufacture of the shoes commences in November; and the order is filled before July.

Dates of delivery are fixed, of course, when orders are taken; but the dates fixed had not been taken very seriously by the manufacturers; and the trade was greatly annoyed by irregularities in delivery. McElwain recognized the business waste and inconvenience attendant upon such unfulfilled promises. He insisted that an agreement to deliver on a certain day was as binding as an agreement to pay a note on a certain day.

He knew that to make punctual delivery possible, careful study and changes in the methods of manufacture and of distribution were necessary. He made the study; he introduced the radical changes found necessary; and he so perfected his organization that customers could rely absolutely upon delivery on the day fixed. Scientific management practically eliminated the recurring obstacles of the unexpected. To attain this result business invention of a high order was of course necessary—invention directed to the departments both of production and of distribution.

The career of the Filenes of Boston affords another example of success in professional business. In 1891 the Filenes occupied two tiny retail stores in Boston. The floor space of each was only twenty feet square. One was a glove stand, the other a women's specialty store. Twenty years later their sales were nearly $5,000,000 a year. In September, 1912, they moved into a new building with more than nine acres of floor space. But the significant thing about their success is not their growth in size or in profits. The trade offers many other examples of similar growth. The preeminence of the Filenes lies in the advance which has been made in the nature, the aims, and the ideals of retailing, due to their courage, initiative, persistence, and fine spirit. They have applied minds of a high order and a fine ethical sense to the prosaic and seemingly uninteresting business of selling women's garments. Instead of remaining petty tradesmen, they have become, in every sense of the word, great merchants.

The Filenes recognized that the function of retail distribution should be undertaken as a social service, equal in dignity and responsibility to the function of production; and that it should be studied with equal intensity in order that the service may be performed with high efficiency, with great economy, and with nothing more than a fair profit to the retailer. They recognized that to serve their own customers properly, the relations of the retailer to the producer must be fairly and scientifically adjusted; and, among other things, that it was the concern of the retailer to know whether the goods which he sold were manufactured under conditions which were fair to the workers—fair as to wages, hours of work, and sanitary conditions.

But the Filenes recognized their obligations to their own employees. They found as the common and accepted conditions in large retail stores, that the employees had no voice as to the conditions or rules under which they were to work; that the employees had no appeal from policies prescribed by the management; and that in the main they were paid the lowest rate of wages possible under competitive conditions.

In order to insure a more just arrangement for those working in their establishment, the Filenes provided three devices:

First. A system of self-government for employees, administered by the store co-operative association. Working through this association, the employees have the right to appeal from and to veto policies laid down by the management. They may adjust the conditions under which employees are to work, and, in effect, prescribe conditions for themselves.

Second. A system of arbitration, through the operation of which individual employees can call for an adjustment of differences that may exist between themselves and the management as to the permanence of em-

ployment, wages; promotion, or conditions of work.

Third. A minimum wage scale, which provided that no woman or girl shall work in their store at a wage less than eight dollars a week, no matter what her age may be or what grade of position she may fill.

The Filenes have thus accepted and applied the principles of industrial democracy and of social justice. But they have done more—they have demonstrated that the introduction of industrial democracy and of social justice is at least consistent with marked financial success. They assert that the greater efficiency of their employees shows industrial democracy and social justice to be money-makers. The so-called "practical business man," the narrow money-maker without either vision or ideals, who hurled against the Filenes, as against McElwain, the silly charge of being "theorists," has been answered even on his own low plane of material success.

McElwain and the Filenes are of course exceptional men; but there are in America to-day many with like perception and like spirit. The paths broken by such pioneers will become the peopled highways. Their exceptional methods will become accepted methods. Then the term "big business" will lose its sinister meaning, and will take on a new significance. "Big business" will then mean business big not in bulk or power, but great in service and grand in manner. "Big business" will mean professionalized business, as distinguished from the occupation of petty trafficking or mere money-making. And as the profession of business develops, the great industrial and social problems expressed in the present social unrest will one by one find solution.

Ida Tarbell

Ida Tarbell (1857–1944), known as a "muck-raking" journalist, exposed the machinations of John D. Rockefeller's rise to monopolistic power in the oil industry. Although Tarbell's father was an oil producer beset by other refiners, she denied that he influenced her ideas. This selection traces Rockefeller's career from his childhood through his youth as an accountant to his early business dealings in which he effectively eliminated his two dozen competitors. The South Improvement Company, discussed here, was voided, but Standard Oil continued to employ its tactics under new guises.

THE RISE OF THE STANDARD OIL COMPANY

Among the many young men of Cleveland who, from the start, had an eye on the oil-refining business and had begun to take an active part in its development as soon as it was demonstrated that there was a reasonable hope of its being permanent, was a young firm of produce commission merchants. Both members of this firm were keen business men, and one of them had remarkable commercial vision—a genius for seeing the possibilities in material things. This man's name was Rockefeller—John D. Rockefeller. He was but twenty-three years old when he first went into the oil business, but he had already got his feet firmly on the business ladder, and had got them there by his own efforts. The habit of driving good bargains and of saving money had started him. He himself once told how he learned these lessons so useful in money-making, in one of his frequent Sunday-school talks to young men on success in business. The value of a good bargain he learned in buying cord-wood for his father: "I knew what a cord of good solid beech and maple wood was. My father told me to select only the solid wood and the straight wood and not to put any limbs in it or any punky wood. That was a good training for me. I did not need any father to tell me or anybody else how many feet it took to make a cord of wood."

And here is how he learned the value of investing money: "Among the early experiences that were helpful to me that I recollect with pleasure was one in working a few days for a neighbour in digging potatoes—a very enterprising, thrifty farmer, who could dig a great many potatoes. I was a boy of perhaps thirteen or fourteen years of age, and it kept me very busy from morning until night. It was a ten-hour day. And as I was saving these little sums I soon learned that I could get as much interest for fifty dollars loaned at seven per cent. —the legal rate in the state of New York at that time for a year—as I could earn by digging potatoes for 100 days. The impression was gaining ground with me that it was a good thing to let the money be my slave and not make myself a slave to money." Here we have the foundation principles of a great financial career.

When young Rockefeller was thirteen years old, his father moved from the farm in Central New York, where the boy had been born (July 8, 1839), to a farm near Cleveland, Ohio. He went to school in Cleveland for three years. In 1855 it became necessary for him to earn his own living. It was a hard year in the West and the boy walked the streets for days looking for work. He was about to give it up and go to the country when, to quote the story as Mr. Rockefeller once told it to his Cleveland Sunday-school, "As good fortune would have it I went down to the dock and made one more application, and I was told that if I would come in after dinner—our noon-day meal was dinner in those days— they would see if I could come to work for them. I went down after dinner and I got the position, and I was permitted to remain in the city." The position, that of a clerk and bookkeeper, was not lucrative. According to a small ledger which has figured frequently in Mr. Rockefeller's religious instructions, he earned from September 26, 1855, to January, 1856, fifty dollars. "Out of that," Mr. Rockefeller told the young men of his Sunday-school class, "I paid my washerwoman and the lady I boarded with, and I saved a little money to put away."

He proved an admirable accountant—one of the early-and-late sort, who saw everything, forgot nothing and never talked. In 1856 his salary was raised to twenty-five dollars a month, and he went on always "saving a little money to put away." In 1858 came a chance to invest his savings. Among his acquaintances was a young Englishman, M. B. Clark. Older by twelve years than Rockefeller he had left a hard life in England when he was twenty to seek fortune in America. He had landed in Boston in 1847, without a penny or a friend, and it had taken three months for him to earn money to get to Ohio. Here he had taken the first job at hand, as man-of-all-work, wood-chopper, teamster. He had found his way to Cleveland, had become a valuable man in the houses where he was employed, had gone to school at nights, had saved money. They were two of a kind, Clark and Rockefeller, and in 1858 they pooled their earnings and started a produce commission business on the Cleveland docks. The venture succeeded. Local historians credit Clark and Rockefeller with doing a business of $450,000 the first year. The war came on, and as neither partner went to the front, they had a full chance to take advantage of the opportunity for produce business a great army gives. A greater chance than furnishing army supplies, lucrative as most people found that, was in the oil business (so Clark and Rockefeller began to think), and in 1862, when an Englishman of ability and energy, one Samuel Andrews, asked them to back him in starting a refinery, they put in $4,000 and promised to give more if necessary. Now Andrews was a mechanical genius. He devised new processes, made a better and better quality of oil, got larger and larger percentages of refined from his crude. The little refinery grew big, and Clark and Rockefeller soon had $100,000 or more in it. In the meantime Cleveland was growing as

a refining centre. The business which in 1860 had been a gamble was by 1865 one of the most promising industries of the town. It was but the beginning—so Mr. Rockefeller thought—and in that year he sold out his share of the commission business and put his money into the oil firm of Rockefeller and Andrews.

In the new firm Andrews attended to the manufacturing. The pushing of the business, the buying and the selling, fell to Rockefeller. From the start his effect was tremendous. He had the frugal man's hatred of waste and disorder, of middlemen and unnecessary manipulation, and he began a vigorous elimination of these from his business. The residuum that other refineries let run into the ground, he sold. Old iron found its way to the junk shop. He bought his oil directly from the wells. He made his own barrels. He watched and saved and contrived. The ability with which he made the smallest bargain furnishes topics to Cleveland story-tellers to-day. Low-voiced, soft-footed, humble, knowing every point in every man's business, he never tired until he got his wares at the lowest possible figure. "John always got the best of the bargain," old men tell you in Cleveland to-day, and they wince though they laugh in telling it. "Smooth," "a *savy* fellow," is their description of him. To drive a good bargain was the joy of his life. "The only time I ever saw John Rockefeller enthusiastic," a man told the writer once, "was when a report came in from the creek that his buyer had secured a cargo of oil at a figure much below the market price. He bounded from his chair with a shout of joy, danced up and down, hugged me, threw up his hat, acted so like a madman that I have never forgotten it."

He could borrow as well as bargain. The firm's capital was limited; growing as they were, they often needed money, and had none. Borrow they must. Rarely if ever did Mr. Rockefeller fail. There is a story handed down in Cleveland from the days of Clark and Rockefeller, produce merchants, which is illustrative of his methods. One day a well-known and rich business man stepped into the office and asked for Mr. Rockefeller. He was out, and Clark met the visitor. "Mr. Clark," he said, "you may tell Mr. Rockefeller, when he comes in, that I think I can use the $10,000 he wants to invest with me for your firm. I have thought it all over."

"Good God!" cried Clark, "we don't want to invest $10,000. John is out right now trying to borrow $5,000 for us."

It turned out that to prepare him for a proposition to borrow $5,000 Mr. Rockefeller had told the gentleman that he and Clark wanted to invest $10,000!

"And the joke of it is," said Clark, who used to tell the story, "John got the $5,000 even after I had let the cat out of the bag. Oh, he was the greatest borrower you ever saw!" . . .

The strides the firm of Rockefeller and Andrews made after the former went into it were attributed for three or four years mainly to his extraordinary capacity for bargaining and borrowing. Then its chief competitors began to suspect something. John Rockefeller might get his oil cheaper now and then, they said, but he could not do it often. He might make close contracts for which they had neither the patience nor the stomach. He might have an unusual mechanical and practical genius in his partner. But these things could not explain all. They believed they bought, on the whole, almost as cheaply as he, and they knew they made as good oil and with as great, or nearly as great, economy. He could sell at no better price than they. Where was his advantage? There was but one place where it could be, and that was in transportation. He must be getting better rates from the railroads than they were. In 1868 or 1869 a member of a rival firm long in the business, which had been prosperous from the start, and which prided itself on its methods, its economy and its energy, Alexander, Scofield and Company, went to the Atlantic and Great Western road, then under the Erie management, and complained. "You are giving others better rates than you are us," said Mr. Alexander, the representative of the firm. "We cannot compete if you do that." The railroad agent did not attempt to deny it—he simply agreed to give Mr. Alexander a rebate also. The arrangement was interesting. Mr. Alexander was to pay the open, or regular, rate on oil from the Oil Regions to Cleveland, which was then forty cents a barrel. At the end of each month he was to send to the railroad vouchers for the amount of oil shipped and paid for at forty cents, and was to get back from the railroad, in money, fifteen cents on each barrel. This concession applied only to oil brought from the wells. He was never able to get a rebate on oil shipped eastward. . . .

What the Standard's rebate on Eastern shipments was in 1870 it is impossible to say. Mr. Alexander says he was never able to get a rate lower than $1.33 a barrel by rail, and that it was commonly believed in Cleveland that the Standard had a rate of ninety cents. Mr. Flagler, however, the only member of the firm who has been examined under oath on that point, showed, by presenting the contract of the Standard Oil Company with the Lake Shore road in 1870, that the rates varied during the year from $1.40 to $1.20 and $1.60, according to the season. When Mr. Flagler was asked if there was no drawback or rebate on this rate he answered, "None whatever."

It would seem from the above as if the one man in the Cleveland oil trade in 1870 who ought to have been satisfied was Mr. Rockefeller. His was the largest firm in the largest refining centre of the country; that is, of the 10,000 to 12,000 daily capacity divided among the twenty-five or twenty-six refiners of Cleveland he controlled 1,500 barrels. . . . But Mr. Rockefeller was far from satisfied. He was a brooding, cautious, secretive man, seeing all the possible dangers as well as all the possible opportunities in things, and he studied, as a player at chess, all the possible combinations which might imperil his supremacy. These twenty-five Cleveland rivals of his—how could he at once and forever put them out of the game? He and his partners had somehow conceived a great idea—the advantages of combination. What might they not do, if they could buy out and absorb the big refineries now competing with them in Cleveland? The possibilities of the idea grew as they discussed it. Finally they began tentatively to sound some of their rivals. But there were other rivals than these at home. There were the Creek refiners! They were there at the mouth of the wells. What might not this geographical advantage do in time? The Oil Regions, in the first years of oil production, had been an unfit place for refining because of its lack of connections with the outside world; now, however, the railroads were in, and refining was going on there on an increasing scale; the capacity of the region had indeed risen to nearly 10,000 barrels a day—equal to that of New York, exceeding that of Pittsburgh by nearly 4,000 barrels, and almost equaling that of Cleveland. . . .

How long could the Standard Oil Company stand against this competition? . . . This was the condition of the refining business as a whole. It was unsatisfactory in many particulars. First, it was overdone. The great profits on refined oil and the growing demand for it had naturally caused a great number to rush into its manufacture. There was at this time a refining capacity of three barrels to every one produced. To be sure, few if any of these plants expected to run the year around. Then, as to-day, there were nearly always some stills in even the most prosperous works shut down. But after making a fair allowance for this fact there was still a much larger amount of refining actually done than the market demanded. The result was that the price of refined oil was steadily falling. Where Mr. Rockefeller had received on an average 58¾ cents a gallon for the oil he exported in 1865, the year he went into business, in 1870 he received but 26½ cents. In 1865 he had a margin of forty-three cents, out of which to pay for transportation, man-

ufacturing, barrelling and marketing and to make his profits. In 1870 he had but 17⅛ cents with which to do all this. To be sure his expenses had fallen enormously between 1865 and 1870, but so had his profits. The multiplication of refiners with the intense competition threatened to cut them down still lower. Naturally Mr. Rockefeller and his friends looked with dismay on this lowering of profits through gaining competition.

Another anxiety of the American refiners was the condition of the export trade. Oil had risen to fourth place in the exports of the United States in the twelve years since its discovery, and every year larger quantities were consumed abroad, but it was crude oil, not refined, which the foreigners were beginning to demand; that is, they had found they could import crude, refine it at home, and sell it cheaper than they could buy American refined. France, to encourage her home refineries, had even put a tax on American refined.

In the fall of 1871, while Mr. Rockefeller and his friends were occupied with all these questions, certain Pennsylvania refiners, it is not too certain who, brought to them a remarkable scheme, the gist of which was to bring together secretly a large enough body of refiners and shippers to persuade all the railroads handling oil to give to the company formed special rebates on its oil, and drawbacks on that of other people. If they could get such rates it was evident that those outside of their combination could not compete with them long and that they would become eventually the only refiners. They could then limit their output to actual demand, and so keep up prices. This done, they could easily persuade the railroads to transport no crude for exportation, so that the foreigners would be forced to buy American refined. They believed that the price of oil thus exported could easily be advanced fifty per cent. The control of the refining interests would also enable them to fix their own price on crude. As they would be the only buyers and sellers, the speculative character of the business would be done away with. In short, the scheme they worked out put the entire oil business in their hands. It looked as simple to put into operation as it was dazzling in its results. Mr. Flagler has sworn that neither he nor Mr. Rockefeller believed in this scheme. But when they found that their friend Peter H. Watson, and various Philadelphia and Pittsburgh parties who felt as they did about the oil business, believed in it, they went in and began at once to work up a company—secretly. It was evident that a scheme which aimed at concentrating in the hands of one company the business now operated by scores, and which proposed to effect this consolidation through a practice of the railroads which was contrary to the spirit of their charters, although freely indulged in, must be worked with fine discretion if it ever were to be effective. . . .

It was on the second of January, 1872, that the organization of the South Improvement Company was completed. The day before the Standard Oil Company of Cleveland increased its capital from $1,000,000 to $2,500,000, "all the stockholders of the company being present and voting therefor." These stockholders were greater by five than in 1870, the names of O. B. Jennings, Benjamin Brewster, Truman P. Handy, Amasa Stone, and Stillman Witt having been added. The last three were officers and stockholders in one or more of the railroads centring in Cleveland. Three weeks after this increase of capital Mr. Rockefeller had the charter and contracts of the South Improvement Company in hand, and was ready to see what they would do in helping him carry out his idea of wholesale combination in Cleveland. There were at that time some twenty-six refineries in the town —some of them very large plants. All of them were feeling more or less the discouraging effects of the last three or four years of railroad discriminations in favour of the Standard Oil Company. To the owners of these refineries Mr. Rockefeller now went one by one, and explained the South Im-

provement Company. "You see," he told them, "this scheme is bound to work. It means an absolute control by us of the oil business. There is no chance for anyone outside. But we are going to give everybody a chance to come in. You are to turn over your refinery to my appraisers, and I will give you Standard Oil Company stock or cash, as you prefer, for the value we put upon it. I advise you to take the stock. It will be for your good." Certain refiners objected. They did not want to sell. They did want to keep and manage their business. Mr. Rockefeller was regretful, but firm. It was useless to resist, he told the hesitating; they would certainly be crushed if they did not accept his offer, and he pointed out in detail, and with gentleness, how beneficent the scheme really was—preventing the creek refiners from destroying Cleveland, ending competition, keeping up the price of refined oil, and eliminating speculation. Really a wonderful contrivance for the good of the oil business. . . .

Under the combined threat and persuasion of the Standard, armed with the South Improvement Company scheme, almost the entire independent oil interest of Cleveland collapsed in three months' time. Of the twenty-six refineries, at least twenty-one sold out. From a capacity of probably not over 1,500 barrels of crude a day, the Standard Oil Company rose in three months' time to one of 10,000 barrels. By this manoeuvre it became master of over one-fifth of the refining capacity of the United States. Its next individual competitor was Sone and Fleming, of New York, whose capacity was 1,700 barrels. The Standard had a greater capacity than the entire Oil Creek Regions, greater than the combined New York refiners. The transaction by which it acquired this power was so stealthy that not even the best informed newspaper men of Cleveland knew what went on. It had all been accomplished in accordance with one of Mr. Rockefeller's chief business principles—"Silence is golden."

Upton Sinclair

Upton Sinclair (1878–1968), who wrote several dozen novels espousing social change, was an active Socialist who ran several times for public office. His biggest success, however, came with publication of The Jungle *in 1906. The scene reprinted here, one of the most dramatic and important in the novel, helped spur the passage of the Pure Food and Drug Act (1906).*

THE STOCKYARDS *

"Bubbly Creek" is an arm of the Chicago River, and forms the southern boundary of the yards; all the drainage of the square mile of packing-houses empties into it, so that it is really a great open sewer a hundred or two feet wide. One long arm of it is blind, and the filth stays there forever and a day. The grease and chemicals that are poured into it undergo all sorts of strange transformations, which are the cause of its name; it is constantly in motion, as if huge fish were feeding in it, or great leviathans disporting themselves in its depths. Bubbles of carbonic acid gas will rise to the surface and burst, and make rings two or three feet wide. Here and there the grease and filth have caked solid, and the creek looks like a bed of lava; chickens walk about on it, feeding, and many times an unwary stranger has started to stroll across, and vanished temporarily. The packers used to leave the creek that way, till every now and then the surface would catch on fire and burn furiously, and the fire department would have to come and put it out. Once, however, an ingenious stranger came and started to gather this filth in scows, to make lard out of; then the packers took the cue, and got out an injunction to stop him, and afterwards gathered it themselves. The banks of "Bubbly Creek" are plastered thick with hairs, and this also the packers gather and clean.

* Editor's title.

And there were things even stranger than this, according to the gossip of the men. The packers had secret mains, through which they stole billions of gallons of the city's water. The newspapers had been full of this scandal—once there had even been an investigation, and an actual uncovering of the pipes; but nobody had been punished, and the thing went right on. And then there was the condemned meat industry, with its endless horrors. The people of Chicago saw the government inspectors in Packingtown, and they all took that to mean that they were protected from diseased meat; they did not understand that these hundred and sixty-three inspectors had been appointed at the request of the packers, and that they were paid by the United States government to certify that all the diseased meat was kept in the state. They had no authority beyond that; for the inspection of meat to be sold in the city and state the whole force in Packingtown consisted of three henchmen of the local political machine! And shortly afterward one of these, a physician, made the discovery that the carcasses of steers which had been condemned as tubercular by the government inspectors, and which therefore contained ptomaines, which are deadly poisons, were left upon an open platform and carted away to be sold in the city; and so he insisted that these carcasses be treated with an injection of kerosene—and was ordered to resign the same week! So indignant were the packers that they went farther, and compelled the mayor to abolish the whole bureau of inspection; so that since then there has not been even a pretence of any interference with the graft. There was said to be two thousand dollars a week hush-money from the tubercular steers alone; and as much again from the hogs which had died of cholera on the trains, and which you might see any day being loaded into boxcars and hauled away to a place called Globe, in Indiana, where they made a fancy grade of lard.

Jurgis heard of these things little by

little, in the gossip of those who were obliged to perpetrate them. It seemed as if every time you met a person from a new department, you heard of new swindles and new crimes. There was, for instance, a Lithuanian who was a cattle-butcher for the plant where Marija had worked, which killed meat for canning only; and to hear this man describe the animals which came to his place would have been worth while for a Dante or a Zola. It seemed that they must have agencies all over the country, to hunt out old and crippled and diseased cattle to be canned. There were cattle which had been fed on "whiskey-malt," the refuse of the breweries, and had become what the men called "steerly"—which means covered with boils. It was a nasty job killing these, for when you plunged your knife into them they would burst and splash foul-smelling stuff into your face; and when a man's sleeves were smeared with blood, and his hands steeped in it, how was he ever to wipe his face, or to clear his eyes so that he could see? It was stuff such as this that made the "embalmed beef" that had killed several times as many United States soldiers as all the bullets of the Spaniards; only the army beef, besides, was not fresh canned, it was old stuff that had been lying for years in the cellars.

Then one Sunday evening, Jurgis sat puffing his pipe by the kitchen stove, and talking with an old fellow whom Jonas had introduced, and who worked in the canning-rooms at Durham's; and so Jurgis learned a few things about the great and only Durham canned goods, which had become a national institution. They were regular alchemists at Durham's; they advertised a mushroom-catsup, and the men who made it did not know what a mushroom looked like. They advertised "potted chicken,"—and it was like the boarding-house soup of the comic papers, through which a chicken had walked with rubbers on. Perhaps they had a secret process for making chickens chemically—who knows? said Jurgis's friend; the things that went into the mixture were

tripe, and the fat of pork, and beef suet, and hearts of beef, and finally the waste ends of veal, when they had any. They put these up in several grades, and sold them at several prices; but the contents of the cans all came out of the same hopper. And then there was "potted game" and "potted grouse," "potted ham," and "devilled ham" —de-vyled, as the men called it. "De-vyled" ham was made out of the waste ends of smoked beef that were too small to be sliced by the machines; and also tripe, dyed with chemicals so that it would not show white; and trimmings of hams and corned beef; and potatoes, skins and all; and finally the hard cartilaginous gullets of beef, after the tongues had been cut out. All this ingenious mixture was ground up and flavored with spices to make it taste like something. Anybody who could invent a new imitation had been sure of a fortune from old Durham, said Jurgis's informant; but it was hard to think of anything new in a place where so many sharp wits had been at work for so long; where men welcomed tuberculosis in the cattle they were feeding, because it made them fatten more quickly; and where they bought up all the old rancid butter left over in the grocery-stores of a continent, and "oxidized" it by a forced-air process, to take away the odor, rechurned it with skim-milk, and sold it in bricks in the cities! Up to a year or two ago it has been the custom to kill horses in the yards—ostensibly for fertilizer; but after long agitation the newspapers had been able to make the public realize that the horses were being canned. Now it was against the law to kill horses in Packingtown, and the law was really complied with—for the present, at any rate. Any day, however, one might see sharp-horned and shaggy-haired creatures running with the sheep—and yet what a job you would have to get the public to believe that a good part of what it buys for lamb and mutton is really goat's flesh!

There was another interesting set of statistics that a person might have gathered in Packingtown—those of the various afflictions of the workers. When Jurgis had first inspected the packing-plants with Szedvilas, he had marvelled while he listened to the tale of all the things that were made out of the carcasses of animals, and of all the lesser industries that were maintained there; now he found that each one of these lesser industries was a separate little inferno, in its way as horrible as the killing-beds, the source and fountain of them all. The workers in each of them had their own peculiar diseases. And the wandering visitor might be sceptical about all the swindles, but he could not be sceptical about these, for the worker bore the evidence of them about on his own person—generally he had only to hold out his hand.

There were the men in the pickle-rooms, for instance, where old Antanas had gotten his death; scarce a one of these that had not some spot of horror on his person. Let a man so much as scrape his finger pushing a truck in the pickle-rooms, and he might have a sore that would put him out of the world; all the joints in his fingers might be eaten by the acid, one by one. Of the butchers and floorsmen, the beef-boners and trimmers, and all those who used knives, you could scarcely find a person who had the use of his thumb; time and time again the base of it had been slashed, till it was a mere lump of flesh against which the man pressed the knife to hold it. The hands of these men would be criss-crossed with cuts, until you could no longer pretend to count them or to trace them. They would have no nails,—they had worn them off pulling hides; their knuckles were swollen so that their fingers spread out like a fan. There were men who worked in the cooking-rooms, in the midst of steam and sickening odors, by artificial light; in these rooms the germs of tuberculosis might live for two years, but the supply was renewed every hour. There were the beef-luggers, who carried two-hundred-pound quarters into the refrigerator-cars; a fearful kind of work, that began at four o'clock in the morning, and that wore out the most powerful men

in a few years. There were those who worked in the chilling-rooms, and whose special disease was rheumatism; the time-limit that a man could work in the chilling-rooms was said to be five years. There were the wool-pluckers, whose hands went to pieces even sooner than the hands of the pickle-men; for the pelts of the sheep had to be painted with acid to loosen the wool, and then the pluckers had to pull out this wool with their bare hands, till the acid had eaten their fingers off. There were those who made the tins for the canned-meat; and their hands, too, were a maze of cuts, and each cut represented a chance for blood-poisoning. Some worked at the stamping-machines, and it was very seldom that one could work long there at the pace that was set, and not give out and forget himself, and have a part of his hand chopped off. There were the "hoisters," as they were called, whose task it was to press the lever which lifted the dead cattle off the floor. They ran along upon a rafter, peering down through the damp and the steam; and as old Durham's architects had not built the killing-room for the convenience of the hoisters, at every few feet they would have to stoop under a beam, say four feet above the one they ran on; which got them into the habit of stooping, so that in a few years they would be walking like chimpanzees. Worst of any, however, were the fertilizer-men, and those who served in the cooking-rooms. These people could not be shown to the visitor,—for the odor of a fertilizer-man would scare any ordinary visitor at a hundred yards, and as for the other men, who worked in tank-rooms full of steam, and in some of which there were open vats near the level of the floor, their peculiar trouble was that they fell into the vats; and when they were fished out, there was never enough of them left to be worth exhibiting, —sometimes they would be overlooked for days, till all but the bones of them had gone out to the world as Durham's Pure Leaf Lard!

John Dos Passos

John Dos Passos (1896–1970), born in Chicago and educated at Harvard, was an idealist concerned with the consequences of bigness and modern technology. This selection from the novel The Big Money *is one of several biographies of famous tycoons interspersed through the narrative. This technique and his impressionistic style gave Dos Passos a reputation as an experimentalist. In "Tin Lizzie" Dos Passos notes the paradox of Henry Ford the mechanical genius, who invented a new manufacturing method—the assembly line—and Henry Ford the country boy, who was confused by the problems of the modern age he helped create, and who retreated into clichés, slogans, and sometimes cruelty in an attempt to escape.*

TIN LIZZIE

"Mr. Ford the automobileer," the featurewriter wrote in 1900,

"Mr. Ford the automobileer began by giving his steed three or four sharp jerks with the lever at the righthand side of the seat; that is, he pulled the lever up and down sharply in order, as he said, to mix air with gasoline and drive the charge into the exploding cylinder. . . . Mr. Ford slipped a small electric switch handle and there followed a puff, puff, puff. . . . The puffing of the machine assumed a higher key. She was flying along about eight miles an hour. The ruts in the road were deep, but the machine certainly went with a dreamlike smoothness. There was none of the bumping common even to a streetcar. . . . By this time the boulevard had been reached, and the automobileer, letting a lever fall a little, let her out. Whiz! She picked up speed with infinite rapidity. As she ran on there was a clattering behind, the new noise of the automobile."

For twenty years or more,

ever since he'd left his father's farm when he was sixteen to get a job in a Detroit machineshop, Henry Ford had been nuts about machinery. First it was watches,

then he designed a steamtractor, then he built a horseless carriage with an engine adapted from the Otto gas-engine he'd read about in *The World of Science*, then a mechanical buggy with a onecyclinder fourcycle motor, that would run forward but not back;

at last, in ninetyeight, he felt he was far enough along to risk throwing up his job with the Detroit Edison Company, where he'd worked his way up from night fireman to chief engineer, to put all his time into working on a new gasoline engine,

(in the late eighties he'd met Edison at a meeting of electriclight employees in Atlantic City. He'd gone up to Edison after Edison had delivered an address and asked him if he thought gasoline was practical as a motor fuel. Edison had said yes. If Edison said it, it was true. Edison was the great admiration of Henry Ford's life);

and in driving his mechanical buggy, sitting there at the lever jauntily dressed in a tightbuttoned jacket and a high collar and a derby hat, back and forth over the level illpaved streets of Detroit,

scaring the big brewery horses and the skinny trotting horses and the sleek-rumped pacers with the motor's loud explosions,

looking for men scatterbrained enough to invest money in a factory for building automobiles.

He was the eldest son of an Irish immigrant who during the Civil War had married the daughter of a prosperous Pennsylvania Dutch farmer and settled down to farming near Dearborn in Wayne County, Michigan;

like plenty of other Americans, young Henry grew up hating the endless sogging through the mud about the chores, the hauling and pitching manure, the kerosene lamps to clean, the irk and sweat and solitude of the farm.

He was a slender, active youngster, a good skater, clever with his hands; what he liked was to tend the machinery and let the others do the heavy work. His mother had told him not to drink, smoke, gamble or go into debt, and he never did.

When he was in his early twenties his father tried to get him back from Detroit, where he was working as mechanic and repairman for the Drydock Engine Company that built engines for steamboats, by giving him forty acres of land.

Young Henry built himself an uptodate square white dwelling-house with a false mansard roof and married and settled down on the farm,

but he let the hired men do the farming;

he bought himself a buzzsaw and rented a stationary engine and cut the timber off the woodlots.

He was a thrifty young man who never drank or smoked or gambled or coveted his neighbor's wife, but he couldn't stand living on the farm.

He moved to Detroit, and in the brick barn behind his house tinkered for years in his spare time with a mechanical buggy that would be light enough to run over the clayey wagonroads of Wayne County, Michigan.

By 1900 he had a practicable car to promote.

He was forty years old before the Ford Motor Company was started and production began to move.

Speed was the first thing the early automobile manufacturers went after. Races advertised the makes of cars.

Henry Ford himself hung up several records at the track at Grosse Pointe and on the ice on Lake St. Clair. In his 999 he did the mile in thirtynine and fourfifths seconds.

But it had always been his custom to hire others to do the heavy work. The speed he was busy with was speed in production, the records were records in efficient output. He hired Barney Oldfield, a stunt bicyclerider from Salt Lake City, to do the racing for him.

Henry Ford had ideas about other things than the designing of motors, carburetors, magnetos, jigs and fixtures, punches and dies; he had ideas about sales,

that the big money was in economical quantity production, quick turnover, cheap interchangeable easilyreplaced standardized parts;

it wasn't until 1909, after years of arguing with his partners, that Ford put out the first Model T.

Henry Ford was right.

That season he sold more than ten thousand tin lizzies, ten years later he was selling almost a million a year.

In these years the Taylor Plan was stirring up plantmanagers and manufacturers all over the country. Efficiency was the word. The same ingenuity that went into improving the performance of a machine could go into improving the performance of the workmen producing the machine.

In 1913 they established the assemblyline at Ford's. That season the profits were something like twentyfive million dollars, but they had trouble in keeping the men on the job, machinists didn't seem to like it at Ford's.

Henry Ford had ideas about other things than production.

He was the largest automobile manufacturer in the world; he paid high wages; maybe if the steady workers thought they were getting a cut (a very small cut) in the profits, it would give trained men an inducement to stick to their jobs,

wellpaid workers might save enough money to buy a tin lizzie; the first day Ford's announced that cleancut properlymarried American workers who wanted jobs had a chance to make five bucks a day (of course it turned out that there were strings to it; always there were strings to it)

such an enormous crowd waited outside the Highland Park plant

all through the zero January night

that there was a riot when the gates were opened; cops broke heads, jobhunters threw bricks; property, Henry Ford's own property, was destroyed. The company dicks had to turn on the firehose to beat back the crowd.

The American Plan; automotive prosperity seeping down from above; it turned out there were strings to it.

But that five dollars a day

paid to good, clean American workmen who didn't drink or smoke cigarettes or read or think,

and who didn't commit adultery

and whose wives didn't take in boarders, made America once more the Yukon of the sweated workers of the world;

made all the tin lizzies and the automotive age, and incidentally,

made Henry Ford, the automobileer, the admirer of Edison, the birdlover,

the great American of his time.

But Henry Ford had ideas about other things besides assemblylines and the livinghabits of his employees. He was full of ideas. Instead of going to the city to make his fortune, here was a country boy who'd made his fortune by bringing the city out to the farm. The precepts he'd learned out of McGuffey's Reader, his mother's prejudices and preconceptions, he had preserved clean and unworn as freshprinted bills in the safe in a bank.

He wanted people to know about his ideas, so he bought the *Dearborn Independent* and started a campaign against cigarettesmoking.

When war broke out in Europe, he had ideas about that too. (Suspicion of armymen and soldiering were part of the midwest farm tradition, like thrift, stickativeness, temperance and sharp practice in money matters.) Any intelligent American mechanic could see that if the Europeans hadn't been a lot of ignorant underpaid foreigners who drank, smoked, were loose about women and wasteful in their methods of production, the war could never have happened.

When Rosika Schwimmer broke through

the stockade of secretaries and servicemen who surrounded Henry Ford and suggested to him that he could stop the war,

he said sure they'd hire a ship and go over and get the boys out of the trenches by Christmas.

He hired a steamboat, the *Oscar II,* and filled it up with pacifists and social-workers,

to go over to explain to the princelings of Europe

that what they were doing was vicious and silly.

It wasn't his fault that Poor Richard's commonsense no longer rules the world and that most of the pacifists were nuts,

goofy with headlines.

When William Jennings Bryan went over to Hoboken to see him off, somebody handed William Jennings Bryan a squirrel in a cage; William Jennings Bryan made a speech with the squirrel under his arm. Henry Ford threw American Beauty roses to the crowd. The band played *I Didn't Raise My Boy to Be a Soldier.* Practical jokers let loose more squirrels. An eloping couple was married by a platoon of ministers in the saloon, and Mr. Zero, the flophouse humanitarian, who reached the dock too late to sail,

dove into the North River and swam after the boat.

The *Oscar II* was described as a floating Chautauqua; Henry Ford said it felt like a middlewestern village, but by the time they reached Christiansand in Norway, the reporters had kidded him so that he had gotten cold feet and gone to bed. The world was too crazy outside of Wayne County, Michigan. Mrs. Ford and the management sent an Episcopal dean after him who brought him home under wraps,

and the pacifists had to speechify without him.

Two years later Ford's was manufacturing munitions, Eagle boats; Henry Ford was planning oneman tanks, and oneman submarines like the one tried out in the

Revolutionary War. He announced to the press that he'd turn over his war profits to the government,

but there's no record that he ever did.

One thing he brought back from his trip

was the Protocols of the Elders of Zion.

He started a campaign to enlighten the world in the *Dearborn Independent;* the Jews were why the world wasn't like Wayne County, Michigan, in the old horse and buggy days;

the Jews had started the war, Bolshevism, Darwinism, Marxism, Nietzsche, short skirts and lipstick. They were behind Wall Street and the international bankers, and the whiteslave traffic and the movies and the Supreme Court and ragtime and the illegal liquor business.

Henry Ford denounced the Jews and ran for senator and sued the *Chicago Tribune* for libel,

and was the laughingstock of the kept metropolitan press;

but when the metropolitan bankers tried to horn in on his business

he thoroughly outsmarted them.

In 1918 he had borrowed on notes to buy out his minority stockholders for the picayune sum of seventyfive million dollars.

In February, 1920, he needed cash to pay off some of these notes that were coming due. A banker is supposed to have called on him and offered him every facility if the bankers' representative could be made a member of the board of directors. Henry Ford handed the banker his hat,

and went about raising the money in his own way:

he shipped every car and part he had in his plant to his dealers and demanded immediate cash payment. Let the other fellow do the borrowing had always been a cardinal principle. He shut down production and canceled all orders from the supplyfirms. Many dealers were ruined,

many supplyfirms failed, but when he reopened his plant,

he owned it absolutely,

the way a man owns an unmortgaged farm with the taxes paid up.

In 1922 there started the Ford boom for President (high wages, waterpower, industry scattered to the small towns) that was skillfully pricked behind the scenes

by another crackerbarrel philosopher, Calvin Coolidge;

but in 1922 Henry Ford sold one million three hundred and thirtytwo thousand two hundred and nine tin lizzies; he was the richest man in the world.

Good roads had followed the narrow ruts made in the mud by the Model T. The great automotive boom was on. At Ford's production was improving all the time: less waste, more spotters, strawbosses, stoolpigeons (fifteen minutes for lunch, three minutes to go to the toilet, the Taylorized speedup everywhere, reach under, adjust washer, screw down bolt, shove in cotterpin, reachunder adjustwasher, screwdown bolt, reachunderadjustscrewdownreachunderadjust until every ounce of life was sucked off into production and at night the workmen went home grey shaking husks).

Ford owned every detail of the process from the ore in the hills until the car rolled off the end of the assemblyline under its own power, the plants were rationalized to the last tenthousandth of an inch as measured by the Johansen scale;

in 1926 the production cycle was reduced to eightyone hours from the ore in the mine to the finished salable car proceeding under its own power,

but the Model T was obsolete.

New Era prosperity and the American Plan

(there were strings to it, always there were strings to it)

had killed Tin Lizzie.

Ford's was just one of many automobile plants.

When the stockmarket bubble burst,

Mr. Ford the crackerbarrel philosopher said jubilantly,

"I told you so.

Serves you right for gambling and getting in debt.

The country is sound."

But when the country on cracked shoes, in frayed trousers, belts tightened over hollow bellies,

idle hands cracked and chapped with the cold of that coldest March day of 1932,

started marching from Detroit to Dearborn, asking for work and the American Plan, all they could think of at Ford's was machineguns.

The country was sound, but they mowed the marchers down.

They shot four of them dead.

Henry Ford as an old man
is a passionate antiquarian,

(lives besieged on his father's farm embedded in an estate of thousands of millionaire acres, protected by an army of servicemen, secretaries, secret agents, dicks under orders of an English exprizefighter,

always afraid of the feet in broken shoes on the roads, afraid the gangs will kidnap his grandchildren,

that a crank will shoot him,

that Change and the idle hands out of work will break through the gates and the high fences;

protected by a private army against the new America of starved children and hollow bellies and cracked shoes stamping on souplines,

that has swallowed up the old thrifty farmlands

of Wayne County, Michigan,

as if they had never been).

Henry Ford as an old man
is a passionate antiquarian.

He rebuilt his father's farmhouse and put it back exactly in the state he remembered it in as a boy. He built a village of museums for buggies, sleighs, coaches, old plows, waterwheels, obsolete models of

motorcars. He scoured the country for fiddlers to play old-fashioned squaredances.

Even old taverns he bought and put back into their original shape, as well as Thomas Edison's early laboratories.

When he bought the Wayside Inn near Sudbury, Massachusetts, he had the new highway where the newmodel cars roared and slithered and hissed oilily past (*the new noise of the automobile*).

moved away from the door,

put back the old bad road,

so that everything might be

the way it used to be,

in the days of horses and buggies.

Harvey Swados

Harvey Swados (1920–1972), novelist, short story writer, and essayist, finds that factory conditions today are not totally unlike those of Upton Sinclair's time. The following story describes the initiation of a young man into the factory assembly line and his acquaintance with Joe, the last of the "rugged individualists."

JOE, THE VANISHING AMERICAN

If Walter had not been so desperately anxious to go away to college he might never have been able to stick it out those first few weeks at the factory. His father, once district sales manager for a bankrupt sewing-machine concern, had come down in the world and was now a continually uneasy clerk in the branch office of a usury outfit called the Friendly Finance Corporation; his mother, who had borne Walter late in life, clung jealously to the fading prestige conferred on her by her many beneficences on behalf of the Ladies' Guild.

Walter had never done anything harder

than shovel the neighbors' snowy driveways and sell magazines to reluctant relatives. But the night of his graduation from high school his father grunted in a choked voice that there was no money to send him to college. Walter swore to himself that he would get a college education if he had to rob a bank. At the commencement exercise a classmate had told him that you could get a job at the new auto assembly plant if you said on your application that you had worked as a garage mechanic. While his parents rocked creakily, proud but miserable, on the porch glider, Walter mounted the narrow steps to his little room and sat down at his desk. If he could work steadily at the plant for a year he ought to be able to save several thousand dollars even after contributing his share of the household expenses. Without saying a word to his parents, he went to the plant the following morning and filled out an application blank. Three days later he received a telegram asking him to report for work at six-thirty A.M.

When he returned, gray and exhausted, from his long day in the body shop to which he had been assigned, Walter found his mother sitting in the parlor and sobbing into a handkerchief. She raised her eyes at the slamming of the door and stared at him in horror.

"Look at you!" she cried, and immediately Walter knew that her first shock was at the way he *looked,* not at how he must have *felt.* Nevertheless Walter felt it his filial duty to explain that he would not have to march past the neighbors in greasy coveralls, but could wear sport clothes to work and change at the plant; furthermore, he hinted, when his mother was preparing his sandwiches for the next day's lunch, he could just as easily carry them in a little paper sack as in a metal lunchbox.

His father, keeping them company in the kitchen, took a different tack, and even blustered a little about the advantages of working for a huge corporation.

"I don't see why Walter couldn't have started with something more pleasant," his mother said plaintively, smoothing mayonnaise across white bread. "In an office he could at least use his brains."

"Don't kid yourself," her husband replied. "There's no shame attached to factory work any more. Besides, Walter has a darned good chance to advance if he shows them the stuff he's got."

Implicit in all this was his parents' fear that Walter had started down a dead-end street, and their own shame at not having been able to send him away to college. Anxious not to inflame their feelings, Walter refrained from defending his decision; even if he were only to point out that he would be making big money, it would be a direct insult to his father, who at fifty-nine was making only five dollars a week more than his son. So he put the case negatively.

"There's just no place else around," he said, "that would pay me anything like what I'm going to be making at the auto plant."

"The boy is right, mother," his father said decisively, much to Walter's satisfaction. "You're doing the smart thing, Walter."

Thus challenged at home, Walter had no alternative but to grit his teeth and swear to himself that nothing would make him quit until he had reached his goal. Like a groggy but game boxer, he measured out his future not with the end of the fight in view, for that would have been too far away, but rather in terms of more immediate accomplishments: his first automatic nickel raise at the end of four weeks, his second automatic nickel raise at the end of eight weeks, his acceptance as a permanent employee at the end of ninety days, and most of all his listing as a metal-finisher, which would mean that he would be in the highest-paid group in the plant and that he would be recognized as a skilled worker, a man who had made the grade.

His surroundings meant nothing to Walter, who had not expected that the factory would look like an art gallery; but the work, and the conditions under which he had to do it, were a nightmare of endless horror from which Walter sometimes thought, stumbling wearily out of the plant after ten hours of unremitting anguish, he would one day awaken with a scream. It was not simply that the idea of working on an endless succession of auto bodies as they came slowly but ineluctably rolling down the assembly line like so many faceless steel robots was both monotonous and stupefying, or that the heavy work of finding bumps and dents in them, knocking them out and filing them down, was in itself too exhausting.

No, it was the strain of having to work both fast and accurately, with the foreman standing over him and glaring through his thick-lensed glasses, that made Walter dread the beginning of each day. Under the best of conditions, he figured, he had three and a half minutes to complete his metal-finishing work from the time he started a job on his line to the time it reached the platform and was swung off on hooks toward the bonderizing booth. If he began at the very beginning, as soon as the inspector had indicated bad spots with a stump of chalk, circling hollows and x-ing high spots, he could finish before the job reached the final inspector at the far end of the line—unless the dents were too deep or too numerous, in which case he was still madly pounding and filing, squatting and straining with the sweat running down his temples and his cheekbones while the solder-flower worked next to him in a tangle of rubber hose, melting lead and a blazing gun with a flame so hot that it scorched dry the running sweat on his face, and the final inspector stood over him, imperturbably chalking newly discovered hollows and pimples in the infuriating metal. Then he would straighten up from his hopeless effort and with a despairing glance at the impassive pick-up man, who had to finish what he had left undone, he would hurry back down the line, praying to dear God that the next car

—he did every third one—would be in fairly decent condition.

Worst of all were the times when he would hear a piercing whistle and would look up from the damnable dent at which he had been rapping blindly with the point of his file, to see Buster the foreman all the way past the platform, waving angrily with his cigar. Hurrying from his unfinished work to his punishment, Walter would try to steel himself against what he knew was coming, but it was no use.

"You call yourself a metal man?" Buster would ask, stuffing the cigar between his teeth with an angry snap. "You want to get metal-finisher's pay and you let a job like that go through?" His eyes glinting with rage behind his thick spectacles, Buster would gesticulate at one of Walter's cars, freshly speckled with chalk marks as it swung in the air. "Get going on it!"

And Walter would hurl himself at the job, dashing the sweat from his brow with the back of his gloved hand and filing away in a clumsy fury.

By the time he had somehow or other repaired what he had left undone, he would find on hastening back to the line that he was far behind once again in his regular work, so far behind that it might take him the better part of an hour to gradually work his way back on the line to where he really belonged, safe for the moment from shouted complaints.

Inevitably the men around him had suggestions as to how Walter might better his condition. Of the two other metal-finishers who worked on the line with him, one was a dour, fattish man, a leader in the opposition of the local union and disgusted because it did nothing to provide security for probationary employees like Walter.

"I'll tell you something else. There's countries where a bright young hard-working fellow like you, that wants to go to college, doesn't have to waste the best years of his life in factory work just to save the money for college fees. He gets sent right through school and the government foots the bills. All he has to do is show that he's got the stuff and his future is secure."

Walter allowed that this sounded fine, although "having the stuff" sounded uncomfortably like his father's eulogies of life in America, but he could not see what practical good it did him here and now—unless he was supposed to get satisfaction from the bitterness of knowing that in mysterious other countries his opposite numbers were better off than he.

The third metal-finisher, a lean efficient sardonic man, had been listening silently to this talk of free college careers. He put his wiry hand inside his open-necked khaki shirt, scratched the coarse curling hair below his throat, and laughed aloud.

"What's the matter?" asked his fattish colleague suspiciously.

"You think your propaganda's going to change this boy's ideas about the other side of the world when everything here tells him he's got it so good?" He tapped the fat man on the shoulder with the butt end of his file as patronizingly as if he were patting him on the head. "Even if he has to suffer for his education in a way that shouldn't be necessary, he's free. He can blunder around and maybe even learn something that isn't listed in the college catalogues. These poor kids you want him to envy, they may be getting their college for nothing, but they're paying a higher price for it than this fellow ever will. And the sad part is that most of them probably don't even know what the price is." And he turned back to his work without giving the fat man a chance to reply.

Fortunately for the three of them, the fat metal-finisher was transferred. He was only replaced, however, by an intense worker with two vertical wrinkles between his brows, who watched Walter's ineffectual work with growing impatience. At last he could stand it no more.

"In this game, kid, the knack of it is in the speed. The speed," he said fiercely, "and the way you concentrate on the job. If you're going to fumble around and just

bitch about your mistakes, you'll be a long time getting straightened out." He greeted his own badly dented job, rolling toward them, with a smile of genuine pleasure. "Size it up quick, pick out the worst dents, and get going on them right away. Leave the high spots for last—the pick-up men don't mind doing them."

The third man, the gray-haired cynic whom everyone liked but no one seemed to know, had been listening quietly, with a strange, mild grin on his long and youthful face. He put a stick of chewing gum in his mouth, ruminated for a moment, and said: "What you really want is for him to enjoy his work, Orrin. Might be more practical if you'd get down and actually show him how to do it. Here, hold on a minute, Walter."

Walter had been squatting on his haunches before the wheel-housing of his job, blindly pounding with a hammer at his hidden screwdriver, trying hopelessly to punch a hole underneath so that with the screwdriver he could dig out a deep dent as the others did, trying so hopelessly that as he smashed the hammer against his left hand, missing the butt end of the screwdriver, he had to squeeze his eyes to keep the tears from starting forth.

"Give me that screwdriver."

Handing up the tool to the laconic man, Walter noticed for the first time that he bore an unusual tattoo, faded like an old flag, on his right forearm: an American eagle, claws gripping his wrist, beak opened triumphantly at the elbow—you could almost hear it screaming. Without a word the man took the screwdriver and swiftly pressed it to a grinding wheel, fashioning a beveled point.

"Try it now."

Walter stuck the screwdriver under the car, rapped at it smartly several times— bang! it was through and resting against the outer skin of the car, just at the very dent. Gratefully, he turned to the gray-haired man, but he was gone, like a mirage.

There was something mirage-like about

him, anyway. He drove to and from work alone, he never engaged in small talk, he never hung around with a group at lunch hour or before work, he kept a paper book in the hip pocket of his khaki trousers, and always when he was not concentrating on his own work, when he was watching Walter or listening to the others handing him advice, he had that mocking irreligious smile on his long narrow youthful face. What was more, his cold blue eyes seemed always to be on Walter, sizing him up, watching not so much his work, as every one else did, but his temperament and his personality. It made him uncomfortable.

Gradually Walter began to sort out the other men around him, the ones who had more common reality in their talk and their tastes. Most companionable of them all was Kevin, the former rural school teacher, now an immigrant hook-man. His accent was so delightful, his turns of speech so happy, that Walter engaged the towering redhead in conversation at every opportunity.

"Hey, Kevin," he shouted at him one day, "how old were those kids you taught in County Kerry?"

"Ah, Walter," Kevin sighed, showing his long white teeth as he spoke, "they weren't *all* such children. If you were to see some of the older girls—quite well developed, they were. Oh, how shameful if they had known what was passing through their schoolmaster's mind!"

Kevin laughed at the memory, Walter at the picture the big fellow conjured up of countryside lust; he turned around and there was the gray-haired metal-finisher, smiling too, but so coldly you would have thought him a scientist observing a successful experiment. It was chilling, and yet not wholly unpleasant. In a way that he could not define, Walter felt that he was being judged and approved.

This third man, reserved and anonymous as ever, continued to observe him as Walter chatted not only with Kevin and the second metal-finisher, but with all of the other men on their line. Conversation was necessarily shouted and fragmentary, but Walter was astonished at how intimacies could be revealed in the course of a few phrases:

"A man's a fool to get married."

"Grab the overtime while you can. In the auto industry you never know when you'll be laid off."

"Happiest time of my life was when I was in the army."

"Only reason I'm here is because I was too stupid to learn a trade."

"I came here out of curiosity, but my curiosity's all used up."

"My wife says if I quit I'll have a better chance to line up a construction job."

"Walter, don't turn out like those college men who can tell you how to do everything but can't do a damn thing themselves."

The only one to rebuff Walter's friendly overtures was Pop, the seamy-faced little inspector with a rooster's ruff of yellowing white hair that rose and tumbled down over his forehead, and sunken old lips from which depended miraculously a heavy, unlit cigar. Wizened, pale and bloodless, he regarded Walter, for no apparent reason, with bottomless contempt. With a little cap perched sideways on his Niagara of a head like a precarious canoe, and a soft brown cloth knotted about the hand with which he probed Walter's work for defects and omissions, he seemed to Walter like some strange and hateful gnome.

"Kids like you," he said in a dry and rusty monotone, "they come and go. Twenty-three years I'm here, and I seen a million like you. Not steady, not reliable, don't want to learn, just out for fun. You'll never make a metal man."

I don't want to be a metal man, Walter wanted to reply; I just want to make my money and get out of here. But this was, he knew, just what Pop was goading him to say, so he held his tongue. A moment later he was glad that he had, for he was startled to hear the third metal-finisher address him.

"Pop is an exception," he said, bending over Walter's car and scrubbing at it with his sandpaper as he spoke. "By and large there is a democracy of age in the factory. Men who have been here since before you were born fought for a union contract guaranteeing equal treatment for you. Ninety days after you start you get the same wage as a worker who's been on the job nineteen years. A man twice your age will treat you as a working partner and an adult. Where else is that true?"

"Yes," Walter replied angrily, "but Pop—"

"He's got reason to be bitter. Some day I'll tell you why."

He straightened up abruptly and walked away to his own job. But the words he had used reverberated in Walter's mind. Who was he, with his young-old face and his expressions like "democracy of age"? Walter asked, but no one seemed to know. Some said he was a seaman and adventurer, and his big tattoo was pointed to as proof, for he had been heard to state himself that he had acquired it in Lourenço Marques; but others, who had themselves come to the assembly line from rural homesteads, were positive from clues he had let fall that he had formerly been an itinerant farm laborer; and there were even those who swore that he was really an educated man, a kind of college professor amusing himself by slumming among them.

Whoever he was, for the time he had nothing more to say. But Walter felt his presence, for he was always ready to lend a hand, always laconically helpful, always silently observing and listening.

One day the younger inspector at the beginning of the line, blowing genial clouds of illegal pipe smoke, gave Walter some frank and cynical advice.

"Been listening to the bosses talking about you, buddy." He took the pipe from his mouth and formed a fat smoke ring. "Want to know what's wrong with what you're doing?"

"I guess so," said Walter dully.

"You try too hard. You're trying to do a good job—that's the worst thing you can do."

Walter stared in bewilderment at the inspector. "But why?"

"They're interested in pulling production. If you're going to be running up and down the line all day trying to make every job perfect, you're just going to get in people's way. What the bosses will do is, they'll look for an excuse to fire you before your probationary period is up, or else they'll stick you in a routine lower-paying job."

"Then . . ."

"I've been here ten years. Believe me," he drew on his pipe once again and smiled disarmingly, "they're not interested in making good cars, they're interested in making cars. You know what production means? Volume. And you know what they hired you for? To camouflage, not to get rid of every flaw. Hide them so they don't show up after the car's been through paint, so the customer doesn't see them at the dealer's, and you'll get along great."

"Camouflage them how?"

"With your sandpaper. With the grinding wheel. If you hit them up and down and then across, final inspection will never know what's underneath. Make it look good, and confusing. Be a camouflage artist and the bosses'll very seldom bother you."

Walter could not help laughing. "Listen, how could you stand it here for ten years? Every day I think maybe I ought to get out and look for something else."

"For six years," the inspector said pleasantly, "I was like you. This was going to be just temporary until I found something with a real future. It took me six years to realize that I was going to be spending the rest of my life here—it's like breaking in a wild horse, only with a human being it takes longer. I got married, had three kids, now I'm building a home near the plant. So I make the best of it, I take it easy and I have as much fun as I can, and I hate to see a guy like you breaking his back all for nothing."

Bending over his work, Walter raised his file and heard the inspector's final shot, lightly enough intended but bearing its own weight of bitterness and resignation: "You'd be surprised how many fellows I've heard talking just like you, couldn't stand the work, going to quit any day, and now they're five and ten year men, starting to think about retirement benefits."

Walter could not clarify in his own mind what it was about the inspector's attitude that increased his desperation, not until his silent partner eased up to him from no-where and said quietly, "Kind of terrified you, didn't he?"

"Not exactly terrified."

"Just the same, it's no fun to be doing time and to be told that your sentence just might turn out to be indefinite. Then if you've got a good imagination you can see yourself gradually getting used to it, even getting to like the routine, so that one day follows another and the first thing you know the wrinkles are there and the kids are grown up and you don't know where it's all gone to, your life."

Walter felt himself shuddering. Was it from the blower overhead that he felt his hot sweat turning cold and drying on his face? He said, "I suppose you have to be cynical if you're going to stay here."

"Day after day your life becomes a joke without any point, a trick that you play on yourself from punching in to punching out."

"But that's only if you're an imaginative or a sensitive person."

For the first time, the man's angular face hardened. "Don't you think somebody like that inspector had his ambitions? Don't you think he still has his man's pride? Did you ever figure the cost of the job in terms of what it does to the personality of a clever intelligent fellow like him? He says if you're going to be trapped you might as well make the best of it, and by his lights he may be right. Anyway don't be too quick to blame him—he probably never had the oppor-tunity to save money and go off to college."

No one had ever, not ever in eighteen years, talked to Walter in such a way. He would never again be able to look at a man like the inspector without compassion. Even at home in the evening with his father, whom he could no longer talk to about anything but baseball or weather (although they both tried clumsily to broach other more serious topics), Walter found that he was viewing this desolate man not just as his father but as a man who had his own miseries; and this, he knew, was a part of growing up that could not have come about as it had without the influence of his strange friend in the factory.

More and more as the weeks passed and exhaustion was gradually overcome by vitality, only to be transformed into monot-ony, Walter came to feel that only this man could explain the real meaning of the as-sembly line. But he remained aloof, insub-stantial as a ghost. The more he held to himself, the more Walter was piqued, and determined to make the ghost speak.

At last one day he ventured to demand: "Say, what does that tattoo of yours stand for, that big bird?"

The man smiled with one side of his mouth. "That old bird is the American eagle." He raised his arm briefly, flexed it, and let it fall to his side. "It's screaming with rage at what's happened to the re-public."

"What *has* happened?"

"Where are the guts? Where's the drive? In a place like this a man's life goes down the drain like scummy water."

"But you're working here too," Walter said boldly.

The man shook his head slowly, with such finality that there was something ele-mental about the gesture. "I'm not a settled-down man, I'm just passing through."

Walter cleared his throat. "I don't even know your name."

"Why should you? Instead of learning names, we refer to the fellow with the bad teeth, or the guy with the blue coveralls. When I work next to a man for months and learn that his wife is being operated on for cancer of the breast and still don't know his name, it tells me something not just about him and me, but about the half-connections that are all the factory allows you in the way of friendships."

"The old-timers are clubby enough, but everybody else claims they're here for a limited time. The place is so big and everything seems so temporary that I suppose we don't feel the need of introducing ourselves."

The older man looked at Walter somberly. "No one who comes here wants to admit that the place has any real connection with his real life. He has to say that he is just putting in his time here, and so no matter how friendly he is by nature he has to think of the people around him as essentially strangers, men whom he can't even trouble to say good-by to when he quits or gets laid off."

"But *your* name—"

"Call me Joe."

Walter pursued him: "Every third guy on the line must be named Joe. Joe what?"

He smiled again, his long Yankee countenance creasing in a cold grin. "Joe, the vanishing American." And he turned his back on Walter and bent to his work as the line resumed its endless progress.

But he was a curious man, a nosey man, and he was there, listening and leering, when Walter found a minute to respond without cursing to a bitter remark of Pop's. Walter turned on him with the anger he had managed to suppress when speaking to the old inspector.

"It's easy for you to stand there and laugh. You think you're better than anybody else in the shop."

Joe hitched up his khaki trousers and replied with deliberate anger, "I never claimed that. I just read a little more and ponder a little more than the average fellow. That's why I don't laugh at them, I feel sorry for them. If I'm a little freer, I've had to make sacrifices for it—no dependents, no ties." He added cryptically, "They punish you one way or they punish you another way."

Walter did not quite understand, but it struck him that these remarks were a prelude to farewell. He asked uneasily, "You're not going to quit?"

"One of these days. Maybe the weather will turn, or I'll hear of something else, or I'll have words with Buster . . ." He added with somewhat more warmth, "But I'll be back—if not here, some place like here. You won't, though. That's why I hope you won't forget what it was like for the people who made the things you'll be buying."

Walter cried indignantly: "How could I? How could I ever forget?" It seemed to him that the thick scurf of silver through which he shuffled as he worked, the glittering waste of lead filings and melted sticks, were so many needles, each carrying its stinging injection of memory—of sweat, exhaustion, harrying, feverish haste, and stupid boredom.

"You forget worse things, don't you? Pain, and even death? You'll think back on the days when you were slaving away to save money for college, and they'll strike you as comical, maybe even romantic."

"God forbid!" Walter laughed. And yet he had suddenly a shivery foretaste of a future beyond the one of which he daydreamed as he worked.

When the siren screamed the end of their nine and a half hours Walter hurled his file and apron into his tool box and trotted down the aisle toward the time clock. Turning the corner of the body shop office just as its lights were extinguished, he ran headlong into the iron antennae of a fork truck and cried aloud with pain as the metal plate struck his shinbone. Tottering backward, Walter was suddenly gripped by the forearm and pulled erect. He turned gratefully and found himself staring into the eyes of Joe.

Smarting with soreness and embarrassment, Walter demanded aggressively, "I suppose that's what you want me to remember!"

A faint stubble glinted along Joe's narrow checks. Graying like his iron hair, it aged him as it grew. He scraped his hand across it wearily and replied quietly, "Never mind the machinery. Remember the men. The men make the machines, and they make their own tragedies too. Once your own life gets easier, you'll take it for granted not only that theirs must be easier too, but that they deserve what they get anyway, that some law of natural selection has put you up where you are and them down where they are."

They had reached the clock bay where they took their place meekly in line, waiting to punch out, shuffling forward every few seconds while they spoke in low voices. Around them a swarm of men surged toward freedom—noisy boys with laughter to spare for the evening, haggard weary men in their forties, surly powerful black men in stained coveralls and scrawny brown men chattering in Spanish, vacant-faced fools with slack jaws and dangling hands, shrewd-eyed men fingering their union contract books, composing their campaign leaflets, and computing their chances of election to positions that would lift them out of the work routine.

"Why do they stay?"

"They're trapped, that's why. They say everybody's supposed to be, one way or another, but it's worse to be stuck here. Spending your life on the production line means counting out the minutes, being grateful that Mondays go fast because you're rested, and hating Tuesdays because the week is so long. It means that you're paying off forever on all the things you've been pressured into buying by getting up every day in order to do something you'd never, never think of doing if it was a matter of choice. It means never having anything to look forward to in all of your working life." Joe took his card from the rack, clicked it in the time clock, and with a wave of his hand was gone.

What was happening, as Walter woke daily to the dawn's dull alarm and went from the still house through the newly washed streets to the waiting assembly line, was that his self-pity, so strong that the page blurred before him when he lay in bed reading himself to sleep, was altering into a maturer concern with the fate of others who could not, like himself, set a term to their labor.

He began to question the men on the line with him, one after another, to find out how many of them felt as he did about what they were doing for a living. More sure of himself with every passing hour, he moved up and down the line, demanding, whenever there was a moment, an answer to his insistent question: "Do you think anybody likes coming in here to work?"

"Everybody does one day a week—payday," said the solder-flower.

"Not even the bosses," said the deck-fitter. "Do you think anybody with sense would knock himself out in this dirt and noise if it wasn't for the money?"

And the door-fitter said wryly, "Do you know what this kind of work is? It's colored man's work. Why, even the colored men are smartening up—they turn up their noses at it too, unless they get strapped."

Saddened and bewildered by this last comment, Walter turned away from the man who had made it, and who had punctuated his bitter remark with a series of thunderous blows on a door that he was fitting. Only Orrin, the second metal-finisher, grudgingly admitted that the work was a challenge to him, that the pay was fair, and that there were worse jobs. Behind them all, long-jawed Joe, caught up with his work as usual, stood casually beveling his screwdriver.

"I hear you've been taking a little poll," he said to Walter.

"What's it to you?" Walter asked truculently. He was in no mood to be mocked.

With apparent irrelevance, Joe replied by demanding, "How come you fixed on being an engineer?"

Walter was taken aback. "Why, that's where everybody says the future is."

"That's not reason enough for a fellow to struggle and sweat to get to college. Damn it, doesn't anybody go out and do what he wants to any more? I'm not saying you wouldn't make a good engineer, or that it wouldn't be fine for a change to have some engineers who care as much about people as they do about gadgets. But supposing you find out after you get to college that you want to spend your time learning something useless—are you going to leave yourself open for it?"

"Boy, you sure are free with advice."

Joe looked at him gravely. His long sad jaw had the hint of a smile. "The men on the line like you, Walter. They don't think you're nosey when you ask questions. They think you're one of them, and in a good way you are. Maybe that's why I've got hopes for you."

Walter fought hard against the influence of the older man, whose crabbed and subversive outlook was so foreign to everything Walter had been taught, but he was forced to admit to himself that more and more he was seeing the factory through Joe's cold discerning eyes; and he began to fear that if Joe were ever to leave, the plant would have no real existence other than as a money-producing nightmare. Not only was there no one else really to talk to about it, but Joe had forced Walter to try to formulate his emerging ideas in an adult and comprehensible way.

"The worst thing about the assembly line is what it does to your self-respect," he said to Joe early one morning as they squatted on their haunches, waiting for the starting siren. "It's hard to keep from feeling like a fool when you know that everybody looks down on what you're doing, even the men who are doing it themselves."

Joe hung his hammer and metal spoon from the brass hook at his belt. "The big pitch has always been that we're a practical people, that we've proved to all the impractical European dreamers that produc-tion can serve people. But instead people are serving production. Look how frightened, how hysterical the bosses get when the line stops—they can't afford to figure what it costs *you* to keep it moving—they only know they've got a production quota. Of course when sales resistance starts building up and they put the cork back in themselves, they give you just the opposite story. Who can blame the poor slob in the middle for suspecting that the whole setup is really as nutty as a fruitcake, and for feeling ashamed of himself for being caught up in it?"

"All right," Walter challenged him. "Who's crazy? You, me, the guys around us, or the board of directors?"

"Anybody who gets suckered into believing that there's anything real behind the billboards they put up to get the show on the road, so that he commits himself to buying the billboard pictures by selling his life on the installment plan. I sympathize with any joker who begins to suspect that the whole world is against him, that he's the victim of a huge conspiracy organized to make his car fall apart before it's been paid off. Doesn't life in the factory seem to be deliberately designed to lower your own self-esteem? What happens when you're knocking down a dent? If you rap it too hard from the inside, you have to file it down that much more, and you hate yourself for it. If you don't rap it hard enough you only find out after it's moved on down the line, and then you have to hurry up and wallop it again. In either case you hate yourself instead of hating the car, or the invisible man that started up the line." He laughed briefly in anticipation of what he was about to add. "It's like the man that hits his thumb with a hammer while he's hanging a picture—only here he keeps hitting his thumb because they're moving the wall as fast as the union will let them. Who does he yell at every time that ball peen comes down on his nail? Himself."

"I wonder," Walter said slowly, "how many people actually feel that way."

"More than you can count. It's always safe to figure that if you feel something, the world must be full of people who feel the same way. Every sensible man realizes as he gets older that his feelings aren't unique. After all, that's the basis of the best art: the fact that you recognize yourself in it, and all those inner experiences that you'd thought no one else but you could know."

Walter was willing to recognize that he was not the only one to cringe when Buster called him back on a badly done job, to swear at himself for the mistakes that made him fall behind, to realize how he was being trapped into swearing at himself and deflecting his anger from what he did to the way he did it. But it was hard for him to believe that there were others who felt as intensely as he did, who beat their heads against the bars as he did, who dreamed of sunlight and freedom as he did, even though Joe tried to persuade him that the difference was often one of degree, or of his being able to express his feelings in a way that others couldn't. This was one of the questions that Walter was eager to argue with Joe, who moved from one extreme position to another, always mocking, always challenging him to learn what he stood for and to defend it like a man.

"You know something," Walter burst out impetuously one day, "I don't know what I would have done here without you."

Instead of laughing, or belittling this praise, Joe's face darkened. The next morning he was not on the line.

By the third day of his absence Walter was beginning to feel as though it had all been a dream, as though he were slipping once again into the awful pit of loneliness, exhaustion and self-doubting despair. As a last resort he sought out the men on the line to learn what they thought of Joe.

"He's irresponsible," said Pop.

"He's the kind of guy that just don't care," said the younger inspector. "No wife, no kids, no wonder he can take off three days without worrying about getting a reprimand or getting fired."

"He knows his work," said Orrin grudgingly. "I don't know where he learned it, but he did. Just the same, he takes off. You can't *afford* to take off like that nowadays, not if you want to hold down a job."

On the fourth day he came back. He told no one where he had been. "Am I glad to see you!" Walter exclaimed—but Joe merely indicated, with a cold grin and a turn of his tattooed arm, that from time to time things came up that were more important than the making of automobiles. He did not set to work, but almost immediately was engaged in serious talk with Buster the foreman and with the union shop steward. The two were arguing vigorously, but suddenly Joe cut them off simply by lifting his hand. He said something very briefly, shoved his hands into his pockets, and the discussion was finished.

To Walter's amazement, he came back to the line, picked up his toolbox, and nodded casually to him.

"I just quit, Walter," he said. "Going to hit the road."

"But—"

"You'll make out all right, no matter what you do. I don't even have to wish you good luck."

Then he was off down the aisle, on his way to the tool crib and the plant police and the parking lot and God alone knew where after that, without so much as a handshake or an inclination of his lean frame. Suddenly Walter remembered something: "Hey!" he shouted. But Joe—if he heard him—did not turn around and soon was out of sight.

You never told me about Pop, he wanted to tell Joe, you never answered all the questions I was going to ask you—but even if Joe had not gone for good, Walter would not have known how to say to him all the things that should have been said, the words of gratitude and self-confidence.

When the relief man came a few minutes later to give him a twelve-minute break, he hurried to the bathroom. There, just beyond the big circular sink that could accommodate half a dozen men, he could see out the tilted window to the vast parking lot.

The dull winter light was gloomy and deceptive, and so vague was the air that the dark ranks of massed automobiles was no more than darker blurs against the background of the grey steel fencing and the lowering sky. One of the cars moved, or was it his imagination? But no, the red tail-light dimmed, glowed, dimmed. Joe, the vanishing American, was swinging out of the lot and away from the production line, out of Walter's life and into someone else's, out of the present and into what lay beyond the gate. He was leaving the future to Walter, who now at last could wave his farewell, with his face pressed to the cool window as he watched the little light disappearing from view.

Then he washed the sweat from his face and returned to his work.

Judson Gooding

In this essay Judson Gooding points out that the majority of workers in American business are white-collar employees. He explores the problems of white-collar work and reports on the programs of education, incentive, and promotion that American businesses are using to make white-collar work more satisfying.

THE FRAYING WHITE COLLAR

There are many groups undergoing transitions in America today, but none more rapidly than the country's white-collar workers. The strong mutual loyalty that has traditionally bound white-collar workers and management is rapidly eroding. These workers—clerks, accountants, bookkeepers, secretaries—were once the elite at every plant, the educated people who worked alongside the bosses and were happily convinced that they made all the wheels go around. Now there are platoons of them instead of a privileged few, and instead of talking to the boss they generally communicate with a machine.

The jobs are sometimes broken down into fragmented components, either for the convenience of those machines or so that the poorly educated graduates of big-city high schools can perform them. Despite their air-conditioned, carpeted offices—certainly the most lavish working quarters ever provided employees in mass—the sense of distance and dissociation from management has increased sharply, and the younger white collars are swept by some of the same restlessness and cynicism that afflict their classmates who opted for manual labor. . . . All too often, the keypunch operator spends the workday feeling more like an automaton than a human being.

The new masses

The white-collar worker is caught in the middle—and indeed is chief actor—in one of the most basic of the trends now sweeping the country. This is the trend toward a predominantly service economy. Already, the clerk rather than the man on the production line is the typical American worker. Under the broad definition of the white-collar category used by the Bureau of Labor Statistics—covering the whole sweep from professional and managerial through clerical and sales workers—the white collars outnumber blue-collar workers, by 38 million to 28 million. In this article, FORTUNE has excluded supervisors, proprietors, and degree-holding technicians and engineers—workers with authority over other employees or for committing company funds—and even by this narrower definition white-collar workers total about 19 million. Until the economy slowed down last winter, employment in these categories had been increasing by an average of 3 percent a year.

Now that they are needed by the millions, white-collar workers are also expendable. The lifetime sinecure is rapidly disappearing as management experts figure out yet another way to streamline the job, get in another machine, and cut down overhead. William Gomberg, a former union official and now a professor at the Wharton School of Finance, says, "White collars are where administrators look to save money, for places to fire. It's the law of supply and demand. Once you're in big supply, you're a bum." When an unprofitable division is closed or a big contract slips away to a competitor, layoffs are measured in thousands, and the workers usually hit the streets with no more severance benefits than management feels willing and able to provide.

Member firms of the New York Stock Exchange cut payrolls from 101,314 to 86,123 nonsales employees during the first seven months of 1970—a deep slash of 15,191 persons. In just one grim week in October, Sylvania Electric Products, Inc., announced it was discontinuing semiconductor operations and the Celanese Corp. disclosed it was cutting 2,000 employees, most of them white-collar. Steel companies are reducing office staffs by the thousands. The unemployment rate for white-collar workers, "usually somewhat more impervious to a general rise in joblessness," according to the Bureau of Labor Statistics, rose a full percentage point during the first nine months of this year, from 2.1 to 3.1 percent.

The pay advantage white-collar workers enjoyed when they were a select group has been eroded along with their job security. Until 1920, white-collar workers got between 50 and 100 percent more pay than blue-collar workers, but by 1952 they had fallen 4 percent behind. The pay gap has grown steadily since then. Raises for clerical workers came to 21.9 percent from 1964 to 1969, while factory workers, already ahead, got raises adding up to 26.2 percent. Production workers made an average of $130 a week last year and clerical workers only $105. A Penn Central station agent with twenty-four years of service complains: "New cleaning men make more than I do, counting overtime, although I'm in charge of running the station and handling the cash." Many white-collar workers feel their status has declined as well. A twenty-nine-year-old secretary in a government agency in Washington says, "We're lower people. Down at our level we're peons, that's what they think of you."

To the labor unions that specialize in white-collar organizing, this is a situation that seems ripe with promise. From 1958 to 1968, the number of white-collar union members increased 46 percent to 3,179,000. With white-collar employment increasing over the long range and factory employment stagnant or declining, union leaders see their white-collar drive as the battle for the future—some would say even for survival.

But the unions are not likely to have it all their own way. There is a countertrend working too. These white-collar masses are, after all, sharing the same quarters with management; their grievances and problems, more often than not, are on conspicuous display. Precisely because most white-collar jobs have never been frozen by union-shop rules, management has maximum flexibility for imaginative improvements. There is additional opportunity for management in the fact that three-fifths of the lower-level white-collar jobs are held by women. Since women quit to get married or have babies, turnover runs to 30 percent or more in big white-collar operations such as insurance companies and banks. While the turnover is a major headache, it also provides natural opportunities for rapid promotion. Enlightened managers are able to move employees out of those dull, entry-level jobs quite rapidly.

The company in loco parentis

"Those companies that have thought in terms of careers, that have counselors available, that practice job posting, that have thought about progression—they seem to be on the right track," says Fred K. Foulkes, an assistant professor and specialist in job improvement at the Harvard Graduate School of Business Administration. And with a little imagination and effort, the content of almost any job can be improved. . . . Even now, the techniques of job enrichment are much more often found in white-collar operations than on factory floors. As union organizers continue to make headway among white-collar workers, managers can be expected to intensify these efforts to retain control of their own staffs through improving the jobs. For management, too, the issue is a vital one.

Generalizations about low-level white-collar workers are difficult, because there are pronounced differences not only between those in harsh environments, like New York City or Los Angeles, and gentler settings like Atlanta and Minneapolis. Both age and geography affect attitudes. Because many of them got their jobs when work was hard to find, the older workers feel more obligated to their employers. The younger ones expect a job as a matter of course, and are far more demanding about working conditions. In the smaller cities, younger workers conform more readily, the men tend to have short hair, and girls dress less eccentrically. In a city like Minneapolis, where only 4 percent of the population is black, there are fewer tensions arising from demands for equal opportunity. There is less militancy on other subjects as well, and young workers tend to accept management dictates more readily. Because of these generational and regional differences, inconsistencies abound.

But in the transaction between management and worker, two developments are evident. Old-fashioned loyalty is declining. A twenty-eight-year-old secretary in a New York City bank said, "Loyalty? That's kind of archaic. It's really if you like your job, if it's what you need and what you want.

The job is not loyal to you." At the same time, the younger workers expect extensive services from their employers. They want the customary advantages like good vacations, health coverage, and a low-priced company cafeteria, but beyond these they want company-paid training given on company time, medical care at the office, even counseling. This is especially true in the big urban centers where many beginning jobs are filled by recruits from the ghettos. To help young men and women who have substandard educations and have never learned office behavior, some major employers even offer lessons in comportment and suggestions on dress and personal habits. The extent to which some employees rely on their companies became clear when liberalization of New York's abortion laws was announced and the medical department of a big company received a telephone call the same day asking if an employee could get an abortion at the office.

Robert Feagles, senior vice president for personnel of the First National City Bank, says that in the 1950's employees resisted and resented any intrusion on their lives by the company that employed them. He explains: "Then, it was 'Stay out of my life.' Now, with the sad state of society, with family, churches, and the schools often disqualified, the job and the employer become central. The employer is almost the last resort now. The company is the only entity that is not disqualified."

The company as schoolmaster

The new employees, while expecting much more, often bring much less in the way of work experience, qualifications, even education. In Minneapolis, C. Marvin Mandery, General Mills corporate personnel manager, says much more company training is required for entry-level clerical employees today because "in addition to teaching them their jobs, there is the whole business of teaching them to work." For many, he says, "this is their first exposure to a work situation, where in the past most kids had worked before graduation and their families had expected them to take more responsibility at home."

The need to train new employees is even more pressing in major urban centers like New York. The First National City Bank finds it necessary to run a school system as large as those of some small towns, with more than 6,000 employees taking courses each year at a new complex in Queens. The center has a staff of sixty-five, and its elaborate equipment, worth $800,000, includes teaching machines, closed-circuit television, and video tape recorders. "The city schools are not preparing young people in New York for the business world, either in the use of business equipment, or in attitude," says Norman Willard Jr., First National City's vice president for training. "Some problems of employee performance—error rate, promptness, and the like—we attribute to the deterioration of the school system. The reading level of the new employees is down, and although this should not be a bank problem, we have to run remedial reading courses."

But imaginative companies are making a virtue of necessity and are using their schools to help attract and hold young workers. If the company school, which seems well on the way to becoming a permanent feature of the American corporation, is a reflection on the state of public education, it is also a tribute to management ingenuity. First National City has already moved dozens of its ghetto recruits up the ladder to teller positions and has found them to be loyal and well-motivated employees.

At the Equitable Life Assurance Society in New York, Edward Robie, senior vice president for personnel, says company training was crucial in making a smooth transition to the computer. Electronic data processing represented "a tremendous technical change in our business, comparable in impact to what happened in industry around the turn of the century when assembly lines were started. Now we grow our own programmers." Alma Sykes, a nineteen-year-old receptionist at Equitable who has combined mornings of classes and afternoons of on-the-job training, explains that she came to Equitable because "I wanted to improve myself. I heard about the training program here and I heard it was a good place to work. It is."

An antidote for frustration

The company school is only one of the tools available for turning on the white-collar worker. Promotion is another, and it is a powerful instrument indeed. Promotion simultaneously improves income, enhances security, and raises status, and promotion is what the younger white-collar workers talk about and dream of more than anything else. Lawrence Porto, nineteen, who started as a check sorter at First National City Bank two years ago, says, "I found there was more to the job than I saw at first, more opportunity, after I was there a while, and talked to people, saw how they progressed. In six months I went up to clearance clerk. There was more money and responsibility. That was when I started liking it and planned to stay."

Conversely, if promotions are not readily forthcoming, frustration develops quickly. Federal office managers and supervisors who were interviewed agreed that promotion policy is the biggest single cause of discontent in federal government jobs. After less than two years with the National Aeronautics and Space Administration in Washington, George Hamilton, twenty-seven, is chafing at the civil-service rules that prevent his moving up. He is a communication-equipment operator, which is considered a clerical job. He believes he deserves a higher classification and more pay, but says, "The civil service does not classify the job as technical. I can't get more money unless the job is reclassified." He likes everything about his job except the feeling of being blocked off from moving up.

"Young people coming in aren't going to sit around and wait for promotions," says Mrs. Doris Wilkins, twenty-eight, a wage-and-hours assistant in the Department of Labor, with eleven years of government service. "They have younger ideas, a different approach. There's a lot of job hopping in the lower grades to get more money. It's the only way to get a promotion. It causes a tremendous amount of moves back and forth. The supervisors lose a lot of good employees and they keep on having vacancies."

All too often, the supervisors themselves are impediments to promotion. A reservation sales agent at American Airlines in Los Angeles, Mrs. Adele Velasquez, twenty-three, describes the problem. "Supervisors don't push people upward because of a fear of losing the best people. There is a delaying tactic which is selfish, to protect themselves. If the group looks good, they look good."

Robie at Equitable terms this behavior "feudal parochialism." He suggests that companies should build some kind of reward into the system for promoting good workers. "As it is, the supervisor is penalized by losing good workers. Short-term pressures on management restrict the success of the promotion policy." Equitable has designated promotion specialists who are continually on the lookout for good openings and good people to put into them. The company also tries to keep its managers under pressure to release good workers to other departments for advancement, unless they have suitable opportunities for them. Parochialism is self-defeating, as Cynthia Crotty, twenty, a typist at Equitable, points out. "If the person is not satisfied, he probably won't stay, and the supervisor will lose him anyway. The more good peo-

ple he can promote, the more it's to his credit—it just shows he has trained people well."

Mobility from both ends of the telescope

Atlanta's Retail Credit Co. has made job advancement the central tenet of its corporate philosophy—perhaps because its president, W. Lee Burge, worked his way up from a beginning job in Retail Credit's mail room starting in 1936. He now directs 13,000 clerical, administrative, and field employees in the largest credit-information business in the country (1969 revenues: $161 million). "Our objective," he says, "is to provide good careers and challenge individual abilities." Jim Slade, a thirty-year-old computer programmer who learned his job during the two years he has worked at Retail Credit, sees things in much the same way, looking at the company from the other end of the telescope. He says he expects to be in management within ten years, likes the emphasis on promotions from within, and believes Retail Credit is an outstanding company because it has "outstanding management people—that's because they train their own."

In attempting to engage the interest of white-collar workers, management has a good deal more flexibility than in factories, where the pace is inexorably set by production lines or quota requirements. Office work can often be done at a more individual pace. Hours can be shortened or lengthened, the four-day week can be introduced, and, as noted, the high turnover provides many openings for promotions.

Equitable used its managerial flexibility to conduct a trial of the four-day work week at one of its New York data-processing offices. The experiment produced a drop in error rates of 20.6 percent, with no decrease in production. Employee satisfaction with work hours improved from 53 percent before the trial to 86 percent, and of course the company obtained more efficient use of equipment because of the longer work hours each day.

Any job can be improved

Many of the techniques used to enrich white-collar jobs are similar in principle to those used with blue-collar jobs. The aim is to increase the worker's role in planning the work, increase his responsibility for its execution, and to broaden his job so that he has a complete unit of work rather than a fragment.

American Telephone & Telegraph has perhaps the most extensive experience in the U.S. in improving white-collar jobs. At the urging of the company's personnel director for manpower utilization, Robert N. Ford, managers all over the country have initiated hundreds of job improvements, all based on concepts of Dr. Frederick Herzberg of Case Western Reserve University, who teaches that the job content, the "work itself," is the most important factor in employee morale. In one exercise, which is still in progress at Pacific Telephone in Los Angeles, commercial-division manager J. M. Suozzo increased the responsibility given to service representatives and their authority to make decisions. He brought turnover down from 62 percent for 1969 to 48 percent for the first half of 1970. This meant better service for customers and a saving of $3,800 in training cost for each service representative who was retained instead of replaced. The saving came to $332,000 for the first eight months of this year. By promoting operators more rapidly to service representative, Pacific Telephone cut turnover among operators in one division by 41 percent.

Service representative Mrs. Marsha Lang, twenty-three, said she liked the Los Angeles office changes because before "you didn't know how well you were doing. I didn't understand the changes at first, but now I know it is a program for developing decision-making abilities. The supervisors are letting out more line and giving more freedom." After all, she said, with a touch of pride, "we are the persons between the customer and the computer."

In St. Louis, American Airlines improved the morale, and the commitment, of twenty of its agents who handle the boarding of flights. In so doing, the airline illustrated that improvements can be made in almost any sort of white-collar job. Two agents had been assigned to each flight, under direction of a supervisor. Now one of the agents is designated "flight coordinator" and is responsible for getting the flight into the air, without need to clear any but the most unusual decisions. One flight coordinator delayed a take-off to accommodate twenty passengers from a competing airline that had canceled its flight, judging that the additional revenues would justify the delay. He got the request five minutes before scheduled take-off, held the flight until the twenty were aboard—and was complimented for his decision. An agent summed up his reaction to the job change by saying, "I have more confidence in myself now that I see the confidence management has in me."

The deterioration in white-collar morale is not just a passing phenomenon born of the economic downturn. Opinion Research Corp. of Princeton, New Jersey, has charted responses to questions on job satisfaction from more than 25,000 white-collar employees in eighty-eight major American companies over the years since 1955. Using attitudes during the 1955–65 period as a base, Opinion Research Vice President Alfred Vogel finds that job satisfaction has declined since 1965 in several crucial areas.

Worker satisfaction with job security has dropped by 17 percent and with pay by 45 percent. There has been a 30 percent decline in the belief that companies deal fairly without playing favorites, and a 39 percent decline in the belief that the company will do something about individual problems and complaints. Some of the sharpest declines in white-collar ratings show up on company communication efforts. Workers feel increasingly cut off. But employees rate their immediate supervisors better by 23 percent than in the earlier period for listening to what employees say. They downgrade supervisors by 19 percent on taking action on worker complaints—action that is often beyond a supervisor's power.

"The most neglected group"

Improvement experiments like those at A.T. & T., Equitable, and American Airlines are still the exceptions in white-collar jobs. The majority of such jobs are standing still, if not deteriorating, in relative pay, in status, and in worker satisfaction. Professor Eric Trist of the Wharton School of Finance, a specialist in the impact of technology on social systems, calls white-collar workers "the most neglected group in the U.S." He points out that "the skilled blue-collar worker is a professional and does unprogrammed work. He is getting more and more money and working less and less hours. He's got it made."

Enlightened managers already proclaim that a central concern in any enterprise must be to provide fulfilling, satisfying work for the people who spend so much of their lives inside company walls. More than economic needs must be met. The importance of this concept is reinforced by the fact that the job, dull as it may be, is the most active involvement that many white-collar workers have with the world around them. Few of those interviewed by FORTUNE claimed much interest in reading, in music, in any cultural activity.

There is a terrible, striking contrast between the fun-filled, mobile existence of the young opulents of America as shown on television, and the narrow, constricting, un-fun existence that is the lot of most white-collar workers at the lower job levels. You can't buy much of what television is selling

on the salaries these young workers earn; about all you do is stay at home watching those good things go by on the screen. The result is frustration, sometimes bitterness, even anger. Workers in this stratum cannot but notice that the federally defined poverty standard is climbing toward their level from below, while above them the salary needed to enjoy the glittery aspects of American life soars ever higher, further and further out of reach. For many, the office is the real world, not only a livelihood but a focus of existence. They expect it, somehow, to be more than it has yet become.

DISCUSSION QUESTIONS

"The Self-Made Man in America"

1. Wyllie quotes John C. Van Dyke saying that success in America means financial success. Do you feel that this is still true, or are newer concepts of success replacing that definition? How would Franklin and Mather have reacted to that statement?

2. Wyllie sees the self-made man as a legendary hero. Compare this hero to the traditional heroes of America such as Washington and Lincoln.

3. Was the argument that poverty provides a strong basis for success ever true? What would Michael Harrington think?

4. What connection does Wyllie make between rural areas and success? Does this connection reinforce our belief in the pastoral ideal?

"Proposals to Rich Men"

1. How, according to Cotton Mather, are the rich especially consecrated by God? Is there any belief in this today?

2. What is the reverse corollary to this assumption? Do we believe that?

3. What, in Mather's view, is the best way to success? What are the spiritual components of his assertions?

4. Mather's philosophy has been called "smug." What basis do you see for this?

"The Way to Wealth"

1. What impression of Franklin do you have from this essay? How is he the epitome of the work ethic?

2. What is important to success beyond work?

3. Do people today still believe Franklin's sayings? Cite some examples.

4. What is the most obvious difference between Franklin's and Mather's ideas on wealth?

"Frank Is Offered a Position"

1. How does the Horatio Alger character embody the teachings of Mather and Franklin and the views of Wyllie?

2. Why were these books so popular? Could they be as popular today if rewritten for the times? What virtues does the main character possess? What is the significance of his name?

3. Could anything like this ever happen? How do you react to the individual characters?

"Richard Cory" and "Bewick Finzer"

1. Richard Cory shows us the paradox of wealth. Why are we left wondering about the cause of his suicide?

2. Bewick Finzer is another casualty of success. What happened to his money? What is "the worm of what-was-not"? Is his decline due solely to his financial reversals?

3. Would Mather or Franklin have some advice for Cory or Finzer?

"nobody loses all the time" and "Try, Try Again"

1. What does Uncle Sol have in common with Bewick Finzer? How are they different?

2. Cummings's attitude toward Uncle Sol's financial problems is satirical. However, can you tell what his views are on why people fail?

3. What is the irony of Uncle Sol's splendid funeral? How does the title apply here?

4. Compare Cummings's view of persistence with the McGuffey Reader's advice, especially noting "Time will bring your reward."

"O Youth and Beauty!"

1. What is success to Cash Bentley?

2. What aspects of success are satirized? How is the American dream of success and its reality shown?

3. What is the role of Louise Bentley in the dream of success? Is Cheever's portrait of the suburban housewife realistic or exaggerated?

4. What really causes Cash's depression?

5. What is your reaction to the ending?

"The Invisible Land"

1. Do the poor in America owe their status to the non-pursuit of success? Can anyone succeed who wants to? What does Harrington suggest about the poverty of tens of millions of Americans?

2. Why are they invisible, and could they become visible through an act of will?

3. How might an imaginary conversation proceed between Mather, Franklin, Alger, and Harrington?

4. What is the difference between poverty now and during the 1930s?

"Business—A Profession"

1. Brandeis's speech on business was delivered in 1912—is his advice applicable today? Do you consider business a profession?

2. Brandeis says that good business practices are consistent with successful money-making. Do you agree?

3. Has "big business" become more socially committed since 1912? If so, what factors caused it to change?

"The Rise of the Standard Oil Company"

1. In Tarbell's view, how much of Rockefeller's success is attributed to luck? prudence? craftiness? Was he bound to succeed?

2. Is he the Alger hero? Could his success be duplicated today?

3. Are his actions part of a larger pattern in the dream of success? Are similar actions occurring today?

4. Do Americans admire men like Rockefeller?

"The Stockyards"

1. Although "The Stockyards" appears in a work of fiction, it is based on Sinclair's observations of meat-packing plants. What details would most horrify the American people?

2. What allowed these conditions to exist?

3. What occupational hazards exist today that might remind one of the things described here?

"Tin Lizzie"

1. What image of Ford does Dos Passos develop by using the quotation from the feature writer?

2. Compare and contrast Ford's success to that of Rockefeller. Were any of Ford's business methods similar to those of Rockefeller?

3. How did Ford's rural background influence him? Does Ford fit Wyllie's description of the self-made man?

4. How did Ford deal with the realities of the Depression?

5. What irony does Dos Passos intend in his last paragraph?

"Joe, The Vanishing American"

1. What are the men on the assembly line like? What does Swados suggest about the nature of the blue-collar worker and the nature of blue-collar jobs?

2. Compare Swados's view of the modern assembly line with Dos Passos's description of the early line.

3. Do you agree with Joe that most people get "trapped" in their jobs? How does Joe escape this trap?

4. How does Joe affect Walter? Is he a real or symbolic character?

"The Fraying White Collar"

1. According to Gooding, what problems are white-collar workers currently facing?

2. What are companies doing to make work more attractive and rewarding?

3. Are there any similarities between the workers' attitudes portrayed in Swados's story and those in Gooding's article? What differences are there?

4. It is said that job satisfaction is becoming more important than wages earned. Does Gooding's article confirm that idea? What is your opinion?

SUGGESTED READINGS

ALLEN, FREDERICK LEWIS. *Since Yesterday.* New York, 1940.

BARNUM, P. T. *The Art of Money-Getting.* New York, 1882.

CARNEGIE, ANDREW. *The Gospel of Wealth.* New York, 1892.

DAVIS, REBECCA HARDING. *Life in the Iron Mills.* New York, 1972.

FITZGERALD, F. SCOTT. *The Great Gatsby.* New York, 1925.

HEMINGWAY, ERNEST. *The Sun Also Rises.* New York, 1926.

HOWELLS, WILLIAM DEAN. *The Rise of Silas Lapham*. 1885.

JOSEPHSON, MATTHEW. *The Robber Barons: The Great American Capitalists, 1861–1901*. New York, 1934.

LYNN, KENNETH. *The Dream of Success: A Study of the Modern American Imagination*. Boston, 1955.

MILLER, ARTHUR. *Death of a Salesman*. New York, 1949.

MILLS, C. WRIGHT. *The Power Elite*. New York, 1956.

O'HARA, JOHN. *Appointment in Samarra*. New York, 1934.

SHANNON, DAVID, ed. *The Great Depression*. Englewood Cliffs, 1960.

PART THREE

THE SHAPING
OF THE LAND

THE GARDEN

The pastoral vision, that is, the desire for the simple, direct, pleasant life of nature, has always been a dream in America. Our interest in ecology, hunting, camping, gardening, "westerns," and other film adventures like *Deliverance* shows the appeal of the pastoral for most Americans. Television commercials for cereals, beer, soft drinks, even aspirin and sleeping pills, depict seacoasts, farms, waterfalls, open prairies, and small town family reunions. Though most Americans now live in metropolitan areas, the city does not have the positive image of the rural landscape; in a recent Gallup survey eight out of ten people said they would leave the commotion of the cities if they could. Even names of city suburbs and streets—Park Ridge, Glenside, Lake Forest, Springfield, Chestnut Street, Walnut Lane, Rolling Pass—reflect our desire for the pastoral. As Leo Marx says in *The Machine in the Garden* (1964), "The soft veil of nostalgia that hangs over our urbanized landscape is largely the vestige of the once dominant image of an undefiled green republic, a quiet land of forest, villages, and farm dedicated to the pursuit of happiness."

However, the pastoral dream is more complex than just the worshipping of nature; it is intertwined with the other aspects of the American dream. Jefferson felt that land ownership was crucial for the governing of the country, since small land holders

173

had a special commitment to American ideals and would be independent of influence. "We are a people of cultivators," said de Crèvecoeur in explaining why Americans are strong and free. In addition to being the base for political democracy, the land was believed to give instant success to those who claimed it, a dream reinforced by the first bumper crop on the prairie in 1841. Utopians used land as a basis for their philosophical principles, and thus between 1820 and 1850, when the dream of the fruitfulness of the land was strongest, over one hundred utopian communities were formed. The dream of the garden also permeated the artistic vision of the nineteenth century, as can be seen, for example, in the work of Thomas Cole, a landscape painter of the Hudson River School, and of Albert Bierstadt, whose gloriously romanticized paintings of the West acted as a magnet to those in the cities. American writers have always drawn extensively upon the American landscape in their works. Here, Robert Frost in "The Gift Outright" expresses emphatically the importance of the land to American history and character, and in "Birches" he uses his New England environment as a metaphor for his philosophical ideas. In *Walden,* our most important document of the pastoral experience, Henry David Thoreau analyzes the benefits of living in nature and, in this passage, explains how one finds solitude. Finally, Mark Twain, whose intimate knowledge of the landscape made him among the first truly American writers, captures the boredom and the excitement in a small riverfront town before the Civil War.

But the dream of the garden often turned into a harsh reality when the land was unaccommodating, as the utopians discovered. The typical commune lasted ten months as the members' inexperience at working the land provided a meager harvest and a bleak winter. The dream was further defiled by land speculators and the arrival of the railroad, the "machine in the garden," as Leo Marx calls it. Then in the 1880s, the cornucopian image of the land was shattered when grasshoppers, droughts, blizzards, low wheat prices, and high freight rates seemed to be in collusion. Still, a half century later, John Steinbeck's protest in *Grapes of Wrath* against the poverty of the Great Depression derives much of its power from his images of the waste and destruction of the land, the desecration of the pastoral ideal.

Though today an urban America looks back nostalgically to the bliss of the small town with its imagined simplicity and neighborliness, writers like Sherwood Anderson and Willie Morris reveal the mixed blessings of small town life. In Anderson's story "Sophistication," from *Winesburg, Ohio,* the beauty of the slower paced life and country pleasures of a small town is tempered by the knowledge that a young man like George Willard must leave the town to realize his dreams. Morris writes affectionately about his home town in Mississippi, remembering the delights it held for him as a boy, but at the same time realizing the dehumanizing effect the town's racist attitudes had on its black citizens.

THE FRONTIER

Two statements made nearly sixty years apart, one at the popular beginning of the frontier and the other at its theoretical closing, suggest the frontier's importance to American history. In 1837 Horace Greely issued his renowned slogan, "Go West, young man," in response to the pressures of poverty and unemployment in that year. But the most important statement about the importance of the frontier was made in 1893 by Frederick Jackson Turner. Turner's thesis was that the frontier had democratized America by providing an abundance of free land for yeoman farmers to settle and work independently, and by allowing thousands of men without means a place to live away from the teeming cities;

that, in fact, the frontier had been a "safety valve" in times of panic and depression. Both the safety-valve idea and the idea that the free land of the frontier formed the basis of American democracy have been questioned by modern historians. It is doubtful, for example, that the unemployed in the cities had either the money for transport to the West or the skills to make the land productive once they got there. Nevertheless, the idea of the frontier as a place where democracy flourished, as the hope and opportunity for immigrants and new generations of Americans, began with Jefferson, continued through decades of settlement, and is believed by many Americans today.

What captured the imagination of Americans most about the frontier were the stories of Wild West heroes, both real and fictional. James Fenimore Cooper's Natty Bumppo, the first of a long line of noble, strong, clear-eyed sharp-shooters, appeared in five Leather-stocking Tales, beginning with *The Pioneer* (1823) and ending with what many consider Cooper's best book, *The Deerslayer* (1841). Biographies and stories of real pioneers like Kit Carson, Daniel Boone, and Davy Crockett (often bearing little resemblance to the men or their exploits) also were very popular. But probably the most successful and most widespread publications were the dime novels, begun by Erastus Beadle in 1860. Popular into the 1890s and numbering in the thousands of titles, the dime novel began the tradition of the adventurous western which later became so popular in movies and on television. Two of the most famous dime novel characters, Deadwood Dick and Calamity Jane, are introduced in chapter one of Edward L. Wheeler's *Deadwood Dick on Deck,* along with the author's strange mixture of slang and formal speech, his confusion over names, and his obvious sentimentality. In reaction to the stereotyped western sheriff-meets-gunfighter, Stephen Crane parodies that tradition in his 1895 story "The Bride Comes to Yellow Sky." Last in this section, E. E. Cummings, a modern poet, looks back into America's past and evokes a sense of sadness at the passing of a hero and a way of life in "Buffalo Bill's."

As the legendary heroes of the forest and frontier clashed with native Indian settlers of America, pushing them farther and farther west, the frontiersman's dream of new game, unspoiled land, and "elbow room" became a nightmare of humiliation and massacre for the Indian. Cooper's adventure stories show this conflict clearly—though from the viewpoint of the dominant white man. It is sadly appropriate that Turner's date of the closing of the frontier, 1890, coincides with the Battle of Wounded Knee, the final extermination of the Indian as a threat.

Other harsh views of the frontier can be seen in Francis Parkman's description of frontier travel and Hamlin Garland's story of downtrodden farmers in "Under the Lion's Paw." A terse summary of reality for many frontier farmers is found in "Jason Edward," another Hamlin Garland story: "So this is the reality of the dream! This is the homestead on the Golden West, embowered in tears beside the purling brook! A shanty on the barren plain, hot and lone as a desert. My God!"

That modern Americans yearn for the frontier or the frontier spirit is suggested in the appeal of John Kennedy's concept of a New Frontier and the challenge of space exploration. But since discovering unknown territory like space now depends on science and technology, the frontiers today are in fields like medicine (heart and cancer research), aeronautical engineering, and oceanographic research, and the pioneer hero works with a team of experts.

THE CITY

By 1900 cities towered over the landscape, and Americans acknowledged the closing of the frontier. Yet, as huge numbers fled from rural areas to the cities, attracted by the dream of continual excitement, variety, anonymity, success, and a sophisticated life style, Americans, as Peter Schrag says in "The End of Innocence," never fully accepted the urbanization of America. The belief that cities are centers of corruption and decay, the reluctance to improve cities, and the flight to the suburbs may be the consequences of our commitment to the pastoral ideal. The American dream, therefore, presents a dilemma: on the one hand, opportunities for success are greatest in the city; yet, on the other hand, peace of mind and independence are to be found in the rural landscape. Many Americans have tried to resolve the dilemma by participating in both worlds, with a job in the city and a home or second home in the country, but this solution does not solve the basic problems troubling the cities. Only a fundamental change in the way Americans view cities—that is, a change in the American dream—will produce significant improvements in our new urban landscape.

The selections in this section show the variety of response to the city experience. Walt Whitman celebrates the magnificence of New York, while Carl Sandburg explores the paradox of Chicago—vital and exciting, yet brutal and dehumanizing. In "Mrs. Manstey's View," written in 1891, Edith Wharton portrays the loneliness and powerlessness of a poor city dweller. In contrast, Joan Didion explains the magnetism of New York for the young and aspiring in her essay. John Updike and Bennett Berger explore the phenomenon of suburbia through fiction and sociology. Updike's Rabbit Angstrom gives us a glimpse of the tensions and conflicts felt by a lower-middle-class working-man as he comes home to the suburbs from his work in the city. And Berger's insightful essay corrects some of the half-truths about suburbs which have been accepted on faith by most observers of modern American life.

THE GARDEN

Thomas P. Rossiter, **Opening of the Wilderness.** *Courtesy Museum of Fine Arts, Boston.*

Robert Frost

Robert Frost (1874–1963), perhaps the most-renowned twentieth-century American poet and four-time winner of the Pulitzer Prize, was born in San Francisco, but at eleven moved back to New England where nine generations of forebears had lived. He was a footloose youth, a college dropout who tramped around the country, a sometime farmer, and a poet who did not achieve popularity until he was thirty-nine. "The Gift Outright" considers the importance of the land to the shaping of the American character, while "Birches" uses nature as a metaphor for the poet's ideas.

THE GIFT OUTRIGHT

The land was ours before we were the
    land's.
She was our land more than a hundred
    years
Before we were her people. She was ours
In Massachusetts, in Virginia,
But we were England's, still colonials,
Possessing what we still were unpossessed
    by,
Possessed by what we now no more
    possessed.
Something we were withholding made us
    weak
Until we found out that it was ourselves
We were withholding from our land of
    living,
And forthwith found salvation in surrender.
Such as we were we gave ourselves outright
(The deed of gift was many deeds of war)
To the land vaguely realizing westward,

But still unstoried, artless, unenhanced,
Such as she was, such as she would become.

BIRCHES

When I see birches bend to left and right
Across the lines of straighter darker trees,
I like to think some boy's been swinging
    them.
But swinging doesn't bend them down to
    stay
As ice storms do. Often you must have seen
    them
Loaded with ice a sunny winter morning
After a rain. They click upon themselves
As the breeze rises, and turn many-colored
As the stir cracks and crazes their enamel.
Soon the sun's warmth makes them shed
    crystal shells
Shattering and avalanching on the snow
    crust—
Such heaps of broken glass to sweep away
You'd think the inner dome of heaven had
    fallen.
They are dragged to the withered bracken
    by the load,
And they seem not to break; though once
    they are bowed
So low for long, they never right themselves:
You may see their trunks arching in the
    woods
Years afterwards, trailing their leaves on the
    ground
Like girls on hands and knees that throw
    their hair
Before them over their heads to dry in the
    sun.
But I was going to say when Truth broke in

With all her matter of fact about the ice
storm,
I should prefer to have some boy bend them
As he went out and in to fetch the cows—
Some boy too far from town to learn base-
ball,
Whose only play was what he found him-
self,
Summer or winter, and could play alone.
One by one he subdued his father's trees
By riding them down over and over again
Until he took the stiffness out of them,
And not one but hung limp, not one was
left
For him to conquer. He learned all there
was
To learn about not launching out too soon
And so not carrying the tree away
Clear to the ground. He always kept his
poise
To the top branches, climbing carefully
With the same pains you use to fill a cup
Up to the brim, and even above the brim.
Then he flung outward, feet first, with a
swish,
Kicking his way down through the air to
the ground.
So was I once myself a swinger of birches.
And so I dream of going back to be.
It's when I'm weary of considerations,
And life is too much like a pathless wood
Where your face burns and tickles with the
cobwebs
Broken across it, and one eye is weeping
From a twig's having lashed across it open.
I'd like to get away from earth awhile
And then come back to it and begin over.
May no fate willfully misunderstand me
And half grant what I wish and snatch me
away
Not to return. Earth's the right place for
love:
I don't know where it's likely to go better.
I'd like to go by climbing a birch tree,
And climb black branches up a snow-white
trunk
Toward heaven, till the tree could bear no
more,
But dipped its top and set me down again.

That would be good both going and coming
back.
One could do worse than be a swinger of
birches.

Henry David Thoreau

*Thoreau went to Walden Pond near Con-
cord, Massachusetts, in 1845 for a two-year
experiment to understand the value and relationship of nature to mankind. In Walden
he suggests an alternative life style for those
who "lead lives of quiet desperation." Thoreau expresses the ideal of pastoral beauty
perhaps better than any other American
writer. (Thoreau is also discussed on page
13.)*

SOLITUDE

This is a delicious evening, when the
whole body is one sense, and imbibes delight through every pore. I go and come
with a strange liberty in Nature, a part of
herself. As I walk along the stony shore of
the pond in my shirt sleeves, though it is
cool as well as cloudy and windy, and I see
nothing special to attract me, all the elements are unusually congenial to me. The
bullfrogs trump to usher in the night, and
the note of the whippoorwill is borne on
the rippling wind from over the water.
Sympathy with the fluttering alder and pop-
lar leaves almost takes away my breath; yet,
like the lake, my serenity is rippled but not
ruffled. These small waves raised by the
evening wind are as remote from storm as
the smooth reflecting surface. Though it is
now dark, the wind still blows and roars in
the wood, the waves still dash, and some
creatures lull the rest with their notes. The
repose is never complete. The wildest animals do not repose, but seek their prey now;
the fox, and skunk, and rabbit, now roam
the fields and woods without fear. They are

Nature's watchmen,—links which connect the days of animated life.

When I return to my house I find that visitors have been there and left their cards, either a bunch of flowers, or a wreath of evergreen, or a name in pencil on a yellow walnut leaf or a chip. They who come rarely to the woods take some little piece of the forest into their hands to play with by the way, which they leave, either intentionally or accidentally. One has peeled a willow wand, woven it into a ring, and dropped it on my table. I could always tell if visitors had called in my absence, either by the bended twigs or grass, or the print of their shoes, and generally of what sex or age or quality they were by some slight trace left, as a flower dropped, or a bunch of grass plucked and thrown away, even as far off as the railroad, half a mile distant, or by the lingering odor of a cigar or pipe. Nay, I was frequently notified of the passage of a traveller along the highway sixty rods off by the scent of his pipe.

There is commonly sufficient space about us. Our horizon is never quite at our elbows. The thick wood is not just at our door, nor the pond, but somewhat is always clearing, familiar and worn by us, appropriated and fenced in some way, and reclaimed from Nature. For what reason have I this vast range and circuit, some square miles of unfrequented forest, for my privacy, abandoned to me by men? My nearest neighbor is a mile distant, and no house is visible from any place but the hill-tops within half a mile of my own. I have my horizon bounded by woods all to myself; a distant view of the railroad where it touches the pond on the one hand, and of the fence which skirts the woodland road on the other. But for the most part it is as solitary where I live as on the prairies. It is as much Asia or Africa as New England. I have, as it were, my own sun and moon and stars, and a little world all to myself. At night there was never a traveller passed my house, or knocked at my door, more than if I were the first or last man; unless it were in the spring, when at long intervals some came from the village to fish for pouts,—they plainly fished much more in the Walden Pond of their own natures, and baited their hooks with darkness,—but they soon retreated, usually with light baskets, and left "the world to darkness and to me," and the black kernel of the night was never profaned by any human neighborhood. I believe that men are generally still a little afraid of the dark, though the witches are all hung, and Christianity and candles have been introduced.

Yet I experienced sometimes that the most sweet and tender, the most innocent and encouraging society may be found in any natural object, even for the poor misanthrope and most melancholy man. There can be no very black melancholy to him who lives in the midst of Nature and has his senses still. There was never yet such a storm but it was Æolian music to a healthy and innocent ear. Nothing can rightly compel a simple and brave man to a vulgar sadness. While I enjoy the friendship of the seasons I trust that nothing can make life a burden to me. The gentle rain which waters my beans and keeps me in the house to-day is not drear and melancholy, but good for me too. Though it prevents my hoeing them, it is of far more worth than my hoeing. If it should continue so long as to cause the seeds to rot in the ground and destroy the potatoes in the low lands, it would still be good for the grass on the uplands, and, being good for the grass, it would be good for me. Sometimes, when I compare myself with other men, it seems as if I were more favored by the gods than they, beyond any deserts that I am conscious of; as if I had a warrant and surety at their hands which my fellows have not, and were especially guided and guarded. I do not flatter myself, but if it be possible they flatter me. I have never felt lonesome, or in the least oppressed by a sense of solitude, but once, and that was a few weeks after I came to the woods, when, for an hour, I doubted if the near neighborhood of man was not essential to a serene and healthy life. To be alone was something unpleasant. But I was at the same time conscious of a slight insanity in my mood, and seemed to foresee my recovery. In the midst of a gentle rain while these thoughts prevailed, I was suddenly sensible of such sweet and beneficent society in Nature, in the very pattering of the drops, and in every sound and sight around my house, an infinite and unaccountable friendliness all at once like an atmosphere sustaining me, as made the fancied advantages of human neighborhood insignificant, and I have never thought of them since. Every little pine needle expanded and swelled with sympathy and befriended me. I was so distinctly made aware of the presence of something kindred to me, even in scenes which we are accustomed to call wild and dreary, and also that the nearest of blood to me and humanest was not a person nor a villager, that I thought no place could ever be strange to me again.—

"Mourning untimely consumes the sad;
    Few are their days in the land of the
        living,
Beautiful daughter of Toscar."

Some of my pleasantest hours were during the long rain storms in the spring or fall, which confined me to the house for the afternoon as well as the forenoon, soothed by their ceaseless roar and pelting; when an early twilight ushered in a long evening in which many thoughts had time to take root and unfold themselves. In those driving north-east rains which tried the village houses so, when the maids stood ready with mop and pail in front entries to keep the deluge out, I sat behind my door in my little house, which was all entry, and thoroughly enjoyed its protection. In one heavy thunder shower the lightning struck a large pitch-pine across the pond, making a very conspicuous and perfectly regular spiral groove from top to bottom, an inch or more deep, and four or five inches wide, as you would groove a walking-stick. I passed it

again the other day, and was struck with awe on looking up and beholding that mark, now more distinct than ever, where a terrific and resistless bolt came down out of the harmless sky eight years ago. Men frequently say to me, "I should think you would feel lonesome down there, and want to be nearer to folks, rainy and snowy days and nights especially." I am tempted to reply to such,—This whole earth which we inhabit is but a point in space. How far apart, think you, dwell the two most distant inhabitants of yonder star, the breadth of whose disk cannot be appreciated by our instruments? Why should I feel lonely? is not our planet in the Milky Way? This which you put seems to me not to be the most important question. What sort of space is that which separates a man from his fellows and makes him solitary? I have found that no exertion of the legs can bring two minds much nearer to one another. What do we want most to dwell near to? Not to many men surely, the depot, the post-office, the bar-room, the meeting-house, the school-house, the grocery, Beacon Hill, or the Five Points, where men most congregate, but to the perennial source of our life, when in all our experience we have found that to issue, as the willow stands near the water and sends out its roots in that direction. This will vary with different natures, but this is the place where a wise man will dig his cellar.

Mark Twain

Mark Twain, pseudonym of Samuel Langhorne Clemens (1835–1910), America's greatest humorist, was a complex personality who wrote boys' adventure books like Tom Sawyer, *far more involved commentaries on society like his most famous novel,* Huckleberry Finn, *essays, journalism, and bitter satire. Twain's fondness for the river towns of his youth and especially for the river itself permeates his writing. He did realize "the boys' ambition" and became a river pilot, which he remembered as the happiest time of his life, but the Civil War ended river trade, and Twain was forced to seek a new profession—writing.*

THE BOYS' AMBITION

When I was a boy, there was but one permanent ambition among my comrades in our village on the west bank of the Mississippi River. That was, to be a steamboatman. We had transient ambitions of other sorts, but they were only transient. When a circus came and went, it left us all burning to become clowns; the first negro minstrel show that came to our section left us all suffering to try that kind of life; now and then we had a hope that if we lived and were good, God would permit us to be pirates. These ambitions faded out, each in its turn; but the ambition to be a steamboatman always remained.

Once a day a cheap, gaudy packet arrived upward from St. Louis, and another downward from Keokuk. Before these events, the day was glorious with expectancy; after them, the day was a dead and empty thing. Not only the boys, but the whole village, felt this. After all these years I can picture that old time to myself now, just as it was then: the white town drowsing in the sunshine of a summer's morning; the streets empty, or pretty nearly so; one or two clerks sitting in front of the Water Street stores, with their splint-bottomed chairs tilted back against the wall, chins on breasts, hats slouched over their faces, asleep—with shingle-shavings enough around to show what broke them down; a sow and a litter of pigs loafing along the sidewalk, doing a good business in watermelon rinds and seeds; two or three lonely little freight piles scattered about the "levee;" a pile of "skids" on the slope of the stone-paved wharf, and the fragrant town drunkard asleep in the shadow of them; two or three wood flats at the head of the wharf, but nobody to listen to the peaceful lapping of the wavelets against

them; the great Mississippi, the majestic, the magnificent Mississippi, rolling its mile-wide tide along, shining in the sun; the dense forest away on the other side; the "point" above the town, and the "point" below, bounding the river-glimpse and turning it into a sort of sea, and withal a very still and brilliant and lonely one. Presently a film of dark smoke appears above one of those remote "points;" instantly a negro drayman, famous for his quick eye and prodigous voice, lifts up the cry, "S-t-e-a-m-boat a-comin'!" and the scene changes! The town drunkard stirs, the clerks wake up, a furious clatter of drays follows, every house and store pours out a human contribution, and all in a twinkling the dead town is alive and moving. Drays, carts, men, boys, all go hurrying from many quarters to a common centre, the wharf. Assembled there, the people fasten their eyes upon the coming boat as upon a wonder they are seeing for the first time. And the boat *is* rather a handsome sight, too. She is long and sharp and trim and pretty; she has two tall, fancy-topped chimneys, with a gilded device of some kind swung between them; a fanciful pilot-house, all glass and "gingerbread," perched on top of the "texas" deck behind them; the paddle-boxes are gorgeous with a picture or with gilded rays above the boat's name; the boiler deck, the hurricane deck, and the texas deck are fenced and ornamented with clean white railings; there is a flag gallantly flying from the jack-staff; the furnace doors are open and the fires glaring bravely; the upper decks are black with passengers; the captain stands by the big bell, calm, imposing, the envy of all; great volumes of the blackest smoke are rolling and tumbling out of the chimneys—a husbanded grandeur created with a bit of pitch pine just before arriving at a town; the crew are grouped on the forecastle; the broad stage is run far out over the port bow, and an envied deck-hand stands picturesquely on the end of it with a coil of rope in his hand; the pent steam is screaming through the gauge-cocks; the captain lifts his hand, a bell rings, the wheels stop; then they turn back, churning the water to foam, and the steamer is at rest. Then such a scramble as there is to get aboard, and to get ashore, and to take in freight and to discharge freight, all at one and the same time; and such a yelling and cursing as the mates facilitate it all with! Ten minutes later the steamer is under way again, with no flag on the jack-staff and no black smoke issuing from the chimneys. After ten more minutes the town is dead again, and the town drunkard asleep by the skids once more.

My father was a justice of the peace, and I supposed he possessed the power of life and death over all men and could hang anybody that offended him. This was distinction enough for me as a general thing; but the desire to be a steamboatman kept intruding, nevertheless. I first wanted to be a cabin-boy, so that I could come out with a white apron on and shake a table-cloth over the side, where all my old comrades could see me; later I thought I would rather be the deck-hand who stood on the end of the stage-plank with the coil of rope in his hand, because he was particularly conspicuous. But these were only day-dreams,—they were too heavenly to be contemplated as real possibilities. By and by one of our boys went away. He was not heard of for a long time. At last he turned up as apprentice engineer or "striker" on a steamboat. This thing shook the bottom out of all my Sunday-school teachings. That boy had been notoriously worldly, and I just the reverse; yet he was exalted to this eminence, and I left in obscurity and misery. There was nothing generous about this fellow in his greatness. He would always manage to have a rusty bolt to scrub while his boat tarried at our town, and he would sit on the inside guard and scrub it, where we could all see him and envy him and loathe him. And whenever his boat was laid up he would come home and swell around the town in his blackest and greasiest clothes, so that nobody could help remembering that he

was a steamboatman; and he used all sorts of steamboat technicalities in his talk, as if he were so used to them that he forgot common people could not understand them. He would speak of the "labboard" side of a horse in an easy, natural way that would make one wish he was dead. And he was always talking about "St. Looy" like an old citizen; he would refer casually to occasions when he "was coming down Fourth Street," or when he was "passing by the Planter's House," or when there was a fire and he took a turn on the brakes of "the old Big Missouri;" and then he would go on and lie about how many towns the size of ours were burned down there that day. Two or three of the boys had long been persons of consideration among us because they had been to St. Louis once and had a vague general knowledge of its wonders, but the day of their glory was over now. They lapsed into a humble silence, and learned to disappear when the ruthless "cub"—engineer approached. This fellow had money, too, and hair oil. Also an ignorant silver watch and a showy brass watch chain. He wore a leather belt and used no suspenders. If ever a youth was cordially admired and hated by his comrades, this one was. No girl could withstand his charms. He "cut out" every boy in the village. When his boat blew up at last, it diffused a tranquil contentment among us such as we had not known for months. But when he came home the next week, alive, renowned, and appeared in church all battered up and bandaged, a shining hero, stared at and wondered over by everybody, it seemed to us that the partiality of Providence for an undeserving reptile had reached a point where it was open to criticism.

This creature's career could produce but one result, and it speedily followed. Boy after boy managed to get on the river. The minister's son became an engineer. The doctor's and the post-master's sons became "mud clerks," the wholesale liquor dealer's son became a bar-keeper on a boat; four sons of the chief merchant, and two sons of the county judge became pilots. Pilot was the grandest position of all. The pilot, even in those days of trivial wages, had a princely salary—from a hundred and fifty to two hundred and fifty dollars a month, and no board to pay. Two months of his wages would pay a preacher's salary for a year. Now some of us were left disconsolate. We could not get on the river—at least our parents would not let us.

So by and by I ran away. I said I never would come home again till I was a pilot and could come in glory. But somehow I could not manage it. I went meekly aboard a few of the boats that lay packed together like sardines at the long St. Louis wharf, and very humbly inquired for the pilots, but got only a cold shoulder and short words from mates and clerks. I had to make the best of this sort of treatment for the time being, but I had comforting day-dreams of a future when I should be a great and honored pilot, with plenty of money, and could kill some of these mates and clerks and pay for them.

Sherwood Anderson

Sherwood Anderson (1876–1941) based his book Winesburg, Ohio *on his own experiences in Clyde, Ohio. Anderson's description of a small town at play is a classic. The stories focus on the frustrations of characters limited by their own personalities and the narrowness of the small town. George Willard, a young newspaper reporter, comes to manhood in Winesburg with feelings of restlessness and loneliness made more acute by his environment.*

SOPHISTICATION

It was early evening of a day in the late fall and the Winesburg County Fair had brought crowds of country people into town. The day had been clear and the night came on warm and pleasant. On the Trun-
ion Pike, where the road after it left town stretched away between berry fields now covered with dry brown leaves, the dust from passing wagons arose in clouds. Children, curled into little balls, slept on the straw scattered on wagon beds. Their hair was full of dust and their fingers black and sticky. The dust rolled away over the fields and the departing sun set it ablaze with colors.

In the main street of Winesburg crowds filled the stores and the sidewalks. Night came on, horses whinnied, the clerks in the stores ran madly about, children became lost and cried lustily, an American town worked terribly at the task of amusing itself.

Pushing his way through the crowds in Main Street, young George Willard concealed himself in the stairway leading to Doctor Reefy's office and looked at the people. With feverish eyes he watched the faces drifting past under the store lights. Thoughts kept coming into his head and he did not want to think. He stamped impatiently on the wooden steps and looked sharply about. "Well, is she going to stay with him all day? Have I done all this waiting for nothing?" he muttered.

George Willard, the Ohio village boy, was fast growing into manhood and new thoughts had been coming into his mind. All that day, amid the jam of people at the Fair, he had gone about feeling lonely. He was about to leave Winesburg to go away to some city where he hoped to get work on a city newspaper and he felt grown up. The mood that had taken possession of him was a thing known to men and unknown to boys. He felt old and a little tired. Memories awoke in him. To his mind his new sense of maturity set him apart, made of him a half-tragic figure. He wanted someone to understand that feeling that had taken possession of him after his mother's death.

There is a time in the life of every boy when he for the first time takes the backward view of life. Perhaps that is the moment when he crosses the line into manhood. The boy is walking through the street of his town. He is thinking of the future and of the figure he will cut in the world. Ambitions and regrets awake within him. Suddenly something happens; he stops under a tree and waits as for a voice calling his name. Ghosts of old things creep into his consciousness; the voices outside of himself whisper a message concerning the limitations of life. From being quite sure of himself and his future he becomes not at all sure. If he be an imaginative boy a door is torn open and for the first time he looks out upon the world, seeing, as though they marched in procession before him, the countless figures of men who before his time have come out of nothingness into the world, lived their lives and again disappeared into nothingness. The sadness of sophistication has come to the boy. With a little gasp he sees himself as merely a leaf blown by the wind through the streets of his village. He knows that in spite of all the stout talk of his fellows he must live and die in uncertainty, a thing blown by the winds, a thing destined like corn to wilt in the sun. He shivers and looks eagerly about. The eighteen years he has lived seem but a moment, a breathing space in the long march of humanity. Already he hears death calling. With all his heart he wants to come close to some other human, touch someone with his hands, be touched by the hand of another. If he prefers that the other be a woman, that is because he believes that a woman will be gentle, that she will understand. He wants, most of all, understanding.

When the moment of sophistication came to George Willard his mind turned to Helen White, the Winesburg banker's daughter. Always he had been conscious of the girl growing into womanhood as he grew into manhood. Once on a summer night when he was eighteen, he had walked with her on a country road and in her presence had given way to an impulse to boast, to make himself appear big and significant in her eyes. Now he wanted to see her for another purpose. He wanted to tell her of the new impulses that had come to him. He had tried to make her think of him as a man when he knew nothing of manhood and now he wanted to be with her and to try to make her feel the change he believed had taken place in his nature.

As for Helen White, she also had come to a period of change. What George felt, she in her young woman's way felt also. She was no longer a girl and hungered to reach into the grace and beauty of womanhood. She had come home from Cleveland, where she was attending college, to spend a day at the Fair. She also had begun to have memories. During the day she sat at the grandstand with a young man, one of the instructors from the college, who was a guest of her mother's. The young man was of a pedantic turn of mind and she felt at once he would not do for her purpose. At the Fair she was glad to be seen in his company as he was well dressed and a stranger. She knew that the fact of his presence would create an impression. During the day she was happy, but when night came on she began to grow restless. She wanted to drive the instructor away, to get out of his presence. While they sat together in the grandstand and while the eyes of former schoolmates were upon them, she paid so much attention to her escort that he grew interested. "A scholar needs money. I should marry a woman with money," he mused.

Helen White was thinking of George Willard even as he wandered gloomily through the crowds thinking of her. She remembered the summer evening when they had walked together and wanted to walk with him again. She thought that the months she had spent in the city, the going to theaters and the seeing of great crowds wandering in lighted thoroughfares, had changed her profoundly. She wanted him to feel and be conscious of the change in her nature.

The summer evening together that had left its mark on the memory of both the young man and woman had, when looked at quite sensibly, been rather stupidly spent.

They had walked out of town along a country road. Then they had stopped by a fence near a field of young corn and George had taken off his coat and let it hang on his arm. "Well, I've stayed here in Winesburg—yes—I've not yet gone away but I'm growing up," he had said. "I've been reading books and I've been thinking. I'm going to try to amount to something in life.

"Well," he explained, "that isn't the point. Perhaps I'd better quit talking."

The confused boy put his hand on the girl's arm. His voice trembled. The two started to walk back along the road toward town. In his desperation George boasted, "I'm going to be a big man, the biggest that ever lived here in Winesburg," he declared. "I want you to do something, I don't know what. Perhaps it is none of my business. I want you to try to be different from other women. You see the point. It's none of my business I tell you. I want you to be a beautiful woman. You see what I want."

The boy's voice failed and in silence the two came back into town and went along the street to Helen White's house. At the gate he tried to say something impressive. Speeches he had thought out came into his head, but they seemed utterly pointless. "I thought—I used to think—I had it in my mind you would marry Seth Richmond. Now I know you won't," was all he could find to say as she went through the gate and toward the door of her house.

On the warm fall evening as he stood in the stairway and looked at the crowd drifting through Main Street, George thought of the talk beside the field of young corn and was ashamed of the figure he had made of himself. In the street the people surged up and down like cattle confined to a pen. Buggies and wagons almost filled the narrow thoroughfare. A band played and small boys raced along the sidewalk, diving between the legs of men. Young men with shining red faces walked awkwardly about with girls on their arms. In a room above one of the stores, where a dance was to be held, the fiddlers tuned their instruments.

The broken sounds floated down through an open window and out across the murmur of voices and the loud blare of the horns of the band. The medley of sounds got on young Willard's nerves. Everywhere, on all sides, the sense of crowding, moving life closed in about him. He wanted to run away by himself and think. "If she wants to stay with that fellow she may. Why should I care? What difference does it make to me?" he growled and went along Main Street and through Hern's Grocery into a side street.

George felt so utterly lonely and dejected that he wanted to weep but pride made him walk rapidly along, swinging his arms. He came to Wesley Moyer's livery barn and stopped in the shadows to listen to a group of men who talked of a race Wesley's stallion, Tony Tip, had won at the Fair during the afternoon. A crowd had gathered in front of the barn and before the crowd walked Wesley, prancing up and down and boasting. He held a whip in his hand and kept tapping the ground. Little puffs of dust arose in the lamplight. "Hell, quit your talking," Wesley exclaimed. "I wasn't afraid, I knew I had 'em beat all the time. I wasn't afraid."

Ordinarily George Willard would have been intensely interested in the boasting of Moyer, the horseman. Now it made him angry. He turned and hurried away along the street. "Old windbag," he sputtered. "Why does he want to be bragging? Why don't he shut up?"

George went into a vacant lot and, as he hurried along, fell over a pile of rubbish. A nail protruding from an empty barrel tore his trousers. He sat down on the ground and swore. With a pin he mended the torn place and then arose and went on. "I'll go to Helen White's house, that's what I'll do. I'll walk right in. I'll say that I want to see her. I'll walk right in and sit down, that's what I'll do," he declared, climbing over a fence and beginning to run.

On the veranda of Banker White's house

Helen was restless and distraught. The instructor sat between the mother and daughter. His talk wearied the girl. Although he had also been raised in an Ohio town, the instructor began to put on the airs of the city. He wanted to appear cosmopolitan. "I like the chance you have given me to study the background out of which most of our girls come," he declared. "It was good of you, Mrs. White, to have me down for the day." He turned to Helen and laughed. "Your life is still bound up with the life of this town?" he asked. "There are people here in whom you are interested?" To the girl his voice sounded pompous and heavy.

Helen arose and went into the house. At the door leading to a garden at the back she stopped and stood listening. Her mother began to talk. "There is no one here fit to associate with a girl of Helen's breeding," she said.

Helen ran down a flight of stairs at the back of the house and into the garden. In the darkness she stopped and stood trembling. It seemed to her that the world was full of meaningless people saying words. Afire with eagerness she ran through a garden gate and, turning a corner by the banker's barn, went into a little side street. "George! Where are you, George?" she cried, filled with nervous excitement. She stopped running, and leaned against a tree to laugh hysterically. Along the dark little street came George Willard, still saying words. "I'm going to walk right into her house. I'll go right in and sit down," he declared as he came up to her. He stopped and stared stupidly. "Come on," he said and took hold of her hand. With hanging heads they walked away along the street under the trees. Dry leaves rustled under foot. Now that he had found her George wondered what he had better do and say.

At the upper end of the Fair Ground, in Winesburg, there is a half decayed old grand-stand. It has never been painted and the boards are all warped out of shape. The Fair Ground stands on top of a low hill rising out of the valley of Wine Creek and from the grand-stand one can see at night, over a cornfield, the lights of the town reflected against the sky.

George and Helen climbed the hill to the Fair Ground, coming by the path past Waterworks Pond. The feeling of loneliness and isolation that had come to the young man in the crowded streets of his town was both broken and intensified by the presence of Helen. What he felt was reflected in her.

In youth there are always two forces fighting in people. The warm unthinking little animal struggles against the thing that reflects and remembers, and the older, the more sophisticated thing had possession of George Willard. Sensing his mood, Helen walked beside him filled with respect. When they got to the grand-stand they climbed up under the roof and sat down on one of the long bench-like seats.

There is something memorable in the experience to be had by going into a fair ground that stands at the edge of a Middle Western town on a night after the annual fair has been held. The sensation is one never to be forgotten. On all sides are ghosts, not of the dead, but of living people. Here, during the day just passed, have come the people pouring in from the town and the country around. Farmers with their wives and children and all the people from the hundreds of little frame houses have gathered within these board walls. Young girls have laughed and men with beards have talked of the affairs of their lives. The place has been filled to overflowing with life. It has itched and squirmed with life and now it is night and the life has all gone away. The silence is almost terrifying. One conceals oneself standing silently beside the trunk of a tree and what there is of a reflective tendency in his nature is intensified. One shudders at the thought of the meaninglessness of life while at the same instant, and if the people of the town are his people, one loves life so intensely that tears come into the eyes.

In the darkness under the roof of the grand-stand, George Willard sat beside Helen White and felt very keenly his own insignificance in the scheme of existence. Now that he had come out of town where the presence of the people stirring about, busy with a multitude of affairs, had been so irritating, the irritation was all gone. The presence of Helen renewed and refreshed him. It was as though her woman's hand was assisting him to make some minute readjustment of the machinery of his life. He began to think of the people in the town where he had always lived with something like reverence. He had reverence for Helen. He wanted to love and to be loved by her, but he did not want at the moment to be confused by her womanhood. In the darkness he took hold of her hand and when she crept close put a hand on her shoulder. A wind began to blow and he shivered. With all his strength he tried to hold and to understand the mood that had come upon him. In that high place in the darkness the two oddly sensitive human atoms held each other tightly and waited. In the mind of each was the same thought. "I have come to this lonely place and here is this other," was the substance of the thing felt.

In Winesburg the crowded day had run itself out into the long night of the late fall. Farm horses jogged away along lonely country roads pulling their portion of weary people. Clerks began to bring samples of goods in off the sidewalks and lock the doors of stores. In the Opera House a crowd had gathered to see a show and further down Main Street the fiddlers, their instruments tuned, sweated and worked to keep the feet of youth flying over a dance floor.

In the darkness in the grand-stand Helen White and George Willard remained silent. Now and then the spell that held them was broken and they turned and tried in the dim light to see into each other's eyes. They kissed but that impulse did not last. At the upper end of the Fair Ground a half dozen men worked over horses that had raced during the afternoon. The men had built a fire and were heating kettles of water. Only their legs could be seen as they passed back and forth in the light. When the wind blew the little flames of the fire danced crazily about.

George and Helen arose and walked away into the darkness. They went along a path past a field of corn that had not yet been cut. The wind whispered among the dry corn blades. For a moment during the walk back into town the spell that held them was broken. When they had come to the crest of Waterworks Hill they stopped by a tree and George again put his hands on the girl's shoulders. She embraced him eagerly and then again they drew quickly back from that impulse. They stopped kissing and stood a little apart. Mutual respect grew big in them. They were both embarrassed and to relieve their embarrassment dropped into the animalism of youth. They laughed and began to pull and haul at each other. In some way chastened and purified by the mood they had been in, they became, not man and woman, not boy and girl, but excited little animals.

It was so they went down the hill. In the darkness they played like two splendid young things in a young world. Once, running swiftly forward, Helen tripped George and he fell. He squirmed and shouted. Shaking with laughter, he rolled down the hill. Helen ran after him. For just a moment she stopped in the darkness. There is no way of knowing what woman's thoughts went through her mind but, when the bottom of the hill was reached and she came up to the boy, she took his arm and walked beside him in dignified silence. For some reason they could not have explained they had both got from their silent evening together the thing needed. Man or boy, woman or girl, they had for a moment taken hold of the thing that makes the mature life of men and women in the modern world possible.

John Steinbeck

John Steinbeck (1902–1968), Nobel prize-winning novelist born in Salinas, California, saw firsthand the problems of the migrant farmers and factory workers. His greatest novel The Grapes of Wrath *blends social protest with a moving portrait of human dignity and endurance. This chapter is a poetic statement of the bountiful land and the pastoral dream ruined by politics and greed.*

from THE GRAPES OF WRATH

The spring is beautiful in California. Valleys in which the fruit blossoms are fragrant pink and white waters in a shallow sea. Then the first tendrils of the grapes, swelling from the old gnarled vines, cascade down to cover the trunks. The full green hills are round and soft as breasts. And on the level vegetable lands are the mile-long rows of pale green lettuce and the spindly little cauliflowers, the gray-green unearthly artichoke plants.

And then the leaves break out on the trees, and the petals drop from the fruit trees and carpet the earth with pink and white. The centers of the blossoms swell and grow and color: cherries and apples, peaches and pears, figs which close the flower in the fruit. All California quickens with produce, and the fruit grows heavy, and the limbs bend gradually under the fruit so that little crutches must be placed under them to support the weight.

Behind the fruitfulness are men of understanding and knowledge and skill, men who experiment with seed, endlessly developing the techniques for greater crops of plants whose roots will resist the million enemies of the earth: the molds, the insects, the rusts, the blights. These men work carefully and endlessly to perfect the seed, the roots. And there are the men of chemistry who spray the trees against pests, who sulphur the grapes, who cut out disease and rots, mildews and sicknesses. Doctors of preventive medicine, men at the borders who look for fruit flies, for Japanese beetle, men who quarantine the sick trees and root them out and burn them, men of knowledge. The men who graft the young trees, the little vines, are the cleverest of all, for theirs is a surgeon's job, as tender and delicate; and these men must have surgeons' hands and surgeons' hearts to slit the bark, to place the grafts, to bind the wounds and cover them from the air. These are great men.

Along the rows, the cultivators move, tearing the spring grass and turning it under to make a fertile earth, breaking the ground to hold the water up near the surface, ridging the ground in little pools for the irrigation, destroying the weed roots that may drink the water away from the trees.

And all the time the fruit swells and the flowers break out in long clusters on the vines. And in the growing year the warmth grows and the leaves turn dark green. The prunes lengthen like little green bird's eggs, and the limbs sag down against the crutches under the weight. And the hard little pears take shape, and the beginning of the fuzz comes out on the peaches. Grape blossoms shed their tiny petals and the hard little beads become green buttons, and the buttons grow heavy. The men who work in the fields, the owners of the little orchards, watch and calculate. The year is heavy with produce. And men are proud, for of their knowledge they can make the year heavy. They have transformed the world with their knowledge. The short, lean wheat has been made big and productive. Little sour apples have grown large and sweet, and that old grape that grew among the trees and fed the birds its tiny fruit has mothered a thousand varieties, red and black, green and pale pink, purple and yellow; and each variety with its own flavor. The men who work in the experimental farms have made new fruits: nectarines and forty kinds of plums, walnuts with paper shells. And always they work, selecting, grafting, changing, driving themselves, driving the earth to produce.

And first the cherries ripen. Cent and a half a pound. Hell, we can't pick 'em for that. Black cherries and red cherries, full and sweet, and the birds eat half of each cherry and the yellow jackets buzz into the holes the birds made. And on the ground the seeds drop and dry with black shreds hanging from them.

The purple prunes soften and sweeten. My God, we can't pick them and dry and sulphur them. We can't pay wages, no matter what wages. And the purple prunes carpet the ground. And first the skins wrinkle a little and swarms of flies come to feast, and the valley is filled with the odor of sweet decay. The meat turns dark and the crop shrivels on the ground.

And the pears grow yellow and soft. Five dollars a ton. Five dollars for forty fifty-pound boxes; trees pruned and sprayed, orchards cultivated—pick the fruit, put it in boxes, load the trucks, deliver the fruit to the cannery—forty boxes for five dollars. We can't do it. And the yellow fruit falls heavily to the ground and splashes on the ground. The yellowjackets dig into the soft meat, and there is a smell of ferment and rot.

Then the grapes—we can't make good wine. People can't buy good wine. Rip the grapes from the vines, good grapes, rotten grapes, wasp-stung grapes. Press stems, press dirt and rot.

But there's mildew and formic acid in the vats.

Add sulphur and tannic acid.

The smell from the ferment is not the rich odor of wine, but the smell of decay and chemicals.

Oh, well. It has alcohol in it, anyway. They can get drunk.

The little farmers watched debt creep up on them like the tide. They sprayed the trees and sold no crop, they pruned and grafted and could not pick the crop. And the men of knowledge have worked, have considered, and the fruit is rotting on the ground, and the decaying mash in the wine vats is poisoning the air. And taste the wine—no grape flavor at all, just sulphur and tannic acid and alcohol.

This little orchard will be a part of a great holding next year, for the debt will have choked the owner.

This vineyard will belong to the bank. Only the great owners can survive, for they own the canneries too. And four pears peeled and cut in half, cooked and canned, still cost fifteen cents. And the canned pears do not spoil. They will last for years.

The decay spreads over the State, and the sweet smell is a great sorrow on the land. Men who can graft the trees and make the seed fertile and big can find no way to let the hungry people eat their produce. Men who have created new fruits in the world cannot create a system whereby their fruits may be eaten. And the failure hangs over the State like a great sorrow.

The works of the roots of the vines, of the trees, must be destroyed to keep up the price, and this is the saddest, bitterest thing of all. Carloads of oranges dumped on the ground. The people came for miles to take the fruit, but this could not be. How would they buy oranges at twenty cents a dozen if they could drive out and pick them up? And men with hoses squirt kerosene on the oranges, and they are angry at the crime, angry at the people who have come to take the fruit. A million people hungry, needing the fruit—and kerosene sprayed over the golden mountains.

And the smell of rot fills the country.

Burn coffee for fuel in the ships. Burn corn to keep warm, it makes a hot fire. Dump potatoes in the rivers and place guards along the banks to keep the hungry people from fishing them out. Slaughter the pigs and bury them, and let the putrescence drip down into the earth.

There is a crime here that goes beyond denunciation. There is a sorrow here that weeping cannot symbolize. There is a failure here that topples all our success. The fertile earth, the straight tree rows, the sturdy trunks, and the ripe fruit. And children dying of pellagra must die because a profit cannot be taken from an orange. And coroners must fill in the certificates—died of malnutrition—because the food must rot, must be forced to rot.

The people come with nets to fish for potatoes in the river, and the guards hold them back; they come in rattling cars to get the dumped oranges, but the kerosene is sprayed. And they stand still and watch the potatoes float by, listen to the screaming pigs being killed in a ditch and covered with quicklime, watch the mountains of oranges slop down to a putrefying ooze; and in the eyes of the people there is the failure; and in the eyes of the hungry there is a growing wrath. In the souls of the people the grapes of wrath are filling and growing heavy, growing heavy for the vintage.

Willie Morris

Willie Morris (b. 1934), born and raised in Mississippi, went to the University of Texas and to Oxford University as a Rhodes scholar. He became editor of Harper's Magazine *at the age of thirty-two. His first book,* North Toward Home, *is an autobiography tracing his coming of age in the South and his working in New York City. This section, the opening of the book, shows Morris's strong attraction to the power and mystery of the Delta landscape, but also his recognition that his childhood views of the South were seen from a different viewpoint by blacks.*

from NORTH TOWARD HOME

Half an hour north of Jackson on U.S. 49, not far beyond the Big Black River, the casual rolling land gives way to a succession of tall, lush hills, one after another for twelve or fifteen miles. In spring and summer the trees and underbrush are of an al-most tropical density, and the whole terrain is grown over with a prolific green creeping vine, right up to the highway, and sometimes onto the concrete itself when the highway workers have let up a day too long. On a quiet day after a spring rain this stretch of earth seems prehistoric—damp, cool, inaccessible, the moss hanging from the giant old trees—and if you ignore the occasional diesel, churning up one of these hills on its way to Greenwood or Clarksdale or Memphis, you may feel you are in one of those sudden magic places of America, known mainly to the local people and merely taken for granted, never written about, not even on any of the tourist maps. To my knowledge this area of abrupt hills and deep descents does not have a name, but if you drive up and down them once on a fine day and never see them again, you will find them hard to forget.

Beyond these hills, if you follow the highway as it forks north and slightly west, the hills suddenly come to an end and there is one long, final descent. Out in the distance, as far as the eye can see, the land is flat, dark, and unbroken, sweeping away in a faint misty haze to the limits of the horizon. This is the great delta. Once it was the very floor under the sea; later knee-deep in waters and covered with primordial forests—a dank shadowy swampland, fetid and rich. There will not be a hill or a rise now until just below Memphis, 180 miles away. In a fast car a man can almost make it to Tennessee on automatic pilot, driving the straight, level road in a kind of euphoria, past the cotton fields and the tenant shacks, the big plantation houses and the primitive little Negro churches, over the muddy creeks and rivers, through the counties with the forgotten Indian names—Leflore, Coahoma, Tallahatchie, Tunica.

The town where I grew up sits there on the edge of the delta, straddling that memorable divide where the hills end and the flat land begins. The town itself was half hills and half delta, only forty miles from the Mississippi as the crow flies. One afternoon when I was ten years old, lounging in front of the Phillips station on the street which came hell-bent out of the hills as the highway, I watched a man and his wife emerge from a Buick with Illinois plates. The woman smoothed out the wrinkles in her dress with her palm, paused for a second to look at the drab vistas of the downtown, and whispered, "My God!"

Its name was Yazoo City, from the river that flows by it from farther up in the delta —a muddy winding stream that takes in the Tallahatchie, the Sunflower, and God knows how many less ambitious creeks and rivers in its southward course before it empties itself into the greater River a few miles north of Vicksburg. "Yazoo," far from being the ludicrous name that others would take it, always meant for me something dark, a little blood-crazy and violent. It is, in fact, an old Indian name that means "Death," or "waters of the dead"; the Indians who once inhabited the region as fighters and hunters had died by the scores of some horrible disease. Stephen Foster at first meant his song to be "Way Down upon the Yazoo River," but it was rumored he found out about the meaning of the word, and felt he had been tricked. Hence the town was "death city" to its detractors, and to my contemporaries when I left the place later for college, I was called "Yazoo," such was the spell the very name exerted on you long after you had left it. When the Greyhound out of Jackson stops at some dilapidated grocery store covered with patent medicine posters to pick up a few Negroes, or a solitary traveler waving a white handkerchief in the middle of nowhere, the driver will ask "Where to?" and the passenger will say "Yazoo," with the accent on the last syllable, rich and bass like a quick rumble of thunder.

In the nineteenth century the cotton growers, adventurous younger sons and brothers, came here from the older South where the land had played out, seeking the rich alluvial earth. Later the merchants came to exploit the commerce of the Yazoo River, where the old river boats were stacked ten and fifteen deep in cotton bales, and steamboats with names like the *Hard Cash*, the *City of Greenwood*, and the *Katie Robbins* plied their trade from the upper delta to Vicksburg. Keel- and flatboats laden with flour and apples started out on the Yazoo River, then entered the Mississippi and went all the way south to New Orleans. These early settlers had names like Beatty, Adams, Bull, Clark, Gray, Howard, Little, Robertson, Sparks, Taylor, Thompson, Walton, Whitehead, Young. The slaves had the names of the masters, and for years the tax lists of the place suggested the old Anglo-Saxon blood-source. Later others came to this lower delta—Italians, Irish, Jews, Syrians, even Chinese—to produce a curious melting pot, black, yellow, and white, and all the gradations known to man.

For a white boy growing up in the 1940s it was a pleasant old town; many of its streets were unpaved, although most of them in the white neighborhoods would be sooner or later. Broadway, the street that came swooping out of the hills, was the most unusual of all. Its angle was so steep, and its descent from the top so long, that ever so often the driver of some doomed car or truck would discover that his brakes were not nearly sufficient to deal with this reckless terrain. His path to death would be an agonizing one, as he whipped 80 or 90 miles an hour out of those hills, usually crashing into another car or truck where the ground leveled off at the intersection with Main Street. Once, as we were told it later as children, a truckful of Negro cottonpickers got out of control coming down that street and crashed into a big pecan tree at 70 miles an hour; the dead and dying were thrown for yards around, even into the broad limbs of the pecan tree.

The main street, stretching its several blocks from the Dixie Theater at Broadway down to the cabin that housed Western Union at the bend of the river, was always narrow and dingy, so that the gaudy colored postcard of the "business district" on display in the drugstore seemed more like another place altogether; and out along the highways where the town began there was that raw, desperate, unsettled look, much like towns I later would know in West Texas and the red-clay parts of Louisiana. But down in the settled places, along the quiet, shady streets with their pecan and elm and magnolia and locust trees were the stately old houses, slightly dark and decaying before the descendants became prosperous enough to have them "restored," which usually meant one coat of white enamel. Even the names of the streets suggested they might have been there for a while: Washington, Jefferson, Madison, Monroe, Jackson, Calhoun, and of course, College, which ran by the high school.

All this was before the advent of a certain middle-class prosperity, before the big supermarkets and the neighborhood "shopping centers," back when the game laws were the only device protecting Republicans, both New ones and Old. Then it was a lazy town, stretched out on its hills and its flat streets in a summer sun, a lethargic dreamy place, green and lush all year except for those four stark months at the end and the beginning, heavy with leafy smells, at night full of rumblings and lost ghosts—the Yankees in the sunken gunboat down in the river, the witch in the cemetery who burned down the whole town in 1904, Casey Jones crashing headlong into that unfortunate Illinois Central freight. So isolated was the place that when a big passenger plane mistook the few lights of the dirt airport for Jackson, circled around town and finally came to a skidding halt in the mud, everyone who heard the motors drove out to the airport before the lost plane landed, and a representative of the chamber of commerce put up a stepladder and said to each passenger climbing down, "Welcome to Yazoo." All over the town, everywhere, the Negro sections surrounded the white, and in that curious fractured pattern which Northerners have never quite comprehended, many Negro and white houses sat side by side. But in the larger, unbroken Negro sections—on Brickyard Hill, in the river bottom with its shacks on stilts, around the town dump and the Cotton Club honky-tonk where all the killings were said to take place Saturday nights—even in these a white boy would wander about any time he felt like it, feeling that damp adventure and pulsing of blood of walking through niggertown alone. I have a vivid image of myself as a child, on the first day the "city bus line" opened, riding all one afternoon in the only bus they owned, paying a nickel every time the rickety old vehicle turned around at the end of the line. We rode in great excitement and pride, having never had a bus line before, down Grand Avenue and Canal to Main, then turned around at the old Western Union station, headed up Main and Canal again and along the rim of Brickyard Hill over the same route: these were the limits of my world.

Somewhere I once saw a roster of the prominent people the place had produced. General Pershing's aide-de-camp. Senator John Sharp Williams, a friend and advisor of Woodrow Wilson. Hershel Brickell, a literary critic in New York, who died the day I finished my last examinations in high school. Who remembers them now, who knows much about them or cares? And who knows, for no one has any records, what Negroes came from this common place, moved to Chicago or Harlem, and remembered in pleasure or anguish what they had left behind? As a boy Richard Wright lived on a tenant farm not far from the town. Once, many years later, when I was full grown and twenty-two, I found myself in Paris; I got Wright's phone number and called him, saying I was a white Yazoo boy. "You're from Yazoo?" he asked. "Well, come on over." We went out to an Arab bar and got a little drunk together, and talked about the place we both had known. I asked him, "Will you ever come back to America?" "No," he said. "I want my children to grow up as human beings." After a time a silence fell between us, like an immense pain—or maybe it was my imagining.

THE FRONTIER

Frederick Jackson Turner

Frederick Jackson Turner (1861–1932), an influential American historian, gave a speech in 1893 in which he explained his "frontier theory" of American democracy. Cornerstones of the theory were that the frontier had provided opportunity to all men regardless of class, thereby creating a more democratic climate, and had acted as a "safety valve" allowing the poor in the cities to escape to the country, thus averting a dangerous revolutionary situation. The closing of the frontier, which Turner felt occurred around 1890, was as a result greeted as an ominous sign for America. Later scholars have examined the claims of frontier opportunity and found many myths and half-truths. Nevertheless, Turner's thesis inspired a whole generation of historians to look to unique American conditions as a source of American character and political thought, rather than to the philosophies and customs of Europeans.

THE SIGNIFICANCE OF THE FRONTIER IN AMERICAN HISTORY

In a recent bulletin of the Superintendent of the Census for 1890 appear these significant words: "Up to and including 1880 the country had a frontier of settlement, but at present the unsettled area has been so broken into by isolated bodies of settlement that there can hardly be said to be a frontier line. In the discussion of its extent, its westward movement, etc., it can not, therefore, any longer have a place in the census reports." This brief official statement marks the closing of a great historic movement. Up to our own day American history has been in a large degree the history of the colonization of the Great West. The existence of an area of free land, its continuous recession, and the advance of American settlement westward, explain American development.

Behind institutions, behind constitutional forms and modifications, lie the vital forces that call these organs into life and shape them to meet changing conditions. The peculiarity of American institutions is, the fact that they have been compelled to adapt themselves to the changes of an expanding people—to the changes involved in crossing a continent, in winning a wilderness, and in developing at each area of this progress out of the primitive economic and political conditions of the frontier into the complexity of city life. Said Calhoun in 1817, "We are great, and rapidly—I was about to say fearfully—growing!" So saying, he touched the distinguishing feature of American life. All peoples show development; the germ theory of politics has been sufficiently emphasized. In the case of most nations, however, the development has occurred in a limited area; and if the nation has expanded, it has met other growing peoples whom it has conquered. But in the case of the United States we have a different phenomenon. Limiting our attention to the Atlantic coast, we have the familiar phenomenon of the evolution of institutions in a limited area, such as the rise of representative government; the differentiation of simple colonial governments into complex organs; the progress from primitive industrial society, without division of labor, up to manufacturing civilization. But we have in addition to this a recurrence of the process of evolution in each western area reached in the process of expansion. Thus American development has exhibited not merely advance along a single line, but a return to primitive conditions on a continually advancing frontier line, and a new development for that area. American social development has been continually beginning over again on the frontier. This perennial rebirth, this fluidity of American life, this expansion westward with its new opportunities, its continuous touch with the simplicity of primitive society, furnish the forces dominating American character. The true point of view in the history of this nation is not the Atlantic coast, it is the great West. Even the slavery struggle, which is made so exclusive an object of attention by writers like Prof. von Holst, occupies its important place in American history because of its relation to westward expansion.

In this advance, the frontier is the outer edge of the wave—the meeting point between savagery and civilization. Much has been written about the frontier from the point of view of border warfare and the chase, but as a field for the serious study of the economist and the historian it has been neglected.

The American frontier is sharply distinguished from the European frontier—a fortified boundary line running through dense populations. The most significant thing about the American frontier is, that it lies at the hither edge of free land. In the census reports it is treated as the margin of that settlement which has a density of two or more to the square mile. The term is an elastic one, and for our purposes does not need sharp definition. We shall consider the whole frontier belt, including the Indian country and the outer margin of the "settled area" of the census reports. This paper will make no attempt to treat the subject exhaustively; its aim is simply to call attention to the frontier as a fertile field

for investigation, and to suggest some of the problems which arise in connection with it.

In the settlement of America we have to observe how European life entered the continent, and how America modified and developed that life and reacted on Europe. Our early history is the study of European germs developing in an American environment. Too exclusive attention has been paid by institutional students to the Germanic origins, too little to the American factors. The frontier is the line of most rapid and effective Americanization. The wilderness masters the colonist. It finds him a European in dress, industries, tools, modes of travel, and thought. It takes him from the railroad car and puts him in the birch canoe. It strips off the garments of civilization and arrays him in the hunting shirt and the moccasin. It puts him in the log cabin of the Cherokee and Iroquois and runs an Indian palisade around him. Before long he has gone to planting Indian corn and plowing with a sharp stick; he shouts the war cry and takes the scalp in orthodox Indian fashion. In short, at the frontier the environment is at first too strong for the man. He must accept the conditions which it furnishes, or perish, and so he fits himself into the Indian clearings and follows the Indian trails. Little by little he transforms the wilderness, but the outcome is not the old Europe, not simply the development of Germanic germs, any more than the first phenomenon was a case of reversion to the Germanic mark. The fact is, that here is a new product that is American. At first, the frontier was the Atlantic coast. It was the frontier of Europe in a very real sense. Moving westward, the frontier became more and more American. As successive terminal moraines result from successive glaciations, so each frontier leaves its traces behind it, and when it becomes a settled area the region still partakes of the frontier characteristics. Thus the advance of the frontier has meant a steady movement away from the influence of Europe, a steady growth of independence on American lines. And to study this advance, the men who grew up under these conditions, and the political, economic, and social results of it, is to study the really American part of our history.

James Fenimore Cooper

James Fenimore Cooper (1789–1851) was America's first great novelist. To the modern reader Cooper's novels seem stilted, romantic, and even racist in their portrayal of Indians; yet his thirty-three novels were enormously popular and formed the "true picture" of the American frontier in the minds of many Americans. The myth of the lone frontiersman—rugged, independent, honest, and loyal—stems from Cooper's portrait of Natty Bumppo, the Deerslayer.

Previous to this chapter, Natty Bumppo, given the name of Deerslayer by the Delaware Indians, has been captured by the Hurons, enemies of the Delawares and allies of the French in the French and Indian Wars. The Hurons have allowed Deerslayer to go free to attempt a mission of peace so long as he agrees to return to face his fate. In this chapter Deerslayer returns to the Huron camp.

THE DEERSLAYER

Rivenoak and the Panther sat side by side, awaiting the approach of their prisoner, as Deerslayer put his moccasined foot on the strand; nor did either move or utter a syllable until the young man had advanced into the centre of the area, and proclaimed his presence with his voice. This was done firmly, though in a simple manner that marked the character of the individual.

"Here I am, Mingos," he said, in the dialect of the Delawares, a language that most present understood; "here I am, and there is the sun. One is not more true to the laws of natur', than the other has proved true to his word. I am your prisoner; do with me what you please. My business with man and 'arth is settled; nothing remains now but to meet the white man's God, accordin' to a white man's duties and gifts."

A murmur of approbation escaped even the women at this address, and, for an instant, there was a strong and pretty general desire to adopt into the tribe one who owned so brave a spirit. Still there were dissenters from this wish, among the principal of whom might be classed the Panther, and his sister, Le Sumach, so called from the number of her children, who was the widow of Le Loup Cervier, now known to have fallen by the hand of the captive. Native ferocity held one in subjection, while the corroding passion of revenge prevented the other from admitting any gentler feeling at the moment. Not so with Rivenoak. This chief arose, stretched his arm before him, in a gesture of courtesy, and paid his compliments with an ease and dignity that a prince might have envied. As, in that band, his wisdom and eloquence were confessedly without rivals, he knew that on himself would properly fall the duty of first replying to the speech of the pale-face.

"Pale-face, you are honest," said the Huron orator. "My people are happy in having captured a man, and not a skulking fox. We now know you; we shall treat you like a brave. If you have slain one of our warriors, and helped to kill others, you have a life of your own ready to give away in return. Some of my young men thought that the blood of a pale-face was too thin; that it would refuse to run under the Huron knife. You will show them it is not so; your heart is stout as well as your body. It is a pleasure to make such a prisoner; should my warriors say that the death of Le Loup Cervier ought not to be forgotten, and that he cannot travel towards the land of spirits alone, that his enemy must be sent to overtake him, they will remember that he fell by the hand of a brave, and send you after him with such signs of our friendship as shall not make him ashamed to keep your company. I have spoken; you know what I have said."

"True enough, Mingo, all true as the Gospel," returned the simple-minded hunter; "you *have* spoken, and I *do* know not only what you have *said*, but, what is still more important, what you *mean*. I dare say your warrior, the Lynx, was a stout-hearted brave, and worthy of your fri'ndship and respect, but I do not feel unworthy to keep his company, without any passport from your hands. Nevertheless, I am ready to receive judgment from your council, if, indeed, the matter was not detarmined among you, afore I got back."

"My old men would not sit in council over a pale-face until they saw him among them," answered Rivenoak, looking around him a little ironically; "they said it would be like sitting in council over the winds; they go where they will, and come back as they see fit, and not otherwise. There was one voice that spoke in your favor, Deerslayer, but it was alone, like the wren whose mate has been struck by the hawk."

"I thank that voice, whosoever it may have been, Mingo, and will say it was as true a voice, as the rest were lying voices. A furlough is as binding on a pale-face, if he be honest, as it is on a redskin; and was it not so, I would never bring disgrace on the Delawares, among whom I may be said to have received my edication. But words are useless, and lead to braggin' feelin's; here I am; act your will on me."

Rivenoak made a sign of acquiescence, and then a short conference was privately held among the chiefs. As soon as the latter ended, three or four young men fell back from among the armed group, and disappeared. Then it was signified to the prisoner that he was at liberty to go at large on the point, until a council was held concerning his fate. There was more of seeming, than of real confidence, however, in this apparent liberality, inasmuch as the young men mentioned already formed a line of sentinels across the breadth of the point, inland, and escape from any

other part was out of the question. Even the canoe was removed beyond this line of sentinels, to a spot where it was considered safe from any sudden attempt. These precautions did not proceed from a failure of confidence, but from the circumstance that the prisoner had now complied with all the required conditions of his parole, and it would have been considered a commendable and honorable exploit to escape from his foes. So nice, indeed, were the distinctions drawn by the savages, in cases of this nature, that they often gave their victims a chance to evade the torture, deeming it as creditable to the captors to overtake, or to outwit a fugitive, when his exertions were supposed to be quickened by the extreme jeopardy of his situation, as it was for him to get clear from so much extraordinary vigilance.

Nor was Deerslayer unconscious of, or forgetful of, his rights, and of his opportunities. Could he now have seen any probable opening for an escape, the attempt would not have been delayed a minute. But the case seemed desperate. He was aware of the line of sentinels, and felt the difficulty of breaking through it, unharmed. The lake offered no advantages, as the canoe would have given his foes the greatest facilities for overtaking him; else would he have found it no difficult task to swim as far as the castle. As he walked about the point, he even examined the spot to ascertain if it offered no place of concealment; but its openness, its size, and the hundred watchful glances that were turned towards him, even while those who made them affected not to see him, prevented any such expedient from succeeding. The dread and disgrace of failure had no influence on Deerslayer, who deemed it ever a point of honor to reason and feel like white men, rather than as an Indian, and who felt it as a sort of duty to do all he could, that did not involve a dereliction from principle, in order to save his life. Still he hesitated about making the effort, for he also felt that he ought to see the chance of success before he committed himself.

In the meantime the business of the camp appeared to proceed in its regular train. The chiefs consulted apart, admitting no one but the Sumach to their councils; for she, the widow of the fallen warrior, had an exclusive right to be heard on such an occasion. The young men strolled about in indolent listlessness, awaiting the result with Indian impatience, while the females prepared the feast that was to celebrate the termination of the affair, whether it proved fortunate or otherwise for our hero. No one betrayed feeling; and an indifferent observer, beyond the extreme watchfulness of the sentinels, would have detected no extraordinary movement or sensation to denote the real state of things. Two or three old women put their heads together, and it appeared unfavorably to the prospect of Deerslayer, by their scowling looks and angry gestures; but a group of Indian girls were evidently animated by a different impulse as was apparent by stolen glances that expressed pity and regret. In this condition of the camp, an hour soon glided away.

Suspense is, perhaps, the feeling of all others, that is most difficult to be supported. When Deerslayer landed, he fully expected in the course of a few minutes to undergo the tortures of an Indian revenge, and he was prepared to meet his fate manfully; but the delay proved far more trying than the nearer approach of suffering, and the intended victim began seriously to meditate some desperate effort at escape, as it might be from sheer anxiety to terminate the scene, when he was suddenly summoned to appear, once more, in front of his judges, who had already arranged the band in its former order, in readiness to receive him.

"Killer of the Deer," commenced Rivenoak, as soon as his captive stood before him, "my aged men have listened to wise words; they are ready to speak. You are a man whose fathers came from beyond the rising sun; we are children of the setting sun; we turn our faces towards the Great Sweet Lakes when we look towards our villages. It may be a wise country and full of riches towards the morning, but it is very pleasant towards the evening. We love most to look in that direction. When we gaze at the east we feel afraid, canoe after canoe bringing more and more of your people in the track of the sun, as if their land was so full as to run over. The redmen are few already; they have need of help. One of our best lodges has lately been emptied by the death of its master; it will be a long time before his son can grow big enough to sit in his place. There is his widow! she will want venison to feed her and her children, for her sons are yet like the young of the robin before they quit the nest. By your hand has this great calamity befallen her. She has two duties; one to Le Loup Cervier, and one to his children. Scalp for scalp, life for life, blood for blood, is one law; to feed her young another. We know you, Killer of the Deer. You are honest; when you say a thing it is so. You have but one tongue, and that is not forked like a snake's. Your head is never hid in the grass; all can see it. What you say that will you do. You are just. When you have done wrong, it is your wish to do right again as soon as you can. Here is the Sumach; she is alone in her wigwam, with children crying around her for food; yonder is a rifle, it is loaded and ready to be fired. Take the gun; go forth and shoot a deer; bring the venison and lay it before the widow of Le Coup Cervier; feed her children; call yourself her husband. After which, your heart will no longer be Delaware but Huron; Le Sumach's ears will not hear the cries of her children; my people will count the proper number of warriors."

"I feared this, Rivenoak," answered Deerslayer, when the other had ceased speaking; "yes, I did dread that it would come to this. Howsever, the truth is soon told, and that will put an end to all expectations on this head. Mingo, I'm white, and Christianborn; 't would ill become me to take a wife, under redskin forms, from among heathen. That which I wouldn't do in peaceable times, and under a bright sun, still less would I do behind clouds, in order to save my life. I may never marry; most likely Providence, in putting me up here in the woods, has intended I should live single, and without a lodge of my own; but should such a thing come to pass, none but a woman of my own color and gifts shall darken the door of my wigwam. As for feeding the young of your dead warrior, I would do that cheerfully, could it be done without discredit; but it cannot, seeing that I can never live in a Huron village. Your own young men must find the Sumach in venison, and the next time she marries, let her take a husband whose legs are not long enough to overrun territory that don't belong to him. We fou't a fair battle, and he fell; in this there is nothin' but what a brave expects, and should be ready to meet. As for getting a Mingo heart, as well might you expect to see gray hairs on a boy, or the blackberry growing on the pine. No, no, Huron; my gifts are white, so far as wives are consarned; it is Delaware in all things touchin' Injins."

These words were scarcely out of the mouth of Deerslayer, before a common murmur betrayed the dissatisfaction with which they had been heard. The aged women, in particular, were loud in their expressions of disgust; and the gentle Sumach herself, a woman quite old enough to be our hero's mother, was not the least pacific in her denunciations. But all the other manifestations of disappointment and discontent were thrown into the background, by the fierce resentment of the Panther. This grim chief had thought it a degradation to permit his sister to become the wife of a pale-face of the Yengeese, at all, and had only given a reluctant consent to the arrangement—one by no means unusual among the Indians, however—at the earnest solicitations of the bereaved widow; and it goaded him to the quick to find his condescension slighted, the honor he had with so much regret been persuaded to

accord, contemned. The animal from which he got his name does not glare on his intended prey with more frightful ferocity, than his eyes gleamed on the captive; nor was his arm backward in seconding the fierce resentment that almost consumed his breast.

"Dog of the pale-faces!" he exclaimed, in Iroquois, "go yell among the curs of your own evil hunting-grounds!"

The denunciation was accompanied by an appropriate action. Even while speaking his arm was lifted and the tomahawk hurled. Luckily the loud tones of the speaker had drawn the eye of Deerslayer towards him, else would that moment have probably closed his career. So great was the dexterity with which this dangerous weapon was thrown, and so deadly the intent, that it would have riven the skull of the prisoner, had he not stretched forth an arm, and caught the handle in one of its turns, with a readiness quite as remarkable as the skill with which the missile had been hurled. The projectile force was so great, notwithstanding, that when Deerslayer's arm was arrested, his hand was raised above and behind his own head, and in the very attitude necessary to return the attack. It is not certain whether the circumstance of finding himself unexpectedly in this menacing posture and armed, tempted the young man to retaliate, or whether sudden resentment overcame his forbearance and prudence. His eye kindled, however, and a small red spot appeared on each check, while he cast all his energy into the effort of his arm, and threw back the weapon at his assailant. The unexpectedness of this blow contributed to its success; the Panther neither raising an arm nor bending his head to avoid it. The keen little axe struck the victim in a perpendicular line with the nose, directly between the eyes, literally braining him on the spot. Sallying forward, as the serpent darts at its enemy even while receiving its own death-wound, this man of powerful frame fell his length into the open area formed by the circle, quivering in death. A common rush to his relief left the captive, for a single instant, quite without the crowd; and, willing to make one desperate effort for life, he bounded off with the activity of a deer. There was but a breathless instant, when the whole band, old and young, women and children, abandoning the lifeless body of the Panther where it lay, raised the yell of alarm, and followed in pursuit.

Sudden as had been the event which induced Deerslayer to make this desperate trial of speed, his mind was not wholly unprepared for the fearful emergency. In the course of the past hour, he had pondered well on the chances of such an experiment, and had shrewdly calculated all the details of success and failure. At the first leap, therefore, his body was completely under the direction of an intelligence that turned all its efforts to the best account, and prevented everything like hesitation or indecision, at the important instant of the start. To this alone was he indebted for the first great advantage, that of getting through the line of sentinels unharmed. The manner in which this was done, though sufficiently simple, merits a description.

Although the shores of the point were not fringed with bushes, as was the case with most of the others on the lake, it was owing altogether to the circumstance that the spot had been so much used by hunters and fishermen. This fringe commenced on what might be termed the mainland, and was as dense as usual, extending in long lines both north and south. In the latter direction, then, Deerslayer held his way; and, as the sentinels were a little without the commencement of this thicket before the alarm was clearly communicated to them, the fugitive had gained its cover. To run among the bushes, however, was out of the question, and Deerslayer held his way for some forty or fifty yards in the water, which was barely knee deep, offering as great an obstacle to the speed of his pursuers as it did to his own. As soon as a favorable spot presented, he darted through the line of bushes, and issued into the open woods.

Several rifles were discharged at Deerslayer while in the water, and more followed as he came out into the comparative exposure of the clear forest. But the direction of his line of flight which partially crossed that of the fire, the haste with which the weapons had been aimed, and the general confusion that prevailed in the camp, prevented any harm from being done. Bullets whistled past him, and many cut twigs from the branches at his side, but not one touched even his dress. The delay caused by these fruitless attempts was of great service to the fugitive, who had gained more than a hundred yards on even the leading men of the Hurons, ere something like concert and order had entered into the chase. To think of following with rifle in hand was out of the question; and after emptying their pieces in vague hope of wounding their captive, the best runners of the Indians threw them aside, calling out to the women and boys to recover and load them again, as soon as possible.

Deerslayer knew too well the desperate nature of the struggle in which he was engaged, to lose one of the precious moments. He also knew that his only hope was to run in a straight line, for as soon as he began to turn, or double, the greater number of his pursuers would put escape out of the question. He held his way, therefore, in a diagonal direction up the acclivity, which was neither very high nor very steep, in this part of the mountain, but which was sufficiently toilsome for one contending for life, to render it painfully oppressive. There, however, he slackened his speed, to recover breath, proceeding even at a quick walk, or a slow trot, along the more difficult parts of the way. The Hurons were whooping and leaping behind him; but this he disregarded, well knowing they must overcome the difficulties he had surmounted, ere they could reach the elevation to which he had attained. The summit of the first hill was now quite near him, and he saw, by the formation of the land, that a deep glen intervened, before the base of a second hill could be reached. Walking deliberately to the summit, he glanced eagerly about him, in every direction, in quest of a cover. None offered in the ground; but a fallen tree lay near him, and desperate circumstances required desperate remedies. This tree lay in a line parallel to the glen, at the brow of the hill; to leap on it, and then to force his person as close as possible under its lower side, took but a moment. Previously to disappearing from his pursuers, however, Deerslayer stood on the height, and gave a cry of triumph, as if exulting at the sight of the descent that lay before him. In the next instant he was stretched beneath the tree.

Walt Whitman

This poem shows Whitman's boundless optimism and passionate involvement with the American frontier spirit. (Whitman is also discussed on page 18.)

PIONEERS! O PIONEERS!

Come my tan-faced children,
Follow well in order, get your weapons ready,
Have you your pistols? have you your sharp-edged axes?
    Pioneers! O pioneers!

For we cannot tarry here,
We must march my darlings, we must bear the brunt of danger,
We the youthful sinewy races, all the rest on us depend,
    Pioneers! O pioneers!

O you youths, Western youths,
So impatient, full of action, full of manly pride and friendship,

Plain I see you Western youths, see you tramping with the foremost.
    Pioneers! O pioneers!

Have the elder races halted?
Do they droop and end their lesson, wearied over there beyond the seas?
We take up the task eternal, and the burden and the lesson,
    Pioneers! O pioneers!

All the past we leave behind,
We debouch upon a newer mightier world, varied world,
Fresh and strong the world we seize, world of labor and the march,
    Pioneers! O pioneers!

We detachments steady throwing,
Down the edges, through the passes, up the mountains steep,
Conquering, holding, daring, venturing as we go the unknown ways,
    Pioneers! O pioneers!

We primeval forests felling,
We the rivers stemming, vexing we and piercing deep the mines within,
We the surface broad surveying, we the virgin soil upheaving,
    Pioneers! O pioneers!

Colorado men are we,
From the peaks gigantic, from the great sierras and the high plateaus,
From the mine and from the gully, from the hunting trail we come,
    Pioneers! O pioneers!

From Nebraska, from Arkansas,
Central inland race are we, from Missouri, with the continental blood inter-vein'd,
All the hands of comrades clasping, all the Southern, all the Northern,
    Pioneers! O pioneers!

O resistless restless race!
O beloved race in all! O my breast aches with tender love for all!

O I mourn and yet exult, I am rapt with
      love for all,
      Pioneers! O pioneers!

Raise the mighty mother mistress,
Waving high the delicate mistress, over all
      the starry mistress, (bend your
      heads all,)
Raise the fang'd and warlike mistress, stern,
      impassive, weapon'd mistress,
      Pioneers! O pioneers!

See my children, resolute children,
By those swarms upon our rear we must
      never yield or falter,
Ages back in ghostly millions frowning
      there behind us urging,
      Pioneers! O pioneers!

On and on the compact ranks,
With accessions ever waiting, with the
      places of the dead quickly fill'd,
Through the battle, through defeat, moving
      yet and never stopping,
      Pioneers! O pioneers!

O to die advancing on!
Are there some of us to droop and die? has
      the hour come?
Then upon the march we fittest die, soon
      and sure the gap is fill'd,
      Pioneers! O pioneers!

All the pulses of the world,
Falling in they beat for us, with the Western
      movement beat,
Holding single or together, steady moving
      to the front, all for us,
      Pioneers! O pioneers!

Life's involv'd and varied pageants,
All the forms and shows, all the workmen
      at their work,
All the seamen and the landsmen, all the
      masters with their slaves,
      Pioneers! O pioneers!

All the hapless silent lovers,
All the prisoners in the prisons, all the
      righteous and the wicked,

All the joyous, all the sorrowing, all the
      living, all the dying,
      Pioneers! O pioneers!

I too with my soul and body,
We, a curious trio, picking, wandering on
      our way,
Through these shores amid the shadows,
      with the apparitions pressing,
      Pioneers! O pioneers!

Lo, the darting bowling orb!
Lo, the brother orbs around, all the cluster-
      ing suns and planets,
All the dazzling days, all the mystic nights
      with dreams,
      Pioneers! O pioneers!

These are of us, they are with us,
All for primal needed work, while the fol-
      lowers there in embryo wait be-
      hind,
We to-day's procession heading, we the
      route for travel clearing,
      Pioneers! O pioneers!

O you daughters of the West!
O you young and elder daughters! O you
      mothers and you wives!
Never must you be divided, in our ranks
      you move united,
      Pioneers! O pioneers!

Minstrels latent on the prairies!
(Shrouded bards of other lands, you may
      rest, you have done your work,)
Soon I hear you coming warbling, soon you
      rise and tramp amid us,
      Pioneers! O pioneers!

Not for delectations sweet,
Not the cushion and the slipper, not the
      peaceful and the studious,
Not the riches safe and palling, not for us
      the tame enjoyment,
      Pioneers! O pioneers!

Do the feasters gluttonous feast?
Do the corpulent sleepers sleep? have they
      lock'd and bolted doors?

Still be ours the diet hard, and the blanket
on the ground,
Pioneers! O pioneers!

Has the night descended?
Was the road of late so toilsome? did we
stop discouraged nodding on our
way?
Yet a passing hour I yield you in your
tracks to pause oblivious,
Pioneers! O pioneers!

Till with sound of trumpet,
Far, far off the daybreak call—hark! how
loud and clear I hear it wind,
Swift! to the head of the army!—swift!
spring to your places,
Pioneers! O pioneers!

Francis Parkman

*Francis Parkman (1823–1893), an historian,
journeyed west in 1846 to study Indians and
improve his health. The result of his journey
was his greatest work,* The Oregon Trail, *the
first work by an American writer which did
not glorify or romanticize the Indian.*

THE FRONTIER

Last spring, 1846, was a busy season in
the city of St. Louis. Not only were emigrants from every part of the country preparing for the journey to Oregon and California, but an unusual number of traders
were making ready their wagons and out-
fits for Santa Fé. The hotels were crowded,
and the gunsmiths and saddlers were kept
constantly at work in providing arms and
equipments for the different parties of
travelers. Steamboats were leaving the levee
and passing up the Missouri, crowded with
passengers on their way to the frontier.

In one of these, the "Radnor," since
snagged and lost, my friend and relative
Quincy Adams Shaw, and myself left St.
Louis on the 28th of April, on a tour of

curiosity and amusement to the Rocky
Mountains. The boat was loaded until the
water broke alternately over her guards.
Her upper-deck was covered with large
wagons of a peculiar form, for the Santa
Fé trade, and her hold was crammed with
goods for the same destination. There were
also the equipments and provisions of a
party of Oregon emigrants, a band of mules
and horses, piles of saddles and harness,
and a multitude of nondescript articles, in-
dispensable on the prairies. Almost hidden
in this medley was a small French cart, of
the sort very appropriately called a "mule-
killer" beyond the frontiers, and not far
distant a tent, together with a miscellaneous assortment of boxes and barrels. The
whole equipage was far from prepossessing
in its appearance; yet, such as it was, it was
destined to a long and arduous journey, on
which the persevering reader will accom-
pany it.

The passengers on board the "Radnor"
corresponded with her freight. In her cabin
were Santa Fé traders, gamblers, speculators, and adventurers of various descrip-
tions, and her steerage was crowded with
Oregon emigrants, "mountain men," negroes, and a party of Kanzas Indians, who
had been on a visit to St. Louis.

Thus laden the boat struggled upward
for seven or eight days against the rapid
current of the Missouri, grating upon
snags, and hanging for two or three hours
at a time upon sand-bars. We entered the
mouth of the Missouri in a drizzling rain,
but the weather soon became clear, and
showed distinctly the broad and turbid
river, with its eddies, its sand-bars, its ragged islands, and forest-covered shores. The
Missouri is constantly changing its course
—wearing away its banks on one side, while
it forms new ones on the other. Its channel
is continually shifting. Islands are formed,
and then washed away; and while the old
forests on one side are undermined and
swept off, a young growth springs up from
the new soil upon the other. With all these
changes the water is so charged with mud

and sand that, in spring, it is perfectly opaque, and in a few minutes deposits a sediment an inch thick in the bottom of a tumbler. The river was now high; but when we descended in the autumn it was fallen very low, and all the secrets of its treacherous shallows were exposed to view. It was frightful to see the dead and broken trees, thick-set as a military abattis, firmly imbedded in the sand, and all pointing down stream, ready to impale any unhappy steamboat that at high water should pass over them.

In five or six days we began to see signs of the great western movement that was taking place. Parties of emigrants, with their tents and wagons, were encamped on open spots near the bank, on their way to the common rendezvous at Independence. On a rainy day, near sunset, we reached the landing of this place, which is some miles from the river, on the extreme frontier of Missouri. The scene was characteristic, for here were represented at one view the most remarkable features of this wild and enterprising region. On the muddy shore stood some thirty or forty dark, slavish-looking Spaniards, gazing stupidly out from beneath their broad hats. They were attached to one of the Santa Fé companies, whose wagons were crowded together on the banks above. In the midst of these, crouching over a smouldering fire, was a group of Indians, belonging to a remote Mexican tribe. One or two French hunters from the mountains, with their long hair and buckskin dresses, were looking at the boat; and seated on a log close at hand were three men, with rifles lying across their knees. The foremost of these, a tall, strong figure, with a clear blue eye and an open, intelligent face, might very well represent that race of restless and intrepid pioneers whose axes and rifles have opened a path from the Alleghanies to the western prairies. He was on his way to Oregon, probably a more congenial field to him than any that now remained on this side of the great plains.

Early on the next morning we reached Kanzas, about five hundred miles from the mouth of the Missouri. Here we landed, and leaving our equipments in charge of Colonel Chick, whose log-house was the substitute for a tavern, we set out in a wagon for Westport, where we hoped to procure mules and horses for the journey.

It was a remarkably fresh and beautiful May morning. The woods, through which the miserable road conducted us, were lighted by the bright sunshine and enlivened by a multitude of birds. We overtook on the way our late fellow-travellers, the Kanzas Indians, who adorned with all their finery were proceeding homeward at a round pace; and whatever they might have seemed on board the boat, they made a very striking and picturesque feature in the forest landscape.

Westport was full of Indians, whose little shaggy ponies were tied by dozens along the houses and fences. Sacs and Foxes, with shaved heads and painted faces, Shawanoes and Delawares, fluttering in calico frocks and turbans, Wyandots dressed like white men, and a few wretched Kanzas wrapped in old blankets, were strolling about the streets or lounging in and out of the shops and houses.

As I stood at the door of the tavern I saw a remarkable-looking personage coming up the street. He had a ruddy face, garnished with the stumps of a bristly red beard and moustache; on one side of his head was a round cap with a knob at the top, such as Scottish laborers sometimes wear; his coat was of a nondescript form, and made of a gray Scotch plaid, with the fringes hanging all about it; he wore trousers of coarse homespun, and hobnailed shoes; and to complete his equipment, a little black pipe was stuck in one corner of his mouth. In this curious attire, I recognized Captain C——, of the British army, who, with his brother, and Mr. R——, an English gentleman, was bound on a hunting expedition across the continent. I had seen the Captain and his companions at

St. Louis. They had now been for some time at Westport, making preparations for their departure, and waiting for a reinforcement, since they were too few in number to attempt it alone. They might, it is true, have joined some of the parties of emigrants who were on the point of setting out for Oregon and California; but they professed great disinclination to have any connection with the "Kentucky fellows."

The Captain now urged it upon us that we should join forces and proceed to the mountains in company. Feeling no greater partiality for the society of the emigrants than they did, we thought the arrangement a good one, and consented to it. Our future fellow-travellers had installed themselves in a little log-house, where we found them surrounded by saddles, harness, guns, pistols, telescopes, knives, and in short their complete appointments for the prairie. R——, who had a taste for natural history, sat at a table stuffing a woodpecker; the brother of the Captain, who was an Irishman, was splicing a trail-rope on the floor. The Captain pointed out, with much complacency, the different articles of their outfit. "You see," said he, "that we are all old travellers. I am convinced that no party ever went upon the prairie better provided." The hunter whom they had employed, a surly-looking Canadian, named Sorel, and their muleteer, an American ruffian from St. Louis, were lounging about the building. In a little log stable close at hand were their horses and mules, selected with excellent judgment by the Captain.

We left them to complete their arrangements, while we pushed our own to all convenient speed. The emigrants, for whom our friends professed such contempt were encamped on the prairie about eight or ten miles distant, to the number of a thousand or more, and new parties were constantly passing out from Independence to join them. They were in great confusion, holding meetings, passing resolutions, and drawing up regulations, but unable to unite in the choice of leaders to conduct them across

the prairie. Being at leisure one day, I rode over to Independence. The town was crowded. A multitude of shops had sprung up to furnish the emigrants and Santa Fé traders with necessaries for their journey; and there was an incessant hammering and banging from a dozen blacksmiths' sheds, where the heavy wagons were being repaired, and the horses and oxen shod. The streets were thronged with men, horses, and mules. While I was in the town, a train of emigrant wagons from Illinois passed through, to join the camp on the prairie, and stopped in the principal street. A multitude of healthy children's faces were peeping out from under the covers of the wagons. Here and there a buxom damsel was seated on horseback, holding over her sunburnt face an old umbrella or a parasol, once gaudy enough, but now miserably faded. The men, very sober-looking countrymen, stood about their oxen; and as I passed I noticed three old fellows, who, with their long whips in their hands, were zealously discussing the doctrine of regeneration. The emigrants, however, are not all of this stamp. Among them are some of the vilest outcasts in the country. I have often perplexed myself to divine the various motives that give impulse to this migration; but whatever they may be, whether an insane hope of a better condition in life, or a desire of shaking off restraints of law and society, or mere restlessness, certain it is that multitudes bitterly repent the journey, and, after they have reached the land of promise, are happy enough to escape from it.

In the course of seven or eight days we had brought our preparations nearly to a close. Meanwhile our friends had completed theirs, and, becoming tired of Westport, they told us that they would set out in advance, and wait at the crossing of the Kanzas till we should come up. Accordingly R—— and the muleteer went forward with the wagon and tent, while the Captain and his brother, together with Sorel and a trapper named Boisverd, who had joined them, followed with the band of horses. The commencement of the journey was ominous, for the captain was scarcely a mile from Westport, riding along in state at the head of his party, leading his intended buffalo horse by a rope, when a tremendous thunder-storm came on and drenched them all to the skin. They hurried on to reach the place, about seven miles off, where R—— was to have had the camp in readiness to receive them. But this prudent person, when he saw the storm approaching, had selected a sheltered glade in the woods, where he pitched his tent, and was sipping a comfortable cup of coffee while the Captain galloped for miles beyond through the rain to look for him. At length the storm cleared away, and the sharp-eyed trapper succeeded in discovering his tent. R—— had by this time finished his coffee, and was seated on a buffalo-robe smoking his pipe. The Captain was one of the most easy-tempered men in existence, so he bore his ill-luck with great composure, shared the dregs of the coffee with his brother, and lay down to sleep in his wet clothes.

We ourselves had our share of the deluge. We were leading a pair of mules to Kanzas when the storm broke. Such sharp and incessant flashes of lightning, such stunning and continuous thunder I had never known before. The woods were completely obscured by the diagonal, sheets of rain that fell with a heavy roar, and rose in spray from the ground, and the streams swelled so rapidly that we could hardly ford them. At length, looming through the rain, we saw the log-house of Colonel Chick, who received us with his usual bland hospitality; while his wife, who, though a little soured and stiffened by a long course of camp-meetings, was not behind him in good-will, supplied us with the means of bettering our drenched and bedraggled condition. The storm clearing away at about sunset opened a noble prospect from the porch of the Colonel's house which stands upon a high hill. The sun streamed from the breaking clouds upon the swift and angry Missouri, and on the vast expanse of forest that stretched from its banks back to the distant bluffs.

Returning on the next day to Westport we received a message from the Captain, who had ridden back to deliver it in person, but finding that we were in Kanzas, had intrusted it to an acquaintance of his, named Vogel, who kept a small grocery and liquor shop. Whiskey, by the way, circulates more freely in Westport than is altogether safe in a place where every man carries a loaded pistol in his pocket. As we passed this establishment we saw Vogel's broad German face thrust from his door. He said he had something to tell us, and invited us to take a dram. Neither his liquor nor his message was very palatable. The Captain had returned to give us notice that R——, who assumed the direction of his party had determined upon another route from that agreed upon between us; and instead of taking the course of the traders, had resolved to pass northward by Fort Leavenworth, and follow the path marked out by the dragoons in their expedition of last summer. To adopt such a plan without consulting us, we looked upon as a high-handed proceeding; but suppressing our dissatisfaction as well as we could, we made up our minds to join them at Fort Leavenworth, where they were to wait for us.

Accordingly, our preparation being now complete, we attempted one fine morning to begin our journey. The first step was an unfortunate one. No sooner were our animals put in harness than the shaft-mule reared and plunged, burst ropes and straps, and nearly flung the cart into the Missouri. Finding her wholly uncontrollable, we exchanged her for another, with which we were furnished by our friend Mr. Boone, of Westport, a grandson of Daniel Boone, the pioneer. This foretaste of prairie experience was very soon followed by another. Westport was scarcely out of sight when we encountered a deep muddy gully, of a species that afterward became but too familiar to us, and here for the space of an hour or more the cart stuck fast. . . .

I pass by the following day or two of our journey, for nothing occurred worthy of record. Should any one of my readers ever be impelled to visit the prairies, and should he choose the route of the Platte (the best, perhaps, that can be adopted), I can assure him that he need not think to enter at once upon the paradise of his imagination. A dreary preliminary, a protracted crossing of the threshold, awaits him before he finds himself fairly upon the verge of the "great American desert,"— those barren wastes, the haunts of the buffalo and the Indian, where the very shadow of civilization lies a hundred leagues behind him. The intervening country, the wide and fertile belt that extends for several hundred miles beyond the extreme frontier, will probably answer tolerably well to his preconceived ideas of the prairie; for this it is from which picturesque tourists, painters, poets, and novelists, who have seldom penetrated farther, have derived their conceptions of the whole region. If he has a painter's eye, he may find his period of probation not wholly void of interest. The scenery, though tame, is graceful and pleasing. Here are level plains too wide for the eye to measure; green undulations, like motionless swells of the ocean; abundance of streams, followed through all their windings by lines of woods and scattered groves. But let him be as enthusiastic as he may, he will find enough to damp his ardor. His wagons will stick in the mud; his horses will break loose; harness will give way; and axle-trees prove unsound. His bed will be a soft one, consisting often of black mud of the richest consistency. As for food, he must content himself with biscuit and salt provisions; for strange as it may seem, this tract of country produces very little game. As he advances, indeed, he will see, mouldering in the grass by his path, the vast antlers of the elk, and farther

on the whitened skulls of the buffalo, once swarming over this now deserted region. Perhaps, like us, he may journey for a fortnight, and see not so much as the hoofprint of a deer; in the spring, not even a prairie-hen is to be had.

Yet, to compensate him for this unlooked for deficiency of game, he will find himself beset with "varmints" innumerable. The wolves will entertain him with a concert at night, and skulk around him by day just beyond rifle-shot; his horse will step into badger-holes; from every marsh and mud-puddle will arise the bellowing, croaking and trilling of legions of frogs, infinitely various in color, shape, and dimensions. A profusion of snakes will glide away from under his horse's feet, or quietly visit him in his tent at night; while the pertinacious humming of unnumbered mosquitoes will banish sleep from his eyelids. When, thirsty with a long ride in the scorching sun over some boundless reach of prairie, he comes at length to a pool of water and alights to drink, he discovers a troop of young tadpoles sporting in the bottom of his cup. Add to this that, all the morning, the sun beats upon him with a sultry, penetrating heat, and that, with provoking regularity, at about four o'clock in the afternoon a thunderstorm rises and drenches him to the skin.

Edward L. Wheeler

This is the first chapter of a "dime novel" popular in the late nineteenth century. Wheeler's characters, Deadwood Dick and Calamity Jane, are two of the most famous dime novel heroes. Calamity Jane is based on the real Martha Jane Canary, who appeared in Deadwood, South Dakota, in 1876 dressed in men's clothes, saying she had been a pony express rider and a scout. She is buried in Deadwood next to Wild Bill Hickok. The real Deadwood Dick, who doesn't appear in recognizable form in Wheeler's novel, was Nat Love, a black cow-

boy, who won a contest in riding, roping, and shooting on July 4, 1876, and later toured the nation in a rodeo.

BARKIN' UP THE WRONG TREE

Dashing along thro' the valley and vale,
From early morn till the day grows pale;
Into the 'pockets' framed in flowers—
Into the woodland's shady bowers;
Stopping anon by babbling streams,
Then darting on into rocky seams;
Free as the eagle in its flight,
Fearless in daylight, happy at night;
Ever unfettered to roam about—
Such is the life of the glorious scout.

Searching for gold in the waters clear,
Running a race with the mountain deer;
Profiting well by the miner's abuse,
Taming with spur the buckin' cayuse;
Paying one's way, taking no 'slack,'
Biting cold lead, and sending it back;
Friendly to friends, but deadly to foes,
Gay as a robin, hoarding no woes;
Such is the life of the scout, gay and free,
Such is the life that is suiting to me.

On the clear air of an August night these words were distinctly wafted in melodious song—a wild, rollicking harmony of weird music, such as none but a cultivated voice could produce. Mountains have their peculiar facility of carrying and retaining sound, and it was long ere the last quivering notes of the midsummer night's song had died out. The tone of the singer had been one of those pure, intoxicating rivals of the flute; clear and strong, with power of sustenation, and capable of instant modulation to the softest, sweetest degree.

Even after the singer had ceased in the song of the gay mountaineer, it seemed as if the long gulches and gloomy mountain defiles had become enthused with the glorious melody, and the spectral pines sighed a weird peculiar sound as if in a diapason accompaniment.

The screams of the night birds had been hushed; the noisy streams and leaping cascades were seemingly less boisterous; two men sitting down in the bottom of a narrow winding canyon or gulch, had ceased smoking, to listen to the song of the unknown nightingale.

A little fire was burning in close proximity to a sharp bend in the course of the canyon, and near by was a single marquee of canvas, and a couple of superannuated-looking mules stretched out on the grass. A few yards to the left, as you looked up toward the bend in the canyon, rolled a wide, shallow stream of water, confined in its course by nearly perpendicular walls of rock, that towered aloft in rugged piles, until in natural grandeur they terminated in misty mountain peaks. The two men alluded to were sitting upon the bank of the stream, and they did not move until the songstress had ceased her melody; then they looked up and exchanged glances.

"Beautiful, wasn't it, Sandy?"

"Yes," replied the younger of the twain, as he resumed his pipe, his eyes roving out over the noisy river, dreamily. "I was not aware you had such musical stars out here in your mining districts. A woman, wa'n't it?"

"Yas, a woman," replied Colonel Joe Tubbs, knocking the ashes out of his pipe, and refilling it with chipped plug. "At least they say she's o' the feminine sex, fer w'ich I can't sw'ar, purtic'lar. An' ef she's a wee-mon, thar ain't many better lukers 'twixt hayr, Deadwood, an' ther risin' sun."

"What reason have you to doubt that she is not a woman, colonel?"

"Wal, Sandy, I ken't say as I really doubt et, fer I 'spect et's a solid fac' that she ar' one o'ther lineal descendents of thet leetle fruitful scrape in a certain garden, yeers ago, afore ther Antediluve. But ye see how it is: in the gelorious State o' Ohio, from which I war imported ter this side o' ther hemisphere, ther female sex ginnerally war begarbed in petticoats, an' left ther male representatives to wear ther breeches!"

"Humph!" and a little smile came to

Sandy's lips, "then this nightingale who has just favored us, wears the breeches herself, does she?"

"You pile up yer chips an' bet thet she do, Sandy, and ef you warn't an Eastern chap, an' but leetle used ter sech weemon as we hev in this delectable Black Hills kentry, I'd say, 'Sandy, galoot, pile yer frunt foot for'a'd, and go in for Janie.' "

"Janie—that is her name, eh?"

"Wal, I reckon—Calamity Jane for short. I don't allow thar's many who do know who she is, aside from her title, Sandy, tho' she don't cum no furder off than up in Nevada. She's a brick, Sandy, and jest let et pop right inter yer noddle right hayr, that she ain't no fool ef she do wear breeches. An' ef ye ever have occasion ter meet ther gal, Sandy, jest remember ther words uv Colorado Joe Tubbs on thes 'ere eventful night —'Ther gal ain't no fool ef she do wear breeches.' "

"I will, pardner. I don't suppose because a woman wears male attire that she is necessarily a fool; though why a female must lower her sex by appearing in man's garb, I see not. She must be an eccentric creature —rather a hard case, is she not?" with a little curl of the lip.

" 'Hard case,' Sandy?" and here the veteran paused to close one eye, and blow out a cloud of fragrant smoke; "wal, no, when ye ask my jedgment in ther matter. She's a woman, Sandy, an' tho' thar's many who lay claim ter that name who ar' below par, I don't reckon Janie ar' quite that fur gone. She's a dare-devil, Sandy, an' no mistake. She ar' the most reckless buchario in ther Hills, kin drink whisky, shute, play keerds, or sw'ar, ef et comes ter et; but, 'twixt you and me, I reckon ther gal's got honor left wi' her grit, out o' ther wreck o' a young life. Oncet an' awhile thar is a story whispered about that she war deserted up at Virginny City, an' tuk ter thes rovin' life ter hunt down her false lover; another thet she hed bin married ter a Nevada brute, an' kim over inter these deestrict ter escape him; then thar's bin sum hard stories o' her

up at Deadwood an' Hayward, but I never b'lieved 'em 'case they were ginneraly invented by a gang o' toughs who hed a grudge ag'in' her. I never b'lieved 'em, Sandy, because she war a woman; an' once I hed a wife an' little golden-haired daughter—she luked like you, Sandy—an' I know'd 'em ter be good; thet's why I nevyr kim ter believe all about Calamity Jane!" and the old man bowed his head on his arm, at some sad recollection.

"No! no!" he went on, after a few moments of silence. "Janie's not as bad as ther world would have her; because she's got grit an' ain't afeared to shute ther galoot as crosses her, people condemn her. I reckon ye kno' how et is, out hayr in ther Hills, Sandy—ef a female ken't stand up and fight for her rights, et's durned little aid she'll git."

"So I should conclude from what observations I have been able to make, since I came West," was the reply of the young miner. "Is this Calamity Jane pretty, colonel?"

"Wal, some might say so, Sandy; I am not partial ter givin' opinions o' ther external merits of ther female line, o' late years. Hed sum experience in thet line a couple o' years ago, afore I left Angelina, my second, ter come out hayr—war just tellin' her how purty a certain widder war, when—well, I never quite knew what struck me, but I finally waked up ter find myself carved up inter steaks an' ther ha'r on top o' my head gone. Likewise, my Angelina. She had eloped wi' another galoot. Since then I allus withhold my opinion on ther beauty or humblyness o' ther oppsite sex."

"Well, I suppose you wa'nt sorry, eh?" observed Sandy, as he arose, with a yawn, and picked up his handsome Sharpe's rifle.

"Wal, no; I ken't say's I am, sence et turns out thet ther Black Hills affords me more comfort an' enjoyment than hum uster wi' Angelina everlastingly browsin' me down wi' a mop-stick. Whar ye goin', Sandy, boy?"

"Just up to the bend and back, colonel,

to see that all is right, before turning in for the night," was the reply, as the stalwart miner strode off, whistling softly some tune which was dear to the home in the East, which he had left to seek gold in the Black Hills country. After he had gone out of view in the darkness of the warm semi-tropical night, laden as it was with a strangely intoxicating perfume of many mountain flowers—for the Black Hills are truly the flower land of America—Colonel Joe Tubbs resumed his pipe, while he gazed thoughtfully out over the noisy, shallow waters of Canyon Creek. "A mighty good feller ar' thet Sandy, an' no mistake, but a queer stick, wi' all. Now, we've bin con-solidated fer a couple o' months as pards, in a s'arch fer ther p'izen they call gold, an' I don't kno' nothin' about ther chap, 'cept thet he claims ter hev cum frum New York, an' ar' one o' the squarest galoots I ever fell in wi'. Quiet an' unobtrusive as a crippled cat—hain't much ov a talker neither; but them's often ther kind as hes got a sleepin' tiger in 'em."

Colonel Joe Tubbs had well described the young miner, Sandy, when he had said he was quiet and unobtrusive. He *was* quiet and unobtrusive—was deep and thoughtful—very seldom in a jolly spirit, though at all times pleasant and agreeable. Twenty-four or five years of life which had passed over his head had left a man in every sense of the word—a man in physical and mental de-velopment—a man in will and great force of character—a man so quiet and retired as to seem almost a recluse; yet, when gazing scrutinizingly at him, you could but be impressed with the peculiar force of the expression—"still waters run deep."

His form was stalwart and iron-cast, with strength delineated to the critical eye in every curve and muscle. His face was plain, yet rather attractive, with its firm mouth shaded by a heavy yellow mustache, eyes of a dusky brown, and hair light and worn long down over the shoulders. A face it was which a lady might admire, and a gentle-man envy, even though Sandy would not

have passed criticism as being handsome. His attire was plain, consisting of a buck-skin suit, knee boots, and a slouch gray felt hat. He wore no belt; no other weapons than his rifle were visible about his person.

Tubbs was a short, stubby man, with a genial face, reddened somewhat by long exposure to the sun, and more so, perhaps, by a love for the miner's favorite, "tarant'ler juice," especially his nose. He was an ec-centric, big-hearted fellow, past the middle age of man's worldly existence, who had had much experience in the Black Hills, and never laid by a cent.

This fact seemed to strike him very forc-ibly now, as he sat waiting for Sandy's re-turn. Sandy was the name the colonel had given the young miner, when they had first met in Cheyenne, in lieu of another which the so-called Sandy had said was not for public ears—nor private, either.

"No, not a durned sum total o' one red hev ye laid by, Joe Tubbs, out o' all ther dust ye've handled. An' supposin' Angelina shed come back on ye fer support in yer old age? Lordy! whar'd ther ha'r be *then?*"

"Then, here's Sandy, too—squarest galoot in ther hills, an' I'll be on't—thar's Sandy; I orter leave him a leetle mite when I shuffle off, fer I got a peep at ther poor cuss's pocket-book, t'other day, an' 'twar flatter'n a flapjack. No use o' talkin'; responsibilities ar' rollin' on ye, Colonel Joe Tubbs, an' ye've got to clap yer hoof down an' bid farewell ter tarant'ler forever. Hello, Sandy, ar' that ye back a'ready?"

"Yes, colonel. Didn't know but I might see the nightingale, but was disappointed," was the reply, as the young miner sat down upon a camp-stool in the firelight. "Guess she did not know of our camp here."

"Don't you fool yourself, Sandy; thet gal knows every krook an' hoel in ther hull Black Hills proper, an' can lay her finger on any chap hayr ye kin name, wi'out any trouble. Hello! w'at hev ye got thar, pard?" —alluding to a small object that Sandy was turning over in his hands and inspecting admiringly.

"A piece o' rock that got dislodged somehow, up there around the bend, and rolled down in my path. Out of curiosity I fetched it in. What do you think of it colonel?" and with a peculiar smile, the young miner tossed the rock over to Tubbs.

"What! thunderation, Sandy, *it's gold! it's gold!*" and the colonel sprung hastily to the fire to examine the prize. "Yes, by thunder! et's gold, Sandy, an' as big as my fist; durn my ducats ef et ain't. Whar'd ye git et, boyee?—for Heaven's sake tell me whar? Why don't ye git exicited, Sandy, you galoot? It's gold! it's gold! Wurth a couple or three thousan' at least calcylation, I s'war!"

"No use of getting excited, is there, colonel?" and the miner stretched out with a yawn. "If it's gold, I don't suppose it will hurt anybody, and if there's gold in the mountain-side around the bend, it will not run away in affright."

"Sandy, ye're a cool 'un, an' no mistake. Ye'd freeze ice in fly-time, I do believe, ef ye were not in a kentry thet is next door neighbor ter purgatory etself. Thunderation, boyee, ef I only had a pint uv stiff old tarant'ler hyar, I'd celebrate over yer discovery uv a rich 'find.' What shall we name et, Sandy?—ther place must have a name right in its infancy, just like leetle infant babbys hev."

"All right, colonel. Call it Satan's Bend. Sometime we may find a better name."

"Agreed. Satan's Bend et is, Sandy, an' but fer the want o' a pint o' good stiff tarant'ler, we'd hev a gelorious celebration."

After the conclusion of the beautiful yet weird mountaineer's song, which Joe Tubbs had declared came from the lips of Calamity Jane, a person on horseback descended a dizzy zig-zag path that led from one of the mountain peaks, into a narrow dark defile, but the matter of a mile or so above Canyon Gulch, and the infant city of Satan's Bend.

"Whoa! Steady, Trick—none o' yer funny business, now. Don't ye perceive thet ef yer were to tumble down this declivity with me, there'd be no guardian angel in the Black Hills?" and here a merry peal of laughter escaped the red lips of the speaker.

"Steady—a little further—there! Good for you, old fellow! We're on safe footing, at last. I wonder if any one's around in these parts?" and the dark eyes peered sharply into every shadow in her immediate vicinity. "No; I reckon the coast is all clear, and we must get a-going for Deadwood, Trick, for there is no telling how soon that delightful population may need us to quell some row or do a suffering pilgrim good."

We have described the eccentric daredevil of the Black Hills in other works of this series, but as some may not have read them, it will require but little time to describe her again.

A female of no given age, although she might have ranged safely anywhere between seventeen and twenty-three, she was the possessor of a form both graceful and womanly, and a face that was peculiarly handsome and attractive, though upon it were lines drawn by the unmistakable hand of dissipation and hard usage, lines never to be erased from a face that in innocent childhood had been a pretty one. The lips and eyes still retained in themselves their girlish beauty; the lips their full, rosy plumpness, and the eyes their dark, magnetic sparkle, and the face proper had the power to become stern, grave or jolly in expression, wreathed partially as it was in a semi-framework of long, raven hair that reached below a faultless waist.

Her dress was buckskin trowsers, met at the knee by fancifully beaded leggings, with slippers of dainty pattern upon the feet; a velvet vest, and one of those luxuries of the mines, a boiled shirt, open at the throat, partially revealing a breast of alabaster purity; a short, velvet jacket, and Spanish broad-brimmed hat, slouched upon one side of a regally beautiful head. There were diamond rings upon her hands, a diamond pin in her shirt-bosom, a massive gold chain strung across her vest front.

For she had riches, this girl, and none knew better than she how to find them in the auriferous earth or at the gaming-table of Deadwood, the third Baden Baden of two continents.

A belt around her waist contained a solitary revolver of large caliber; and this, along with a rifle strapped to her back, comprised her outfit, except we mention the fiery little Mexican black she rode, and the accompanying trappings, which were richly decorated and bespangled, after lavish Mexican taste.

"I guess the coast is clear, Trick; so go ahead," and a jerk at the cruel Spanish bit and an application of spurs sent the spiteful cayuse clattering wildly down the canyon, while Calamity Jane rocked not ungracefully from side to side with the reckless freedom peculiar to the California bucharío. Indeed, I think that any person who has witnessed the dare-devil riding of this eccentric girl, in her mad career through the Black Hills country, will agree with me that she has of her sex no peer in the saddle or on horseback.

The first time it was ever my fortune to see her, was when Deadwood was but an infant city of a few shanties, but many tents.

She dashed madly down through the gulch one day, standing erect upon the back of her unsaddled cayuse, and the animal running at the top of its speed, leaping sluices and other obstructions—still the dare-devil retained her position as if glued to the animal's back, her hair flowing wildly back from beneath her slouch hat, her eyes dancing occasionally with excitement, as she recognized some wondering pilgrim, every now and then her lips giving vent to a ringing whoop, which was creditable in imitation if not in volume and force to that of a full-blown Comanche warrior.

Now, she dashed away through the narrow gulch, catching with delight long breaths of the perfume of flowers which met her nostrils at every onward leap of her horse, piercing the gloom of the night with her dark lovely eyes, searchingly, lest she should be surprised; lighting a cigar at full motion—dashing on, on, this strange girl of the Hills went, on her flying steed.

The glowing end of her cigar attracted the notice of four men who were crouching in the dense shadows, further down the gulch, even as the hoofstrokes broke upon their hearing.

"That's her!" growled one, knocking the ashes out of his pipe, with an oath. "Reckoned she wouldn't be all night, ef we only hed patience. Grab yer weepons, an' git ready, boys. She mustn't escape us this time."

Calamity Jane came on; she was not aware of her danger, until she saw four dark shadows cross her path, and her cayuse reared upon its haunches.

"Whoa! Trick; don't git skeered; hold up, you devils. I reckon you're barkin' up ther wrong tree!" she cried.

Then there were three flashes of light in the darkness followed by as many pistol-shots—howls of pain and rage, and curses too vile to repeat here—a yell, wild and clear, a snort from the horse—then the dare-devil rode down the man at the bits, and dashed away down the canyon, with a yell of laughter that echoed and re-echoed up and down the canyon walls.

"I wonder who composed thet worthy quartette?" Calamity mused, as she gazed back over her shoulder. "Reckon at least a couple of 'em bit ther dust, ef not more. Could it have been—but no! I do not believe so. Deadwood Dick's men ain't on the rampage any more, and it couldn't hev been them. Whoever it was wanted my life, that's plain, and I shall have to look out fer breakers ahead, or next time I shall not get oft with a simple scratch."

Stephen Crane

*Though Stephen Crane (1871–1900) began
his brilliant, brief writing career as a journalist, he was soon writing fiction which was
more truly modern than that of any of his
contemporaries. His first popular success,*
The Red Badge of Courage (1894), *was the
first impressionistic novel by an American.
A western trip the following year gave him
the background for "The Bride Comes to
Yellow Sky," a story illustrating the end of
the frontier myth.*

THE BRIDE COMES TO
YELLOW SKY

I

The great Pullman was whirling onward
with such dignity of motion that a glance
from the window seemed simply to prove
that the plains of Texas were pouring eastward. Vast flats of green grass, dull-hued
spaces of mesquite and cactus, little groups
of frame houses, woods of light and tender
trees, all were sweeping into the east, sweeping over the horizon, a precipice.

A newly married pair had boarded this
coach at San Antonio. The man's face was
reddened from many days in the wind and
sun, and a direct result of his new black
clothes was that his brick-colored hands
were constantly performing in a most conscious fashion. From time to time he looked
down respectfully at his attire. He sat with
a hand on each knee, like a man waiting in
a barber's shop. The glances he devoted to
other passengers were furtive and shy.

The bride was not pretty, nor was she
very young. She wore a dress of blue cash-
mere, with small reservations of velvet here
and there and with steel buttons abound-
ing. She continually twisted her head to
regard her puff sleeves, very stiff, straight,
and high. They embarrassed her. It was
quite apparent that she had cooked, and
that she expected to cook, dutifully. The
blushes caused by the careless scrutiny of
some passengers as she had entered the car
were strange to see upon this plain, underclass countenance, which was drawn in
placid, almost emotionless lines.

They were evidently very happy. "Ever
been in a parlor-car before?" he asked, smiling with delight.

"No," she answered. "I never was. It's
fine, ain't it?"

"Great! And then after a while we'll go
forward to the diner and get a big lay-out.
Finest meal in the world. Charge a dollar."

"Oh, do they?" cried the bride. "Charge
a dollar? Why, that's too much—for us—
ain't it, Jack?"

"Not this trip, anyhow," he answered
bravely. "We're going to go the whole
thing."

Later, he explained to her about the
trains. "You see, it's a thousand miles from
one end of Texas to the other, and this train
runs right across it and never stops but four
times." He had the pride of an owner. He
pointed out to her the dazzling fittings of
the coach, and in truth her eyes opened
wider as she contemplated the sea-green figured velvet, the shining brass, silver, and
glass, the wood that gleamed as darkly brilliant as the surface of a pool of oil. At one
end a bronze figure sturdily held a support
for a separated chamber, and at convenient
places on the ceiling were frescoes in olive
and silver.

To the minds of the pair, their surroundings reflected the glory of their marriage that morning in San Antonio. This
was the environment of their new estate,
and the man's face in particular beamed
with an elation that made him appear
ridiculous to the negro porter. This individual at times surveyed them from afar with
an amused and superior grin. On other occasions he bullied them with skill in ways
that did not make it exactly plain to them
that they were being bullied. He subtly used
all the manners of the most unconquerable
kind of snobbery. He oppressed them, but
of this oppression they had small knowledge, and they speedily forgot that infre-

quently a number of travelers covered them with stares of derisive enjoyment. Historically there was supposed to be something infinitely humorous in their situation.

"We are due in Yellow Sky at 3.42," he said, looking tenderly into her eyes.

"Oh, are we?" she said, as if she had not been aware of it. To evince surprise at her husband's statement was part of her wifely amiability. She took from a pocket a little silver watch, and as she held it before her and stared at it with a frown of attention, the new husband's face shone.

"I bought it in San Anton' from a friend of mine," he told her gleefully.

"It's seventeen minutes past twelve," she said, looking up at him with a kind of shy and clumsy coquetry. A passenger, noting this play, grew excessively sardonic, and winked at himself in one of the numerous mirrors.

At last they went to the dining-car. Two rows of negro waiters in glowing white suits surveyed their entrance with the interest and also the equanimity of men who had been forewarned. The pair fell to the lot of a waiter who happened to feel pleasure in steering them through their meal. He viewed them with the manner of a fatherly pilot, his countenance radiant with benevolence. The patronage entwined with the ordinary deference was not plain to them. And yet as they returned to their coach they showed in their faces a sense of escape.

To the left, miles down a long purple slope, was a little ribbon of mist where moved the keening Rio Grande. The train was approaching it at an angle, and the apex was Yellow Sky. Presently it was apparent that as the distance from Yellow Sky grew shorter, the husband became commensurately restless. His brick-red hands were more insistent in their prominence. Occasionally he was even rather absent-minded and far-away when the bride leaned forward and addressed him.

As a matter of truth, Jack Potter was beginning to find the shadow of a deed weigh upon him like a leaden slab. He, the town marshal of Yellow Sky, a man known, liked, and feared in his corner, a prominent person, had gone to San Antonio to meet a girl he believed he loved, and there, after the usual prayers, had actually induced her to marry him, without consulting Yellow Sky for any part of the transaction. He was now bringing his bride before an innocent and unsuspecting community.

Of course, people in Yellow Sky married as it pleased them in accordance with a general custom; but such was Potter's thought of his duty to his friends, or of their idea of his duty, or of an unspoken form which does not control men in these matters, that he felt he was heinous. He had committed an extraordinary crime. Face to face with this girl in San Antonio, and spurred by his sharp impulse, he had gone headlong over all the social hedges. At San Antonio he was like a man hidden in the dark. A knife to sever any friendly duty, any form, was easy to his hand in that remote city. But the hour of Yellow Sky, the hour of daylight, was approaching.

He knew full well that his marriage was an important thing to his town. It could only be exceeded by the burning of the new hotel. His friends would not forgive him. Frequently he had reflected on the advisability of telling them by telegraph, but a new cowardice had been upon him. He feared to do it. And now the train was hurrying him toward a scene of amazement, glee, reproach. He glanced out of the window at the line of haze swinging slowly in toward the train.

Yellow Sky had a kind of brass band which played painfully to the delight of the populace. He laughed without heart as he thought of it. If the citizens could dream of his prospective arrival with his bride, they would parade the band at the station and escort them, amid cheers and laughing congratulations, to his adobe home.

He resolved that he would use all the devices of speed and plains-craft in making the journey from the station to his house. Once within that safe citadel, he could issue some sort of a vocal bulletin, and then not go among the citizens until they had time to wear off a little of their enthusiasm.

The bride looked anxiously at him. "What's worrying you, Jack?"

He laughed again. "I'm not worrying, girl. I'm only thinking of Yellow Sky."

She flushed in comprehension.

A sense of mutual guilt invaded their minds and developed a finer tenderness. They looked at each other with eyes softly aglow. But Potter often laughed the same nervous laugh. The flush upon the bride's face seemed quite permanent.

The traitor to the feelings of Yellow Sky narrowly watched the speeding land-scape. "We're nearly there," he said.

Presently the porter came and announced the proximity of Potter's home. He held a brush in his hand and, with all his airy superiority gone, he brushed Potter's new clothes as the latter slowly turned this way and that way. Potter fumbled out a coin and gave it to the porter as he had seen others do. It was a heavy and muscle-bound business, as that of a man shoeing his first horse.

The porter took their bag, and as the train began to slow they moved forward to the hooded platform of the car. Presently the two engines and their long string of coaches rushed into the station of Yellow Sky.

"They have to take water here," said Potter, from a constricted throat and in mournful cadence as one announcing death. Before the train stopped his eye had swept the length of the platform, and he was glad and astonished to see there was none upon it but the station-agent, who, with a slightly hurried and anxious air, was walking to-ward the water-tanks. When the train had halted, the porter alighted first and placed in position a little temporary step.

"Come on, girl," said Potter hoarsely. As he helped her down they each laughed on a false note. He took the bag from the negro, and bade his wife cling to his arm. As they slunk rapidly away, his hang-dog glance perceived that they were unloading the two trunks, and also that the station-agent far ahead near the baggage-car had turned and was running toward him, making gestures. He laughed, and groaned as he laughed, when he noted the first effect of his marital bliss upon Yellow Sky. He gripped his wife's arm firmly to his side, and they fled. Behind them the porter stood chuckling fatuously.

II

The California Express on the Southern Railway was due at Yellow Sky in twenty-one minutes. There were six men at the bar of the Weary Gentleman saloon. One was a drummer who talked a great deal and rapidly; three were Texans who did not care to talk at that time; and two were Mexican sheep-herders who did not talk as a general practice in the Weary Gentleman saloon. The bar-keeper's dog lay on the board-walk that crossed in front of the door. His head was on his paws, and he glanced drowsily here and there with the constant vigilance of a dog that is kicked on occasion. Across the sandy street were some vivid green grass plots, so wonderful in appearance amid the sands that burned near them in a blazing sun that they caused a doubt in the mind. They exactly resem-bled the grass mats used to represent lawns on the stage. At the cooler end of the rail-way station a man without a coat sat in a tilted chair and smoked his pipe. The fresh-cut bank of the Rio Grande circled near the town, and there could be seen beyond it a great plum-colored plain of mesquite.

Save for the busy drummer and his com-panions in the saloon, Yellow Sky was doz-ing. The new-comer leaned gracefully upon the bar, and recited many tales with the confidence of a bard who has come upon a new field.

"——and at the moment that the old man fell down stairs with the bureau in his arms, the old woman was coming up with two scuttles of coal, and, of course——"

The drummer's tale was interrupted by

a young man who suddenly appeared in the open door. He cried: "Scratchy Wilson's drunk, and has turned loose with both hands." The two Mexicans at once set down their glasses and faded out of the rear entrance of the saloon.

The drummer, innocent and jocular, answered: "All right, old man. S'pose he has. Come in and have a drink, anyhow."

But the information had made such an obvious cleft in every skull in the room that the drummer was obliged to see its importance. All had become instantly morose. "Say," said he, mystified, "what is this?" His three companions made the introductory gesture of eloquent speech, but the young man at the door forestalled them.

"It means, my friend," he answered, as he came into the saloon, "that for the next two hours this town won't be a health resort."

The bar-keeper went to the door and locked and barred it. Reaching out of the window, he pulled in heavy wooden shutters and barred them. Immediately a solemn, chapel-like gloom was upon the place. The drummer was looking from one to another.

"But say," he cried, "what is this, anyhow? You don't mean there is going to be a gun-fight?"

"Don't know whether there'll be a fight or not," answered one man grimly. "But there'll be some shootin'—some good shootin'."

The young man who had warned them waved his hand. "Oh, there'll be a fight fast enough, if anyone wants it. Anybody can get a fight out there in the street. There's a fight just waiting."

The drummer seemed to be swayed between the interest of a foreigner and a perception of personal danger.

"What did you say his name was?" he asked.

"Scratchy Wilson," they answered in chorus.

"And will he kill anybody? What are you going to do? Does this happen often? Does he rampage around like this once a week or so? Can he break in that door?"

"No, he can't break down that door," replied the bar-keeper. "He's tried it three times. But when he comes you'd better lay down on the floor, stranger. He's dead sure to shoot at it, and a bullet may come through."

Thereafter the drummer kept a strict eye upon the door. The time had not yet been called for him to hug the floor, but as a minor precaution he sidled near to the wall. "Will he kill anybody?" he said again.

The men laughed low and scornfully at the question.

"He's out to shoot, and he's out for trouble. Don't see any good in experimentin' with him."

"But what do you do in a case like this? What do you do?"

A man responded: "Why, he and Jack Potter——"

But, in chorus, the other men interrupted: "Jack Potter's in San Anton'."

"Well, who is he? What's he got to do with it?"

"Oh, he's the town marshal. He goes out and fights Scratchy when he gets on one of these tears."

"Wow," said the drummer, mopping his brow. "Nice job he's got."

The voices had toned away to mere whisperings. The drummer wished to ask further questions which were born of an increasing anxiety and bewilderment; but when he attempted them, the men merely looked at him in irritation and motioned him to remain silent. A tense waiting hush was upon them. In the deep shadows of the room their eyes shone as they listened for sounds from the street. One man made three gestures at the bar-keeper, and the latter, moving like a ghost, handed him a glass and a bottle. The man poured a full glass of whisky, and set down the bottle noiselessly. He gulped the whisky in a swallow, and turned again toward the door in immovable silence. The drummer saw that the bar-keeper, without a sound, had taken a Winchester from beneath the bar. Later he saw this individual beckoning to him, so he tiptoed across the room.

"You better come with me back of the bar."

"No, thanks," said the drummer, perspiring. "I'd rather be where I can make a break for the back door."

Whereupon the man of bottles made a kindly but peremptory gesture. The drummer obeyed it, and finding himself seated on a box with his head below the level of the bar, balm was laid upon his soul at sight of various zinc and copper fittings that bore a resemblance to armor-plate. The bar-keeper took a seat comfortably upon an adjacent box.

"You see," he whispered, "this here Scratchy Wilson is a wonder with a gun— a perfect wonder—and when he goes on the war trail, we hunt our holes—naturally. He's about the last one of the old gang that used to hang out along the river here. He's a terror when he's drunk. When he's sober he's all right—kind of simple—wouldn't hurt a fly—nicest fellow in town. But when he's drunk—whoo!"

There were periods of stillness. "I wish Jack Potter was back from San Anton'," said the bar-keeper. "He shot Wilson up once—in the leg—and he would sail in and pull out the kinks in this thing."

Presently they heard from a distance the sound of a shot, followed by three wild yowls. It instantly removed a bond from the men in the darkened saloon. There was a shuffling of feet. They looked at each other. "Here he comes," they said.

III

A man in a maroon-colored flannel shirt, which had been purchased for purposes of decoration and made, principally, by some Jewish women on the east side of New York, rounded a corner and walked into the middle of the main street of Yellow Sky. In either hand the man held a long, heavy blue-black revolver. Often he yelled, and these cries rang through a semblance of a deserted village, shrilly flying over the roofs in a volume that seemed to have no relation to the ordinary vocal strength of a man. It was as if the surrounding stillness formed the arch of a tomb over him. These cries of ferocious challenge rang against walls of silence. And his boots had red tops with gilded imprints, of the kind beloved in winter by little sledding boys on the hillsides of New England.

The man's face flamed in a rage begot of whisky. His eyes, rolling and yet keen for ambush, hunted the still door-ways and windows. He walked with the creeping movement of the midnight cat. As it occurred to him, he roared menacing information. The long revolvers in his hands were as easy as straws; they were moved with an electric swiftness. The little fingers of each hand played sometimes in a musician's way. Plain from the low collar of the shirt, the cords of his neck straightened and sank, straightened and sank, as passion moved him. The only sounds were his terrible invitations. The calm adobes preserved their demeanor at the passing of this small thing in the middle of the street.

There was no offer of fight; no offer of fight. The man called to the sky. There were no attractions. He bellowed and fumed and swayed his revolvers here and everywhere.

The dog of the bar-keeper of the Weary Gentleman saloon had not appreciated the advance of events. He yet lay dozing in front of his master's door. At sight of the dog, the man paused and raised his revolver humorously. At sight of the man, the dog sprang up and walked diagonally away, with a sullen head and growling. The man yelled, and the dog broke into a gallop. As it was about to enter an alley, there was a loud noise, a whistling, and something spat the ground directly before it. The dog screamed, and, wheeling in terror, galloped headlong in a new direction. Again there was a noise, a whistling, and sand was kicked viciously before it. Fear-stricken, the dog turned and flurried like an animal in a pen. The man stood laughing, his weapons at his hips.

Ultimately the man was attracted by the closed door of the Weary Gentleman saloon. He went to it, and hammering with a revolver, demanded drink.

The door remaining imperturbable, he picked a bit of paper from the walk and nailed it to the framework with a knife. He then turned his back contemptuously upon this popular resort, and walking to the opposite side of the street, and spinning there on his heel quickly and lithely, fired at the bit of paper. He missed it by a half inch. He swore at himself, and went away. Later, he comfortably fusilladed the windows of his most intimate friend. The man was playing with this town. It was a toy for him.

But still there was no offer of fight. The name of Jack Potter, his ancient antagonist, entered his mind, and he concluded that it would be a glad thing if he should go to Potter's house and by bombardment induce him to come out and fight. He moved in the direction of his desire, chanting Apache scalp-music.

When he arrived at it, Potter's house presented the same still, calm front as had the other adobes. Taking up a strategic position, the man howled a challenge. But this house regarded him as might a great stone god. It gave no sign. After a decent wait, the man howled further challenges, mingling with them wonderful epithets.

Presently there came the spectacle of a man churning himself into deepest rage over the immobility of a house. He fumed at it as the winter wind attacks a prairie cabin in the North. To the distance there should have gone the sound of a tumult like the fighting of two hundred Mexicans. As necessity bade him, he paused for breath or to reload his revolvers.

IV

Potter and his bride walked sheepishly and with speed. Sometimes they laughed together shamefacedly and low.

"Next corner, dear," he said finally.

They put forth the efforts of a pair walking bowed against a strong wind. Potter was about to raise a finger to point the first appearance of the new home when, as they circled the corner, they came face to face with a man in a maroon-colored shirt who was feverishly pushing cartridges into a large revolver. Upon the instant the man dropped this revolver to the ground, and, like lightning, whipped another from its holster. The second weapon was aimed at the bridegroom's chest.

There was a silence. Potter's mouth seemed to be merely a grave for his tongue. He exhibited an instinct to at once loosen his arm from the woman's grip, and he dropped the bag to the sand. As for the bride, her face had gone as yellow as old cloth. She was a slave to hideous rites gazing at the apparitional snake.

The two men faced each other at a distance of three paces. He of the revolver smiled with a new and quiet ferocity. "Tried to sneak up on me," he said. "Tried to sneak up on me!" His eyes grew more baleful. As Potter made a slight movement, the man thrust his revolver venomously forward. "No, don't you do it, Jack Potter. Don't you move a finger toward a gun just yet. Don't you move an eyelash. The time has come for me to settle with you, and I'm goin' to do it my own way and loaf along with no interferin'. So if you don't want a gun bent on you, just mind what I tell you."

Potter looked at his enemy. "I ain't got a gun on me, Scratchy," he said. "Honest, I ain't." He was stiffening and steadying, but yet somewhere at the back of his mind a vision of the Pullman floated, the sea-green figured velvet, the shining brass, silver, and glass, the wood that gleamed as darkly brilliant as the surface of a pool of oil—all the glory of the marriage, the environment of the new estate. "You know I fight when it comes to fighting, Scratchy Wilson, but I ain't got a gun on me. You'll have to do all the shootin' yourself."

His enemy's face went livid. He stepped forward and lashed his weapon to and fro before Potter's chest. "Don't you tell me you ain't got no gun on you, you whelp. Don't tell me no lie like that. There ain't a man in Texas ever seen you without no gun. Don't take me for no kid." His eyes blazed with light, and his throat worked like a pump.

"I ain't takin' you for no kid," answered Potter. His heels had not moved an inch backward. "I'm takin' you for a ——— fool. I tell you I ain't got a gun, and I ain't. If you're goin' to shoot me up, you better begin now. You'll never get a chance like this again."

So much enforced reasoning had told on Wilson's rage. He was calmer. "If you ain't got a gun, why ain't you got a gun?" he sneered. "Been to Sunday-school?"

"I ain't got a gun because I've just come from San Anton' with my wife. I'm married," said Potter. "And if I'd thought there was going to be any galoots like you prowling around when I brought my wife home, I'd had a gun, and don't you forget it."

"Married!" said Scratchy, not all comprehending.

"Yes, married. I'm married," said Potter distinctly.

"Married?" said Scratchy. Seemingly for the first time he saw the drooping drowning woman at the other man's side. "No!" he said. He was like a creature allowed a glimpse of another world. He moved a pace backward, and his arm with the revolver dropped to his side. "Is this—is this the lady?" he asked.

"Yes, this is the lady," answered Potter.

There was another period of silence.

"Well," said Wilson at last, slowly, "I s'pose it's all off now."

"It's all off if you say so, Scratchy. You know I didn't make the trouble." Potter lifted his valise.

"Well, I 'low it's off, Jack," said Wilson. He was looking at the ground. "Married!" He was not a student of chivalry; it was merely that in the presence of this foreign condition he was a simple child of the earlier plains. He picked up his starboard revolver, and placing both weapons in their holsters, he went away. His feet made funnel-shaped tracks in the heavy sand.

Hamlin Garland

Hamlin Garland (1860–1940) focused his attention on the region of his childhood, which he called the Middle Border (Minnesota, Wisconsin, North Dakota, South Dakota, and Nebraska). His stories picture the hard life of the yeoman farmer who must endure not only the privations of nature but also the greed of the "money men." Though Garland's rural landscape is naturalistic, most of his stories end somewhat optimistically.

UNDER THE LION'S PAW

It was the last of autumn and first day of winter coming together. All day long the ploughmen on their prairie farms had moved to and fro in their wide level fields through the falling snow, which melted as it fell, wetting them to the skin—all day, notwithstanding the frequent squalls of snow, the dripping, desolate clouds, and the muck of the furrows, black and tenacious as tar.

Under their dripping harness the horses swung to and fro silently, with that marvellous uncomplaining patience which marks the horse. All day the wild geese, honking wildly, as they sprawled sidewise down the wind, seemed to be fleeing from an enemy behind, and with neck outthrust and wings extended, sailed down the wind, soon lost to sight.

Yet the ploughman behind his plough, though the snow lay on his ragged great-coat, and the cold clinging mud rose on his heavy boots, fettering him like gyves, whistled in the very beard of the gale. As day passed, the snow, ceasing to melt, lay along the ploughed land, and lodged in the depth of the stubble, till on each slow round the last furrow stood out black and shining as jet between the ploughed land and the gray stubble.

When night began to fall, and the geese, flying low, began to alight invisibly in the near corn-field, Stephen Council was still at work "finishing a land." He rode on his sulky plough when going with the wind, but walked when facing it. Sitting bent and cold but cheery under his slouch hat, he talked encouragingly to his four-in-hand.

"Come round there, boys!—Round agin! We got t' finish this land. Come in there, Dan! *Stiddy*, Kate,—stiddy! None o' y'r tantrums, Kittie. It's purty tuff, but got a be did. *Tchk! tchk!* Step along, Pete! Don't let Kate git y'r single-tree on the wheel. *Once* more!"

They seemed to know what he meant, and that this was the last round, for they worked with greater vigor than before.

"Once more, boys, an' then, sez I, oats an' a nice warm stall, an' sleep f'r all."

By the time the last furrow was turned on the land it was too dark to see the house, and the snow was changing to rain again. The tired and hungry man could see the light from the kitchen shining through the leafless hedge, and he lifted a great shout, "Supper f'r a half a dozen!"

It was nearly eight o'clock by the time he had finished his chores and started for supper. He was picking his way carefully through the mud, when the tall form of a man loomed up before him with a premonitory cough.

"Waddy ye want?" was the rather startled question of the farmer.

"Well, ye see," began the stranger, in a deprecating tone, "we'd like t' git in f'r the night. We've tried every house f'r the last two miles, but they hadn't any room f'r us. My wife's jest about sick, 'n' the children are cold and hungry——"

"Oh, y' want 'o stay all night, eh?"

"Yes, sir; it 'ud be a great accom——"

"Waal, I don't make it a practice t' turn anybuddy way hungry, not on sech nights as this. Drive right in. We ain't got much, but sech as it is——"

But the stranger had disappeared. And soon his steaming, weary team, with drooping heads and swinging single-trees, moved past the well to the block beside the path. Council stood at the side of the "schooner" and helped the children out—two little half-sleeping children—and then a small woman with a babe in her arms.

"There ye go!" he shouted jovially, to the children. "*Now* we're all right! Run right along to the house there, an' tell Mam' Council you wants sumpthin' t' eat. Right this way, Mis'—keep right off t' the right there. I'll go an' git a lantern. Come," he said to the dazed and silent group at his side.

"Mother," he shouted, as he neared the fragrant and warmly lighted kitchen, "here are some wayfarers an' folks who need sumpthin' t' eat an' a place t' snooze." He ended by pushing them all in.

Mrs. Council, a large, jolly, rather coarse-looking woman, took the children in her arms. "Come right in, you little rabbits. 'Most asleep, hey? Now here's a drink o' milk f'r each o' ye. I'll have s'm tea in a minute. Take off y'r things and set up t' the fire."

While she set the children to drinking milk, Council got out his lantern and went out to the barn to help the stranger about his team, where his loud, hearty voice could be heard as it came and went between the haymow and the stalls.

The woman came to light as a small, timid, and discouraged-looking woman, but still pretty, in a thin and sorrowful way.

"Land sakes! An' you've travelled all the way from Clear Lake t'-day in this mud! Waal! waal! No wonder you're all tired

out. Don't wait f'r the men, Mis' ———"
She hesitated, waiting for the name.

"Haskins."

"Mis' Haskins, set right up to the table an' take a good swig o' tea whilst I make y' s'm toast. It's green tea, an' it's good. I tell Council as I git older I don't seem to enjoy Young Hyson n'r Gunpowder. I want the reel green tea, jest as it comes off'n the vines. Seems t' have more heart in it, some way. Don't s'pose it has. Council says it's all in m' eye."

Going on in this easy way, she soon had the children filled with bread and milk and the woman thoroughly at home, eating some toast and sweet-melon pickles, and sipping the tea.

"See the little rats!" she laughed at the children. "They're full as they can stick now, and they want to go to bed. Now, don't git up, Mis' Haskins; set right where you are an' let me look after 'em. I know all about young ones, though I'm all alone now. Jane went an' married last fall. But, as I tell Council, it's lucky we keep our health. Set right there, Mis' Haskins; I won't have you stir a finger."

It was an unmeasured pleasure to sit there in the warm, homely kitchen, the jovial chatter of the housewife driving out and holding at bay the growl of the impotent, cheated wind.

The little woman's eyes filled with tears which fell down upon the sleeping baby in her arms. The world was not so desolate and cold and hopeless, after all.

"Now I hope. Council won't stop out there and talk politics all night. He's the greatest man to talk politics an' read the *Tribune*—How old is it?"

She broke off and peered down at the face of the babe.

"Two months 'n' five days," said the mother, with a mother's exactness.

"Ye don't say! I want 'o know! The dear little pudzy-wudzy!" she went on, stirring it up in the neighborhood of the ribs with her fat forefinger.

"Pooty tough on 'oo to go gallivant'n' 'cross lots this way——"

"Yes, that's so; a man can't lift a mountain," said Council, entering the door. "Mother, this is Mr. Haskins, from Kansas. He's been eat up 'n' drove out by grasshoppers."

"Glad t' see yeh!—Pa, empty that washbasin 'n' give him a chance t' wash."

Haskins was a tall man, with a thin, gloomy face. His hair was a reddish brown, like his coat, and seemed equally faded by the wind and sun, and his sallow face, though hard and set, was pathetic somehow. You would have felt that he had suffered much by the line of his mouth showing under his thin, yellow mustache.

"Hain't Ike got home yet, Sairy?"

"Hain't seen 'im."

"W-a-a-l, set right up, Mr. Haskins; wade right into what we've got; 'taint much, but we manage to live on it—she gits fat on it," laughed Council, pointing his thumb at his wife.

After supper, while the women put the children to bed, Haskins and Council talked on, seated near the huge cooking-stove, the steam rising from their wet clothing. In the Western fashion Council told as much of his own life as he drew from his guest. He asked but few questions, but by and by the story of Haskins' struggles and defeat came out. The story was a terrible one, but he told it quietly, seated with his elbows on his knees, gazing most of the time at the hearth.

"I didn't like the looks of the country, anyhow," Haskins said, partly rising and glancing at his wife. "I was ust t' northern Ingyannie, where we have lots o' timber 'n' lots o' rain, 'n' I didn't like the looks o' that dry prairie. What galled me the worst was goin' s' far away acrosst so much fine land layin' all through here vacant."

"And the 'hoppers eat ye four years, hand runnin', did they?"

"Eat! They wiped us out. They chawed everything that was green. They jest set around waitin' f'r us to die t' eat us, too. My God! I ust t' dream of 'em 'round on the bedpost, six feet long, workin' their jaws. They eet the fork-handles. They got worse 'n' worse till they jest rolled on one another, piled up like snow in winter. Well, it ain't no use. If I was t' talk all winter I couldn't tell nawthin'. But all the while I couldn't help thinkin' of all that land back here that nobuddy was usin' that I ought 'o had 'stead o' bein' out there in that cussed country."

"Waal, why didn't ye stop an' settle here?" asked Ike, who had come in and was eating his supper.

"Fer the simple reason that you fellers wantid ten 'r fifteen dollars an acre fer the bare land, and I hadn't no money fer that kind o' thing."

"Yes, I do my own work," Mrs. Council was heard to say in the pause which followed. "I'm a gettin' purty heavy t' be on m'laigs all day, but we can't afford t' hire, so I keep rackin' around somehow, like a foundered horse. S' lame—I tell Council he can't tell how lame I am, f'r I'm jest as lame in one laig as t' other." And the good soul laughed at the joke on herself as she took a handful of flour and dusted the biscuit-board to keep the dough from sticking.

"Well, I hain't *never* been very strong," said Mrs. Haskins. "Our folks was Canadians an' small-boned, and then since my last child I hain't got up again fairly. I don't like t' complain. Tim has about all he can bear now—but they was days this week when I jest wanted to lay right down an' die."

"Waal, now, I'll tell ye," said Council, from his side of the stove, silencing everybody with his good-natured roar, "I'd go down and *see* Butler, *anyway*, if I was you. I guess he'd let you have his place purty cheap; the farm's all run down. He's ben anxious t' let t' somebuddy next year. It 'ud be a good chance fer you. Anyhow, you go to bed and sleep like a babe. I've got

some ploughing t' do, anyhow, an' we'll see if somethin' can't be done about your case. Ike, you go out an' see if the horses is all right, an' I'll show the folks t' bed."

When the tired husband and wife were lying under the generous quilts of the spare bed, Haskins listened a moment to the wind in the eaves, and then said, with a slow and solemn tone,

"There are people in this world who are good enough t' be angels, an' only haff t' die to *be* angels."

II

Jim Butler was one of those men called in the West "land poor." Early in the history of Rock River he had come into the town and started in the grocery business in a small way, occupying a small building in a mean part of the town. At this period of his life he earned all he got, and was up early and late sorting beans, working over butter, and carting his goods to and from the station. But a change came over him at the end of the second year when he sold a lot of land for four times what he paid for it. From that time forward he believed in land speculation as the surest way of getting rich. Every cent he could save or spare from his trade he put into land at forced sale, or mortgages on land, which were "just as good as the wheat," he was accustomed to say.

Farm after farm fell into his hands, until he was recognized as one of the leading landowners of the county. His mortgages were scattered all over Cedar County, and as they slowly but surely fell in he sought usually to retain the former owner as tenant.

He was not ready to foreclose; indeed, he had the name of being one of the "easiest" men in the town. He let the debtor off again and again, extending the time whenever possible.

"I don't want y'r land," he said. "All I'm after is the int'rest on my money—that's all. Now, if y' want 'o stay on the farm, why,

I'll give y' a good chance. I can't have the land layin' vacant." And in many cases the owner remained as tenant.

In the meantime he had sold his store; he couldn't spend time in it; he was mainly occupied now with sitting around town on rainy days smoking and "gassin' with the boys," or in riding to and from his farms. In fishing-time he fished a good deal. Doc Grimes, Ben Ashley, and Cal Cheatham were his cronies on these fishing excursions or hunting trips in the time of chickens or partridges. In winter they went to Northern Wisconsin to shoot deer.

In spite of all these signs of easy life Butler persisted in saying he "hadn't enough money to pay taxes on his land," and was careful to convey the impression that he was poor in spite of his twenty farms. At one time he was said to be worth fifty thousand dollars, but land had been a little slow of sale of late, so that he was not worth so much.

A fine farm, known as the Higley place, had fallen into his hands in the usual way the previous year, and he had not been able to find a tenant for it. Poor Higley, after working himself nearly to death on it in the attempt to lift the mortgage, had gone off to Dakota, leaving the farm and his curse to Butler.

This was the farm which Council advised Haskins to apply for; and the next day Council hitched up his team and drove down to see Butler.

"You jest let *me* do the talkin'," he said. "We'll find him wearin' out his pants on some salt barrel somew'ers; and if he thought you *wanted* a place he'd sock it to you hot and heavy. You jest keep quiet; I'll fix 'im."

Butler was seated in Ben Ashley's store telling fish yarns when Council sauntered in casually.

"Hello, But; lyin' agin, hey?"

"Hello, Steve! How goes it?"

"Oh, so-so. Too dang much rain these days. I thought it was goin' t' freeze up f'r good last night. Tight squeak if I get m'

ploughin' done. How's farmin' with *you* these days?"

"Bad. Ploughin' ain't half done."

"It 'ud be a religious idee f'r you t' go out an' take a hand y'rself."

"I don't haff to," said Butler, with a wink.

"Got anybody on the Higley place?"

"No. Know of anybody?"

"Waal, no; not eggsackly. I've got a relation back t' Michigan who's ben hot an' cold on the idee o' comin' West f'r some time. *Might* come if he could get a good layout. What do you talk on the farm?"

"Well, I d' know. I'll rent it on shares or I'll rent it money rent."

"Waal, how much money, say?"

"Well, say ten per cent, on the price—two-fifty."

"Wall, that ain't bad. Wait on 'im till 'e thrashes?"

Haskins listened eagerly to this important question, but Council was coolly eating a dried apple which he had speared out of a barrel with his knife. Butler studied him carefully.

"Well, knocks me out of twenty-five dollars interest."

"My relation'll need all he's got t' git his crops in," said Council, in the same, indifferent way.

"Well, all right; *say* wait," concluded Butler.

"All right; this is the man. Haskins, this is Mr. Butler—no relation to Ben—the hardest-working man in Cedar County."

On the way home Haskins said: "I ain't much better off. I'd like that farm; it's a good farm, but it's all run down, an' so 'am I. I could make a good farm of it if I had half a show. But I can't stock it n'r seed it."

"Waal, now, don't you worry," roared Council in his ear. "We'll pull y' through somehow till next harvest. He's agreed t' hire it ploughed, an' you can earn a hundred dollars ploughin' an' y' c'n git the seed o' me, an' pay me back when y' can."

Haskins was silent with emotion, but at last he said, "I ain't got nothin' t' live on."

"Now, don't you worry 'bout that. You jest make your headquarters at ol' Steve Council's. Mother'll take a pile o' comfort in havin' y'r wife an' children 'round. Y' see, Jane's married off lately, an' Ike's away a good 'eal, so we'll be darn glad t' have y' stop with us this winter. Nex' spring we'll see if y' can't git a start agin." And he chirruped to the team, which sprang forward with the rumbling, clattering wagon.

"Say, looky here, Council, you can't do this. I never saw——" shouted Haskins in his neighbor's ear.

Council moved about uneasily in his seat and stopped his stammering gratitude by saying: "Hold on, now; don't make such a fuss over a little thing. When I see a man down, an' things all on top of 'm, I jest like t' kick 'em off an' help 'm up. That's the kind of religion I got, an' it's about the *only* kind."

They rode the rest of the way home in silence. And when the red light of the lamp shone out into the darkness of the cold and windy night, and he thought of this refuge for his children and wife, Haskins could have put his arm around the neck of his burly companion and squeezed him like a lover. But he contented himself with saying, "Steve Council, you'll git y'r pay f'r this some day."

"Don't want any pay. My religion ain't run on such business principles."

The wind was growing colder, and the ground was covered with a white frost, as they turned into the gate of the Council farm, and the children came rushing out, shouting, "Papa's come!" They hardly looked like the same children who had sat at the table the night before. Their torpidity, under the influence of sunshine and Mother Council, had given way to a sort of spasmodic cheerfulness, as insects in winter revive when laid on the hearth.

III

Haskins worked like a fiend, and his wife, like the heroic woman that she was, bore also uncomplainingly the most terrible burdens. They rose early and toiled without intermission till the darkness fell on the plain, then tumbled into bed, every bone and muscle aching with fatigue, to rise with the sun next morning to the same round of the same ferocity of labor.

The eldest boy drove a team all through the spring, ploughing and seeding, milked the cows, and did chores innumerable, in most ways taking the place of a man.

An infinitely pathetic but common figure —this boy on the American farm, where there is no law against child labor. To see him in his coarse clothing, his huge boots, and his ragged cap, as he staggered with a pail of water from the well, or trudged in the cold and cheerless dawn out into the frosty field behind his team, gave the city-bred visitor a sharp pang of sympathetic pain. Yet Haskins loved his boy, and would have saved him from this if he could, but he could not.

By June the first year the result of such Herculean toil began to show on the farm. The yard was cleaned up and sown to grass, the garden ploughed and planted, and the house mended.

Council had given them four of his cows.

"Take 'em an' run 'em on shares. I don't want 'o milk s' many. Ike's away s' much now, Sat'd'ys an' Sund'ys, I can't stand the bother anyhow."

Other men, seeing the confidence of Council in the newcomer, had sold him tools on time; and as he was really an able farmer, he soon had round him many evidences of his care and thrift. At the advice of Council he had taken the farm for three years, with the privilege of re-renting or buying at the end of the term.

"It's a good bargain, an' y' want 'o nail it," said Council. "If you have any kind ov a crop, you c'n pay y'r debts, an' keep seed an' bread."

The new hope which now sprang up in the heart of Haskins and his wife grew almost as a pain by the time the wide field of wheat began to wave and rustle and swirl in the winds of July. Day after day he would snatch a few moments after supper to go and look at it.

"Have ye seen the wheat t'-day, Nettie?" he asked one night as he rose from supper.

"No, Tim, I ain't had time."

"Well, take time now. Le's go look at it."

She threw an old hat on her head—Tommy's hat—and looking almost pretty in her thin, sad way, went out with her husband to the hedge.

"Ain't it grand, Nettie? Just look at it."

It was grand. Level, russet here and there, heavy-headed, wide as a lake, and full of multitudinous whispers and gleams of wealth, it stretched away before the gazers like the fabled field of the cloth of gold.

"Oh, I think—I *hope* we'll have a good crop, Tim; and oh, how good the people have been to us!"

"Yes; I don't know where we'd be t'-day if it hadn't been f'r Council and his wife."

"They're the best people in the world," said the little woman, with a great sob of gratitude.

"We'll be in the field on Monday sure," said Haskins, gripping the rail on the fences as if already at the work of the harvest.

The harvest came, bounteous, glorious, but the winds came and blew it into tangles, and the rain matted it here and there close to the ground, increasing the work of gathering it threefold.

Oh, how they toiled in those glorious days! Clothing dripping with sweat, arms aching, filled with briers, fingers raw and bleeding, backs broken with the weight of heavy bundles, Haskins and his man toiled on. Tommy drove the harvester, while his father and a hired man bound on the machine. In this way they cut ten acres every day, and almost every night after supper, when the hand went to bed, Haskins returned to the field shocking the bound grain in the light of the moon. Many a night he worked till his anxious wife came out at ten o'clock to call him in to rest and lunch.

At the same time she cooked for the men, took care of the children, washed and ironed, milked the cows at night, made the butter, and sometimes fed the horses and watered them while her husband kept at the shocking.

No slave in the Roman galleys could have toiled so frightfully and lived, for this man thought himself a free man, and that he was working for his wife and babes.

When he sank into his bed with a deep groan of relief, too tired to change his grimy, dripping clothing, he felt that he was getting nearer and nearer to a home of his own, and pushing the wolf of want a little farther from his door.

There is no despair so deep as the despair of a homeless man or woman. To roam the roads of the country or the streets of the city, to feel there is no rood of ground on which the feet can rest, to halt weary and hungry outside lighted windows and hear laughter and song within,—these are the hungers and rebellions that drive men to crime and women to shame.

It was the memory of this homelessness, and the fear of its coming again, that spurred Timothy Haskins and Nettie, his wife, to such ferocious labor during that first year.

IV

" 'M, yes; 'm, yes; first-rate," said Butler, as his eye took in the neat garden, the pig-pen, and the well-filled barnyard. "You're gitt'n' quite a stock around yeh. Done well, eh?"

Haskins was showing Butler around the place. He had not seen it for a year, having spent the year in Washington and Boston with Ashley, his brother-in-law, who had been elected to Congress.

"Yes, I've laid out a good deal of money durin' the last three years. I've paid out three hundred dollars f'r fencin.' "

"Um–h'm! I see, I see," said Butler, while Haskins went on:

"The kitchen there cost two hundred; the barn ain't cost much in money, but I've put a lot o' time on it. I've dug a new well, and I——"

"Yes, yes, I see. You've done well. Stock worth a thousand dollars," said Butler, picking his teeth with a straw.

"About that," said Haskins, modestly. "We begin to feel's if we was gitt'n' a home f'r ourselves; but we've worked hard. I tell you we begin to feel it, Mr. Butler, and we're goin' t' begin to ease up purty soon. We've been kind o' plannin' a trip back t' *her* folks after the fall ploughin's done."

"*Eggs-actly!*" said Butler, who was evidently thinking of something else. "I suppose you've kind o' calc'lated on stayin' here three years more?"

"Well, yes. Fact is, I think I c'n buy the farm this fall, if you'll give me a reasonable show."

"Um—m! What do you call a reasonable show?"

"Well, say a quarter down and three years' time."

Butler looked at the huge stacks of wheat, which filled the yard, over which the chickens were fluttering and crawling, catching grasshoppers, and out of which the crickets were singing innumerably. He smiled in a peculiar way as he said, "Oh, I won't be hard on yeh. But what did you expect to pay f'r the place?"

"Why, about what you offered it for before, two thousand five hundred, or *possibly* three thousand dollars," he added quickly, as he saw the owner shake his head.

"This farm is worth five thousand and five hundred dollars," said Butler, in a careless and decided voice.

"*What!*" almost shrieked the astounded Haskins. "What's that? Five thousand? Why, that's double what you offered it for three years ago."

"Of course, and it's worth it. It was all run down then; now it's in good shape.

You've laid out fifteen hundred dollars in improvements, according to your own story."

"But *you* had nothin' t' do about that. It's my work an' my money."

"You bet it was; but it's my land."

"But what's to pay me for all my——"

"Ain't you had the use of 'em?" replied Butler, smiling calmly into his face.

Haskins was like a man struck on the head with a sandbag; he couldn't think; he stammered as he tried to say: "But—I never'd git the use—You'd rob me! More'n that: you agreed—you promised that I could buy or rent at the end of three years at——"

"That's all right. But I didn't say I'd let you carry off the improvements, nor that I'd go on renting the farm at two-fifty. The land is doubled in value, it don't matter how; it don't enter into the question; an' now you can pay me five hundred dollars a year rent, or take it on your own terms at fifty-five hundred, or—git out."

He was turning away when Haskins, the sweat pouring from his face, fronted him, saying again:

"But *you've* done nothing to make it so. You hain't added a cent. I put it all there myself, expectin' to buy. I worked an' sweat to improve it. I was workin' for myself an' babes——"

"Well, why didn't you buy when I offered to sell? What y' kickin' about?"

"I'm kickin' about payin' you twice f'r my own things,—my own fences, my own kitchen, my own garden."

Butler laughed. "You're too green t' eat, young feller. *Your* improvements! The law will sing another tune."

"But I trusted your word."

"Never trust anybody, my friend. Besides, I didn't promise not to do this thing. Why, man, don't look at me like that. Don't take me for a thief. It's the law. The reg'lar thing. Everybody does it."

"I don't care if they do. It's stealin' jest the same. You take three thousand dollars of my money—the work o' my hands and my wife's." He broke down at this point. He was not a strong man mentally. He could face hardship, ceaseless toil, but he could not face the cold and sneering face of Butler.

"But I don't take it," said Butler, coolly. "All you've got to do is to go on jest as you've been a-doin,' or give me a thousand dollars down, and a mortgage at ten per cent on the rest."

Haskins sat down blindly on a bundle of oats near by, and with staring eyes and drooping head went over the situation. He was under the lion's paw. He felt a horrible numbness in his heart and limbs. He was hid in a mist, and there was no path out.

Butler walked about, looking at the huge stacks of grain, and pulling now and again a few handfuls out, shelling the heads in his hands and blowing the chaff away. He hummed a little tune as he did so. He had an accommodating air of waiting.

Haskins was in the midst of the terrible toil of the last year. He was walking again in the rain and the mud behind his plough; he felt the dust and dirt of the threshing. The ferocious husking-time, with its cutting wind and biting, clinging snows, lay hard upon him. Then he thought of his wife, how she had cheerfully cooked and baked, without holiday and without rest.

"Well, what do you think of it?" inquired the cool, mocking, insinuating voice of Butler.

"I think you're a thief and a liar!" shouted Haskins, leaping up. "A black-hearted houn'!" Butler's smile maddened

him; with a sudden leap he caught a fork in his hands, and whirled it in the air. "You'll never rob another man, damn ye!" he grated through his teeth, a look of pitiless ferocity in his accusing eyes.

Butler shrank and quivered, expecting the blow; stood, held hypnotized by the eyes of the man he had a moment before despised—a man transformed into an avenging demon. But in the deadly hush between the lift of the weapon and its fall there came a gush of faint, childish laughter and then across the range of his vision, far away and dim, he saw the sun-bright head of his baby girl, as, with the pretty, tottering run of a two-year-old, she moved across the grass of the dooryard. His hands relaxed: the fork fell to the ground; his head lowered.

"Make out y'r deed an' mor'gage, an' git off'n my land, an' don't ye never cross my line again; if y' do, I'll kill ye."

Butler backed away from the man in wild haste, and climbing into his buggy with trembling limbs drove off down the road, leaving Haskins seated dumbly on the sunny pile of sheaves, his head sunk into his hands.

E. E. Cummings

This poem captures the lyrical qualities of a Wild West hero eclipsed by death. Cummings is described on page 121.

BUFFALO BILL'S

          Buffalo Bill's
          defunct
                    who used to
                    ride a watersmooth-silver

                              stallion
          and break onetwothreefourfive pigeonsjustlikethat
                                        Jesus

          he was a handsome man
                              and what i want to know is
          how do you like your blueeyed boy
          Mister Death

THE CITY

Walt Whitman

In this poem, Whitman shows his love for New York City with its exciting views of harbors, skyscrapers, and busy people. (Whitman is described on page 18.)

MANNAHATTA

I was asking for something specific and
    perfect for my city,
Whereupon lo! upsprang the aboriginal
    name.

Now I see what there is in a name, a word,
    liquid, sane, unruly, musical self-suf-
    ficient,
I see that the word of my city is that word
    from of old,
Because I see that word nested in nests of
    water-bays, superb,
Rich, hemm'd thick all around with
    sailships and steamships, an island
    sixteen miles long, solid-founded,
Numberless crowded streets, high growths
    of iron, slender, strong, light, splendidly
    uprising toward clear skies,
Tides swift and ample, well-loved by me,
    toward sundown,
The flowing sea-currents, the little islands,
    larger adjoining islands, the heights,
    the villas,
The countless masts, the white shore-steam-
    ers, the lighters, the ferry-boats, the
    black sea-steamers well-model'd,
The down-town streets, the jobbers' houses
    of business, the houses of business of
    the ship-merchants and money-brokers,
    the river-streets,

Immigrants arriving, fifteen or twenty
    thousand in a week,
The carts hauling goods, the manly race
    of drivers of horses, the brown-faced
    sailors,
The summer air, the bright sun shining,
    and the sailing clouds aloft,
The winter snows, the sleigh-bells, the
    broken ice in the river, passing along
    up or down with the flood-tide or
    ebb-tide,
The mechanics of the city, the masters,
    well-form'd, beautiful-faced, looking
    you straight in the eyes,
Trottoirs throng'd, vehicles, Broadway, the
    women, the shops and shows,
A million people—manners free and superb
    —open voices—hospitality—the most
    courageous and friendly young men,
City of hurried and sparkling waters! city
    of spires and masts!
City nested in bays! my city!

Carl Sandburg

Carl Sandburg (1878–1967), influenced by the spirit of Whitman (though not his poetic equal), celebrates America in the power of its landscape, architecture, history, and people. As a youth he had a variety of experiences, from being a hobo in the west to a soldier in the Spanish-American War to a newspaper reporter and correspondent. His six-volume biography of Abraham Lincoln won a Pulitzer Prize. The two following poems show Sandburg's ambivalence towards the rise of the city around the turn of the twentieth century, for though he recognizes

230

*a special vitality in the city, he also sees it
as absorbing the spirit of individualism.*

CHICAGO

Hog Butcher for the World,
Tool Maker, Stacker of Wheat,
Player with Railroads and the Nation's
    Freight Handler;
Stormy, husky, brawling,
City of the Big Shoulders:

They tell me you are wicked and I believe
them, for I have seen your painted women
under the gas lamps luring the farm boys.
And they tell me you are crooked and I
answer: Yes, it is true I have seen the
gunman kill and go free to kill again.
And they tell me you are brutal and my
reply is: On the faces of women and
children I have seen the marks of wanton
hunger.
And having answered so I turn once more
to those who sneer at this my city, and I
give them back the sneer and say to them:
Come and show me another city with lifted
head singing so proud to be alive and
coarse and strong and cunning.
Flinging magnetic curses amid the toil of
piling job on job, here is a tall slugger set
vivid against the little soft cities;
Fierce as a dog with tongue lapping for
action, cunning as a savage pitted against
the wilderness,
    Bareheaded,
    Shoveling,
    Wrecking,
    Planning,
    Building, breaking, rebuilding,
Under the smoke, dust all over his mouth,
laughing with white teeth,
Under the terrible burden of destiny laughing as a young man laughs,
Laughing even as an ignorant fighter laughs
who has never lost a battle,

Bragging and laughing that under his wrist
is the pulse, and under his ribs the heart
of the people,

Laughing!
Laughing the stormy, husky, brawling
laughter of Youth, half-naked, sweating,
proud to be Hog Butcher, Tool Maker,
Stacker of Wheat, Player with Railroads
and Freight Handler to the Nation.

SKYSCRAPER

By day the skyscraper looms in the smoke
and sun and has a soul.
Prairie and valley, streets of the city, pour
people into it and they mingle among
its twenty floors and are poured out again
back to the streets, prairies and valleys.
It is the men and women, boys and girls
so poured in and out all day that they
give the building a soul of dreams and
thoughts and memories.
(Dumped in the sea or fixed in a desert,
who would care for the building or speak
its name or ask a policeman the way to
it?)

Elevators slide on their cables and tubes
catch letters and parcels and iron pipes
carry gas and water in and sewage out.
Wires climb with secrets, carry light and
carry words, and tell terrors and profits
and loves—curses of men grappling plans
of business and questions of women in
plots of love.

Hour by hour the caissons reach down to
the rock of the earth and hold the building to a turning planet.
Hour by hour the girders play as ribs and
reach out and hold together the stone
walls and floors.
Hour by hour the hand of the mason and
the stuff of the mortar clinch the pieces
and parts to the shape an architect voted.
Hour by hour the sun and the rain, the
air and the rust, and the press of time
running into centuries, play on the building inside and out and use it.

Men who sunk the pilings and mixed the

mortar are laid in graves where the wind whistles a wild song without words.

And so are men who strung the wires and fixed the pipes and tubes and those who saw it rise floor by floor.

Souls of them all are here, even the hod carrier begging at back doors hundreds of miles away and the bricklayer who went to state's prison for shooting another man while drunk.

(One man fell from a girder and broke his neck at the end of a straight plunge—he is here—his soul has gone into the stones of the building.)

On the office doors from tier to tier— hundreds of names and each name standing for a face written across with a dead child, a passionate lover, a driving ambition for a million dollar business or a lobster's ease of life.

Behind the signs on the doors they work and the walls tell nothing from room to room.

Ten-dollar-a-week stenographers take letters from corporation officers, lawyers, efficiency engineers, and tons of letters go bundled from the building to all ends of the earth.

Smiles and tears of each office girl go into the soul of the building just the same as the master-men who rule the building.

Hands of clocks turn to noon hours and each floor empties its men and women who go away and eat and come back to work.

Toward the end of the afternoon all work slackens and all jobs go slower as the people feel day closing on them.

One by one the floors are emptied. . . . The uniformed elevator men are gone. Pails clang. . . . Scrubbers work, talking in foreign tongues. Broom and water and mop clean from the floors human dust and spit, and machine grime of the day.

Spelled in electric fire on the roof are words telling miles of houses and people where to buy a thing for money. The sign speaks till midnight.

Darkness on the hallways. Voices echo. Silence holds. . . . Watchmen walk slow from floor to floor and try the doors. Revolvers bulge from their hip pockets. . . . Steel safes stand in corners. Money is stacked in them.

A young watchman leans at a window and sees the lights of barges butting their way across a harbor, nets of red and white lanterns in a railroad yard, and a span of blooms splashed with lines of white and blurs of crosses and clusters over the sleeping city.

By night the skyscraper looms in the smoke and the stars and has a soul.

Edith Wharton

Edith Wharton (1862–1937) was primarily a novelist of manners who wrote about societal mores and customs, often satirically. In this story she portrays the plight of an individual trapped in a society more complex than she can handle, a society best symbolized by the impersonal buildings in a city.

MRS. MANSTEY'S VIEW

The view from Mrs. Manstey's window was not a striking one, but to her at least it was full of interest and beauty. Mrs. Manstey occupied the back room on the third floor of a New York boardinghouse, in a street where the ash barrels lingered late on the sidewalk and the gaps in the pavement would have staggered a Quintus Curtius. She was the widow of a clerk in a large wholesale house, and his death had left her alone, for her only daughter had married in California, and could not afford the long journey to New York to see her mother. Mrs. Manstey, perhaps, might have joined her daughter in the West, but they had now been so many years apart that they had ceased to feel any need of each other's society, and their intercourse had long been limited by the exchange of a few perfunctory letters, written with indifference by the daughter, and with difficulty by Mrs. Manstey, whose right hand was growing stiff with gout. Even had she felt a stronger desire for her daughter's companionship, Mrs. Manstey's increasing infirmity, which caused her to dread the three flights of stairs between her room and the street, would have given her pause on the eve of undertaking so long a journey; and without perhaps formulating these reasons she had long accepted as a matter of course her solitary life in New York.

She was, indeed, not quite lonely, for a few friends still toiled up now and then to her room; but their visits grew rare as the years went by. Mrs. Manstey had never been a sociable woman, and during her husband's lifetime his companionship had been all-sufficient to her. For many years she had cherished a desire to live in the country, to have a henhouse and a garden; but this longing had faded with age, leaving only in the breast of the uncommunicative old woman a vague tenderness for plants and animals. It was, perhaps, this tenderness which made her cling so fervently to her view from her window, a view in which the most optimistic eye would at first have failed to discover anything admirable.

Mrs. Manstey, from her coign of vantage (a slightly projecting bow window where she nursed an ivy and a succession of unwholesome-looking bulbs), looked out first upon the yard of her own dwelling, of which, however, she could get but a restricted glimpse. Still, her gaze took in the topmost boughs of the ailanthus below her window, and she knew how early each year the clump of dicentra strung its bending stalk with hearts of pink.

But of greater interest were the yards beyond. Being for the most part attached to boardinghouses they were in a state of chronic untidiness and fluttering, on certain days of the week, with miscellaneous garments and frayed tablecloths. In spite of this Mrs. Manstey found much to admire in the long vista which she commanded. Some of the yards were, indeed, but stony wastes, with grass in the cracks of the pavement and no shade in spring save that afforded by the intermittent leafage of the clotheslines. These yards Mrs. Manstey disapproved of, but the others, the green ones, she loved. She had grown used to their disorder; the broken barrels, the empty bottles and paths unswept no longer annoyed her; hers was the happy faculty of dwelling on the pleasanter side of the prospect before her.

In the very next enclosure did not a magnolia open its hard white flowers against the watery blue of April? And was there not, a little way down the line, a fence foamed over every May by lilac waves of wisteria? Farther still, a horse chestnut lifted its candelabra of buff and pink blossoms above broad fans of foliage; while in the opposite yard June was sweet with the breath of a neglected syringa, which persisted in growing in spite of the countless obstacles opposed to its welfare.

But if nature occupied the front rank in Mrs. Manstey's view, there was much of a more personal character to interest her in the aspect of the houses and their inmates. She deeply disapproved of the mustard-colored curtains which had lately been hung in the doctor's window opposite; but she glowed with pleasure when the house farther down had its old bricks washed with a coat of paint. The occupants of the houses did not often show themselves at the back windows, but the servants were always in sight. Noisy slatterns, Mrs. Manstey pronounced the greater number; she knew their ways and hated them. But to the quiet cook in the newly-painted house, whose mistress bullied her, and who secretly fed the stray cats at nightfall, Mrs. Manstey's warmest sympathies were given. On one occasion her feelings were racked by the

234 / THE SHAPING OF THE LAND: The City

neglect of a housemaid, who for two days forgot to feed the parrot committed to her care. On the third day, Mrs. Manstey, in spite of her gouty hand, had just penned a letter, beginning: "Madam, it is now three days since your parrot has been fed," when the forgetful maid appeared at the window with a cup of seed in her hand.

But in Mrs. Manstey's more meditative moods it was the narrowing perspective of far-off yards which pleased her best. She loved, at twilight, when the distant brownstone spire seemed melting in the fluid yellow of the west, to lose herself in vague memories of a trip to Europe, made years ago, and now reduced in her mind's eye to a pale phantasmagoria of indistinct steeples and dreamy skies. Perhaps at heart Mrs. Manstey was an artist; at all events she was sensible of many changes of color unnoticed by the average eye and, dear to her as the green of early spring was, the black lattice of branches against a cold sulphur sky at the close of a snowy day. She enjoyed, also, the sunny thaws of March, when patches of earth showed through the snow, like ink spots spreading on a sheet of white blotting paper; and, better still, the haze of boughs, leafless but swollen, which replaced the clear-cut tracery of winter. She even watched with a certain interest the trail of smoke from a far-off factory chimney, and missed a detail in the landscape when the factory was closed and the smoke disappeared.

Mrs. Manstey, in the long hours which she spent at her window, was not idle. She read a little, and knitted numberless stockings; but the view surrounded and shaped her life as the sea does a lonely island. When her rare callers came it was difficult for her to detach herself from the contemplation of the opposite window washing, or the scrutiny of certain green points in a neighboring flower bed which might, or might not, turn into hyacinths, while she feigned an interest in her visitor's anecdotes about some unknown grandchild. Mrs. Manstey's real friends were the denizens of the yards, the hyacinths, the magnolia, the green parrot, the maid who fed the cats, the doctor who studied late behind his mustard-colored curtains; and the confidant of her tenderer musings was the church spire floating in the sunset.

One April day, as she sat in her usual place, with knitting cast aside and eyes fixed on the blue sky mottled with round clouds, a knock at the door announced the entrance of her landlady. Mrs. Manstey did not care for her landlady, but she submitted to her visits with ladylike resignation. Today, however, it seemed harder than usual to turn from the blue sky and the blossoming magnolia to Mrs. Sampson's unsuggestive face, and Mrs. Manstey was conscious of a distinct effort as she did so.

"The magnolia is out earlier than usual this year, Mrs. Sampson," she remarked, yielding to a rare impulse, for she seldom alluded to the absorbing interest of her life. In the first place it was a topic not likely to appeal to her visitors and, besides, she lacked the power of expression and could not have given utterance to her feelings had she wished to.

"The what, Mrs. Manstey?" inquired the landlady, glancing about the room as if to find there the explanation of Mrs. Manstey's statement.

"The magnolia in the next yard—in Mrs. Black's yard," Mrs. Manstey repeated.

"Is it, indeed? I didn't know there was a magnolia there," said Mrs. Sampson, carelessly. Mrs. Manstey looked at her; she did not know that there was a magnolia in the next yard!

"By the way," Mrs. Sampson continued, "speaking of Mrs. Black reminds me that the work on the extension is to begin next week."

"The what?" it was Mrs. Manstey's turn to ask.

"The extension," said Mrs. Sampson, nodding her head in the direction of the ignored magnolia. "You knew, of course, that Mrs. Black was going to build an extension to her house? Yes, ma'am. I hear it is to run right back to the end of the yard. How she can afford to build an extension in these hard times I don't see; but she always was crazy about building. She used to keep a boardinghouse in Seventeenth Street, and she nearly ruined herself then by sticking out bow windows and what not; I should have thought that would have cured her of building, but I guess it's a disease, like drink. Anyhow, the work is to begin on Monday."

Mrs. Manstey had grown pale. She always spoke slowly, so the landlady did not heed the long pause which followed. At last Mrs. Manstey said: "Do you know how high the extension will be?"

"That's the most absurd part of it. The extension is to be built right up to the roof of the main building; now, did you ever?"

Mrs. Manstey paused again. "Won't it be a great annoyance to you, Mrs. Sampson?" she asked.

"I should say it would. But there's no help for it; if people have got a mind to build extensions there's no law to prevent 'em, that I'm aware of." Mrs. Manstey, knowing this, was silent. "There is no help for it," Mrs. Sampson repeated, "but if I *am* a church member, I wouldn't be so sorry if it ruined Eliza Black. Well, good day, Mrs. Manstey; I'm glad to find you so comfortable."

So comfortable—so comfortable! Left to herself the old woman turned once more to the window. How lovely the view was that day! The blue sky with its round clouds shed a brightness over everything; the ailanthus had put on a tinge of yellow-green, the hyacinths were budding, the magnolia flowers looked more than ever like rosettes carved in alabaster. Soon the wisteria would bloom, then the horse chestnut; but not for her. Between her eyes and them a barrier of brick and mortar would swiftly rise; presently even the spire would disappear, and all her radiant world be blotted out. Mrs. Manstey sent away untouched the dinner tray brought to her that evening. She lingered in the window until the windy

sunset died in bat-colored dusk; then, going to bed, she lay sleepless all night.

Early the next day she was up and at the window. It was raining, but even through the slanting gray gauze the scene had its charm—and then the rain was so good for the trees. She had noticed the day before that the ailanthus was growing dusty.

"Of course I might move," said Mrs. Manstey aloud, and turning from the window she looked about her room. She might move, of course; so might she be flayed alive; but she was not likely to survive either operation. The room, though far less important to her happiness than the view, was as much a part of her existence. She had lived in it seventeen years. She knew every stain on the wallpaper, every rent in the carpet; the light fell in a certain way on her engravings, her books had grown shabby on their shelves, her bulbs and ivy were used to their window and knew which way to lean to the sun. "We are all too old to move," she said.

That afternoon it cleared. Wet and radiant the blue reappeared through torn rags of cloud; the ailanthus sparkled; the earth in the flower borders looked rich and warm. It was Thursday, and on Monday the building of the extension was to begin.

On Sunday afternoon a card was brought to Mrs. Black, as she was engaged in gathering up the fragments of the boarders' dinner in the basement. The card, black-edged, bore Mrs. Manstey's name.

"One of Mrs. Sampson's boarders; wants to move, I suppose. Well, I can give her a room next year in the extension. Dinah," said Mrs. Black, "tell the lady I'll be upstairs in a minute."

Mrs. Black found Mrs. Manstey standing in the long parlor garnished with statuettes and antimacassars; in that house she could not sit down.

Stooping hurriedly to open the register, which let out a cloud of dust, Mrs. Black advanced to her visitor.

"I'm happy to meet you, Mrs. Manstey; take a seat, please," the landlady remarked in her prosperous voice, the voice of a woman who can afford to build extensions. There was no help for it; Mrs. Manstey sat down.

"Is there anything I can do for you, ma'am?" Mrs. Black continued. "My house is full at present, but I am going to build an extension, and—"

"It is about the extension that I wish to speak," said Mrs. Manstey, suddenly. "I am a poor woman, Mrs. Black, and I have never been a happy one. I shall have to talk about myself first to—to make you understand."

Mrs. Black, astonished but imperturbable, bowed at this parenthesis.

"I never had what I wanted," Mrs. Manstey continued. "It was always one disappointment after another. For years I wanted to live in the country. I dreamed and dreamed about it; but we never could manage it. There was no sunny window in our house, and so all my plants died. My daughter married years ago and went away —besides, she never cared for the same things. Then my husband died and I was left alone. That was seventeen years ago. I went to live at Mrs. Sampson's and I have been there ever since. I have grown a little infirm, as you see, and I don't get out often; only on fine days, if I am feeling very well. So you can understand my sitting a great deal in my window—the back window on the third floor—"

"Well, Mrs. Manstey," said Mrs. Black, liberally, "I could give you a back room, I dare say; one of the new rooms in the ex—"

"But I don't want to move; I can't move," said Mrs. Manstey, almost with a scream. "And I came to tell you that if you build that extension I shall have no view from my window—no view! Do you understand?"

Mrs. Black thought herself face to face with a lunatic, and she had always heard that lunatics must be humored.

"Dear me, dear me," she remarked, pushing her chair back a little way, "that is too bad, isn't it? Why, I never thought of that.

To be sure, the extension *will* interfere with your view, Mrs. Manstey."

"You do understand?" Mrs. Manstey gasped.

"Of course I do. And I'm real sorry about it, too. But there, don't you worry, Mrs. Manstey. I guess we can fix that all right."

Mrs. Manstey rose from her seat, and Mrs. Black slipped toward the door.

"What do you mean by fixing it? Do you mean that I can induce you to change your mind about the extension? Oh, Mrs. Black, listen to me. I have two thousand dollars in the bank and I could manage, I know I could manage, to give you a thousand if—" Mrs. Manstey paused; the tears were rolling down her cheeks.

"There, there, Mrs. Manstey, don't you worry," repeated Mrs. Black, soothingly. "I am sure we can settle it. I am sorry that I can't stay and talk about it any longer, but this is such a busy time of day, with supper to get—"

Her hand was on the doorknob, but with sudden vigor Mrs. Manstey seized her wrist.

"You are not giving me a definite answer. Do you mean to say that you accept my proposition?"

"Why, I'll think it over, Mrs. Manstey, certainly I will. I wouldn't annoy you for the world—"

"But the work is to begin tomorrow, I am told," Mrs. Manstey persisted.

Mrs. Black hesitated. "It shan't begin, I promise you that; I'll send word to the builder this very night." Mrs. Manstey tightened her hold.

"You are not deceiving me, are you?" she said.

"No—no," stammered Mrs. Black. "How can you think such a thing of me, Mrs. Manstey?"

Slowly Mrs. Manstey's clutch relaxed, and she passed through the open door. "One thousand dollars," she repeated, pausing in the hall; then she let herself out of the house and hobbled down the steps, supporting herself on the cast-iron railing.

"My goodness," exclaimed Mrs. Black, shutting and bolting the hall door, "I never knew the old woman was crazy! And she looks so quiet and ladylike, too."

Mrs. Manstey slept well that night, but early the next morning she was awakened by a sound of hammering. She got to her window with what haste she might and, looking out, saw that Mrs. Black's yard was full of workmen. Some were carrying loads of brick from the kitchen to the yard, others beginning to demolish the old-fashioned wooden balcony which adorned each story of Mrs. Black's house. Mrs. Manstey saw that she had been deceived. At first she thought of confiding her trouble to Mrs. Sampson, but a settled discouragement soon took possession of her and she went back to bed, not caring to see what was going on.

Toward afternoon, however, feeling that she must know the worst, she rose and dressed herself. It was a laborious task, for her hands were stiffer than usual, and the hooks and buttons seemed to evade her.

When she seated herself in the window, she saw that the workmen had removed the upper part of the balcony, and that the bricks had multiplied since morning. One of the men, a coarse fellow with a bloated face, picked a magnolia blossom and, after smelling it, threw it to the ground; the next man, carrying a load of bricks, trod on the flower in passing.

"Look out, Jim," called one of the men to another who was smoking a pipe, "if you throw matches around near those barrels of paper you'll have the old tinderbox burning down before you know it." And Mrs. Manstey, leaning forward, perceived that there were several barrels of paper and rubbish under the wooden balcony.

At length the work ceased and twilight fell. The sunset was perfect and a roseate light, transfiguring the distant spire, lingered late in the west. When it grew dark Mrs. Manstey drew down the shades and proceeded, in her usual methodical manner, to light her lamp. She always filled it

and lit it with her own hands, keeping a kettle of kerosene on a zinc-covered shelf in a closet. As the lamplight filled the room it assumed its usual peaceful aspect. The books and pictures and plants seemed, like their mistress, to settle themselves down for another quiet evening, and Mrs. Manstey, as was her wont, drew up her armchair to the table and began to knit.

That night she could not sleep. The weather had changed and a wild wind was abroad, blotting the stars with close-driven clouds. Mrs. Manstey rose once or twice and looked out the window; but of the view nothing was discernible save a tardy light or two in the opposite windows. These lights at last went out, and Mrs. Manstey, who had watched for their extinction, began to dress herself. She was in evident haste, for she merely flung a thin dressing gown over her nightdress and wrapped her head in a scarf; then she opened her closet and cautiously took out the kettle of kerosene. Having slipped a bundle of wooden matches into her pocket she proceeded, with increasing precautions, to unlock her door, and a few moments later she was feeling her way down the dark staircase, led by a glimmer of gas from the lower hall. At length she reached the bottom of the stairs and began the more difficult descent into the utter darkness of the basement. Here, however, she could move more freely, as there was less danger of being overheard; and without much delay she contrived to unlock the iron door leading into the yard. A gust of cold wind smote her as she stepped out and groped shiveringly under the clotheslines.

That morning at three o'clock an alarm of fire brought the engines to Mrs. Black's door, and also brought Mrs. Sampson's startled boarders to their windows. The wooden balcony at the back of Mrs. Black's house was ablaze, and among those who watched the progress of the flames was Mrs. Manstey, leaning in her thin dressing gown from the open window.

The fire, however, was soon put out, and

the frightened occupants of the house, who had fled in scant attire, reassembled at dawn to find that little mischief had been done beyond the cracking of windowpanes and smoking of ceilings. In fact, the chief sufferer by the fire was Mrs. Manstey, who was found in the morning gasping with pneumonia, a not unnatural result, as everyone remarked, of her having hung out of an open window at her age in a dressing gown. It was easy to see that she was very ill, but no one had guessed how grave the doctor's verdict would be, and the faces gathered that evening about Mrs. Sampson's table were awestruck and disturbed. Not that any of the boarders knew Mrs. Manstey well; she "kept to herself," as they said, and seemed to fancy herself too good for them; but then it is always disagreeable to have anyone dying in the house and, as one lady observed to another: "It might just as well have been you or me, my dear."

But it was only Mrs. Manstey; and she was dying, as she had lived, lonely if not alone. The doctor had sent a trained nurse, and Mrs. Sampson, with muffled step, came in from time to time; but both, to Mrs. Manstey, seemed remote and unsubstantial as the figures in a dream. All day she said nothing; but when she was asked for her daughter's address she shook her head. At times the nurse noticed that she seemed to be listening attentively for some sound which did not come; then again she dozed.

The next morning at daylight she was very low. The nurse called Mrs. Sampson and as the two bent over the old woman they saw her lips move.

"Lift me up—out of bed," she whispered.

They raised her in their arms, and with her stiff hand she pointed to the window.

"Oh, the window—she wants to sit in the window. She used to sit there all day," Mrs. Sampson explained. "It can do her no harm, I suppose?"

"Nothing matters now," said the nurse.

They carried Mrs. Manstey to the window and placed her in her chair. The dawn was abroad, a jubilant spring dawn; the spire had already caught a golden ray, though the magnolia and horse chestnut still slumbered in shadow. In Mrs. Black's yard all was quiet. The charred timbers of the balcony lay where they had fallen. It was evident that since the fire the builders had not returned to their work. The magnolia had unfolded a few more sculptural flowers; the view was undisturbed.

It was hard for Mrs. Manstey to breathe; each moment it grew more difficult. She tried to make them open the window, but they would not understand. If she could have tasted the air, sweet with the penetrating ailanthus savor, it would have eased her; but the view at least was there—the spire was golden now, the heavens had warmed from pearl to blue, day was alight from east to west, even the magnolia had caught the sun.

Mrs. Manstey's head fell back and smiling she died.

That day the building of the extension was resumed.

Joan Didion

Joan Didion (b. 1934), born and educated in California, describes the attractiveness of New York City to the national consciousness and shows her personal disillusionment with that city.

GOODBYE TO ALL THAT

How many miles to Babylon?
Three score miles and ten—
Can I get there by candlelight?
Yes, and back again—
If your feet are nimble and light
You can get there by candlelight.

It is easy to see the beginnings of things, and harder to see the ends. I can remember now, with a clarity that makes the nerves in the back of my neck constrict, when New York began for me, but I cannot lay my finger upon the moment it ended, can never cut through the ambiguities and second starts and broken resolves to the exact place on the page where the heroine is no longer as optimistic as she once was. When I first saw New York I was twenty, and it was summertime, and I got off a DC-7 at the old Idlewild temporary terminal in a new dress which had seemed very smart in Sacramento but seemed less smart already, even in the old Idlewild temporary terminal, and the warm air smelled of mildew and some instinct, programmed by all the movies I had ever seen and all the songs I had ever heard sung and all the stories I had ever read about New York, informed me that it would never be quite the same again. In fact it never was. Some time later there was a song on all the jukeboxes on the upper East Side that went "but where is the school-girl who used to be me," and if it was late enough at night I used to wonder that. I know now that almost everyone wonders something like that, sooner or later and no matter what he or she is doing, but one of the mixed blessings of being twenty and twenty-one and even twenty-three is the conviction that nothing like this, all evidence to the contrary notwithstanding, has ever happened to anyone before.

Of course it might have been some other city, had circumstances been different and the time been different and had I been different, might have been Paris or Chicago or even San Francisco, but because I am talking about myself I am talking here about New York. That first night I opened my window on the bus into town and watched for the skyline, but all I could see were the wastes of Queens and the big signs that said MIDTOWN TUNNEL THIS LANE and then a flood of summer rain (even that seemed remarkable and exotic, for I had come out of the West where there was no summer rain), and for the next three days I sat wrapped in blankets in a hotel room air-conditioned to 35° and tried to get over a bad cold and a high fever. It did not occur to me to call a doctor, because I knew none, and although it did occur to me to call the desk and ask that the air conditioner be turned off, I never called, because I did not know how much to tip whoever might come—was anyone ever so young? I am here to tell you that someone was. All I could do during those three days was talk long-distance to the boy I already knew I would never marry in the spring. I would stay in New York, I told him, just six months, and I could see the Brooklyn Bridge from my window. As it turned out the bridge was the Triborough, and I stayed eight years.

In retrospect it seems to me that those days before I knew the names of all the bridges were happier than the ones that came later, but perhaps you will see that as we go along. Part of what I want to tell you is what it is like to be young in New York, how six months can become eight years with the deceptive ease of a film dissolve, for that is how those years appear to me now, in a long sequence of sentimental dissolves and old-fashioned trick shots—the Seagram Building fountains dissolve into snowflakes, I enter a revolving door at twenty and come out a good deal older, and on a different street. But most particularly I want to explain to you, and in the process perhaps to myself, why I no longer live in New York. It is often said that New York is a city for only the very rich and the very poor. It is less often said that New York is also, at least for those of us who came there from somewhere else, a city for only the very young.

I remember once, one cold bright December evening in New York, suggesting to a friend who complained of having been around too long that he come with me to a party where there would be, I assured him with the bright resourcefulness of twenty-three, "new faces." He laughed literally until he choked, and I had to roll down the taxi window and hit him on the back. "New faces," he said finally, "don't tell me about *new faces*." It seemed that the last time he had gone to a party where he had been promised "new faces," there had been fifteen people in the room, and he had already slept with five of the women and owed money to all but two of the men. I laughed with him, but the first snow had just begun to fall and the big Christmas trees glittered yellow and white as far as I could see up Park Avenue and I had a new dress and it would be a long while before I would come to understand the particular moral of the story.

It would be a long while because, quite simply, I was in love with New York. I do not mean "love" in any colloquial way, I mean that I was in love with the city, the way you love the first person who ever touches you and never love anyone quite that way again. I remember walking across Sixty-second Street one twilight that first spring, or the second spring, they were all alike for a while. I was late to meet someone but I stopped at Lexington Avenue and bought a peach and stood on the corner eating it and knew that I had come out of the West and reached the mirage. I could taste the peach and feel the soft air blowing from a subway grating on my legs and I could smell lilac and garbage and expensive perfume and I knew that it would cost something sooner or later—because I did not belong there, did not come from there— but when you are twenty-two or twenty-three, you figure that later you will have a high emotional balance, and be able to pay whatever it costs. I still believed in possibilities then, still had the sense, so peculiar to New York, that something extraordinary would happen any minute, any day, any month. I was making only $65 or $70 a week then ("Put yourself in Hattie Carnegie's hands," I was advised without the slightest trace of irony by an editor of the magazine for which I worked), so little money that some weeks I had to charge food at Bloomingdale's gourmet shop in order to eat, a fact which went unmentioned in the letters I wrote to California. I never told my father that I needed money because then he would have sent it, and I would never

know if I could do it by myself. At that time making a living seemed a game to me, with arbitrary but quite inflexible rules. And except on a certain kind of winter evening—six-thirty in the Seventies, say, already dark and bitter with a wind off the river, when I would be walking very fast toward a bus and would look in the bright windows of brownstones and see cooks working in clean kitchens and imagine women lighting candles on the floor above and beautiful children being bathed on the floor above that—except on nights like those, I never felt poor; I had the feeling that if I needed money I could always get it. I could write a syndicated column for teenagers under the name "Debbi Lynn" or I could smuggle gold into India or I could become a $100 call girl, and none of it would matter.

Nothing was irrevocable; everything was within reach. Just around every corner lay something curious and interesting, something I had never before seen or done or known about. I could go to a party and meet someone who called himself Mr. Emotional Appeal and ran The Emotional Appeal Institute or Tina Onassis Blandford or a Florida cracker who was then a regular on what he called "the Big C," the Southampton–El Morocco circuit ("I'm well-connected on the Big C, honey," he would tell me over collard greens on his vast borrowed terrace), or the widow of the celery king of the Harlem market or a piano salesman from Bonne Terre, Missouri, or someone who had already made and lost two fortunes in Midland, Texas. I could make promises to myself and to other people and there would be all the time in the world to keep them. I could stay up all night and make mistakes, and none of it would count.

You see I was in a curious position in New York: it never occurred to me that I was living a real life there. In my imagination I was always there for just another few months, just until Christmas or Easter or the first warm day in May. For that reason I was most comfortable in the company of

Southerners. They seemed to be in New York as I was, on some indefinitely extended leave from wherever they belonged, disinclined to consider the future, temporary exiles who always knew when the flights left for New Orleans or Memphis or Richmond or, in my case, California. Someone who lives always with a plane schedule in the drawer lives on a slightly different calendar. Christmas, for example, was a difficult season. Other people could take it in stride, going to Stowe or going abroad or going for the day to their mothers' places in Connecticut; those of us who believed that we lived somewhere else would spend it making and canceling airline reservations, waiting for weatherbound flights as if for the last plane out of Lisbon in 1940, and finally comforting one another, those of us who were left, with the oranges and mementos and smoked-oyster stuffings of childhood, gathering close, colonials in a far country.

Which is precisely what we were. I am not sure that it is possible for anyone brought up in the East to appreciate entirely what New York, the idea of New York, means to those of us who came out of the West and the South. To an Eastern child, particularly a child who has always had an uncle on Wall Street and who has spent several hundred Saturdays first at F. A. O. Schwarz and being fitted for shoes at Best's and then waiting under the Biltmore clock and dancing to Lester Lanin, New York is just a city, albeit *the* city, a plausible place for people to live. But to those of us who came from places where no one had heard of Lester Lanin and Grand Central Station was a Saturday radio program, where Wall Street and Fifth Avenue and Madison Avenue were not places at all but abstractions ("Money," and "High Fashion," and "The Hucksters"), New York was no mere city. It was instead an infinitely romantic notion, the mysterious nexus of all love and money and power, the shining and perishable dream itself. To think of "living" there was to reduce the miraculous to the mundane; one does not "live" at Xanadu.

In fact it was difficult in the extreme for me to understand those young women for whom New York was not simply an ephemeral Estoril but a real place, girls who bought toasters and installed new cabinets in their apartments and committed themselves to some reasonable future. I never bought any furniture in New York. For a year or so I lived in other people's apartments; after that I lived in the Nineties in an apartment furnished entirely with things taken from storage by a friend whose wife had moved away. And when I left the apartment in the Nineties (that was when I was leaving everything, when it was all breaking up) I left everything in it, even my winter clothes and the map of Sacramento County I had hung on the bedroom wall to remind me who I was, and I moved into a monastic four-room floor-through on Seventy-fifth Street. "Monastic" is perhaps misleading here, implying some chic severity; until after I was married and my husband moved some furniture in, there was nothing at all in those four rooms except a cheap double mattress and box springs, ordered by telephone the day I decided to move, and two French garden chairs lent me by a friend who imported them. (It strikes me now that the people I knew in New York all had curious and self-defeating sidelines. They imported garden chairs which did not sell very well at Hammacher Schlemmer or they tried to market hair straighteners in Harlem or they ghosted exposés of Murder Incorporated for Sunday supplements. I think that perhaps none of us was very serious, *engagé* only about our most private lives.)

All I ever did to that apartment was hang fifty yards of yellow theatrical silk across the bedroom windows, because I had some idea that the gold light would make me feel better, but I did not bother to weight the curtains correctly and all that summer the long panels of transparent golden silk would blow out the windows and get tangled and drenched in the afternoon thunderstorms. That was the year, my twenty-eighth, when I was discovering that not all of the promises would be kept, that some things are in fact irrevocable and that it had counted after all, every evasion and every procrastination, every mistake, every word, all of it.

That is what it was all about, wasn't it? Promises? Now when New York comes back to me it comes in hallucinatory flashes, so clinically detailed that I sometimes wish that memory would effect the distortion with which it is commonly credited. For a lot of the time I was in New York I used a perfume called *Fleurs de Rocaille,* and then *L'Air du Temps,* and now the slightest trace of either can short-circuit my connections for the rest of the day. Nor can I smell Henri Bendel jasmine soap without falling back into the past, or the particular mixture of spices used for boiling crabs. There were barrels of crab boil in a Czech place in the Eighties where I once shopped. Smells, of course, are notorious memory stimuli, but there are other things which affect me the same way. Blue-and-white striped sheets. Vermouth cassis. Some faded nightgowns which were new in 1959 or 1960, and some chiffon scarves I bought about the same time.

I suppose that a lot of us who have been young in New York have the same scenes on our home screens. I remember sitting in a lot of apartments with a slight headache about five o'clock in the morning. I had a friend who could not sleep, and he knew a few other people who had the same trouble, and we would watch the sky lighten and have a last drink with no ice and then go home in the early morning light, when the streets were clean and wet (had it rained in the night? we never knew) and the few cruising taxis still had their headlights on and the only color was the red and green of traffic signals. The White Rose bars opened very early in the morning; I recall waiting in one of them to watch an astronaut go

into space, waiting so long that at the moment it actually happened I had my eyes not on the television screen but on a cockroach on the tile floor. I liked the bleak branches above Washington Square at dawn, and the monochromatic flatness of Second Avenue, the fire escapes and the grilled storefronts peculiar and empty in their perspective.

It is relatively hard to fight at six-thirty or seven in the morning without any sleep, which was perhaps one reason we stayed up all night, and it seemed to me a pleasant time of day. The windows were shuttered in that apartment in the Nineties and I could sleep a few hours and then go to work. I could work then on two or three hours' sleep and a container of coffee from Chock Full O' Nuts. I liked going to work, liked the soothing and satisfactory rhythm of getting out a magazine, liked the orderly progression of four-color closings and two-color closings and black-and-white closings and then The Product, no abstraction but something which looked effortlessly glossy and could be picked up on a newsstand and weighed in the hand. I liked all the minutiae of proofs and layouts, liked working late on the nights the magazine went to press, sitting and reading *Variety* and waiting for the copy desk to call. From my office I could look across town to the weather signal on the Mutual of New York Building and the lights that alternately spelled out TIME and LIFE above Rockefeller Plaza; that pleased me obscurely, and so did walking uptown in the mauve eight o'clocks of early summer evenings and looking at things, Lowestoft tureens in Fifty-seventh Street windows, people in evening clothes trying to get taxis, the trees just coming into full leaf, the lambent air, all the sweet promises of money and summer.

Some years passed, but I still did not lose that sense of wonder about New York. I began to cherish the loneliness of it, the sense that at any given time no one need know where I was or what I was doing. I liked walking, from the East River over to the Hudson and back on brisk days, down around the Village on warm days. A friend would leave me the key to her apartment in the West Village when she was out of town, and sometimes I would just move down there, because by that time the telephone was beginning to bother me (the canker, you see, was already in the rose) and not many people had that number. I remember one day when someone who did have the West Village number came to pick me up for lunch there, and we both had hangovers, and I cut my finger opening him a beer and burst into tears, and we walked to a Spanish restaurant and drank Bloody Marys and *gazpacho* until we felt better. I was not then guilt-ridden about spending afternoons that way, because I still had all the afternoons in the world.

And even that late in the game I still liked going to parties, all parties, bad parties, Saturday-afternoon parties given by recently married couples who lived in Stuyvesant Town, West Side parties given by unpublished or failed writers who served cheap red wine and talked about going to Guadalajara, Village parties where all the guests worked for advertising agencies and voted for Reform Democrats, press parties at Sardi's, the worst kinds of parties. You will have perceived by now that I was not one to profit by the experience of others, that it was a very long time indeed before I stopped believing in new faces and began to understand the lesson in that story, which was that it is distinctly possible to stay too long at the Fair.

I could not tell you when I began to understand that. All I know is that it was very bad when I was twenty-eight. Everything that was said to me I seemed to have heard before, and I could no longer listen. I could no longer sit in little bars near Grand Central and listen to someone complaining of his wife's inability to cope with the help while he missed another train to Connecticut. I no longer had any interest in hearing about the advances other people

had received from their publishers, about plays which were having second-act trouble in Philadelphia, or about people I would like very much if only I would come out and meet them. I had already met them, always. There were certain parts of the city which I had to avoid. I could not bear upper Madison Avenue on weekday mornings (this was a particularly inconvenient aversion, since I then lived just fifty or sixty feet east of Madison), because I would see women walking Yorkshire terriers and shopping at Gristede's, and some Veblenesque gorge would rise in my throat. I could not go to Times Square in the afternoon, or to the New York Public Library for any reason whatsoever. One day I could not go into a Schrafft's; the next day it would be Bonwit Teller.

I hurt the people I cared about, and insulted those I did not. I cut myself off from the one person who was closer to me than any other. I cried until I was not even aware when I was crying and when I was not, cried in elevators and in taxis and in Chinese laundries, and when I went to the doctor he said only that I seemed to be depressed, and should see a "specialist." He wrote down a psychiatrist's name and address for me, but I did not go.

Instead I got married, which as it turned out was a very good thing to do but badly timed, since I still could not walk on upper Madison Avenue in the mornings and still could not talk to people and still cried in Chinese laundries. I had never before understood what "despair" meant, and I am not sure that I understand now, but I understood that year. Of course I could not work. I could not even get dinner with any degree of certainty, and I would sit in the apartment on Seventy-fifth Street paralyzed until my husband would call from his office and say gently that I did not have to get dinner, that I could meet him at Michael's Pub or at Toots Shor's or at Sardi's East. And then one morning in April (we had been married in January) he called and told me that he wanted to get out of New

York for a while, that he would take a six-month leave of absence, that we would go somewhere.

It was three years ago that he told me that, and we have lived in Los Angeles since. Many of the people we knew in New York think this a curious aberration, and in fact tell us so. There is no possible, no adequate answer to that, and so we give certain stock answers, the answers everyone gives. I talk about how difficult it would be for us to "afford" to live in New York right now, about how much "space" we need. All I mean is that I was very young in New York, and that at some point the golden rhythm was broken, and I am not that young any more. The last time I was in New York was in a cold January, and everyone was ill and tired. Many of the people I used to know there had moved to Dallas or had gone on Antabuse or had bought a farm in New Hampshire. We stayed ten days, and then we took an afternoon flight back to Los Angeles, and on the way home from the airport that night I could see the moon on the Pacific and smell jasmine all around and we both knew that there was no longer any point in keeping the apartment we still kept in New York. There were years when I called Los Angeles "the Coast," but they seem a long time ago.

Peter Schrag

Peter Schrag (b. 1931), a noted commentator on contemporary America, is the author of several books including The Decline of the Wasp. *In this article, taken from his latest book,* The End of the American Future, *Schrag explores America's ambivalence toward the city and the problem of reconciling the "myth of the garden" with the reality of modern urban life.*

* Editor's title.

THE END OF INNOCENCE *

Even before Jefferson warned about the urban mobs of decadent Europe, Americans had been ambivalent about cities and, in a larger sense, about the meaning of progress itself. If the settlements of New England constituted the New Jerusalem, and if the independent yeoman farmer of the eighteenth century was the ultimate in a democratic civilization, which way was up? The city was opportunity, growth and success, but it was also temptation, sin and corruption. You could play the theology both ways: going there was Good; being there was questionable. Yet on one assumption the theology was (and still is) consistent: the city was, all demography aside, the exception; the country and its ethic were the norm, and every time you flew across the country or looked at the ads on television, the vision returned: Down there was the real America, on the wheat fields of Kansas, in the small crossroads towns with their helpful banker and their friendly Mutual of Omaha insurance agent, in the shopping centers where the farmers congregated on Saturday afternoon and the women came to have their hair set, in the new developments of Topeka or Quincy or Macon or Rapid City, neighborhoods clustered around cities of twenty thousand or seventy-five thousand where they manufactured trailers or hardboard or bricks or Thermopane windows, or where they refined beet sugar, packed meat or milled flour, places where women ran washing machines and men bought tires and where things always went better with Coke. By the census definition, most of them were "urban places"—meaning any town of twenty-five hundred or more—and America was a nation that was seventy-five percent urban, but if one also understood that the census defined places like St. Joseph, Missouri, Saginaw, Michigan, Billings, Montana, Gadsden, Alabama, and York, Pennsylvania, as "Standard Statistical Metropolitan Areas," then the distinctions between rural and urban became more complex and a whole landscape reappeared that had no comfortable place in any of the conventional categories of American sociology. The cliché was Middle America, but that suggested church suppers, clambakes, hard work and thrift, a whole network, indeed, of intrinsic "traditional" values, and not the concomitant suburbanization with its easy credit, its packaged food and packaged culture, or its near-total dependence on economic decisions and forces beyond local control. By the time the sixties came to an end, most of that country was simply defining itself as non-New York (even while it was buying the stuff that New York sold) and commiserating with anyone forced to live in a jungle where white people couldn't walk the streets after dark or sit in the parks without the risk of rape. Herman Kahn, the philosopher of thermonuclear war, echoed the conventional wisdom when he said that the American middle class had been split in two. "We are having a kind of religious war," he had said. "The upper middle class is forcing its religion—call it Secular Humanism—on the middle class, which is basically nationalistic and fundamentalist. The result is that the middle class has begun to feel it has lost the country." What the description ignored was the schizophrenia of each; the traditional values were there, all right, but anyone with half an eye could perceive that the newsstands of Main Street were doing better with *Playboy* than with *Church News* or *American Opinion,* the monthly magazine of the John Birch Society, and that while there were still local entrepreneurs, the big opportunity lay in a fast-food franchise or a service station or dealership dependent on the products and advertising of a national corporation. Every day you could see the salesmen and conventioneers from hicktown around the Americana or the Belmont Plaza or the Waldorf in New York picking up the hookers, every week you could see the ads

in the swingers' magazines seeking compatible couples in El Paso and Tucson, in Albany and Joplin, and every morning you could hear the "California girls" on a San Francisco radio station or on similar phone-in programs on scores of other stations—housewives, thousands of them, in solid Middle American developments like Hayward and San José and Daly City—discussing their affairs with the milkman, the TV repairman, or their husband's best friend. They all had good marriages, they said (meaning that the husband was a good provider), but sex with the other guy was more fun. What you learned in Middle America was that it wasn't merely the kids of the Eastern upper middle class or the Ivy intellectuals who were smoking dope or screwing after the homecoming game, it was the high-school quarterback.

They had lost the country not because the elite had stolen it from them or because the media were prone to orgies of misrepresentation, but because they had chosen to live in a world for which they had no ethic. They lived neither in big cities nor in small towns, were not the sinful people or the crime-besieged victims of urban rot that they imagined the residents of New York to be, nor were they the honest yeomen of national myth. They were increasingly cut off from the security and motivations of the old middle class (and therefore deprived of its sense of the future), yet they retained enough of its ethic to be uncomfortable with the national culture which replaced it. Even in supposedly safe places people had started feeling besieged. New York was spreading. In Mason City, Iowa, the River City of Meredith Wilson's *Music Man,* people were talking about Waterloo, Iowa, as an industrial place with a rising crime rate and a population of bad credit risks who couldn't be trusted to pay their bills; in Sioux Falls it was Minneapolis; in Tracy, California (pop. 14,000), it was Stockton, and in Stockton it was Oakland. Nearly all of them had their "urban problem"—slum housing, decaying business districts, ghettoes of blacks or Chicanos or Indians, drugs, unemployment, welfare—yet the idea that they were in fact urban, or that there was an urban problem, became a nearly unthinkable proposition. Not that they denied everything; the tax bills told them that something was wrong, even if nothing else did. Yet to make common cause with New York, Chicago or St. Louis in confronting social decay was like inviting contamination. John Lindsay didn't speak for them. The big cities were hopeless—beyond repair or salvation—and the only reasonable policy was to diversify, to get the industry out of the big cities and back to the middle-sized towns. "The smaller communities need the plants and the people that are polluting the urban centers—not in large doses, but steadily, surely," wrote the editor of the Mason City *Globe Gazette,* and the words were familiar in other towns. "The small communities are geared up. They have comprehensive plans. They know they can't stand still or they will be passed by." It was a rare place, however, where local enterprise and local investors were able or willing to take the risk themselves. In places like Hannibal, Missouri, which was now trying to promote Huck Finn and Tom Sawyer into a tourist industry, the entrepreneurs of the nineteenth century grew prosperous by buying lumber in Wisconsin, floating it down the Mississippi, cutting it up in locally owned mills, and shipping it west on a locally owned railroad. By 1970 the barges passed most of the river towns by, the mills were closed, and the presence of the river as a great promise of romance and growth had become, on the one hand, an abstraction of international commerce and, on the other, a fading memory of the past.

You saw what you were supposed to see, and then you began to see things you were not: the Civil War monument in the square; the First National Bank; Osco's Self-Service Drugs; the shoestore and the movie theaters; Damon's and Younkers' ("Satis-

faction Always"); Maize's and Penney's; Sears and Monkey Ward. They debated about the construction of a new mall or the possible renewal of the downtown business area, fought about one-way streets, and told you, depending on the region, that when the crops were good you couldn't find a parking space in town.

There seemed to be a common feeling that anyone, even a writer from New York, was, somewhere in his heart, a small-town boy come home. New York was something you put on, but Main Street was something you remained forever. They took you in, absorbed you, soaked you up; they knew whom you'd seen, what you'd done. In the back country of Mississippi, the sheriff used to follow you around; here it was the word. . . . Hannibal, Quincy, Keokuk, Sheboygan, Paducah, Sioux Falls, Rapid City, Mason City, Sandusky, Bristol, Haverhill, Greenfield, Bethlehem, Tracy . . . *Small towns co-opt, you told yourself, and nice small towns co-opt absolutely.* Nostalgia helped make the connections, for how could you be fully American unless you could be part of this? Yes, you were willing to come to dinner, to visit the Club, to suspend your suspicion that all this was some sort of Chamber of Commerce trick. Often they were delighted that you were not surprised that they had a local television station or perhaps two or even three, that there was a decent library in town and a community orchestra, and that you didn't assume that civilization stopped at the Hudson or (going the other way) in the foothills behind the Berkeley campus. They had heard about that other world out there—that's why they commiserated with you—yet they couldn't understand why the things that seemed to work here didn't work everywhere else, nor could they consider the idea that many times they didn't even work at home. The space, the land, the incessant reminders of physical normalcy made it possible to defer almost anything. Church on Sunday, football on Friday and the cycle of parties, dinners and cookouts remained more visible (not to say comprehensible) than the subtle-ties of cultural change or violence overseas or political repression. The answer to an economic problem, the official answer, was to work harder, to take a second job, or to send your wife to work, usually as a clerk or a waitress. On the radio, Junior Achieve-ment made its peace with modernism by setting its jingle to "Get with It" to a rock beat, but the message of adolescent enter-prise was the same, and around the lunch tables in places called the Green Mill or the Chart House or the City Café it was difficult to persuade anyone that sometimes even people with a normal quota of ambi-tion couldn't make it.

What they didn't discuss was what the president of one Midwestern NAACP chap-ter called "the secret places": the subtle dis-crimination in housing and jobs, the out-of-sight dilapidated houses on the edge of town or in places called the Bottoms, build-ings surrounded with little piles of lumber, rusting metal chairs, and decaying junk cars once slated for repair; the lingering aroma of personal defeat; and the peculiar mix of arrogance and apathy that declared, "There are no poor people in this area." On Sundays, while most people were pack-ing their campers for the trip home, or making the transition between church and television football, the old, who had noth-ing to do, wandered into the Park Inn for lunch (hot roast beef sandwiches cost $1.65) and discussed Medicare; while people talked about discipline and hard work around the high school ("Add umph to try and you have triumph"), the star quarterback was paying a brainy junior to take his college board tests for him so that he could get an athletic scholarship (a fact known to the school's college counselor, and to most of the students, who said nothing); and while the football-happy citizens celebrated another victory, the kids attending the dance after the game broke out the joints and turned on. There were, in many of these towns, ghosts of old patriarchs—the general, the founder of the mill, the people

who donated the land for the park or built the YMCA—and, along with them, the re-membrance, perhaps real, perhaps fantasy, of a lost heroic age when bank clerks be-came corporation presidents, the railroad workers boozed and brawled through the cafés on Water Street, and every year brought a new achievement, another monu-ment of modern construction and another thriving business. The ethic remained, often the shadow survived the man, but only at the price of increasing tension and neglect, tension between the temptations of the na-tional culture and the rhetoric of local be-lief, neglect of the secret places of destitu-tion, poverty and frustration which under-lay the illusions of local achievement. The sons of the founders were selling out to na-tional corporations and exchanging control for shares in a conglomerate, and, while they spoke fondly about the wild times in the old days, they were not sure that even the state university was a safe place for their children. Sooner or later the world could come back here, they believed, because the cities were unlivable, and enough people had come—often for that very reason—to sustain the belief. In Mason City, Jack Mac-Nider, the son of one of those local patri-archs, talks about the gradual movement of the "iron triangle," the Midwestern indus-trial region, into north-central Iowa (as if the movement of industry were a law of his-tory but the accompanying problems were not), and in the old towns along the Missis-sippi the Chamber of Commerce promotes clean air and good hunting and fishing. Given enough time, people would come to their senses and rush back to places where life was decent and space remained.

So much for heroic visions and high am-bition. The future lay in the past, and the big city was a mad aberration which was, at long last, coming to its unnatural end. The writers of the fifties had talked exten-sively about the lowering of personal ambi-tion, about people more interested in se-curity, pensions and a modestly decent life than in making it big or in taking big chances. But that older form of modesty assumed a general benevolence in the social order, or, at any rate, a continuing belief that the laws of nature and society were progressive. By the early seventies a great deal of that faith was gone, and, while the behavior of individuals often reverted to the patterns of the Eisenhower era, fewer people were talking about progress or the universal affluence just around the corner. The country had seen enough of the failures of social reform and had discovered enough of the dark underside of national "progress" to understand that segregation and inequality—economic and social—seemed to be the rule of history. (For many, of course, there was nothing new about that discovery; but once again it was becoming fashionable). The mythic Middle American was not only trying to come to terms with change and complexity or to adapt his small-town ethic to the realities of technocracy and bureaucracy; he was also engaged in a paradoxical search to reestablish his historic innocence, to flee from the appearance of *knowing,* and he tried to use bureaucracy for precisely that purpose. Despite the official rhetoric about the new federalism or the talk about decentralization, the national response to the events of the late sixties and early seventies was to try to enlarge the distance between the decisions and their consequences, to make the old ethic viable by restricting perspective to local concerns, and to "trust the President" on other matters. To vote for McGovern was, in a sense, to accept some moral responsibility for those distant decisions and become a participant in national affairs—the ethic of the small town applied to Washington and the world; to vote for Nixon was to sever the ethic from global applications—to preserve it by keeping it local. Nixon offered his constituents the luxury of maintaining their purity at home and getting the dirty work done away from home. Official secrecy (in regard to the Pentagon Papers, for example, or the war in Laos, or My Lai, or the infringement of

civil liberties at home) therefore functioned as a means of keeping the moral illusion intact; brutality and repression could be delegated, and bureaucracies could take the rap. The secrecy existed because most people did not want to know; the President became stronger and the Congress weaker because the amorphous middle, suspended between its old ethic and its desire to live modern, was happy to delegate the responsibility. The advantage of that middle world was in its double standard. The old and the new coexisted, and one could change worlds at will: big technology without slums, poverty or bureaucracy, the amenities of modern life without the political and social complications that accompanied their production and use. Time frames could be juxtaposed, like film running backward, or double-exposed negatives, the simple and the sophisticated, the natural and the contrived. Here, too, people wanted the simple life of the land without giving up their Head skis or their stereos or their campers or their washing machines, and the affairs of Main Street became like the business of the commune, small decisions severed from the larger decisions of corporations and government that would, in the long run, make all the difference.

John Updike

John Updike (b. 1932), one of America's most significant contemporary writers, is concerned with the pressures and problems of modern life. In Rabbit Redux *Updike returns to Harry "Rabbit" Angstrom, the young man in* Rabbit, Run, *who is now in his thirties, a working-class man. In this passage Rabbit leaves his work at a printing plant in the city (based on Reading, Pennsylvania) and heads for home in the suburbs. Poetically Updike describes Rabbit's racial fears and confusions, his patriotism, and the suburban development in which he lives.*

from **RABBIT REDUX**

The bus has too many Negroes. Rabbit notices them more and more. They've been here all along, as a tiny kid he remembers streets in Brewer you held your breath walking through, though they never hurt you, just looked; but now they're noisier. Instead of bald-looking heads they're bushy. That's O.K., it's more Nature, Nature is what we're running out of. Two of the men in the shop are Negroes, Farnsworth and Buchanan, and after a while you didn't even notice; at least they remember how to laugh. Sad business, being a Negro man, always underpaid, their eyes don't look like our eyes, bloodshot, brown, liquid in them about to quiver out. Read somewhere some anthropologist thinks Negroes instead of being more primitive are the latest thing to evolve, the newest men. In some ways tougher, in some ways more delicate. Certainly dumber but then being smart hasn't amounted to so much, the atom bomb and the one-piece aluminum beer can. And you can't say Bill Cosby's stupid.

But against these educated tolerant thoughts rests a certain fear; he doesn't see why they have to be so noisy. The four seated right under him, jabbing and letting their noise come out in big silvery hoops; they know damn well they're bugging the fat Dutchy wives pulling their shopping bags home. Well, that's kids of any color: but strange. They are a strange race. Not only their skins but the way they're put together, loose-jointed like lions, strange about the head, as if their thoughts are a different shape and come out twisted even when they mean no menace. It's as if, all these Afro hair bushes and gold earrings and hoopy noise on buses, seeds of some tropical plant sneaked in by the birds were taking over the garden. His garden. Rabbit knows it's his garden and that's why he's put a flag decal on the back window of the Falcon even though Janice says it's corny and fascist. In the papers you read about these houses in Connecticut where the par-

ents are away in the Bahamas and the kids come in and smash it up for a party. More and more this country is getting like that. As if it just grew here instead of people laying down their lives to build it.

The bus works its way down Weiser and crosses the Running Horse River and begins to drop people instead of taking them on. The city with its tired five and dimes (that used to be a wonderland, the counters as high as his nose and the Big Little Books smelling like Christmas) and its Kroll's Department Store (where he once worked knocking apart crates behind the furniture department) and its flowerpotted traffic circle where the trolley tracks used to make a clanging star of intersection and then the empty dusty windows where stores have been starved by the suburban shopping malls and the sad narrow places that come and go called Go-Go or Boutique and the funeral parlors with imitation granite faces and the surplus outlets and a shoe parlor that sells hot roasted peanuts and Afro newspapers printed in Philly crying MBOYA MARTYRED and a flower shop where they sell numbers and protection and a variety store next to a pipe-rack clothing retailer next to a corner dive called JIMBO's *Friendly* LOUNGE, cigarette ends of the city snuffed by the bridge—the city gives way, after the flash of open water that in his youth was choked with coal silt (a man once tried to commit suicide from this bridge but stuck there up to his hips until the police pulled him out) but that now has been dredged and supports a flecking of moored pleasure boats, to West Brewer, a gappy imitation of the city, the same domino-thin houses of brick painted red, but spaced here and there by the twirlers of a car lot, the pumps and blazoned overhang of a gas station, the lake-like depth of a supermarket parking lot crammed with shimmering fins. Surging and spitting, the bus, growing lighter, the Negroes vanishing, moves toward a dream of spaciousness, past residential fortresses with sprinkled lawn around all four sides and clipped hydrangeas above newly pointed retaining walls, past a glimpse of the museum whose gardens were always in blossom and where the swans ate the breadcrusts schoolchildren threw them, then a glimpse of the sunstruck windows, pumpkin orange blazing in reflection, of the tall new wing of the County Hospital for the Insane. Closer at hand, the West Brewer Dry Cleaners, a toy store calling itself Hobby Heaven, a Rialto movie house with a stubby marquee: 2001 SPACE OD'SEY. Weiser Street curves, becomes a highway, dips into green suburbs where in the Twenties little knights of industry built half-timbered dreamhouses, pebbled mortar and clinker brick, stucco flaky as pie crust, witch's houses of candy and hardened cookie dough with two-car garages and curved driveways. In Brewer County, but for a few baronial estates ringed by iron fences and moated by miles of lawn, there is nowhere higher to go than these houses; the most successful dentists may get to buy one, the pushiest insurance salesmen, the suavest opthalmologists. This section even has another name, distinguishing itself from West Brewer: Penn Park. Penn Villas echoes the name hopefully, though it is not incorporated into this borough but sits on the border of Furnace Township, looking in. The township, where once charcoal-fed furnaces had smelted the iron for Revolutionary muskets, is now still mostly farmland, and its few snowplows and single sheriff can hardly cope with this ranch-house village of muddy lawns and potholed macadam and sub-code sewers the developers suddenly left in its care.

Rabbit gets off at a stop in Penn Park and walks down a street of mock Tudor, Emberly Avenue, to where the road surface changes at the township line, and becomes Emberly Drive in Penn Villas. He lives on Vista Crescent, third house from the end. Once there may have been here a vista, a softly sloped valley of red barns and field-stone farmhouses, but more Penn Villas had been added and now the view from any window is as into a fragmented mirror, of houses like this, telephone wires and tele-vision aerials showing where the glass cracked. His house is faced with apple-green aluminum clapboards and is numbered 26. Rabbit steps onto his flagstone porchlet and opens his door with its three baby windows arranged like three steps, echoing the door-chime of three stepped tones.

Bennett Berger

Bennett Berger, a sociologist at the University of California at Davis, here analyzes the backgrounds and implications of the various stereotypes that have arisen around suburbia and its inhabitants.

THE MYTH OF SUBURBIA

In recent years a veritable myth of suburbia has developed in the United States. I am not referring to the physical facts of large-scale population movement to the suburbs: these are beyond dispute. But the social and cultural "revolution" that suburban life supposedly represents is far from being an established fact. Nevertheless, newspapers and magazines repeatedly characterize suburbia as "a new way of life," and one recent textbook refers to the rise of suburbia as "one of the major social changes of the twentieth century."

To urban sociologists, "suburbs" is an ecological term, distinguishing these settlements from cities, rural villages, and other kinds of communities. "Suburbia," on the other hand, is a cultural term, intended to connote a way of life, or, rather, the intent of those who use it is to connote a way of life. The ubiquity of the term in current discourse—suggests that its meaning is well on the way to standardization—that what it is supposed to connote is widely enough accepted to permit free use of the term with a reasonable amount of certainty that it will convey the image or images intended. Over the last dozen years, these images have coalesced into a full-blown myth, complete with its articles of faith, its sacred symbols, its rituals, its promise for the future, and its resolution of ultimate questions. The details of the myth are rife in many popular magazines as well as in more highbrow periodicals and books; and although the details should be familiar to almost everyone interested in contemporary cultural trends, it may be well to summarize them briefly.

The elements of the myth

Approaching the myth of suburbia from the outside, one is immediately struck by rows of new "ranch-type" houses, either identical in design or with minor variations built into a basic plan, winding streets, neat lawns, two-car garages, infant trees, and bicycles and tricycles lining the sidewalks. Nearby is the modern ranch-type school and the even more modern shopping center dominated by the department store branch or the giant super market, itself flanked by a pastel-dotted expanse of parking lot. Beneath the television antennas and behind the modestly but charmingly landscaped entrance to the tract home resides the suburbanite and his family. I should say *"temporarily resides"* because perhaps the most prominent element of the myth is that residence in a tract suburb is temporary; suburbia is a "transient center" because its breadwinners are upwardly mobile, and live there only until a promotion or a company transfer permits or requires something more opulent in the way of a home. The suburbanites are upwardly mobile because they are predominantly young (most commentators seem to agree that they are almost all between twenty-five and thirty-five, well educated, and have a promising place in some organizational hierarchy—promising because of a continuing expansion of the economy and with no serious slowdown in sight). They are engineers, middle-management men, young lawyers, salesmen, insurance agents, teachers, civil service bureau-

crats—groups sometimes designated as Organization Men, and sometimes as "the new middle class." Most such occupations require some college education, so it comes as no surprise to hear and read that the suburbanites are well educated. Their wives, too, seem well educated; their reported conversation, their patois, and especially their apparently avid interest in theories of child development all suggest exposure to higher education.

According to the myth, a new kind of hyperactive social life has developed in suburbia. Not only is informal visiting or "neighboring" said to be rife, but a lively organizational life also goes on. Clubs, associations, and organizations allegedly exist for almost every conceivable hobby, interest, or preoccupation. An equally active participation in local civic affairs is encouraged by the absence of an older generation, who, in other communities, would normally be the leaders.

The rich social and civic life is fostered by the homogeneity of the suburbanites: they are in the same age range, they have similar jobs and incomes, their children are around the same age, their problems of housing and furnishing are similar. In short, a large number of similar interests and preoccupations promotes their solidarity. This very solidarity and homogeneity, on top of the physical uniformities of the suburb itself, is often perceived as the source of the problem of "conformity" in suburbia; aloofness or detachment is frowned upon. The "involvement of everyone in everyone else's life" subjects one to the constant scrutiny of the community, and everything from an unclipped lawn to an unclipped head of hair may be cause for invidious comment. On the other hand, the uniformity and homogeneity make suburbia classless, or one-class (variously designated as middle or upper-middle class). For those interlopers who arrive in the suburbs bearing the unmistakable marks of a more deprived upbringing, suburbia is said to serve as a kind of "second melting pot" in which those who are on the way up learn to take on the appropriate folkways of the milieu to which they aspire.

The widely commented upon "return to religion" is said to be most visible in suburbia. Clergymen are swamped, not only with their religious duties but with problems of marriage family counseling and other family problems as well. The revivified religious life in suburbia is not merely a matter of the increasing size of Sunday congregations, for the church is not only a house of worship but a local civic institution also. As such it benefits from the generally active civic life of the suburbanites.

On week-days, suburbia is a manless society that is almost wholly given over to the business of child rearing. Well-educated young mothers, free from the interference of tradition (represented by doting grandparents), can rear their children according to the best modern methods. "In the absence of older people, the top authorities on child guidance (in suburbia) are two books: Spock's *Infant Care,* and Gesell's *The First Five Years of Life.* You hear frequent references to them."

Part of the myth of suburbia has been deduced from the fact of commuting. For a father, commuting means an extra hour or two away from the family—with debilitating effects upon the relationship between father and children. Sometimes this means that Dad leaves for work before the children are up and comes home after they are put to bed. Naturally, these extra hours put a greater burden upon the mother, and have implications for the relationship between husband and wife.

The commuter returns in the morning to the place where he was bred, for the residents of suburbia are apparently former city people who "escaped" to the suburbs. By moving to suburbia, however, the erstwhile Democrat from the "urban ward" [1]

becomes the suburban **Republican.** The voting shift has been commented on or worried about at length; there seems to be something about suburbia that makes **Re**publicans out of people who were Democrats while they lived in the city. But the political life of suburbia is characterized not only by the voting shift, but by the vigor with which it is carried on. Political *activity* takes its place beside other civic and organizational activity, intense and spirited.

The sources of the myth

This brief characterization is intended neither as ethnography nor as caricature, but it does not, I think, misrepresent the image of suburbia that has come to dominate the minds of most Americans, including intellectuals. Immediately, however, a perplexing question arises: why should a group of tract houses, mass produced and quickly thrown up on the outskirts of a large city, apparently generate so unique and distinctive a way of life? What is the logic that links tract living with suburbia as a way of life?

If suburban homes were all within a limited price range, one might expect them to be occupied by families of similar income, and this might account for some of the homogeneity of the neighborhood ethos. But suburban developments are themselves quite heterogeneous. The term "suburbia" has not only been used to refer to tract housing developments as low as $8,000 per unit and as high as $65,000 per unit, but also to rental developments whose occupants do not think of themselves as homeowners. The same term has been used to cover old rural towns (such as those in the Westchester–Fairfield County complex around New York City) which, because of the expansion of the city and improvements in transportation, have only gradually become suburban in character. It has been applied also to gradually developing

---

[1] William Whyte has a way of making the phrase "urban ward" resound with connotations of poverty, deprivation, soot, and brick—as if "urban ward" were a synonym for "slum."

residential neighborhoods on the edges of the city itself. The ecological nature of the suburbs cannot justify so undifferentiated an image as that of "suburbia."

If we limit the image of suburbia to the mass produced tract developments, we might regard the fact of commuting as the link between suburban residence and "suburbanism as a way of life." Clearly, the demands of daily commuting create certain common conditions which might go far to explain some of the ostensible uniformities of suburban living. But certainly commuting is not a unique feature of suburban living: many suburbanites are not commuters, many urban residents are. It may be true that the occupations of most suburbanites presently require a daily trip to and from the central business district of the city, but it is likely to be decreasingly true with the passage of time: The pioneers to the suburban residential frontier have been followed not only by masses of retail trade outlets, but by industry also. Modern mass production technology has made obsolete many two- and three-story plants in urban areas. Today's modern factories are vast one-story operations that require wide expanses of land, which are either unavailable or too expensive in the city itself. With the passage of time, "industrial parks" will increasingly dot suburban areas, and the proportions of suburbanites commuting to the city each day will decrease.

If the occupations of most suburbanites were similar in their demands, then this might help account for the development of a generic way of life. And, indeed, if suburbia were populated largely by Organization Men and their families, or, lacking this, if Organization Men, as Whyte puts it, gave the prevailing *tone* to life in suburbia, then one could more readily understand the prevalence of his model in the writing on suburbia. But there is no real reason to believe this. Perhaps the typical Organization Man is a suburbanite. But it is one thing to assert this and quite another thing to say that the typical tract suburb is populated or dominated by an Organization way of life.

Clearly, then, one suburb (or *kind* of suburb) is likely to differ from another not only in terms of the cost of its homes, the income of its residents, their occupations and commuting patterns, but also in terms of its educational levels, the character of the region, the size of the suburb, the social and geographical origin of its residents, and countless more indices—all of which, presumably, may be expected to lead to differences in "way of life."

But we not only have good reason to expect suburbs to *differ* markedly from one another; we have reason to expect striking *similarities* between life in urban residential neighborhoods and tract suburbs of a similar social cast. In large cities many men "commute" to work, that is, take subways, buses, or other forms of public transportation to their jobs which may be over on the other side of town. There are thousands of blocks in American cities with rows of identical or similar houses within a limited rental or price range, and presumably occupied by families in a similar income bracket. The same fears for massification and conformity were once felt regarding these urban neighborhoods as are now felt for the mass produced suburbs. Certainly, urban neighborhoods have always had a class character and a "way of life" associated with them. Certainly, too, the whole image of the problem of "conformity" in suburbia closely parallels the older image of the tyranny of gossip in the American small town.

In continually referring to "the myth of suburbia" I do not mean to imply that the reports on the culture of suburban life have been falsified; and it would be a mistake to interpret the tone of my remarks as a debunking one. *I mean only to say that the reports of suburbia we have had so far have been extremely selective.* They are based for the most part, upon life in Levittown, N.Y., Park Forest, Ill., Lakewood, near Los

Angeles, and, most recently (the best study so far) a fashionable suburb of Toronto, Canada. The studies that have given rise to the myth of suburbia have been studies of *white collar suburbs* of large cities. If the phrase "middle-class suburb" or "white collar suburb" strikes the eye as redundant, it is testimony to the efficacy of the myth. Large tracts of suburban housing, in many respects indistinguishable from those in Levittown and Park Forest have gone up and are continuing to go up all over the country, not only near large cities, but near middle sized and small ones as well. In many of these tracts, the homes fall within the $12,000 to $16,000 price range, a range well within the purchasing abilities of large numbers of semi-skilled and skilled factory workers in unionized heavy industry. Many of these working-class people are migrating to these new suburbs—which are not immediately and visibly characterizable as "working class," but which, to all intents and purposes, look from the outside like the fulfillment of the "promise of America" symbolized in the myth. Even more of them will be migrating to new suburbs as increasing numbers of factories move out of the city to the hinterlands. Many of these people are either rural-bred, or urban–working class bred, with relatively little education, and innocent of white collar status or aspiration. And where this is true, as it is in many low-price tracts, one may expect sharp differences between their social and cultural life and that of their more sophisticated counterparts in white collar suburbs.

This should be no surprise; indeed, the fact that it should have to be asserted at all is still further testimony to the vitality of the myth I have been describing. My own research among auto workers in a new, predominantly "working-class" suburb in California demonstrates how far removed their style of life is from that suggested by the myth of suburbia. The group I interviewed still vote 81% Democratic; there has been no "return to religion"

among them—more than half of the people I spoke to said they went to church rarely or not at all. On the whole, they have no great hopes of getting ahead in their jobs, and an enormous majority regard their new suburban homes not as a temporary resting place, but as paradise permanently gained. Of the group I interviewed, 70% belonged to not a single club, organization, or association (with the exception of the union), and their mutual visiting or "neighboring" was quite rare except if relatives lived nearby. Let me summarize, then, by saying that the group of auto workers I interviewed has, for the most part, maintained its working class attitudes and style of life in the context of the bright new suburb.

The functions of the myth

Similar conditions probably prevail in many of the less expensive suburbs; in any case, semi-skilled "working-class" suburbs probably constitute a substantial segment of the reality of suburban life. Why, then, is the myth still so potent in our popular culture? Suburbia today is a public issue—something to talk about, everywhere from the pages of learned journals to best sellers, from academic halls to smoke-filled political rooms, from the pulpits of local churches to Hollywood production lots.[2]

---

[2] In the movie version of the novel *No Down Payment,* ostensibly a fictional account of life in the new suburbia, Hollywood makes a pointed comment on social stratification. The sequence of violence, rape, and accidental death is set in motion by the only important character in the story who is not a white-collar man: the rural Tennessee-bred service station manager. Frustrated at being denied the job of police chief (because of his lack of education), he drinks himself into a stupor, rapes his upper-middle-class, college-educated neighbor, and then is accidentally killed (symbolically enough) under the wheels of his new Ford. The film closes with his blonde, nymphomaniacal widow leaving the suburb for good on a Sunday morning, while the white-collar people are seen leaving the Protestant church (denomination ambiguous) with looks of quiet illumination on their faces.

One source of the peculiar susceptibility of "suburbia" to the manufacture of myth is the fact that a large supply of visible symbols are ready at hand. Picture windows, patios and barbecues, power lawn mowers, the problems of commuting, and the armies of children manning their mechanized vehicles down the sidewalks, are only secondarily facts; primarily they are symbols whose function is to evoke an image of a way of life for the nonsuburban public. These symbols of suburbia can be fitted neatly into the total pattern of the "spirit" of this "age." Suburbia is the locus of gadgetry, shopping centers, and "station wagon culture"; its grass grows greener, its chrome shines brighter, its lines are clean and new and modern. Suburbia is America in its drip-dry Sunday clothes, standing before the bar of history fulfilled, waiting for its judgment. But like Mr. Dooley's court, which kept its eyes on the election returns, the "judgments of history" are also affected by contemporary ideological currents, and the myth of suburbia is enabled to flourish precisely because it fits into the general outlook of at least four otherwise divergent schools of opinion whose function it is to shape the "judgment of history."

To realtor-chamber of commerce defenders of the American Way of Life suburbia represents the fulfillment of the American middle-class dream; it is identified with the continuing possibility of upward mobility, with expanding opportunities in middle-class occupations, with rising standards of living and real incomes, and with the gadgeted good life as it is represented in the full-color ads in the mass circulation magazines.

To a somewhat less sanguine group— for example, architects, city planners, estheticians, and designers—suburbia represents a dreary blight on the American landscape, the epitome of American standardization and vulgarization, with its row upon monotonous row of mass produced cheerfulness masquerading as homes, whole agglomerations or "scatterations" of them masquerading as communities. To these eyes, the new tract suburbs of today are the urban slums of tomorrow.

Third, the myth of suburbia seems important to sociologists and other students of contemporary social and cultural trends. David Riesman says that John R. Seeley et al., the authors of *Crestwood Heights,* "collide like Whyte, with a problem their predecessors only brushed against, for they are writing about *us,* about the professional upper middle class and its businessmen allies. . . . They are writing, as they are almost too aware, about themselves, their friends, their 'type'." There are, obviously, personal pleasures in professionally studying people who are much like oneself; more important, the myth of suburbia conceptualizes for sociologists a microcosm in which some of the apparently major social and cultural trends of our time (other-direction, social mobility, neoconservatism, status anxiety, etc.) flow together, and may be conveniently studied.

Finally, for a group consisting largely of left-wing and formerly left-wing critics of American society, the myth of suburbia provides an up-to-date polemical vocabulary. "Suburb" and "suburban" have replaced the now embarrassingly obsolete "bourgeois" as a packaged rebuke to the whole tenor of American life. What used to be condemned as "bourgeois style," "bourgeois values," and "bourgeois hypocrisy," are now simply designated as "suburban."[3]

But while the myth of suburbia is useful to each of these four groups, it cannot be written off simply as "ruling class propaganda," or as an attempt to see only the sunny side of things, or for that matter, as an attempt to see only the darker side of things—or even as a furtive attempt to peer into a mirror. Too many responsible intellectuals, while uncritically accepting the *myth* of suburbia, are nevertheless extremely critical of what they "see" in it.

3 In 1970, "plastic" seems to be the most common term of general rebuke.

But precisely *what* is it that they see that they are critical of? Is it conformity? status anxiety? chrome? tail fins? gadgetry? gray flannel suits? No doubt, these are symbols powerful enough to evoke images of an enemy. But the nature of this "enemy" remains peculiarly elusive. Surely, there is nothing specifically "suburban" about conformity, status anxiety, and the rest; nor is there anything necessarily diabolical about mass-produced domestic comfort and conservatively cut clothes. It is extraordinary that, with the single exception of William H. Whyte's attempt to trace the "web of friendship" on the basis of the physical structure of the Park Forest "courts," no one, to my knowledge, has come to grips with the problem of defining what is specifically *suburban* about suburbia. Instead, most writers are reduced to the use of hackneyed stereotypes not of suburbia, but of the upper middle class. When most commentators say "suburbia," they really mean "middle class."

The sources of this way of life, however, lie far deeper than mere residence in a suburb. These sources have been much discussed in recent years, most notably perhaps, by Mills, Riesman, Fromm, and Galbraith. They go beyond suburbs to questions of wealth, social status, and corporate organization. Even Whyte's famous discussion of suburbia (upon which so much of the myth is founded) was undertaken in the context of his larger discussion of the Organization Man, a social type created by the structure of corporate opportunity in the United States—something a good deal more profound than the folkways of suburbanites. Seen in this light, suburbia may be nothing but a scapegoat; by blaming "it" for the consequences of our commitment to chrome idols, we achieve ritual purity without really threatening anything or anyone—except perhaps the poor suburbanites, who can't understand why they're always being satirized.

But heaping abuse on suburbia instead of on the classic targets of American social criticism ("success," individual and corporate greed, corruption in high and low places, illegitimate power, etc.) has its advantages for the not-quite-completely-critical intellectual. His critical stance places him comfortably in the great tradition of American social criticism, and at the same time his targets render him respectable and harmless—because, after all, the critique of suburbia is essentially a "cultural" critique; unlike a political or economic one, it threatens no entrenched interests, and contains no direct implications for agitation or concerted action. Indeed, it may be, as Edward Shils has suggested, that a "cultural" critique is all that is possible today from a left-wing point of view; the American economy and political process stand up fairly well under international comparisons, but American "culture" is fair game for anyone.

Despite the epithets that identify suburbia as the citadel of standardization ·and vulgarization and conformity, suburbia is also testimony to the fact that Americans are living better than ever before. What needs emphasis is that this is true not only for the traditionally comfortable white collar classes, but for the blue collar, frayed collar, and turned collar classes also. Even families in urban slums are likely to be paying upward of $85 a month in rent these days, and for this or only slightly more, they can "buy" a new tract home in the suburbs. There is an irony, therefore, in the venom that left-wing critics inject into their discussions of suburbia because the criticism of suburbia tends to become a criticism of industrialization, "rationality," and "progress," and thus brings these critics quite close to the classic conservatives, whose critique of industrialization was also made in terms of its cultural consequences. It is almost as if left-wing critics feared the seduction of the working class by pie—not in the sky, not even on the table, but right in the freezer.

DISCUSSION QUESTIONS

"The Gift Outright" and *"Birches"*

1. What does Frost mean when he says "The land was ours before we were the land's"? What made us belong to the land?

2. When we finally "gave ourselves outright," what was the condition of the land? What does Frost mean by "unstoried, artless, unenhanced"? Who would remedy that condition?

3. The first part of "Birches" is a celebration of the pastoral experience. Describe what a boy does who swings birches. How does the effect of that activity differ from the effects of an ice storm?

4. The last part of "Birches" uses the image of birch swinging as a metaphor for escaping from "considerations." Nature represents here both the dream of escape and the reality of life. Find lines which show these two aspects.

5. How does Frost emphasize the spiritual quality of the land?

"Solitude"

1. In this selection the pastoral is almost a religious experience. What are the qualities of nature that create this spiritual mood?

2. How does Thoreau answer people who ask if he is lonely?

3. What benefits does Thoreau feel nature provides? Compare his ideas with Frost's views of nature.

4. Does Thoreau's nature exist today or has man destroyed it? What would Thoreau's reaction be to the modern world?

"The Boys' Ambition"

1. Why is the steamboatman a kind of god? What qualities of the American hero does he possess?

2. Describe the life in a river town as seen in this essay. Does it seem idyllic?

3. Does Twain see the steamboat as the "machine in the garden," that is, a destroyer of the serenity of nature? Would Thoreau? Why?

"Sophistication"

1. The pastoral experience has often been allied with the small town. What elements of the dream of the pastoral do you see in this story? What elements suggest a harsher reality?

2. Why does sophistication occur?

3. What does the last sentence suggest about the pastoral experience?

4. Does the story offer any insights into why young people leave the small town for the city?

from *"The Grapes of Wrath"*

1. Describe both the virginal and cultivated nature in this selection. Do these two types of nature harmonize or are they discordant?

2. How is the cornucopian image of America described?

3. What is it that destroys the dream of the garden? Whose fault is it? Point out images of control.

4. Is Steinbeck's outrage justified?

from *"North Towards Home"*

1. What is the difference between the way Morris and Richard Wright look at Yazoo? From the details Morris gives, can you understand what Wright meant when he said he would not come back to America?

2. Compare Morris's recollections of Yazoo with Sherwood Anderson's views of Winesburg or Mark Twain's picture of Hannibal. Though the accounts are years

apart, what similarities are there? What specific differences do you note?

"The Significance of the Frontier in American History"

1. What is Turner's definition of the frontier?

2. Why does he say the frontier was "the distinguishing feature of American life"?

3. Compare Turner's ideas of what makes a European into an American with those of de Crèvecoeur.

from "The Deerslayer"

1. What qualities of character do most Americans associate with the frontier and frontier heroes? Is the Deerslayer heroic? Is he similar to Wheeler's Calamity Jane?

2. What is Deerslayer's attitude towards Indians?

3. Compare Rivenoak's speech to Deerslayer ("We are the children of the setting sun") with Black Elk's speech in "Wounded Knee."

"Pioneers! O Pioneers!"

1. What is Whitman's conception of the frontier and of the people who settled it? Is he realistic or romantic in this view?

2. What contrast does he see between the pioneers and the citizens used to luxury? Is the belief that hardship is a virtue a common American belief?

3. Would Hamlin Garland or Francis Parkman share Whitman's enthusiasm? Why?

"The Frontier"

1. What evidence is there in Parkman's 1846 account that the present frontier was getting too crowded for some people?

2. What does Parkman think of the emigrants?

3. What realities does he suggest about frontier travel?

4. Is his frontier the frontier most Americans believe in?

"Barkin' Up the Wrong Tree"

1. What similarities does this dime novel chapter have with Cooper's tale? What differences?

2. What idea of frontier women do we get from the description of Calamity Jane and Colonel Tubbs's wife Angelina?

3. What picture of the West would readers of dime novels get? Compare and contrast this to Parkman's frontier.

"The Bride Comes to Yellow Sky"

1. Describe the personalities of the Marshal and Scratchy Wilson. How are they a parody of the lawman and the bandit?

2. What details in this story suggest the closing of the frontier? For example, what is the importance of the train in the story?

3. What is the significance of the title and the importance of the bride?

4. Compare Crane's portrait of the West with other writers' views in this section.

"Under the Lion's Paw"

1. What were the realities of life for the prairie farmer as suggested by this story?

2. What help was available to the farmer? How dependable do you think that was? Is Steve Council too good to be true?

3. Does Garland's story contradict the Turner thesis of free land providing a basis for equality and independence? Explain.

4. Is Garland's portrait of Jim Butler a fair one? How do you react to him? What terms or business practices could he have adopted? Have laws changed or would a modern-day Haskins face much the same financial difficulty?

"Buffalo Bill's"

1. What qualities of the frontier hero does Cummings emphasize in this poem?

2. What point about death is he trying to make?

3. What is he saying about the frontier and the frontier spirit?

"Mannahatta," "Chicago," and "Skyscraper"

1. Why does Whitman find the city appealing?

2. Sandburg is both dreamer and realist. How is he able to be both simultaneously?

3. How does Sandburg show the city as the new landscape?

"Mrs. Manstey's View"

1. In this story how is the impersonality of the city shown?

2. What details show the yearning for the pastoral? In what way does Mrs. Manstey link success with the pastoral?

3. How does Mrs. Manstey cope with her problem? Is there some insight into crime in cities?

4. Could a story like this be written today?

"Goodbye to All That"

1. How does Joan Didion describe the sense of unlimited possibilities of New York? She calls the city "Xanadu"—to what is she referring?

2. What is the lure of the city for young people?

3. Can you account for her depression which caused her to leave New York?

4. What does she mean when she says that one can "stay too long at the Fair"?

"The End of Innocence"

1. Compare Schrag's statements that Americans are ambivalent toward cities with Wyllie's remarks about the city and success.

2. Why do Americans reject New York, in Schrag's opinion? Compare with Joan Didion's essay.

3. What are the "secret places" people don't talk about in most towns?

4. What evidence is there that the "national culture" has become dominant over "local culture"? What change in American values has that produced, if any?

from *"Rabbit Redux"*

1. Rabbit tells us a great deal about himself on his bus ride home. What are his racial attitudes? What direction is America taking, according to him?

2. What has happened to the city where he works? What is the suburb like where he lives?

3. What contrast is noted between the suburban street "Vista Crescent" and the pastoral ideal?

4. Can you tell what class of Americans Rabbit represents? Explain.

"The Myth of Suburbia"

1. What aspects of the suburban myth, as described by Berger, did you take as "facts" about suburbs?

2. In Berger's opinion, why have these half-truths gone generally unchallenged for so long?

3. Compare the suburbia of John Cheever's "O Youth and Beauty!" to Berger's ideas on the suburbs. Does Cheever perpetuate the myth? What about John Updike's brief portrait; is it representative?

SUGGESTED READINGS

BABCOCK, C. MERTON, ed. *The American Frontier: A Social and Literary Record.* New York, 1965.

BELLOW, SAUL. *Herzog.* New York, 1961.

———. *Seize the Day.* New York, 1956.

BRAUTIGAN, RICHARD. *Trout Fishing in America.* New York, 1969.

CATHER, WILLA. *My Antonia.* Boston, 1918.

COOPER, JAMES FENIMORE. *Last of the Mohicans.* 1826.

DE VOTO, BERNARD. *Across the Wide Missouri.* Boston, 1947.

FAULKNER, WILLIAM. "The Bear" in *Go Down, Moses, and Other Stories.* New York, 1942.

GANS, HERBERT J. *The Urban Villagers.* New York, 1962.

HARTE, BRET. *The Luck of Roaring Camp and Other Sketches.* 1870.

HAZARD, LUCY. *The Frontier in American Literature.* New York, 1927.

HOLLOWAY, MARK. *Heavens on Earth: Utopian Communities in America 1680–1880.* New York, 1966.

JACOBS, JANE. *The Death and Life of Great American Cities.* New York, 1961.

LEWIS, R. W. B. *The American Adam.* Chicago, 1955.

LEWIS, SINCLAIR. *Main Street.* New York, 1920.

MARX, LEO. *The Machine in the Garden: Technology and the Pastoral Ideal in America.* New York, 1964.

SMITH, HENRY NASH. *Virgin Land: The American West as Symbol and Myth.* Cambridge, Mass., 1950.

STEFFENS, LINCOLN. *The Shame of the Cities.* New York, 1902.

TERKEL, STUDS. *Division Street: America.* New York, 1967.

TWAIN, MARK. *Roughing It.* 1872.

WILLIAMS, WILLIAM CARLOS. *Paterson.* New York, 1948.

PART FOUR

WHERE DO WE GO FROM HERE?

Where do we go from here? In order to shape the future, one must understand the past and the present. As the modern philosopher George Santayana cautioned, those who fail to learn from the past are doomed to repeat it. What then has been our past, as presented in this book? It has been one of ideals and hopes: for political freedom, for economic opportunity, and for a productive, satisfying environment. Though these ideals have not been fully realized, Americans have not abandoned them for others. What will be the future for these ideals, the American dream? The selections presented here were chosen to touch on problems and solutions of current interest, ranging from the influence of the military-industrial complex, the position of women in American society, and progress in ecology and technology, to what Allan Nevins calls our unwavering faith in the future. These selections should provoke the reader to explore further the condition of the American dream. After all, if we know where we were and where we are, then we may know where we will be.

Thomas Griffith

*Thomas Griffith (b. 1915) was born and
educated in the state of Washington. He
began his career in journalism as a reporter
for the Seattle* Times *and eventually became
a senior editor for* Time Magazine. *He
brings to his analysis of American culture
the perceptions of a man who has spent a
lifetime reporting the achievements and
failures of the American way of life.*

THE AMERICAN IMAGE

Just as the sky over a city, when seen from
afar at night, is lit by a reflected luminosity
that is the merged glow of the city's many
lights, so does a culture give off a halation.
That halation, which is not a true sum of
all its parts but only a visual effect which
can sometimes be misleading, might be
called its image. What is the American
Image?

I think that it is first of all an image of
immense energy. On the day of Pearl Harbor, when Americans themselves were
stunned by the blow, Winston Churchill
was in quite a different mood. He thought
of a remark that Edward Grey had made
to him more than thirty years before—that
the United States is like "a gigantic boiler.
Once the fire is lighted under it there is no
limit to the power it can generate." With
such an ally, and no longer condemned to
fight alone, Churchill went to bed "and
slept the sleep of the saved and thankful."
In the few short years since Pearl Harbor,
our capacity to generate power has increased in strides that in turn appear to

be but timid, mincing steps compared to
what scientists intend for us.

A rich and prodigious giant, we seem
impulsively improvident to those peoples
whose barren hillsides yield a hard living,
or whose crabbed space requires a meticul-
ous tilling of terraced hillsides: we dust
crops by plane, reap by machine and think
in vast acreages. Much of what they call our
wastefulness we regard as a mere excess of
our energy, and if we are sometimes prod-
igal of resources, we are also cognizant of
how much science has multiplied the
energy of our waterfalls and the usefulness
of our coal, and of how much a seeming
squandering often returns far more than
was spent. This knowledge of our productive wealth inhabits our characters and influences our conduct; it makes us so generous a people. We are freed by our wealth
from that pinched, selfish and guarded outlook so prevalent in Europe: the foundation of our generosity is our belief that
"there's more where that came from." In
Palm Springs live men who consider themselves only a little better off than most, but
who outdo ancient kings in their holdings.
Our awareness of plenty governs our restless quest for more; we are not dulled by
a sense of limitations nor made grasping
by a feeling that we are all taking from a
diminishing pile. The way to great wealth
in America is not to be a Tiffany to the few
but a Henry Ford to the many. Part of the
dynamism of the American capitalist (and
the reason he is more esteemed than despised) is that he is an energizer whose ambition multiplies opportunities for others.
This is a far cry from the view put forward

by Karl Marx, of an inevitable and squalid conflict between classes for a share of the common wealth; Americans are apt to find Marx not only a pernicious guide but a bad prophet, even if his theories were perhaps explicable in the practices which he saw in his day and which still persist in other parts of the world. To read any classic American 19th Century success story today is not to be left aglow with admiration but appalled by its avarice. We no longer believe in squeezing nickels, but in rotating dollars.

The American lives in waste and accepts the principle of the discard pile. We can chance; if we fail it was "worth trying"; we have a margin. The American credo holds that activity has a value all its own, and that corrections can be made along the way. This pragmatic optimism—the spirit of it-can-be-done—helps explain how much does get done. The easy American confidence is sometimes mistaken for bragging by those who miss the humor in our self-assurance: hyperbole is our style; our folk stories are tall tales, not small ones.

To the wider world, to which every nation makes its useful contribution (Britain, its political institutions and trade patterns; France, its cuisine, its style of living and thought; Germany, its science and commercial impulse; Russia, its military might and political influence), America contributes organization, efficiency, commercial imagination, dynamism and optimism. There are defects to these American qualities: an overriding and sometimes insensitive propulsion to change often takes insufficient account of the values of habit, comfort and simplicity in the old ways, and our missionary-minded enthusiasm is sometimes determined that others must imitate us. But we bring to the world an inventive spirit, prepared to try anything: a boldness that can be seen in our engineering and heard in our jazz. Our science may not be as inherently creative as the German, but it achieves more by being linked to great organizations and vast resources. We bring attractive business practices: openness of wallet and openness of mind; a random experimentalism that prizes new ways: our builders casually make cost estimates on the backs of envelopes as they go about their jobs, and corporals and sergeants in our armies may be restrained by their instructions but always feel free to improvise.

A vital working confidence is the essential American trait, but its sunny outlook has become clouded over of late, because of increased doubts over what use our energy is put to, and fears of an uncertain future. Exuberance is no longer our national image as a people; politically, the halation radiating from us, as seen from abroad, is of selfishness threatened, and inclined to panic. It is an image that does less than justice to us. The capacities that produced our turbulent creativity are still there, and still being used: our productive dynamism has not dried up. Our trouble, as a people that has always been given to anxious self-examination, is that we have begun to doubt our ends.

It was simpler in the 19th Century, when so many massive tasks confronted us—wildernesses to be settled, slums to be torn down, poverty and malnutrition to be conquered, illiteracy to be overcome. If some of the ardor that went into attacking these evils was too expectant, if enthusiasts believed that literacy would make men enlightened, prosperity would make them unselfish and education would make them virtuous, we can be grateful for what, less than the dreams, was achieved. Those immigrants who struggled and denied themselves so that their children might lead better lives may have been avaricious and clutching, but was it their children who gained most, in inheriting it all—or the immigrants themselves, who along with their drudgery and saving were also pursuing, as their children perhaps are not, a goal beyond themselves?

As a nation we have worked hard—for we are not a lazy people—for goals that are nearly in sight. Easy Street now stretches from coast to coast, even if it has its rough spots, and our economy its lurches. The President's Council of Economic Advisers talks of a "diffusion of well-being," which may be another way of saying that our goal has become a life of amiable sloth. Once we chased happiness; our national ambition now seems diminished to life, liberty and the pursuit of ease. We once talked of the greatest good of the greatest number, but now think of the greatest pleasure of the most people, and the distinction is significant. We have television for those who do not even actively seek pleasure any more but are satisfied with distractions. (What is so deadening about mass entertainment, as compared to a past age's aimless conversation and card playing, is that it is all intake and no outgo, involving no effort of response.)

Working at jobs that often do not require or inspire our best, we demand the right to relax as we will. Is the tension of incentive disappearing from our lives? When, like Chinese peasants in a paddy, one must work all day, rest becomes necessity and one does not worry about "what to do with the time." The American woman, freed from an arduous day of preparing food as her grandmother did, is not fully satisfied with the time saved, and elaborates her meals and her preparations to take up the slack, pursues curiosities of cuisine and "balanced meals," is busy in the community or taxiing her family about, and giving luncheons which must look as if they were no work at all. Or else she ceases to struggle. See her now "slaving" over a hot rotisserie with a prepared chicken inside while the dessert needs only thawing from the deep freeze and the automatic dishwasher waits at the ready and the TV baby-sits for the children; then comes that time of day known as "the children's hour": mommy and daddy are having their martini. And ahead, after a lifetime of this, what awaits—a vision of gray hair, rouged cheeks and tartan slacks, drink in hand, playing the slots at Vegas? Or for the quieter ones, shuffleboard and bragging on a Florida park bench?

We are the first people to be freed from the need for overwork: before, there were only individuals, or a class, so freed—and either they became indolent and declined as a culture, or took on duties and responsibilities in return for their privileges. Will it be said of us that we had the greatest of opportunities, and merely enjoyed them?

Allen Ginsberg

Allen Ginsberg (b. 1926) first came to national prominence with the publication of Howl *in 1956 and the subsequent censorship trial in 1957. The poem involved the psychological experiences of the "Beat" poets of the 1950s. "America" deals more with external commentary, and is a difficult, fragmented, apocalyptic vision of contemporary society.*

AMERICA

America I've given you all and now I'm
    nothing.
America two dollars and twentyseven cents
    January 17, 1956.
I can't stand my own mind.
America when will we end the human war?
Go fuck yourself with your atom bomb.
I don't feel good don't bother me.
I won't write my poem till I'm in my right
    mind.
America when will you be angelic?
When will you take off your clothes?
When will you look at yourself through
    the grave?
When will you be worthy of your million
    Trotskyites?
America why are your libraries full of tears?
America when will you send your eggs to
    India?
I'm sick of your insane demands.
When can I go into the supermarket and
    buy what I need with my good looks?

America after all it is you and I who are
perfect not the next world.
Your machinery is too much for me.
You made me want to be a saint.
There must be some other way to settle
this argument.
Burroughs is in Tangiers I don't think he'll
come back it's sinister.
Are you being sinister or is this some form
of practical joke?
I'm trying to come to the point.
I refuse to give up my obsession.
America stop pushing I know what I'm
doing.
America the plum blossoms are falling.
I haven't read the newspapers for months,
everyday somebody goes on trial for
murder.
America I feel sentimental about the
Wobblies.
America I used to be a communist when I
was a kid I'm not sorry.
I smoke marijuana every chance I get.
I sit in my house for days on end and stare
at the roses in the closet.
When I go to Chinatown I get drunk and
never get laid.
My mind is made up there's going to be
trouble.
You should have seen me reading Marx.
My psychoanalyst thinks I'm perfectly right.
I won't say the Lord's Prayer.
I have mystical visions and cosmic vibra-
tions.
America I still haven't told you what you
did to Uncle Max after he came over
from Russia.

I'm addressing you.
Are you going to let your emotional life
be run by Time Magazine?
I'm obsessed by Time Magazine.
I read it every week.
Its cover stares at me every time I slink
past the corner candystore.
I read it in the basement of the Berkeley
Public Library.
It's always telling me about responsibility.
Businessmen are serious. Movie pro-

ducers are serious. Everybody's serious
but me.
It occurs to me that I am America.
I am talking to myself again.

Asia is rising against me.
I haven't got a chinaman's chance.
I'd better consider my national resources.
My national resources consist of two joints
of marijuana millions of genitals an
unpublishable private literature that
goes 1400 miles an hour and twenty-
five thousand mental institutions.
I say nothing about my prisons nor the
millions of underprivileged who live
in my flowerpots under the light of
five hundred suns.
I have abolished the whorehouses of France,
Tangiers is the next to go.
My ambition is to be President despite the
fact that I'm a Catholic.

America how can I write a holy litany in
your silly mood?
I will continue like Henry Ford my
strophes are as individual as his automobiles more so they're all different
sexes.
America I will sell you strophes $2500
apiece $500 down on your old strophe
America free Tom Mooney
America save the Spanish Loyalists
America Sacco & Vanzetti must not die
America I am the Scottsboro boys.
America when I was seven momma took me
to Communist Cell meetings they sold
us garbanzos a handful per ticket a
ticket costs a nickel and the speeches
were free everybody was angelic and
sentimental about the workers it was
all so sincere you have no idea what a
good thing the party was in 1835 Scott
Nearing was a grand old man a real
mensch Mother Bloor made me cry I
once saw Israel Amter plain. Everybody
must have been a spy.
America you don't really want to go to war.
America it's them bad Russians.
Them Russians them Russians and them
Chinamen. And them Russians.

The Russia wants to eat us alive. The Russia's power mad. She wants to take our cars from out our garages.

Her wants to grab Chicago. Her needs a Red Readers' Digest. Her wants our auto plants in Siberia. Him big bureaucracy running our fillingstations.

That no good. Ugh. Him make Indians learn read. Him need big black niggers. Hah. Her make us all work sixteen hours a day. Help.

America this is quite serious.

America this is the impression I get from looking in the television set.

America is this correct?

I'd better get right down to the job.

It's true I don't want to join the Army or turn lathes in precision parts factories, I'm nearsighted and psychopathic anyway.

America I'm putting my queer shoulder to the wheel.

Carl Sandburg

In this last section of a long poem Sandburg shows his faith in the common man. (Sandburg is described on page 230.)

THE PEOPLE WILL LIVE ON

The people will live on.

The learning and blundering people will live on.

They will be tricked and sold and again sold

And go back to the nourishing earth for rootholds.

The people so peculiar in renewal and comeback,

You can't laugh off their capacity to take it.

The mammoth rests between his cyclonic dramas.

The people so often sleepy, weary, enigmatic,

is a vast huddle with many units saying:

"I earn my living.

I make enough to get by

and it takes all my time.

If I had more time

I could do more for myself

and maybe for others.

I could read and study

and talk things over

and find out about things.

It takes time.

I wish I had the time."

The people is a tragic and comic two-face:

hero and hoodlum: phantom and gorilla twist-

ing to moan with a gargoyle mouth: "They

buy me and sell me . . . it's a game . . .

sometime I'll break loose. . . ."

Once having marched

Over the margins of animal necessity,

Over the grim line of sheer subsistence,

Then man came

To the deeper rituals of his bones,

To the lights lighter than any bones,

To the time for thinking things over,

To the dance, the song, the story,

Or the hours given over to dreaming,

Once having so marched.

Between the finite limitations of the five senses

and the endless yearnings of man for the beyond

the people hold to the humdrum bidding of work and food

while reaching out when it comes their way

for lights beyond the prison of the five senses,

for keepsakes lasting beyond any hunger or death.

This reaching is alive.

The panderers and liars have violated and smutted it.

Yet this reaching is alive yet

for lights and keepsakes.

The people know the salt of the sea
and the strength of the winds
lashing the corners of the earth.
The people take the earth
as a tomb of rest and a cradle of hope.
Who else speaks for the Family of Man?
They are in tune and step
with constellations of universal law.

The people is a polychrome,
a spectrum and a prism
held in a moving monolith,
a console organ of changing themes,
a clavilux of color poems
wherein the sea offers fog
and the fog moves off in rain
and the labrador sunset shortens
to a nocturne of clear stars
serene over the shot spray
of northern lights.

The steel mill sky is alive.
The fire breaks white and zigzag
shot on a gun-metal gloaming.
Man is a long time coming.
Man will yet win.
Brother may yet line up with brother:

This old anvil laughs at many broken
    hammers.
There are men who can't be bought.
The fireborn are at home in fire.
The stars make no noise.
You can't hinder the wind from blowing.
Time is a great teacher.
Who can live without hope?
In the darkness with a great bundle of grief
    the people march.
In the night, and overhead a shovel of stars
    for keeps, the people march:
"Where to? what next?"

Dwight D. Eisenhower

*Dwight D. Eisenhower (1890–1969), Ameri-
can general and President of the United
States 1953–1961, was known chiefly for his
success as Supreme Commander of the Allied
Expeditionary Force in World War II and
for his genial, moderate Presidency. During
his terms in the White House, his speeches
were often criticized for their flat, colorless
character. This address, however, has attracted much attention in recent years because it is the first public warning by a major
official (and military man) of the dangers of
a military-industrial complex. The interdependence of the military and the business
world, natural in Eisenhower's time, has become an issue of crucial importance today.*

FAREWELL ADDRESS

Three days from now, after half a century
in the service of our country, I shall lay
down the responsibilities of office as, in
traditional and solemn ceremony, the authority of the Presidency is vested in my
successor.

This evening I come to you with a message of leavetaking and farewell, and to
share a few final thoughts with you, my
countrymen.

Like every other citizen, I wish the new
President, and all who will labor with him,
Godspeed. I pray that the coming years
will be blessed with peace and prosperity
for all.

Our people expect their President and
the Congress to find essential agreement on
issues of great moment, the wise resolution
of which will better shape the future of
the nation.

My own relations with the Congress,
which began on a remote and tenuous basis
when, long ago, a member of the Senate
appointed me to West Point, have since
ranged to the intimate during the war and
immediate post-war period, and finally to
the mutually interdependent during these
past eight years.

In this final relationship, the Congress
and the Administration have, on most vital
issues, cooperated well, to serve the nation's
good rather than mere partisanship, and so
have assured that the business of the nation
should go forward. So my official relation-

ship with the Congress ends in a feeling, on my part, of gratitude that we have been able to do so much together.

We now stand ten years past the midpoint of a century that has witnessed four major wars among great nations—three of these involved our own country.

Despite these holocausts America is today the strongest, the most influential and most productive nation in the world. Understandably proud of this pre-eminence, we yet realize that America's leadership and prestige depend, not merely upon our unmatched material progress, riches and military strength, but on how we use our power in the interests of world peace and human betterment.

Throughout America's adventure in free government, our basic purposes have been to keep the peace; to foster progress in human achievement, and to enhance liberty, dignity and integrity among peoples and among nations.

To strive for less would be unworthy of a free and religious people.

Any failure traceable to arrogance or our lack of comprehension or readiness to sacrifice would inflict upon us grievous hurt, both at home and abroad.

Crises there will continue to be. In meeting them, whether foreign or domestic, great or small, there is a recurring temptation to feel that some spectacular and costly action could become the miraculous solution to all current difficulties. A huge increase in newer elements of our defenses; development of unrealistic programs to cure every ill in agriculture; a dramatic expansion in basic and applied research—these and many other possibilities, each possibly promising in itself, may be suggested as the only way to the road we wish to travel.

But each proposal must be weighed in the light of a broader consideration; the need to maintain balance in and among national programs—balance between the private and the public economy, balance between the cost and hoped for advantages—balance between the clearly necessary and the comfortably desirable; balance between our essential requirements as a nation and the duties imposed by the nation upon the individual; balance between actions of the moment and the national welfare of the future. Good judgment seeks balance and progress; lack of it eventually finds imbalance and frustration.

The record of many decades stands as proof that our people and their Government have, in the main, understood these truths and have responded to them well in the face of threat and stress.

But threats, new in kind or degree, constantly arise. Of these, I mention two only.

A vital element in keeping the peace is our military establishment. Our arms must be mighty, ready for instant action, so that no potential aggressor may be tempted to risk his own destruction.

Our military organization today bears little relation to that known of any of my predecessors in peacetime—or, indeed, by the fighting men of World War II or Korea.

Until the latest of our world conflicts, the United States had no armaments industry. American makers of plowshares could, with time and as required, make swords as well.

But we can no longer risk emergency improvisation of national defense. We have been compelled to create a permanent armaments industry of vast proportions. Added to this, three and a half million men and women are directly engaged in the defense establishment. We annually spend on military security alone more than the net income of all United States corporations.

Now this conjunction of an immense military establishment and a large arms industry is new in the American experience. The total influence—economic, political, even spiritual—is felt in every city, every state house, every office of the Federal Government. We recognize the imperative need for this development. Yet we must not fail to comprehend its grave implications. Our toil, resources and livelihood are all involved; so is the very structure of our society.

In the councils of Government, we must guard against the acquisition of unwarranted influence, whether sought or unsought, by the military-industrial complex. The potential for the disastrous rise of misplaced power exists and will persist.

We must never let the weight of this combination endanger our liberties or democratic processes. We should take nothing for granted. Only an alert and knowledgeable citizenry can compel the proper meshing of the huge industrial and military machinery of defense with our peaceful methods and goals, so that security and liberty may prosper together.

Akin to, and largely responsible for the sweeping changes in our industrial-military posture has been the technological revolution during recent decades.

In this revolution research has become central. It also becomes more formalized, complex and costly. A steadily increasing share is conducted for, by, or at the direction of the Federal Government.

Today the solitary inventor, tinkering in his shop, has been overshadowed by task forces of scientists, in laboratories and testing fields. In the same fashion, the free university, historically the fountainhead of free ideas and scientific discovery, has experienced a revolution in the conduct of research. Partly because of the huge costs involved, a Government contract becomes virtually a substitute for intellectual curiosity.

For every old blackboard there are now hundreds of new electronic computers.

The prospect of domination of the nation's scholars by Federal employment, project allocations and the power of money is ever present, and is gravely to be regarded.

Yet, in holding scientific research and discovery in respect, as we should, we must also be alert to the equal and opposite danger that public policy could itself become the captive of a scientific-technological elite.

It is the task of statesmanship to mold, to balance, and to integrate these and other forces, new and old, within the principles of our democratic system—ever aiming toward the supreme goals of our free society.

Another factor in maintaining balance involves the element of time. As we peer into society's future, we—you and I, and our Government—must avoid the impulse to live only for today, plundering, for our own ease and convenience, the precious resources of tomorrow.

We cannot mortgage the material assets of our grandchildren without risking the loss also of their political and spiritual heritage. We want democracy to survive for all generations to come, not to become the insolvent phantom of tomorrow.

During the long lane of the history yet to be written America knows that this world of ours, ever growing smaller, must avoid becoming a community of dreadful fear and hate, and be, instead, a proud confederation of mutual trust and respect.

Such a confederation must be one of equals. The weakest must come to the conference table with the same confidence as do we, protected as we are by our moral, economic and military strength. That table, though scarred by many past frustrations, cannot be abandoned for the certain agony of the battlefield.

Disarmament, with mutual honor and confidence, is a continuing imperative. Together we must learn how to compose differences—not with arms, but with intellect and decent purpose. Because this need is so sharp and apparent, I confess that I lay down my official responsibilities in this field with a definite sense of disappointment. As one who has witnessed the horror and the lingering sadness of war, as one who knows that another war could utterly destroy this civilization which has been so slowly and painfully built over thousands of years, I wish I could say tonight that a lasting peace is in sight.

Happily, I can say that war has been avoided. Steady progress toward our ultimate goal has been made. But so much remains to be done. As a private citizen, I shall never cease to do what little I can to help the world advance along that road.

So, in this, my last good night to you as your President, I thank you for the many opportunities you have given me for public service in war and in peace.

I trust that in you—that, in that service, you find some things worthy. As for the rest of it, I know you will find ways to improve performance in the future.

You and I—my fellow citizens—need to be strong in our faith that all nations, under God, will reach the goal of peace with justice. May we be ever unswerving in devotion to principle, confident but humble with power, diligent in pursuit of the nation's great goals.

To all the peoples of the world, I once more give expression to America's prayerful and continuing aspiration:

We pray that peoples of all faiths, all races, all nations, may have their great human needs satisfied; that those now denied opportunity shall come to enjoy it to the full; that all who yearn for freedom may experience its spiritual blessings, those who have freedom will understand, also, its heavy responsibility; that all who are insensitive to the needs of others, will learn charity, and that the sources—scourges of poverty, disease and ignorance—will be made to disappear from the earth; and that in the goodness of time, all peoples will come to live together in a peace guaranteed by the binding force of mutual respect and love.

Now, on Friday noon, I am to become a private citizen. I am proud to do so. I look forward to it.

Thank you, and, good night.

James Wright

James Wright (b. 1927), winner of the Pulitzer Prize for his Selected Poems in 1972, was born in Martin's Ferry, Ohio, graduated from Kenyon College, and served with the Occupation Army in Japan after World War II. Later he continued his studies at the University of Washington where he received his Ph.D. In addition to five books of his own poetry, Wright has published several translations and has taught in college. His early poems show an interest in people who are outcasts of society, like the characters in Edwin Arlington Robinson's poems, while his later work shows more interest in political subjects. In this poem Wright examines the military power of the President of the United States and the moral implications of that power.

EISENHOWER'S VISIT TO FRANCO, 1959

> *. . . we die of cold, and not*
> *of darkness.*—Unamuno

The American hero must triumph over
The forces of darkness.
He has flown through the very light of
    heaven
And come down in the slow dusk
Of Spain.

Franco stands in a shining circle of police.
His arms open in welcome.
He promises all dark things
Will be hunted down.

State police yawn in the prisons.
Antonio Machado follows the moon
Down a road of white dust,
To a cave of silent children
Under the Pyrenees.
Wine darkens in stone jars in villages.
Wine sleeps in the mouths of old men, it is
    a dark red color.

Smiles glitter in Madrid.
Eisenhower has touched hands with Franco,
    embracing
In a glare of photographers.
Clean new bombers from America muffle
    their engines
And glide down now.

Their wings shine in the searchlights
Of bare fields,
In Spain.

Joseph Heller

*Joseph Heller (b. 1923), advertising writer,
teacher, novelist, and playwright, uses a
World War II air base as a setting for his
satiric account of modern American military
and civilian life in* Catch-22. *This chapter
shows what happens when the success ethic
goes beserk, when American pragmatism becomes the highest moral law. Though set in
the past, "Milo" is a warning of the impact
of amoral bureaucracy on present and future
American culture.*

MILO

April had been the best month of all for
Milo. Lilacs bloomed in April and fruit
ripened on the vine. Heartbeats quickened
and old appetites were renewed. In April
a livelier iris gleamed upon the burnished
dove. April was spring, and in the spring
Milo Minderbinder's fancy had lightly
turned to thoughts of tangerines.

"Tangerines?"

"Yes, sir."

"My men would love tangerines," admitted the colonel in Sardinia who commanded four squadrons of B-25s.

"There'll be all the tangerines they can
eat that you're able to pay for with money
from your mess fund," Milo assured him.

"Casaba melons?"

"Are going for a song in Damascus."

"I have a weakness for casaba melons.
I've always had a weakness for casaba
melons."

"Just lend me one plane from each squadron, just one plane, and you'll have all the
casabas you can eat that you've money to
pay for."

"We buy from the syndicate?"

"And everybody has a share."

"It's amazing, positively amazing. How
can you do it?"

"Mass purchasing power makes the big
difference. For example, breaded veal cutlets."

"I'm not so crazy about breaded veal
cutlets," grumbled the skeptical B-25 commander in the north of Corsica.

"Breaded veal cutlets are very nutri-
tious," Milo admonished him piously.
"They contain egg yolk and bread crumbs.
And so are lamb chops."

"Ah, lamp chops," echoed the B-25 commander. "Good lamb chops?"

"The best," said Milo, "that the black
market has to offer."

"Baby lamb chops?"

"In the cutest little pink paper panties
you ever saw. Are going for a song in
Portugal."

"I can't send a plane to Portugal. I
haven't the authority."

"I can, once you lend the plane to me.
With a pilot to fly it. And don't forget—
you'll get General Dreedle."

"Will General Dreedle eat in my mess
hall again?"

"Like a pig, once you start feeding him
my best white fresh eggs fried in my pure
creamery butter. There'll be tangerines too,
and casaba melons, honeydews, filet of
Dover sole, baked Alaska, and cockles and
mussels."

"And everybody has a share?"

"That," said Milo, "is the most beautiful
part of it."

"I don't like it," growled the uncooperative fighter-plane commander, who didn't
like Milo either.

"There's an uncooperative fighter-plane
commander up north who's got it in for
me," Milo complained to General Dreedle.
"It takes just one person to ruin the whole
thing, and then you wouldn't have your
fresh eggs fried in my pure creamery butter
any more."

General Dreedle had the uncooperative
fighter-plane commander transferred to the
Solomon Islands to dig graves and replaced

him with a senile colonel with bursitis and a craving for litchi nuts who introduced Milo to the B-17 general on the mainland with a yearning for Polish sausage.

"Polish sausage is going for peanuts in Cracow," Milo informed him.

"Polish sausage," sighed the general nostalgically. "You know, I'd give just about anything for a good hunk of Polish sausage. Just about anything."

"You don't have to give *anything*. Just give me one plane for each mess hall and a pilot who will do what he's told. And a small down payment on your initial order as a token of good faith."

"But Cracow is hundreds of miles behind the enemy lines. How will you get to the sausage?"

"There's an international Polish sausage exchange in Geneva. I'll just fly the peanuts into Switzerland and exchange them for Polish sausage at the open market rate. They'll fly the peanuts back to Cracow and I'll fly the Polish sausage back to you. You buy only as much Polish sausage as you want through the syndicate. There'll be tangerines too, with only a little artificial coloring added. And eggs from Malta and Scotch from Sicily. You'll be paying the money to yourself when you buy from the syndicate, since you'll own a share, so you'll really be getting everything you buy for nothing. Doesn't that make sense?"

"Sheer genius. How in the world did you ever think of it?"

"My name is Milo Minderbinder. I am twenty-seven years old."

Milo Minderbinder's planes flew in from everywhere, the pursuit planes, bombers, and cargo ships streaming into Colonel Cathcart's field with pilots at the controls who would do what they were told. The planes were decorated with flamboyant squadron emblems illustrating such laudable ideals as Courage, Might, Justice, Truth, Liberty, Love, Honor and Patriotism that were painted out at once by Milo's mechanics with a double coat of flat white and replaced in garish purple with the stenciled name M & M ENTERPRISES, FINE FRUITS AND PRODUCE. The "M & M" in "M & M ENTERPRISES" stood for Milo & Minderbinder, and the & was inserted, Milo revealed candidly, to nullify any impression that the syndicate was a one-man operation. Planes arrived for Milo from airfields in Italy, North Africa and England, and from Air Transport Command stations in Liberia, Ascension Island, Cairo and Karachi. Pursuit planes were traded for additional cargo ships or retained for emergency invoice duty and small-parcel service; trucks and tanks were procured from the ground forces and used for short-distance road hauling. Everybody had a share, and men got fat and moved about tamely with toothpicks in their greasy lips. Milo supervised the whole expanding operation by himself. Deep otter-brown lines of preoccupation etched themselves permanently into his careworn face and gave him a harried look of sobriety and mistrust. Everybody but Yossarian thought Milo was a jerk, first for volunteering for the job of mess officer and next for taking it so seriously. Yossarian also thought that Milo was a jerk; but he also knew that Milo was a genius.

One day Milo flew away to England to pick up a load of Turkish halvah and came back from Madagascar leading four German bombers filled with yams, collards, mustard greens and black-eyed Georgia peas. Milo was dumfounded when he stepped down to the ground and found a contingent of armed M.P.s waiting to imprison the German pilots and confiscate their planes. *Confiscate!* The mere word was anathema to him, and he stormed back and forth in excoriating condemnation, shaking a piercing finger of rebuke in the guilt-ridden faces of Colonel Cathcart, Colonel Korn and the poor battle-scarred captain with the submachine gun who commanded the M.P.s.

"Is this Russia?" Milo assailed them incredulously at the top of his voice. "*Confiscate?*" he shrieked, as though he could not believe his own ears. "Since when is it the policy of the American government to confiscate the private property of its citizens? Shame on you! Shame on all of you for even thinking such a horrible thought."

"But Milo," Major Danby interrupted timidly, "we're at war with Germany, and those are German planes."

"They are no such thing!" Milo retorted furiously. "Those planes belong to the syndicate, and everybody has a share. *Confiscate?* How can you possibly confiscate your own private property? *Confiscate,* indeed! I've never heard anything so depraved in my whole life."

And sure enough, Milo was right, for when they looked, his mechanics had painted out the German swastikas on the wings, tails and fuselages with double coats of flat white and stenciled in the words M & M ENTERPRISES, FINE FRUITS AND PRODUCE. Right before their eyes he had transformed his syndicate into an international cartel.

Milo's argosies of plenty now filled the air. Planes poured in from Norway, Denmark, France, Germany, Austria, Italy, Yugoslavia, Romania, Bulgaria, Sweden, Finland, Poland—from everywhere in Europe, in fact, but Russia, with whom Milo refused to do business. When everybody who was going to had signed up with M & M Enterprises, Fine Fruits and Produce, Milo created a wholly owned subsidiary, M & M Enterprises, Fancy Pastry, and obtained more airplanes and more money from the mess funds for scones and crumpets from the British Isles, prune and cheese Danish from Copenhagen, éclairs, cream puffs, Napoleons and *petits fours* from Paris, Reims and Grenoble, *Kugelhopf,* pumpernickel and *Pfefferkuchen* from Berlin, *Linzer* and *Dobos Torten* from Vienna, *Strudel* from Hungary and *baklava* from Ankara. Each morning Milo sent planes aloft all over Europe and North Africa hauling long red tow signs advertising the day's specials in large square letters: "EYE ROUND, 79¢ . . .WHITING, 21¢." He boosted cash income for the syndicate

by leasing town signs to Pet Milk, Gaines Dog Food, and Noxzema. In a spirit of civic enterprise, he regularly allotted a certain amount of free aerial advertising space to General Peckem for the propagation of such messages in the public interest as NEATNESS COUNTS, HASTE MAKES WASTE, and THE FAMILY THAT PRAYS TOGETHER STAYS TOGETHER. Milo purchased spot radio announcements on Axis Sally's and Lord Haw Haw's daily propaganda broadcasts from Berlin to keep things moving. Business boomed on every battlefront.

Milo's planes were a familiar sight. They had freedom of passage everywhere, and one day Milo contracted with the American military authorities to bomb the German-held highway bridge at Orvieto and with the German military authorities to defend the highway bridge at Orvieto with antiaircraft fire against his own attack. His fee for attacking the bridge for America was the total cost of the operation plus six percent, and his fee from Germany for defending the bridge was the same cost-plus-six agreement augmented by a merit bonus of a thousand dollars for every American plane he shot down. The consummation of these deals represented an important victory for private enterprise, he pointed out, since the armies of both countries were socialized institutions. Once the contracts were signed, there seemed to be no point in using the resources of the syndicate to bomb and defend the bridge, inasmuch as both governments had ample men and material right there to do so and were perfectly happy to contribute them, and in the end Milo realized a fantastic profit from both halves of his project for doing nothing more than signing his name twice.

The arrangements were fair to both sides. Since Milo did have freedom of passage everywhere, his planes were able to steal over in a sneak attack without alerting the German antiaircraft gunners; and since Milo knew about the attack, he was able to alert the German antiaircraft gunners in sufficient time for them to begin firing accurately the moment the planes came into range. It was an ideal arrangement for everyone but the dead man in Yossarian's tent, who was killed over the target the day he arrived.

"I didn't kill him!" Milo kept replying passionately to Yossarian's angry protest. "I wasn't even there that day, I tell you. Do you think I was down there on the ground firing an antiaircraft gun when the planes came over?"

"But you organized the whole thing, didn't you?" Yossarian shouted back at him in the velvet darkness cloaking the path leading past the still vehicles of the motor pool to the open-air movie theater.

"And I didn't organize anything," Milo answered indignantly, drawing great agitated sniffs of air in through his hissing, pale, twitching nose. "The Germans have the bridge, and we were going to bomb it, whether I stepped into the picture or not. I just saw a wonderful opportunity to make some profit out of the mission, and I took it. What's so terrible about that?"

"What's so terrible about it? Milo, a man in my tent was killed on that mission before he could even unpack his bags."

"But I didn't kill him."

"You got a thousand dollars extra for it."

"But I didn't kill him. I wasn't even there, I tell you. I was in Barcelona buying olive oil and skinless and boneless sardines, and I've got the purchase orders to prove it. And I didn't get the thousand dollars. That thousand dollars went to the syndicate, and everybody got a share, even you." Milo was appealing to Yossarian from the bottom of his soul. "Look, I didn't start this war, Yossarian, no matter what that lousy Wintergreen is saying. I'm just trying to put it on a businesslike basis. Is anything wrong with that? You know, a thousand dollars ain't such a bad price for a medium bomber and a crew. If I can persuade the Germans to pay me a thousand dollars for every plane they shoot down, why shouldn't I take it?"

"Because you're dealing with the enemy, that's why. Can't you understand that we're fighting a war? People are dying. Look around you, for Christ's sake!"

Milo shook his head with weary forbearance. "And the Germans are not our enemies," he declared. "Oh, I know what you're going to say. Sure, we're at war with them. But the Germans are also members in good standing of the syndicate, and it's my job to protect their rights as shareholders. Maybe they did start the war, and maybe they are killing millions of people, but they pay their bills a lot more promptly than some allies of ours I could name. Don't you understand that I have to respect the sanctity of my contract with Germany? Can't you see it from my point of view?"

"No," Yossarian rebuffed him harshly.

Milo was stung and made no effort to disguise his wounded feelings. It was a muggy, moonlit night filled with gnats, moths, and mosquitoes. Milo lifted his arm suddenly and pointed toward the open-air theater, where the milky, dust-filled beam bursting horizontally from the projector slashed a conelike swath in the blackness and draped in a fluorescent membrane of light the audience tilted on the seats there in hypnotic sags, their faces focused upward toward the aluminized movie screen. Milo's eyes were liquid with integrity, and his artless and uncorrupted face was lustrous with a shining mixture of sweat and insect repellent.

"Look at them," he exclaimed in a voice choked with emotion. "They're my friends, my countrymen, my comrades in arms. A fellow never had a better bunch of buddies. Do you think I'd do a single thing to harm them if I didn't have to? Haven't I got enough on my mind? Can't you see how upset I am already about all that cotton piling up on those piers in Egypt?" Milo's voice splintered into fragments, and he clutched at Yossarian's shirt front as though drowning. His eyes were throbbing visibly like brown caterpillars. "Yossarian, what am I going to do with so much cotton? It's all your fault for letting me buy it."

The cotton was piling up on the piers in Egypt, and nobody wanted any. Milo had never dreamed that the Nile Valley could be so fertile or that there would be no market at all for the crop he had bought. The mess halls in his syndicate would not help; they rose up in uncompromising rebellion against his proposal to tax them on a per capita basis in order to enable each man to own his own share of the Egyptian cotton crop. Even his reliable friends the Germans failed him in this crisis: they preferred ersatz. Milo's mess halls would not even help him store the cotton, and his warehousing costs skyrocketed and contributed to the devastating drain upon his cash reserves. The profits from the Orvieto mission were sucked away. He began writing home for the money he had sent back in better days; soon that was almost gone. And new bales of cotton kept arriving on the wharves at Alexandria every day. Each time he succeeded in dumping some on the world market for a loss it was snapped up by canny Egyptian brokers in the Levant, who sold it back to him at the original contract price, so that he was really worse off than before.

M & M Enterprises verged on collapse. Milo cursed himself hourly for his monumental greed and stupidity in purchasing the entire Egyptian cotton crop, but a contract was a contract and had to be honored, and one night, after a sumptuous evening meal, all Milo's fighters and bombers took off, joined in formation directly overhead and began dropping bombs on the group. He had landed another contract with the Germans, this time to bomb his own outfit. Milo's planes separated in a well-co-ordinated attack and bombed the fuel stocks and the ordnance dump, the repair hangars and the B-25 bombers resting on the lollipop-shaped hardstands at the field. His crews spared the landing strip and the mess halls so that they could land safely when their work was done and enjoy a hot snack before retiring. They bombed with their landing lights on, since no one was shooting back. They bombed all four squadrons, the officers' club and the Group Headquarters building. Men bolted from their tents in sheer terror and did not know in which direction to turn. Wounded soon lay screaming everywhere. A cluster of fragmentation bombs exploded in the yard of the officers' club and punched jagged holes in the side of the wooden building and in the bellies and backs of a row of lieutenants and captains standing at the bar. They doubled over in agony and dropped. The rest of the officers fled toward the two exits in panic and jammed up the doorways like a dense, howling dam of human flesh as they shrank from going farther.

Colonel Cathcart clawed and elbowed his way through the unruly, bewildered mass until he stood outside by himself. He stared up at the sky in stark astonishment and horror. Milo's planes, ballooning serenely in over the blossoming treetops with their bomb bay doors open and wing flaps down and with their monstrous bug-eyed, blinding, fiercely flickering, eerie landing lights on, were the most apocalyptic sight he had ever beheld. Colonel Cathcart let go a stricken gasp of dismay and hurled himself headlong into his jeep, almost sobbing. He found the gas pedal and the ignition and sped toward the airfield as fast as the rocking car would carry him, his huge flabby hands clenched and bloodless on the wheel or blaring his horn tormentedly. Once he almost killed himself when he swerved with a banshee screech of tires to avoid plowing into a bunch of men running crazily toward the hills in their underwear with their stunned faces down and their thin arms pressed high around their temples as puny shields. Yellow, orange and red fires were burning on both sides of the road. Tents and trees were in flames, and Milo's planes kept coming around interminably with their blinking white landing lights on and their bomb bay doors open. Colonel Cathcart almost turned the jeep over when he slammed the brakes on at the control tower. He leaped from the car while it was still skidding dangerously and hurtled up the flight of steps inside, where three men were busy at the instruments and the controls. He bowled two of them aside in his lunge for the nickel-plated microphone, his eyes glittering wildly and his beefy face contorted with stress. He squeezed the microphone in a bestial grip and began shouting hysterically at the top of his voice,

"Milo, you son of a bitch! Are you crazy? What the hell are you doing? Come down! Come down!"

"Stop hollering so much, will you?" answered Milo, who was standing there right beside him in the control tower with a microphone of his own. "I'm right here." Milo looked at him with reproof and turned back to his work. "Very good, men, very good," he chanted into his microphone. "But I see one supply shed still standing. That will never do, Purvis—I've spoken to you about that kind of shoddy work before. Now, you go right back there this minute and try it again. And this time come in slowly . . . slowly. Haste makes waste, Purvis. Haste makes waste. If I've told you that once, I must have told you that a hundred times. Haste makes waste."

The loud-speaker overhead began squawking. "Milo, this is Alvin Brown. I've finished dropping my bombs. What should I do now?"

"Strafe," said Milo.

"*Strafe?*" Alvin Brown was shocked.

"We have no choice," Milo informed him resignedly. "It's in the contract."

"Oh, okay, then," Alvin Brown acquiesced. "In that case I'll strafe."

This time Milo had gone too far. Bombing his own men and planes was more than even the most phlegmatic observer could stomach, and it looked like the end for him. High-ranking government officials poured in to investigate. Newspapers inveighed against Milo with glaring headlines, and Congressmen denounced the atrocity in stentorian wrath and clamored for punishment. Mothers with children in the service organized into militant groups and demanded revenge. Not one voice was raised in his defense. Decent people everywhere were affronted, and Milo was all washed up until he opened his books to the public and disclosed the tremendous profit he had made. He could reimburse the government for all the people and property he had destroyed and still have enough money left over to continue buying Egyptian cotton. Everybody, of course, owned a share. And the sweetest part of the whole deal was that there really was no need to reimburse the government at all.

"In a democracy, the government is the people," Milo explained. "We're people, aren't we? So we might just as well keep the money and eliminate the middleman. Frankly, I'd like to see the government get out of the war altogether and leave the whole field to private industry. If we pay the government everything we owe it, we'll only be encouraging government control and discouraging other individuals from bombing their own men and planes. We'll be taking away their incentive."

Milo was correct, of course, as everyone soon agreed but a few embittered misfits like Doc Daneeka, who sulked cantankerously and muttered offensive insinuations about the morality of the whole venture until Milo mollified him with a donation, in the name of the syndicate, of a lightweight aluminum collapsible garden chair that Doc Daneeka could fold up conveniently and carry outside his tent each time Chief White Halfoat came inside his tent and carry back inside his tent each time Chief White Halfoat came out. Doc Daneeka had lost his head during Milo's bombardment; instead of running for cover, he had remained out in the open and performed his duty, slithering along the ground through shrapnel, strafing and incendiary bombs like a furtive, wily lizard from casualty to casualty, administering tourniquets, morphine, splints and sulfanilamide with a dark and doleful visage, never saying one word more than he had to and reading in each man's bluing wound a dreadful portent of his own decay. He worked himself relentlessly into exhaustion before the long night was over and came down with a sniffle the next day that sent him hurrying querulously into the medical tent to have his temperature taken by Gus and Wes and to obtain a mustard plaster and vaporizer.

Doc Daneeka tended each moaning man that night with the same glum and profound and introverted grief he showed at the airfield the day of the Avignon mission when Yossarian climbed down the few steps of his plane naked, in a state of utter shock, with Snowden smeared abundantly all over his bare heels and toes, knees, arms and fingers, and pointed inside wordlessly toward where the young radio-gunner lay freezing to death on the floor beside the still younger tail-gunner who kept falling back into a dead faint each time he opened his eyes and saw Snowden dying.

Doc Daneeka draped a blanket around Yossarian's shoulders almost tenderly after Snowden had been removed from the plane and carried into an ambulance on a stretcher. He led Yossarian toward his jeep. McWatt helped, and the three drove in silence to the squadron medical tent, where McWatt and Doc Daneeka guided Yossarian inside to a chair and washed Snowden off him with cold wet balls of absorbent cotton. Doc Daneeka gave him a pill and a shot that put him to sleep for twelve hours. When Yossarian woke up and went to see him, Doc Daneeka gave him another pill and a shot that put him to sleep for another twelve hours. When Yossarian woke up again and went to see him, Doc Daneeka made ready to give him another pill and a shot.

"How long are you going to keep giving me those pills and shots?" Yossarian asked him.

"Until you feel better."

"I feel all right now."

Doc Daneeka's fragile suntanned forehead furrowed with surprise. "Then why don't you put some clothes on? Why are you walking around naked?"

"I don't want to wear a uniform anymore."

Doc Daneeka accepted the explanation and put away his hypodermic syringe. "Are you sure you feel all right?"

"I feel fine. I'm just a little logy from all those pills and shots you've been giving me."

Yossarian went about his business with no clothes on all the rest of that day and was still naked late the next morning when Milo, after hunting everywhere else, finally found him sitting up a tree a small distance in back of the quaint little military cemetery at which Snowden was being buried. Milo was dressed in his customary business attire—olive-drab trousers, a fresh olive-drab shirt and tie, with one silver first lieutenant's bar gleaming on the collar, and a regulation dress cap with a stiff leather bill.

"I've been looking all over for you," Milo called up to Yossarian from the ground reproachfully.

"You should have looked for me in this tree," Yossarian answered. "I've been up here all morning."

"Come on down and taste this and tell me. if it's good. It's very important."

Yossarian shook his head. He sat nude on the lowest limb of the tree and balanced himself with both hands grasping the bough directly above. He refused to budge, and Milo had no choice but to stretch both arms about the trunk in a distasteful hug and start climbing. He struggled upward clumsily with loud grunts and wheezes, and his clothes were squashed and crooked by the time he pulled himself up high enough to hook a leg over the limb and pause for breath. His dress cap was askew and in danger of falling. Milo caught it just in time when it began slipping. Globules of perspiration glistened like transparent pearls around his mustache and swelled like opaque blisters under his eyes. Yossarian watched him impassively. Cautiously Milo worked himself around in a half circle so that he could face Yossarian. He unwrapped tissue paper from something soft, round and brown and handed it out to Yossarian.

"Please taste this and let me know what you think. I'd like to serve it to the men."

"What is it?" asked Yossarian, and took a big bite.

"Chocolate-covered cotton."

Yossarian gagged convulsively and sprayed his big mouthful of chocolate-covered cotton right out into Milo's face. "Here, take it back!" he spouted angrily. "Jesus Christ! Have you gone crazy? You didn't even take the goddam seeds out."

"Give it a chance, will you?" Milo begged. "It can't be that bad. Is it really that bad?"

"It's even worse."

"But I've got to make the mess halls feed it to the men."

"They'll never be able to swallow it."

"They've got to swallow it," Milo ordained with dictatorial grandeur, and almost broke his neck when he let go with one arm to wave a righteous finger in the air.

"Come on out here," Yossarian invited him. "You'll be much safer, and you can see everything."

Gripping the bough above with both hands, Milo began inching his way out on the limb sideways with utmost care and apprehension. His face was rigid with tension, and he sighed with relief when he found himself seated securely beside Yossarian. He stroked the tree affectionately. "This is a pretty good tree," he observed admiringly with proprietary gratitude.

"It's the tree of life," Yossarian answered, waggling his toes, "and of knowledge of good and evil, too."

Milo squinted closely at the bark and branches. "No it isn't," he replied. "It's a chestnut tree. I ought to know. I sell chestnuts."

"Have it your way."

They sat in the tree without talking for several seconds, their legs dangling and their hands almost straight up on the bough above, the one completely nude but for a pair of crepe-soled sandals, the other completely dressed in a coarse olive-drab woolen uniform with his tie knotted tight. Milo studied Yossarian diffidently through the corner of his eye, hesitating tactfully.

"I want to ask you something," he said at last. "You don't have any clothes on. I don't want to butt in or anything, but I just want to know. Why aren't you wearing your uniform?"

"I don't want to."

Milo nodded rapidly like a sparrow pecking. "I see, I see," he stated quickly with a look of vivid confusion. "I understand perfectly. I heard Appleby and Captain Black say you had gone crazy, and I just wanted to find out." He hesitated politely again, weighing his next question. "Aren't you ever going to put your uniform on again?"

"I don't think so."

Milo nodded with spurious vim to indicate he still understood and then sat silent, ruminating gravely with troubled misgiving. A scarlet-crested bird shot by below, brushing sure dark wings against a quivering bush. Yossarian and Milo were covered in their bower by tissue-thin tiers of sloping green and largely surrounded by other gray chestnut trees and a silver spruce. The sun was high overhead in a vast sapphire-blue sky beaded with low, isolated, puffy clouds of dry and immaculate white. There was no breeze, and the leaves about them hung motionless. The shade was feathery. Everything was at peace but Milo, who straightened suddenly with a muffled cry and began pointing excitedly.

"Look at that!" he exclaimed in alarm. "Look at that! That's a funeral going on down there. That looks like the cemetery. Isn't it?"

Yossarian answered him slowly in a level voice. "They're burying the kid who got killed in my plane over Avignon the other day. Snowden."

"What happened to him?" Milo asked in a voice deadened with awe.

"He got killed."

"That's terrible," Milo grieved, and his

large brown eyes filled with tears. "That poor kid. It really is terrible." He bit his trembling lip hard, and his voice rose with emotion when he continued. "And it will get even worse if the mess halls don't agree to buy my cotton. Yossarian, what's the matter with them? Don't they realize it's their syndicate? Don't they know they've all got a share?"

"Did the dead man in my tent have a share?" Yossarian demanded caustically.

"Of course he did," Milo assured him lavishly. "Everybody in the squadron has a share."

"He was killed before he even got into the squadron."

Milo made a deft grimace of tribulation and turned away. "I wish you'd stop picking on me about that dead man in your tent," he pleaded peevishly. "I told you I didn't have anything to do with killing him. Is it my fault that I saw this great opportunity to corner the market on Egyptian cotton and got us into all this trouble? Was I supposed to know there was going to be a glut? I didn't even know what a glut was in those days. An opportunity to corner a market doesn't come along very often, and I was pretty shrewd to grab the chance when I had it." Milo gulped back a moan as he saw six uniformed pallbearers lift the plain pine coffin from the ambulance and set it gently down on the ground beside the yawning gash of the freshly dug grave. "And now I can't get rid of a single penny's worth," he mourned.

Yossarian was unmoved by the fustian charade of the burial ceremony, and by Milo's crushing bereavement. The chaplain's voice floated up to him through the distance tenuously in an unintelligible, almost inaudible monotone, like a gaseous murmur. Yossarian could make out Major Major by his towering and lanky aloofness and thought he recognized Major Danby mopping his brow with a handkerchief. Major Danby had not stopped shaking since his run-in with General Dreedle. There were strands of enlisted men molded in a curve around the three officers, as inflexible as lumps of wood, and four idle gravediggers in streaked fatigues lounging indifferently on spades near the shocking, incongruous heap of loose copper-red earth. As Yossarian stared, the chaplain elevated his gaze toward Yossarian beatifically, pressed his fingers down over his eyeballs in a manner of affliction, peered upward again toward Yossarian searchingly, and bowed his head, concluding what Yossarian took to be a climactic part of the funeral rite. The four men in fatigues lifted the coffin on slings and lowered it into the grave. Milo shuddered violently.

"I can't watch it," he cried, turning away in anguish. "I just can't sit here and watch while those mess halls let my syndicate die." He gnashed his teeth and shook his head with bitter woe and resentment. "If they had any loyalty, they would buy my cotton till it hurts so that they can keep right on buying my cotton till it hurts some more. They would build fires and burn up their underwear and summer uniforms just to create a bigger demand. But they won't do a thing. Yossarian, try eating the rest of this chocolate-covered cotton for me. Maybe it will taste delicious now."

Yossarian pushed his hand away. "Give up, Milo. People can't eat cotton."

Milo's face narrowed cunningly. "It isn't really cotton," he coaxed. "I was joking. It's really cotton candy, delicious cotton candy. Try it and see."

"Now you're lying."

"I never lie!" Milo rejoindered with proud dignity.

"You're lying now."

"I only lie when it's necessary," Milo explained defensively, averting his eyes for a moment and blinking his lashes winningly. "This stuff is better than cotton candy, really it is. It's made out of real cotton. Yossarian, you've got to help me make the men eat it. Egyptian cotton is the finest cotton in the world."

"But it's indigestible," Yossarian emphasized. "It will make them sick, don't you understand? Why don't you try living on it yourself if you don't believe me?"

"I did try," admitted Milo gloomily. "And it made me sick."

The graveyard was yellow as hay and green as cooked cabbage. In a little while the chaplain stepped back, and the beige crescent of human forms began to break up sluggishly, like flotsam. The men drifted without haste or sound to the vehicles parked along the side of the bumpy dirt road. With their heads down disconsolately, the chaplain, Major Major and Major Danby moved toward their jeeps in an ostracized group, each holding himself friendlessly several feet away from the other two.

"It's all over," observed Yossarian.

"It's the end," Milo agreed despondently. "There's no hope left. And all because I left them free to make their own decisions. That should teach me a lesson about discipline the next time I try something like this."

"Why don't you sell your cotton to the government?" Yossarian suggested casually, as he watched the four men in streaked fatigues shoveling heaping bladefuls of the copper-red earth back down inside the grave.

Milo vetoed the idea brusquely. "It's a matter of principle," he explained firmly. "The government has no business in business, and I would be the last person in the world to ever try to involve the government in a business of mine. But the business of government is business," he remembered alertly, and continued with elation. "Calvin Coolidge said that, and Calvin Coolidge was a President, so it must be true. And the government does have the responsibility of buying all the Egyptian cotton I've got that no one else wants so that I can make a profit, doesn't it?" Milo's face clouded almost as abruptly, and his spirits descended into a state of sad anxiety. "But how will I get the government to do it?"

"Bribe it," Yossarian said.

"Bribe it!" Milo was outraged and almost lost his balance and broke his neck again.

"Shame on you!" he scolded severely, breathing virtuous fire down and upward into his rusty mustache through his billowing nostrils and prim lips. "Bribery is against the law, and you know it. But it's not against the law to make a profit, is it? So it can't be against the law for me to bribe someone in order to make a fair profit, can it? No, of course not!" He fell to brooding again, with a meek, almost pitiable distress. "But how will I know who to bribe?"

"Oh, don't you worry about that," Yossarian comforted him with a toneless snicker as the engine of the jeeps and ambulance fractured the drowsy silence and the vehicles in the rear began driving away backward. "You make the bribe big enough and they'll find you. Just make sure you do everything right out in the open. Let everyone know exactly what you want and how much you're willing to pay for it. The first time you act guilty or ashamed, you might get into trouble."

"I wish you'd come with me," Milo remarked. "I won't feel safe among people who take bribes. They're no better than a bunch of crooks."

"You'll be all right," Yossarian assured him with confidence. "If you run into trouble, just tell everybody that the security of the country requires a strong domestic Egyptian-cotton speculating industry."

"It does," Milo informed him solemnly. "A strong Egyptian-cotton speculating industry means a much stronger America."

"Of course it does. And if that doesn't work, point out the great number of American families that depend on it for income."

"A great many American families do depend on it for income."

"You see?" said Yossarian. "You're much better at it than I am. You almost make it sound true."

"It is true," Milo explained with a strong trace of the old hauteur.

"That's what I mean. You do it with just the right amount of conviction."

"You're sure you won't come with me?"

Yossarian shook his head.

Milo was impatient to get started. He stuffed the remainder of the chocolate-covered cotton ball into his shirt pocket and edged his way back gingerly along the branch to the smooth gray trunk. He threw his arms about the trunk in a generous and awkward embrace and began shimmying down, the sides of his leather-soled shoes slipping constantly so that it seemed many times he would fall and injure himself. Halfway down, he changed his mind and climbed back up. Bits of tree bark stuck to his mustache, and his straining face was flushed with exertion.

"I wish you'd put your uniform on instead of going around naked that way," he confided pensively before he climbed back down again and hurried away. "You might start a trend, and then I'll never get rid of all this goldarned cotton."

Philip E. Slater

Philip Slater's book The Pursuit of Loneliness *has been acclaimed as a seminal work in the study of contemporary American culture. Slater examines our most cherished ideals and assesses how well they meet the needs of modern Americans. In this section he looks at individualism and competition.*

from THE PURSUIT OF LONELINESS

We are so accustomed to living in a society that stresses individualism that we need to be reminded that "collectivism" in a broad sense has always been the more usual lot of mankind, as well as of most other species. Most people in most societies have been born into and died in stable communities in which the subordination of the individual to the welfare of the group was taken for granted, while the aggrandizement of the individual at the expense of his fellows was simply a crime.

This is not to say that competition is an American invention—all societies involve some sort of admixture of cooperative and competitive institutions. But our society lies near or on the competitive extreme, and although it contains cooperative institutions I think it is fair to say that Americans suffer from their relative weakness and peripherality. Studies of business executives have revealed, for example, a deep hunger for an atmosphere of trust and fraternity with their colleagues (with whom they must, in the short run, engage in what Riesman calls "antagonistic cooperation"). The competitive life is a lonely one, and its satisfactions are very short-lived indeed, for each race leads only to a new one.

In the past, as so many have pointed out, there were in our society many oases in which one could take refuge from the frenzied invidiousness of our economic system—institutions such as the extended family and the stable local neighborhood in which one could take pleasure from something other than winning a symbolic victory over one of his fellows. But these have disappeared one by one, leaving the individual more and more in a situation in which he must try to satisfy his affiliative and invidious needs in the same place. This has made the balance a more brittle one—the appeal of cooperative living more seductive, and the need to suppress our longing for it more acute.

In recent decades the principal vehicle for the tolerated expression of this longing has been the mass media. Popular songs and film comedies have continually engaged in a sentimental rejection of the dominant mores, maintaining that the best things in life are free, that love is more important than success, that keeping up with the Joneses is absurd, that personal integrity should take precedence over winning, and so on. But these protestations must be understood for what they are: a safety valve for the dissatisfactions that the modal American experiences when he behaves as he thinks he should. The same man who chuckles and sentimentalizes over a happy-go-lucky hero in a film would view his real-life counterpart as frivolous and irresponsible, and suburbanites who philosophize over their back fence with complete sincerity about their "dog-eat-dog-world," and what-is-it-all-for, and you-can't-take-it-with-you, and success-doesn't-make-you-happy-it-just-gives-you-ulcers-and-a-heart-condition—would be enraged should their children pay serious attention to such a viewpoint. Indeed, the degree of rage is, up to a point, a function of the degree of sincerity: if the individual did not feel these things he would not have to fight them so vigorously. The peculiarly exaggerated hostility that hippies tend to arouse suggests that the life they strive for is highly seductive to middle-aged Americans.

The intensity of this reaction can in part be attributed to a kind of circularity that characterizes American individualism. When a value is as strongly held as is individualism in America the illnesses it produces tend to be treated by increasing the dosage, in the same way an alcoholic treats a hangover or a drug addict his withdrawal symptoms. Technological change, mobility, and the individualistic ethos combine to rupture the bonds that tie each individual to a family, a community, a kinship network, a geographical location—bonds that give him a comfortable sense of himself. As this sense of himself erodes, he seeks ways of affirming it. But his efforts at self-enhancement automatically accelerate the very erosion he seeks to halt.

It is easy to produce examples of the many ways in which Americans attempt to minimize, circumvent, or deny the interdependence upon which all human societies are based. We seek a private house, a private means of transportation, a private garden, a private laundry, self-service stores, and do-it-yourself skills of every kind. An enormous technology seems to have set itself the task of making it unnecessary for one human being ever to ask anything of another in the course of going about his daily business. Even within the family Americans are unique in their feeling that each member

should have a separate room, and even a separate telephone, television, and car, when economically possible. We seek more and more privacy, and feel more and more alienated and lonely when we get it. What accidental contacts we do have, furthermore, seem more intrusive, not only because they are unsought but because they are unconnected with any familiar pattern of interdependence.

Most important, our encounters with others tend increasingly to be competitive as a result of the search for privacy. We less and less often meet our fellow man to share and exchange, and more and more often encounter him as an impediment or a nuisance: making the highway crowded when we are rushing somewhere, cluttering and littering the beach or park or wood, pushing in front of us at the supermarket, taking the last parking space, polluting our air and water, building a highway through our house, blocking our view, and so on. Because we have cut off so much communication with each other we keep bumping into each other, and thus a higher and higher percentage of our interpersonal contacts are abrasive.

We seem unable to foresee that the gratification of a wish might turn out to be something of a monkey's paw if the wish were shared by many others. We cheer the new road that initially shaves ten minutes off the drive to our country retreat but ultimately transforms it into a crowded resort and increases both the traffic and the time. We are continually surprised to find, when we want something, that thousands or millions of others want it, too—that other human beings get hot in summer and cold in winter. The worst traffic jams occur when a mass of vacationing tourists departs for home early to "beat the traffic." We are too enamored of the individualistic fantasy that everyone is, or should be, different—that each person could somehow build his entire life around some single, unique eccentricity without boring himself and everyone else to death. Each of us of course has his quirks, which provide a surface variety that is briefly entertaining, but aside from this human beings have little basis for their persistent claim that they are not all members of the same species.

Since our contacts with others are increasingly competitive, unanticipated, and abrasive, we seek still more apartness and accelerate the trend. The desire to be somehow special inaugurates an even more competitive quest for progressively more rare and expensive symbols—a quest that is ultimately futile since it is individualism itself that produces uniformity.

This is poorly understood by Americans, who tend to confuse uniformity with "conformity," in the sense of compliance with or submission to group demands. Many societies exert far more pressure on the individual to mold himself to fit a particularized segment of a total group pattern, but there is variation among these circumscribed roles. Our society gives far more leeway to the individual to pursue his own ends, but, since *it* defines what is worthy and desirable, everyone tends, independently but monotonously, to pursue the same things in the same way. The first pattern combines cooperation, conformity, and variety; the second, competition, individualism, and uniformity.

These relationships are exemplified by two familiar processes in contemporary America: the flight to the suburb and the do-it-yourself movement. Both attempt to deny human interdependence and pursue unrealistic fantasies of self-sufficiency. The first tries to overlook our dependence upon the city for the maintenance of the level of culture we demand. "Civilized" means, literally, "citified," and the state of the city is an accurate index of the condition of the culture as a whole. We behave toward our cities like an irascible farmer who never feeds his cow and then kicks her when she fails to give enough milk. But the flight to the suburb is in any case self-defeating, its goals subverted by the mass quality of the exodus. The suburban dweller seeks peace, privacy, nature, community, and a child-rearing environment which is healthy and culturally optimal. Instead he finds neither the beauty and serenity of the countryside, the stimulation of the city, nor the stability and sense of community of the small town, and his children are exposed to a cultural deprivation equaling that of any slum child with a television set. Living in a narrow age-graded and class-segregated society, it is little wonder that suburban families have contributed so little to the national talent pool in proportion to their numbers, wealth, and other social advantages.[1] And this transplantation, which has caused the transplants to atrophy, has blighted the countryside and impoverished the city. A final irony of the suburban dream is that, for many Americans, reaching the pinnacle of one's social ambitions (owning a house in the suburbs) requires one to perform all kinds of menial tasks (carrying garbage cans, mowing lawns, shoveling snow, and so on) that were performed for him when he occupied a less exalted status.

Some of this manual labor, however, is voluntary—an attempt to deny the elaborate division of labor required in a complex society. Many Americans seem quite willing to pay this price for their reluctance to engage in interpersonal encounters with servants and artisans—a price which is rather high unless the householder particularly relishes the work (some find in it a tangible relief from the intangibles they manipulate in their own jobs) or is especially good at

[1] Using cities, small towns, and rural areas for comparison. The small Midwestern town achieves its legendary dullness by a process akin to evaporation—all the warm and energetic particles depart for coastal cities, leaving their place of origin colder and flatter than they found it. But the restless spirit in a small town knows he lives in the sticks and has a limited range of experience, while his suburban counterpart can sustain an illusion of cosmopolitanism in an environment which is far more constricted (a small town is a microcosm, a suburb merely a layer).

it, or cannot command a higher rate of pay in the job market than the servant or artisan.

The do-it-yourself movement has accompanied, paradoxically, increasing specialization in the occupational sphere. As one's job narrows, perhaps, one seeks the challenge of new skill-acquisition in the home. But specialization also means that one's interpersonal encounters with artisans in the home proliferate and become more impersonal. It is not a matter of a familiar encounter with the local smith or grocer—a few well-known individuals performing a relatively large number of functions, and with whom one's casual interpersonal contacts may be a source of satisfaction, and are in any case a testimony to the stability and meaningful interrelatedness of human affairs. One finds instead a multiplicity of narrow specialists—each perhaps a stranger (the same type of repair may be performed by a different person each time). Every relationship, such as it is, must start from scratch, and it is small wonder that the householder turns away from such an unrewarding prospect in apathy and despair.

Americans thus find themselves in a vicious cycle, in which their extrafamilial relationships are increasingly arduous, competitive, trivial, and irksome, in part as a result of efforts to avoid or minimize potentially irksome or competitive relationships. As the few vestiges of stable and familiar community life erode, the desire for a simple, cooperative life style grows in intensity. The most seductive appeal of radical ideologies for Americans consists in the fact that all in one way or another attack the competitive foundations of our society. Each touches a responsive doubt, and the stimuli arousing this doubt must be carefully unearthed and rooted out, just as the Puritan must unearth and root out the sexual stimuli that excite him.[2]

Now it may be objected that American society is far less competitive than it once was, and the appeal of radical ideologies should hence be diminished. A generation of critics has argued that the entrepreneurial individualist of the past has been replaced by a bureaucratic, security-minded, Organization Man. Much of this historical drama was written through the simple device of comparing yesterday's owner-president with today's assistant sales manager; certainly these nostalgia-merchants never visited a nineteenth-century company town. Another distortion is introduced by the fact that it was only the most ruthlessly competitive robber barons who survived to tell us how it was. Little is written about the neighborhood store that extended credit to the poor, or the small town industry that refused to lay off local workers in hard times—they all went under together. And as for the organization men—they left us no sagas.

Despite these biases real changes have undoubtedly occurred, but even if we grant that the business world as such was more competitive, the total environment contained more cooperative, stable, and personal elements. The individual worked in a smaller firm with lower turnover in which his relationships were more enduring and less impersonal, and in which the ideology of Adam Smith was tempered by the fact that the participants were neighbors and might have been childhood playmates. Even if the business world was as "dog-eat-dog" as we imagine it (which seems highly unlikely), one encountered it as a deviant episode in what was otherwise a more comfort-

---

[2] Both efforts are ambivalent, since the "seek and destroy" process is in part a quest for the stimulus itself. The Puritanical censor both wants the sexual stimulus and wants to destroy it, and his job enables him to gratify both of these "contradictory" desires. There is a similar prurience in the efforts of groups such as the House UnAmerican Activities Committee to "uncover subversion." Just as the censor gets to experience far more pornography than the average man, so the Congressional red-baiter gets to hear as much Communist ideology as he wants, which is apparently quite a lot.

able and familiar environment than the organization man can find today in or out of his office. The organization man complex is simply an attempt to restore the personal, particularistic, paternalistic environment of the family business and the company town; and the other-directed "group-think" of the suburban community is a desperate attempt to bring some old-fashioned small-town collectivism into the transient and impersonal life-style of the suburb. The social critics of the 1950's were so preoccupied with assailing these rather synthetic substitutes for traditional forms of human interdependence that they lost sight of the underlying pathogenic forces that produced them. Medical symptoms usually result from attempts made by the body to counteract disease, and attacking such symptoms often aggravates and prolongs the illness. This appears to be the case with the feeble and self-defeating efforts of twentieth-century Americans to find themselves a viable social context.

Carl Degler

Carl Degler (b. 1921), noted historian and author, has taught at several colleges. His books include Economic Revolution *(1967),* Affluence and Anxiety *(1968),* Out of Our Past *(1969), and* Neither Black Nor White *(1971). In this essay Degler provides a historical perspective of the women's rights movement and asks a provocative question about the future of the current women's liberation movement.*

THE CHANGING PLACE OF WOMEN IN AMERICA

If feminism is defined as the belief that women are human beings and entitled to the same opportunities for self-expression as men, then America has harbored a feminist bias from the beginning. In both the eighteenth and nineteenth centuries foreign travelers remarked on the freedom for women in America. "A paradise for women," one eighteenth-century German called America, and toward the close of the nineteenth century Lord Bryce wrote that in the United States "it is easier for women to find a career, to obtain work of an intellectual as of a commercial kind, than in any part of Europe."

Certainly the long history of a frontier in America helps to account for this feminist bias. In a society being carved out of a wilderness, women were active and important contributors to the process of settlement and civilization. Moreover, because women have been scarce in America they have been highly valued. During almost the whole of the colonial period men outnumbered women, and even in the nineteenth century women remained scarce in the West. As late as 1865, for example, there were three men for each woman in California; in Colorado the ratio was as high as 20 to 1. Such disparities in the sex ratio undoubtedly account for the West's favorable attitude toward women as in an Oregon law of 1850 that granted land to single women and, even more significant for the time, to married women: or in the willingness of western territories like Wyoming (1869) and Utah (1870) to grant the suffrage to women long before other regions where the sex ratio was more nearly equal.

Another measure of women's high esteem in American society was the rapidity with which the doors of higher education opened to women. Even without counting forerunners like Oberlin College, which admitted women in 1837, the bars against women came down faster and earlier in America than anywhere. The breakthrough came during the Civil War era, when women's colleges like Elmira, Vassar and Smith were founded, and universities like Michigan and Cornell became coeducational. The process was later and slower in Europe. Girton College, Cambridge, for example, which opened in 1869, was the sole English institution of higher education available to women until London University accorded women full privileges in 1879. Heidelberg, which was the first German university to accept women, did not do so until 1900. More striking was the fact that at its opening Girton provided six places for young women; Vassar alone, when it opened in 1865, counted some 350 students in residence. Another indication of the American feminist bias was that at the end of the century girls outnumbered boys among high school graduates.

But if the frontier experience of America helped to create a vague feminist bias that accorded women more privileges than in settled Europe, the really potent force changing women's place had little to do with the frontier or the newness of the country. It was the industrial revolution that provided the impetus to women's aspirations for equality of opportunity; it was the industrial revolution that carried through the first stage in the changing position of women—the removal of legal and customary barriers to women's full participation in the activities of the world.

Today it is axiomatic that men work outside the home. But before the industrial revolution of the nineteenth century, the great majority of men and women were co-workers on the land and in the home. Women worked in the fields when the chores of the home and child-rearing permitted, so that there was not only close association between work and home for both sexes, but even a certain amount of overlap in the sexual division of labor. The coming of machine production changed all that. For a time, it is true, many unmarried women and children—the surplus labor of the day—were the mainstay of the new factory system, but that was only temporary. By the middle of the nineteenth century the bulk of industrial labor was male. The coming of the factory and the city thus wholly changed the nature of men's work. For the first time in history, work for most men was something done outside the family, psycho-

logically as well as physically separated from the home.

The same industrial process that separated work and home also provided the opportunities for women to follow men out of the home. For that reason the feminist movement, both socially and intellectually, was a direct consequence of the industrial changes of the nineteenth century. Furthermore, just as the new industrial system was reshaping the rural men who came under its influence, so it reshaped the nature of women.

The process began with the home, which in the early years of industrialization, was still the site of most women's work. Because of high land values, the city home was smaller than the farm house, and with less work for children, the size of the urban family was smaller than the rural. Moreover, in the city work in the home changed. Machines in factories now performed many of the tasks that had long been women's. In truth, the feminist movement began not when women felt a desire for men's jobs, but when men in factories began to take away women's traditional work. Factory-produced clothing, commercial laundries, prepared foods (e.g. prepared cereals, canned vegetables, condensed milk, bakery bread) were already available in the years after the Civil War. Toward the end of the century an advanced feminist like Charlotte Perkins Gilman, impressed by the accelerating exodus of women's chores from the middle-class home, predicted that the whole kitchen would soon be gone. She was wrong there, but even today the flight continues with precooked and frozen foods, TV dinners, cake mixes, special packaging for easy disposal, diaper services and the like.

Middle-class women were the main beneficiaries of the lightening of the chores of the home; few working-class or immigrant women could as yet take advantage of the new services and products. These middle-class women became the bone and sinew of the feminist movement, which was almost entirely an urban affair. They joined the women's clubs, organized the temperance crusades and marched in the suffrage parades. With an increasing amount of time available to them in the city, and imbued with the historic American value of work, they sought to do good. And there was much to be done in the raw, sometimes savage, urban environment of the late nineteenth century. For example, public playgrounds in the United States began in Boston only in the 1880's, when two public-spirited middle-class women caused a cartload of sand to be piled on an empty lot and set the neighborhood children loose upon it. Many a city and small town at the turn of the century owed its public library or its park to the dedicated work of women's clubs. The venerable giant redwood trees of northern California survive today because clubwomen of San Francisco and nearby towns successfully campaigned in 1900 to save them from being cut down for lumber. The saloon and prostitution were two other prevalent urban blights that prompted study and action by women's organizations.

More important than women's opposition to social evils was the widening of women's knowledge and concerns that inevitably accompanied it. What began as a simple effort to rid the community of a threat to its purity often turned into a discovery of the economic exploitation that drove young working girls into brothels and harried working men into saloons. Frances Willard for example, while head of the Women's Christian Temperance Union, broadened the WCTU's reform interests far beyond the liquor question, causing it to advocate protective legislation for working women, kindergartens and training programs for young working girls. Jane Addams, at Hull-House in Chicago's slums, quickly learned what historians have only recently discovered, that it was the urban boss's undeniable services to the immigrants that were the true sources of his great political power and the real secret of his suc-

cessful survival of municipal reform campaigns.

The most direct way in which industrialization altered the social function of women was by providing work for women outside the home. Production by machine, of course, widened enormously the uses to which women's labor could be put once physical strength was no longer a consideration. And toward the end of the century, as business enterprises grew and record-keeping, communications and public relations expanded, new opportunities for women opened up in business offices. The telephone operator, the typist, the clerical worker and the stenographer now took places beside the seamstress, the cotton mill operator and the teacher.

As workers outside the home, women buried the Victorian stereotype of the lady under a mountain of reality. After all, it was difficult to argue that women as a sex were weak, timid, incompetent, fragile vessels of spirituality when thousands of them could be seen trudging to work in the early hours of the day in any city of the nation. Nor could a girl who worked in a factory or office help but become more worldly. A young woman new to a shop might have been embarrassed to ask a male foreman for the ladies' room, as some working girls' autobiographies report, but such maidenly reticence could hardly survive very long. Even gentle, naïve farm girls soon found out how to handle the inevitable, improper advances of foremen. They also learned the discipline of the clock, the managing of their own money, the excitement of life outside the home, the exhilaration of financial independence along with the drudgery of machine labor. Having learned something of the ways of the world, women could not be treated then, nor later in marriage, as the hopeless dependents Victorian ideals prescribed.

In time work transformed the outer woman, too. First to go were the hobbling, trailing skirts, which in a factory were a hazard and a nuisance. Even before the Civil War, Amelia Bloomer and other feminists had pointed out that women, if they were to work in the world as human beings, needed looser and lighter garments than those then in fashion. Until working women were numbered in the millions, no change took place. After 1890 women's skirts gradually crept up from the floor, and the neat and simple shirtwaist became the uniform of the working girl. A costume very like the original bloomer was widely worn by women factory workers during the First World War. Later the overall and the coverall continued the adaptation of women's clothes to the machine.

The most dramatic alteration in the image of woman came after the First World War, when there was a new upsurge in women's employment. The twenties witnessed the emergence of the white-collar class, and women were a large part of it. Over twice as many women entered the labor force that decade as in the previous one: the number of typists alone in 1930 was three-quarters of a million, a tenfold increase since 1900. And woman's appearance reflected the requirements of work. Except for some of the extreme flapper fashions, which were transient, the contemporary woman still dresses much as the woman of the 1920's did. In the 1920's women threw out the corset and the numerous petticoats in favor of light undergarments, a single slip, silk or rayon stockings, short skirts and bobbed hair. So rapid and widespread was the change that an investigation in the 1920's revealed that even most working-class girls no longer wore corsets, and the new interest in bobbed hair resulted between 1920 and 1930 in an increase of 400 percent in the number of women hair dressers.

The physical freedom of dress that women acquired during the 1920's was but the superficial mark of a new social equality. The social forces behind this new equality are several. Some of these forces, like the growing number of college-trained women and the increasing number of women in the working force, go back far into the past; others, like the impact of the war and the arduous campaign for women's suffrage, were more recent. But whatever the causes, the consequences were obvious. Indeed, what is generally spoken of as the revolution in morals of the 1920's is more accurately a revolution in the position of women. Within a few short years a spectrum of taboos was shed. For the first time women began to smoke and drink in public; cigarette manufacturers discovered and exploited in advertising a virtually untouched market. As recently as 1918 it was considered daring for a New York hotel to permit women to sit at a bar. In the twenties, despite prohibition, both sexes drank in public.

Perhaps most significant, as well as symbolic, of the new stage in the position of women was their new sexual freedom. The twenties have long been associated with the discovery of Freud and a fresh, publicly acknowledged interest in sex. But insofar as these attitudes were new they represented changes in women, particularly those of the middle and upper classes. Premarital and extramarital sexuality by men had never been severely criticized, and discussion of sexual matters was commonplace wherever men gathered. Now, though, middle-class women also enjoyed that freedom. For the first time, it has been said, middle-class men carried on their extramarital affairs with women of their own social class instead of with cooks, maids and prostitutes.

An easier sexuality outside of marriage was only the most sensational side of the revolution in morals; more important, if only because more broadly based, was a new, informal, equal relationship between the sexes, culminating in a new conception of marriage. The day was long since past when Jennie June Croly could be barred, as she was in 1868, from a dinner in honor of Charles Dickens at a men's club even though her husband was a member and she was a professional writer. (Indeed, so thoroughly has such separation of the sexes been abandoned that the new Princeton Club in New York City has closed all but one of its public rooms to any man who is not accompanied by a woman!) And at least in the gatherings of the educated middle class, talk between the sexes was often free, frank and wide-ranging. The same mutual acceptance of the sexes was visible in the prevalent talk about the "new marriage," in which the woman was a partner and a companion, not simply a mother, a social convenience and a housekeeper.

The reality of the new conception of marriage was reflected in the sharp increase in the divorce rate. Because marriage, legally as well as socially, in the nineteenth century was more confining for women than for men, the early feminist had often advocated more liberal divorce laws. And even though divorce in the nineteenth century was more common in the United States than in any European country, the divorce rate in the 1920's shot up 50 per cent over what it had been only ten years before. One sign that women in the 1920's were seeking freedom from marriage if they could not secure equality in marriage was that two thirds of the divorces in that decade were instituted by women.

By the close of the twenties the ordinary woman in America was closer to a man in the social behavior expected of her, in the economic opportunities open to her and in the intellectual freedom enjoyed by her than at any time in history. To be sure there still was a double standard, but now its existence was neither taken for granted nor confidently asserted by men.

In truth, the years since the twenties have witnessed few alterations in the position of women that were not first evident in that crucial decade. The changes have penetrated more deeply and spread more widely through the social structure, but their central tendency was then already spelled out. Even the upsurge in women's

employment, which was so striking in the twenties, continued in subsequent years. Each decade thereafter has counted a larger number of working women than the previous one. During the depression decade of the 1930's, even, half a million more women entered the labor force than in the prosperous twenties. By 1960 some 38 per cent of all women of working age—almost two out of five women—were employed outside the home.

The movement of women out of the home into remunerative work, however, has been neither steady nor unopposed. Undoubtedly one of the underlying conditions is an expanding economy's need for labor. But something more than that is needed to break society's traditional habits of mind about the proper work for women. Certainly here the feminist demands for equality for women played a part. But a social factor of equal importance was war. By their very disruption of the steady pulse of everyday living, wars break the cake of custom, shake up society and compel people to look afresh at old habits and attitudes. It is not accidental, for instance, that women's suffrage in England, Russia and Germany, as well as the United States, was achieved immediately after the First World War and in France and Italy after the Second.

At the very least, by making large and new demands upon the established work force, war draws hitherto unused labor into the economic process. During the Civil War, for example, young women assumed new roles in the economy as workers in metal and munitions factories, as clerks in the expanded bureaucracy in Washington and as nurses in war hospitals. Moreover, when the war was over women had permanently replaced men as the dominant sex in the teaching profession. Furthermore, since many women found a new usefulness in the Sanitary Fairs and other volunteer work, the end of hostilities left many women unwilling to slip back into the seclusion of the Victorian home. It is not simply coincidental that the women's club movement began very soon after the war.

When the First World War came to the United States, feminist leaders, perhaps recalling the gains of the Civil War, anticipated new and broad advances for their sex. And the demand for labor, especially after the United States entered the war, did open many jobs to women, just as it was doing in contemporary Great Britain and Germany. All over the United States during the war customary and legal restrictions on the employment of women fell away. Women could be seen doing everything from laying railroad ties to working in airplane factories. The war also brought to a successful climax the struggle for the suffrage. Pointedly women had argued that a war for democracy abroad should at least remedy the deficiencies of democracy at home.

If politically the war was a boon to women, economically it failed to live up to feminist anticipations. The First World War, unlike the Civil War, did not result in a large permanent increase in the number of working women. Indeed, by 1920 there were only 800,000 more women working than in 1910. But as a result of wartime demands, women did get permanent places in new job categories, like elevator operators and theater ushers. (But women street car conductors disappeared soon after the armistice.) Certain traditional professions for women, like music teaching, lost members between 1910 and 1920, while professions that required more training and provided steadier income, like library and social work and college teaching, doubled or tripled their numbers in the same period.

The Second World War, with its even more massive demands for labor and skills, brought almost four million new women workers into the nation's factories and offices. Once again jobs usually not filled by women were opened to them. For example, the number of women bank officers rose 40 per cent during the four years of the war and the number of women employees in finance has continued to rise ever since. Furthermore, unlike the situation after the First World War, the female work force after 1945 not only stayed up but then went higher.

Measured in the number of women working, the changes in the economic position of women add up to a feminist success. Twenty-four million working women cannot be ignored. But weighed in the scales of quality instead of quantity, the change in women's economic status is not so striking. It is true that women now work in virtually every job listed by the Bureau of the Census. Moreover, the popular press repeatedly tells of the inroads women are making into what used to be thought of as men's jobs. Three years ago, for example, a woman won a prize as the mutual fund salesman of the year. Women are widely represented in advertising and in real estate, and even women taxicab drivers are no longer rare. Yet the fact remains that the occupations in which the vast majority of women actually engage are remarkably similar to those historically held by women. In 1950 almost three quarters of all employed women fell into twenty occupational categories, of which the largest was stenographers, typists and secretaries—a category that first became prominent as a woman's occupation over a half century ago. Other occupations which have traditionally been women's, like domestic service, teaching, clerical work, nursing and telephone service, are also conspicuous among the twenty categories. Further than that, the great majority of women are employed in occupations in which they predominate. This sexual division of labor is clearly evident in the professions, even though women are only a small proportion of total professional workers. Two thirds of all professional women are either nurses or teachers; and even in teaching there is a division between the sexes. Most women teach in the primary grades; most men teach in high school. Women are notoriously underrepresented in the top professions like law, medicine, engineering and scientific re-search. No more than 7 per cent of all pro-fessional women in 1950 were in the four of these categories together. Only 6 per cent of medical doctors and 4 per cent of law-yers and judges were women. In contrast, almost three quarters of medical doctors are women in the Soviet Union; in England the figure is 16 per cent. In both France and Sweden women make up a high pro-portion of pharmacists and dentists; neither of those professions attracts many women in the United States.

One consequence as well as manifesta-tion of the sexual division of labor in the United States has been the differences in pay for men and women. That difference has been a historical complaint of feminist leaders. In 1900 one study found women's wages to be, on the average, only 53 per cent of men's. The reason was, of course, that women were concentrated in the poorer paying jobs and industries of the economy. The disparity in pay between the sexes has been somewhat reduced today, but not very much. In 1955 among full-time women workers of all types the median wage was about two thirds of that for men. In short, women are still supplying the low-paid labor in the economy just as they were in the last century. (In substance, women workers and Negroes of both sexes perform a similar function in the economy.) The willingness of women to supply cheap labor may well account for their getting the large number of jobs they do; men often will not work for the wages that women will accept.

Today, there does not seem to be very much disparity between men's and women's wages for the same work, though the sexual division of labor is so nearly complete that it is difficult to find comparable jobs of the two sexes to make a definitive study.

There has been no improvement in women's position in higher education; in-deed, it can be argued that women have failed to maintain the place reached much earlier. As we have seen, the United States led the world in opening higher education

to women. This country also led to broad-ening the social base of education for women. No other country educated such a large proportion of women in its univer-sities and colleges as did the United States. At the close of the nineteenth century, one third of American college students were women; by 1937 women made up almost 40 per cent of the students in American institutions of higher learning. In Germany just before Hitler took power, no more than one out of ten university students was a woman; in Swedish universities in 1937 only 17 per cent of the students were women; in British universities the ratio was 22 per cent.

But since the Second World War the gap between American and European pro-portions of women in higher education has narrowed considerably. In 1952-1953 women constituted only 35 per cent of the Amer-ican college population, while France counted women as 36 per cent of its univer-sity students and Sweden 26 per cent. The *number* of women in American colleges, of course, is considerably greater than it was in the 1920's and 1930's, but in pro-portion to men, women have lost ground in America while gaining it in Europe.

A further sign of the regression in the educational position of women in the United States is that in the early 1950's women earned about 10 per cent of the doc-toral degrees in this country as compared with almost 15 per cent in the 1920's.

How is one to explain this uneven, al-most contradictory record of women in America? How does it happen that a coun-try with a kind of built-in feminism from the frontier falls behind more traditional countries in its training of college women; that a country with one of the highest pro-portions of working women in the world ends up with such a small proportion of its women in medicine, in law and in the sciences? Perhaps the correct answer is that the question should not be asked—at least not by Americans. For like so much else in American society, such contradictions are a manifestation of the national avoidance of any ideological principle, whether it be in feminist reform or in anything else. To be sure there has been no lack of feminist argument or rationale for women's work outside the home, for women's education and for other activities by women. But American women, like American society in general, have been more concerned with individual practice than with a consistent feminist ideology. If women have entered the labor force or taken jobs during a war they have done so for reasons related to the immediate individual or social circumstances and not for reasons of feminist ideology. The women who have been concerned about showing that women's capabilities can match men's have been the exception. As the limited, and low-paying, kind of jobs women occupy demonstrate, there is not now and never has been any strong feminist push behind the massive and continuing movement of women into jobs. Most American women have been interested in jobs, not careers. To say, as many feminists have, that men have opposed and resisted the opening of opportunities to women is to utter only a half truth. The whole truth is that American society in general, which includes women, shuns like a disease any feminist ideology.

Another way of showing that the historical changes in the status of women in America bear little relation to a feminist ideology is to examine one of those rare instances when women did effect a social improvement through an appeal to ideology, for instance, the struggle for the suffrage. By the early twentieth century the feminist demand for the vote overrode every other feminist goal. Once women achieved the vote, it was argued, the evils of society would be routed, for women, because of their peculiar attributes, would bring a fresh, needed and wholesome element into political life. In form, and in the minds of many women leaders, the arguments for the suffrage came close to being a full-blown ideology of feminism.

In point of fact, of course, the Nineteenth Amendment ushered in no millenium. But that fact is of less importance than the reason why it did not. When American women obtained the vote they simply did not use it ideologically; they voted not as women but as individuals. Evidence of this was the failure of many women to vote at all. At the end of the first decade of national suffrage women still did not exercise the franchise to the extent that men did. Nor did many women run for or hold political offices. The first woman to serve in Congress was elected in 1916; in 1920, the first year of national women's suffrage, four women were elected to Congress, but until 1940 no more than nine women served at one time in the House of Representatives and the Senate together. That we are here observing an American and not simply a sexual phenomenon is shown by a comparison with European countries. In nonfeminist Germany, where the ballot came to women at about the same time as in the United States, the first Reichstag after suffrage counted forty-one women as members. In 1951 seventeen women sat in the British House of Commons as compared with ten in the United States House of Representatives. Twice the number of women have served as cabinet ministers in Britain between 1928 and 1951 as have served in the United States down to the present.

Another instance in which social change was effected by feminist ideology was prohibition. The achievement of national prohibition ran second only to the suffrage movement as a prime goal of the organized women's movement; the Eighteenth Amendment was as much a product of feminist ideology as the Nineteenth. Yet like the suffrage movement, prohibition, despite its feminist backing, failed to receive the support of women. It was *after* prohibition was enacted, after all, that women drank in public.

In the cases of both suffrage and prohibition, women acted as individuals, not as members of a sex. And so they have continued to act. It is not without relevance that the women's political organization that is most respected—the League of Women Voters—is not only nonpartisan but studiously avoids questions pertaining only to women. To do otherwise would be feminist and therefore ideological.

One further conclusion might be drawn from this examination of the nonideological character of American women. That the changes that have come to the position of women have been devoid of ideological intent may well explain why there has been so little opposition to them. The most successful of American reforms have always been those of an impromptu and practical nature. The great revolution of the New Deal is a classic example. The American people, like F.D.R. himself, simply tried one thing after another, looking for something—anything—that would get the nation out of the depression. If lasting reforms took place, so much the better. On the other hand, reforms that have been justified by an elaborate rationale or ideology, like abolition, have aroused strong and long-drawn-out opposition. By the same token, when women became ideological in support of suffrage and prohibition, they faced their greatest opposition and scored their most disappointing triumphs.

The achievement of the suffrage in 1920 is a convenient date for marking the end of the first phase in the changing position of women, for by then women were accorded virtually the same rights as men even if they did not always exercise them. The second phase began at about the same time. It was the participation of married women in the work force. During the nineteenth century few married women worked; when they did it was because they were childless or because their husbands were inadequate providers. Even among the poor, married women normally did not work. A survey of the slum districts in five large cities in 1893 revealed that no more than 5 percent of the wives were employed.

Only Negro wives in the South and immigrant wives in big northern cities provided any significant exceptions to this generalization.

Before the First World War, the movement of wives into the working force was barely noticeable. During the 1920's there was an acceleration, but as late as 1940 less than 17 percent of all married women were working. Among working women in 1940, 48 percent were single and only 31 percent were married. The Second World War dramatically reversed these proportions—another instance of the influence of war on the position of women. By 1950 the proportion of married women living with their husbands had risen to 48 percent of all working women while that of single women had fallen to 32 percent. In 1960 the Census reported that almost 32 percent of all married women were employed outside the home and that they comprised 54 percent of all working women. No industrial country of Europe, with the exception of the Soviet Union, counted such a high proportion. Today, married women are the greatest source of new labor in the American economy. Between 1949 and 1959, for example, over four million married women entered the labor force, some 60 percent of *all* additions, male and female.

Such a massive movement of married women out of the home was a development few of the early feminists could have anticipated. That it has taken place is at once a sign and a yardstick of the enormous change in women's position in society and in the family. In the nineteenth century work outside the home was unthinkable for the married women. Not only were there children to care for, but there were objections from husbands and society to consider. That is why the convinced feminist of the nineteenth century often spurned marriage. Indeed, it is often forgotten that the feminist movement was a form of revolt against marriage. For it was through marriage, with the legal and social dominance of the husband, that women were most obviously denied opportunities for self-expression. Even after the legal superiority of the husband had been largely eliminated from the law, middle-class social conventions could still scarcely accommodate the working wife. To the woman interested in realizing her human capabilities, marriage in the nineteenth century was not an opportunity but a dead end. And it was indeed a minor scandal of the time that many of the "new women" did in fact reject marriage. The tendency was most pronounced, as was to be expected, among highly educated women, many of whom felt strongly their obligation to serve society through careers. Around 1900 more than one fourth of women who graduated from college never married; more than half of the women medical doctors in 1890 were single.

Like other changes in the position of women, the movement of married women into the work force—the reconciliation of marriage and work—must be related to the social changes of the last three decades. One of these social changes was the increase in contraceptive knowledge, for until married women could limit their families they could not become steady and reliable industrial workers. Information about contraceptive techniques which had been known for a generation or more to educated middle-class women did not seep down to the working class until the years of the Great Depression. In 1931, for instance, there were only 81 clinics disseminating birth control information in the United States; in 1943 there were 549, of which 166 were under public auspices. As the number of public clinics suggest, by the end of the 1930's birth control was both socially and religiously acceptable, at least among Protestants. And a method was also available then to Roman Catholics, since it was in the same decade that the rhythm method, the only one acceptable to the Roman Catholic Church, was first brought to popular attention with the approval of ecclesiastical authorities.

Another social force underlying the movement of wives and mothers in the work force was the growing affluence of an industrialized society, especially after 1940. Higher health standards, enlarged incomes of husbands and a better standard of living in general permitted a marked alteration in the temporal cycle of women's lives. Women now lived longer, stayed in school later and married earlier. In 1890 half the girls left school at 14 or before—that is, when they finished grammar school; in 1957 the median age was 18—after graduation from high school. The girl of 1890, typically, did not marry until she was 22; the age of her counterpart in 1957 was 20, leaving no more than two years for work between the end of school and marriage. Among other things this fact explains the fall in the proportion of single women in the work force in the United States as compared with other industrial societies. Few other countries have such an early median age of marriage for girls.

Early marriages for women produce another effect. With knowledge of contraceptive techniques providing a measure of control over child-bearing, women are now having their children early and rapidly. When this tendency is combined with a younger age of marriage, the result is an early end to child-bearing. In 1890 the median age of a mother when her last child was born was 32; in 1957 it was 26. A modern mother thus has her children off to school by the time she is in her middle thirties, leaving her as much as thirty-five years free for work outside the home. And the fact is that almost half of working women today are over forty years of age. Put another way, 34 per cent of married women between the ages of thirty-five and forty-four years are gainfully employed.

Unquestionably, as the practical character of the woman's movement would lead us to expect, an important force behind the influx of married women into the work force is economic need. But simple poverty is not the only force. Several studies, for example, have documented the conclusion that many women who work are married to men who earn salaries in the upper income brackets, suggesting that poverty is not the controlling factor in the wife's decision to work. A similar conclusion is to be drawn from the positive correlation between education and work for married women. The more education a wife has (and therefore the better salary her husband is likely to earn) the more likely she is to be working herself. Many of these women work undoubtedly in order to raise an adequate standard of living to a comfortable one. Many others work probably because they want to realize their potentialities in the world. But that women are so poorly represented in the professions and other careers suggests that most married women who work are realizing their full capabilities neither for themselves nor for society.

Over sixty years ago, in *Women and Economics,* the feminist Charlotte Perkins Gilman cogently traced the connection between work and the fulfillment of women as human beings. In subsequent writings she grappled with the problem of how this aim might be realized for married women. As a mother herself, raising a child under the trying circumstances of divorce, Gilman knew first hand that work outside the home and child-rearing constituted *two* full-time jobs. No man, she knew, was expected or required to shoulder such a double burden. Gilman's remedies of professional domestic service and kitchenless apartments never received much of a hearing, and considering the utopian if not bizarre character of her solutions, that is not surprising. Yet the problem she raised remained without any solution other than the eminently individualistic and inadequate one of permitting a woman to assume the double burden if she was so minded. Meanwhile, as the economy has grown, the problem has entered the lives of an ever increasing number of women. Unlike most of her feminist contemporaries, who were mainly concerned with the suffrage and the final elimination of legal and customary barriers to women's opportunities, Gilman recognized that the

logic of feminism led unavoidably to the working mother as the typical woman. For if women were to be free to express themselves, then they should be able to marry as well as to work. Women should not have to make a choice any more than men. To make that possible, though, would require that some way be found to mitigate the double burden which biology and society had combined to place only on women.

As women moved into the second stage of their development—the reconciliation of work and marriage—the problem which Gilman saw so early was increasingly recognized as the central issue. Virginia Collier, for example, in a book *Marriage and Careers,* published in 1926, wrote that since so many married women were working, "The question therefore is no longer should women combine marriage with careers, but how do they manage it and how does it work." Interestingly enough, her study shows that what today Betty Friedan, in *The Feminine Mystique,* has called the "problem that has no name," was already apparent in the 1920's. One working wife explained her reasons for taking a job in these words, "I am burning up with energy and it is rather hard on the family to use it up in angry frustration." Another said, "I had done everything for Polly for six years. Suddenly she was in school all day and I had nothing to do. My engine was running just as hard as ever, but my car was standing still." A year after Collier's book appeared, President William A. Nielson of Smith College observed "that the outstanding problem confronting women is how to reconcile a normal life of marriage and motherhood with intellectual activity such as her college education has fitted her for." That the issue was taken seriously is attested by an action of the Board of Trustees of Barnard College in 1932. The board voted to grant six months' maternity leave pay to members of the staff and faculty. In announcing the decision, Dean Virginia Gildersleeve clearly voiced its import. "Neither the men nor the women of our staff," she said, "should be forced into celibacy, and cut off from that great source of experience, of joy, sorrow and wisdom which marriage and parenthood offer."

With one out of three married women working today, the problem of reconciling marriage and work for women is of a social dimension considerably larger than in the days of Charlotte Gilman or even in the 1930's. But the fundamental issue is still the same: how to make it possible, as Dean Gildersleeve said, to pursue a career or hold a job while enjoying the "experience . . . joy, sorrow and wisdom" of marriage and parenthood. The practical solutions to this central problem of the second stage in the changing position of women seem mainly collective or governmental, not individual. Child-care centers, efficient and readily available house-keeping services, and emergency child-care service such as the Swedes have instituted are obviously a minimal requirement if women are to have the double burdens of homemaking and employment lightened. The individual working woman cannot be expected to compensate for the temporary disabilities consequent upon her role as mother any more than the individual farmer or industrial worker can be expected single-handedly to overcome the imbalance between himself and the market. Today both farmers and workers have government and their own organizations to assist them in righting the balance.

But as the history of farmers and industrial labor makes evident, to enact legislation or to change mores requires persuasion of those who do not appreciate the necessity for change. Those who would do so must organize the like-minded and mobilize power, which is to say they need a rationale, an ideology. And here is the rub; in pragmatic America, as we have seen, any ideology must leap high hurdles. And one in support of working wives is additionally handicapped because women themselves, despite the profound changes in their status in the last century, do not acknowledge such an ideology. Most American women simply do not want work outside the home to be

justified as a normal activity for married women. Despite the counter-argument of overwhelming numbers of working wives, they like to think of it as special and exceptional. And so long as they do not advance such an ideology, American society surely will not do so, though other societies, like Israel's and the Soviet Union's, which are more ideological than ours, obviously have.

Perhaps the kind of gradual, piecemeal advance toward a feminist ideology that Mrs. Rossi proposes in other pages of this issue may contain the seeds of change. But a reading of the past reminds us forcefully that in America the soil is thin and the climate uncongenial for the growth of any seedlings of ideology.

John G. Mitchell

John G. Mitchell, editor of Sierra Club books, optimistically suggests in this article about the cleanup of the Hudson River that ecological problems can be solved if there is a commitment by both the people and the government. The people of Oregon under the leadership of Governor Tom McCall have found a basis for similar optimism in their cleanup of the badly polluted Willamette River.

THE RESTORATION OF A RIVER

On the west-facing slopes of Mount Marcy, the snow lies crisp and deep, tons of it, acres of it, anchored above the precipitous ice garden of Feldspar Brook, and locked in each crystal is the stuff that a river is made of. Soon the Adirondack snows will begin to melt—crystals into drops of water, drops into rivulets, down Feldspar Brook to the Opalescent and out across the Flowed Land to the Hudson itself. Rushing south clear and cold, the river trips over a limestone ledge at Glens Falls. It is not quite the same thereafter, for downstream, after swirling into turgid confluence with the Mohawk, the Hudson is made of sterner stuff than water, such stuff as cadmium and coliform bacteria and polychlorinated biphenyls, the concentrations of which in recent years have prompted some observers to speculate that man overboard will rot to death before he can drown. So they say. And yet in this seventh year of the People's Crusade to Save the Hudson, after all the false starts, the empty promises, and the political persiflage, there are signs that drowning may again become practicable south of the Mohawk. In fact, even the most cynical environmentalists would have to concede that, for all its prevailing ills, the river at last is getting cleaned up.

This is no mean achievement. Like most of the nation's major waterways, the Hudson has been growing dirtier and dirtier ever since towns and factories first appeared along its banks. A return to cleanliness became a beckoning hope in 1965 when a $1-billion New York State bond issue was passed for a statewide "Pure Waters Program." Economic, political, and organizational barriers to purifying the Hudson's waters have since proved to be immense, and many remain. Yet dozens of new water-treatment plants are now in the works or operating along the Hudson. Citizen groups have become increasingly active in sniffing out polluters. So has the law, primarily in the person of the polluter-chasing U.S. Attorney for the southern district of New York, Whitney North Seymour, Jr. The net effect has been some distinctly promising movement in the direction of cleaning up one of the nation's most celebrated, most heavily used, and dirtiest of waterways.

"You really can't see the difference with the eye," says Seymour, whose jurisdiction covers most of the Hudson's filthiest stretch, south of Albany. "But at least we know what is—and isn't—going into it." One thing that isn't going into the Hudson as freely and profusely as it has in the past is industrial waste, thanks in part to Seymour himself and to a dusted-off, seventy-three-year-

old federal statute that is proving to be a powerful weapon in bringing industrial polluters to bay. This is the Refuse Act of 1899, which Seymour's office has successfully used to prosecute nearly twenty industrial violators over the past two years, to bring others voluntarily into line, and to encourage private citizens to become pollution policemen.

The act prohibits the unlicensed dumping of wastes in a navigable waterway, provides for violators to be fined, and stipulates that part of the fine be turned over to the person or persons who supplied the evidence leading to conviction. So far, the bounty system has rewarded a Manhattan housewife with $12,500 for reporting violations by a cement-mix company and the Hudson River Fishermen's Association with $3,000 for blowing the whistle on fuel discharges by the Penn Central Railroad and on pollution emanating from a pharmaceutical plant. In addition, the fishermen may reap a reward of $25,000 for developing evidence that the Anaconda Company was polluting the Hudson. Anaconda was convicted and fined $200,000 late last year and has now installed treatment facilities to bring its effluents up to standards acceptable to the government.

"We're receiving good complaints," says Seymour about the siege of citizen activism on behalf of the Hudson. "People have begun to get the message, they're more alert, and they know they have agencies they can turn to." Last summer a group of high school students from Shrub Oak, New York, turned to the U.S. Attorney's office when they discovered that a tidal marsh on the Hudson had been partially filled with debris. The students had been using the marsh as an outdoor ecological laboratory. But the New York National Guard at Camp Smith, which adjoins the marsh near Peekskill, had apparently decided that the wetland would serve a higher purpose if it were turned into a parking lot, and toward that end the guardsmen had deposited the necessary landfill of masonry and rubble. Invoking the Refuse Act, Seymour compelled the guard to seek a dumping permit from the U.S. Army Corps of Engineers and the U.S. Bureau of Sport Fisheries and Wildlife. Those agencies, in turn, declined the request for a permit, and the guard was ordered to remove the debris and restore the marsh to its natural condition.

Having demonstrated the almost unfailing applicability of the Refuse Act to cases involving landfill or the direct discharge of industrial waste, Attorney Seymour and his staff recently set out to take a closer look at industrial installations along the Hudson south of Albany. More than 1,300 firms were surveyed on such matters as production materials, intake of water, and treatment of discharges.

From the survey, U.S. prosecutors compiled a list of those industries discharging wastes directly into the Hudson or its tributaries. Minor offenders requiring some kind of administrative action were referred to the state Department of Environmental Conservation. The more serious ones were referred to the Corps of Engineers for investigation. Thus Seymour believes that, with the possible exception of an occasional new source of pollution or a few willfully surreptitious violators, all direct and untreated industrial discharges in New York south of Albany, are now under some form of abatement proceedings, either an existing state order with a deadline for compliance or a federal sanction instituted by his office.

Cleaning up the river's direct industrial discharges is just a start, however. "Indirect" discharge of industrial waste—from factories into municipal sewer systems and then into the Hudson—continues barely abated. "There's the new frontier," says Seymour. "We're still in the midst of analyzing what happens to those effluents. Our jurisdiction is cloudy, because the Refuse Act exempts sewage passing from streets or sewers in a liquid state. So we're talking to local officials, encouraging them to enforce their own regulations." Fortunately,

some areas have required little suasion. Across the Hudson from Seymour's district, where industry is a prolific polluter, the New Jersey state Senate recently passed a bill requiring manufacturers to pretreat their waste before discharging it into a local sewer system. What prompted this measure was not so much the fact that most North Jersey's sewage, treated or otherwise, finds its way eventually to the interstate water of the Hudson and New York Bay as that there is the specter of toxic metals and acids savaging the delicate systems of modern sewage plants, on which the taxpayers of New Jersey belatedly are laying some fairly precious investments.

Cleaning up municipal pollution itself remains another frontier. Throughout the Hudson Valley, the exorbitant costs of secondary sewage treatment facilities, and the decreasing availability of federal funds to help finance them, continue to frustrate those who would strive to achieve the most difficult goal of all: the elimination of human waste from the river. New York City, for example, expects to spend nearly $2-billion over the next six years completing two new treatment plants and upgrading and expanding twelve others. But the city, like many another community, had also expected the federal government to live up to the promise in water-quality legislation that authorizes the federal government to pay up to 55 per cent of construction costs. So far the United States has contributed only 1.5 percent of the $770-million cost of a huge plant designated to sanitize a raw outpouring of sewage that the city now disgorges directly into the Hudson. And New York State has been stuck with a large part of the bill. "The federal government has been putting up about ten percent of costs statewide," says Henry Diamond, commissioner of the state's Department of Environment Conservation. "We've had the choice of either waiting until the federal money becomes available or prefinancing the federal share ourselves. We've chosen to prefinance. The federal government now owes us one and three-tenths billion dollars."

But there is a limit to how much plant construction New York State can prefinance. It has channeled funds into fifty-one new treatment plants on the Hudson since the voters approved the $1-billion "Pure Waters" bond issue in 1965 (twenty-seven of the plants are already operating), and now the level of the clean-up kitty is falling low. Earlier this year, Diamond's department was forced to abandon its plans to help finance eight projects along the Hudson River. One of these would have sealed forever the forty-seven outfalls in Rensselaer County that now pour raw wastes, both human and industrial, into the river and enhance that region's reputation as having the second-foulest stretch of water along the Hudson's entire 315-mile length.

The ultimate in pollution occurs along the sludge-stained shores and under the rotting piers of the terminal city at the Hudson's mouth. Each day New Yorkers produce some 1.3 billion gallons of raw sewage, of which 450 million gallons is discharged untreated. Completion of the city's $2-billion secondary treatment program will eliminate this frightful flow of waste entirely—but not for at least another six years. And across the moribund river, New Jersey likewise looks forward to the day when all of its municipal sewage plants, now mostly of a primitive primary type, will have been upgraded to add oxygen to the effluent, and reduce bacteria as well as more solids. That will be sometime after 1976. In the meantime, the Passaic Valley Sewage District will continue to pump 300 million gallons of primary effluent to an underwater outfall at Robbin's Reef in New York Harbor, hard by the very spot where the adventurous Verrazano and Henry Hudson first spied the broad river trenching down from the northern mountains.

Yet for all the work that remains before the Hudson becomes, say, swimmable along its whole length, the river of late has offered some encouraging signs of resurgent cleanliness. Some say that Hudson inhabitants of old, say as striped bass and sturgeon, are more plentiful these days. And a recent, carefully conducted test showed some actual, measurable improvement in water quality. Last summer representatives of the New York-New Jersey Interstate Sanitation Commission took water samples from a long stretch of the river north of the New York City line. Purposely they had waited for a hot spell, when the dissolved oxygen content of the water—because of reduced run-off and increased evaporation—normally would be at its lowest, and least capable of sustaining aquatic life. "To our surprise," recalls Commission Director Thomas Glenn, "dissolved oxygen in the river was as high as four to six parts per million—well above our standard of what's acceptable. We also found that the fecal coliform density was lower than it had been in the past."

A truly cleaner Hudson will never be ensured simply by swapping fecal coliform for dissolved oxygen, by bounty-hunting the surreptitious spoilers, and by building bigger and better treatment plants. The Hudson is a complex river with a complex of problems, many of which are not directly associated with conventional water pollution. And today the solutions to *these* problems are as far from men's grasps as pollution abatement appeared to be a decade ago.

The most complicated problem, perhaps, is the increasing potential for overloading the river with waste heat from power plants. "Nuclear plants are proliferating in the Hudson Valley," says Alfred Forsyth, an environmental attorney and vice president of the Sierra Club. "And no one knows what, in the aggregate, their thermal discharges might do to the life of the river." Consolidated Edison Company's nuclear plants at Indian Point on the river south of Peekskill have already been credited with a number of prodigious fish kills. On several occasions white perch and other species have been crushed against the wire mesh screens of the power plants' cooling water intakes. With a flair for the kind of anti-septic language certain people are given to these days, one Con Ed official refers to these incidents as "an impingement of fish."

There is also the continuing problem of shore-line development, best symbolized perhaps by the Federal Power Commission's approval of Con Ed's application to build a pumped storage hydroelectric facility at Storm King Mountain in the beautiful Hudson Highlands. Indeed, if the Scenic Hudson Preservation Conference should fail in its efforts to scuttle this decision, some environmentalists fear resource exploiters will then have a green light to assault other scenic landmarks along the river.

And finally, there is the important question of water-resource development in the Hudson River watershed. New Yorkers are accustomed to taking their water—generally free and unmetered—from upstate streams and impoundments that are tributary to the Hudson and Delaware rivers. But now the water planners are looking farther afield, specifically to the Hudson's headwaters in the Adirondacks. Their latest scheme has been exposed by Robert H. Boyle, a senior editor of *Sports Illustrated* and cofounder of the Hudson River Fishermen's Association. In *The Water Hustlers*, published last fall, Boyle reports that the Corps of Engineers is planning to place the entire Hudson watershed "under siege" by constructing a series of drawn-down reservoirs to regulate fresh-water flow downstream. The idea, he writes, is to release the impounded waters when natural runoff is slack, thereby preventing the intrusion of tidal brine into proposed water withdrawal facilities along the lower Hudson. Some of these impoundments, according to Boyle, would flood out scenic wild forges on the upper Hudson and its tributaries and leave the great river "spread out 'like a patient etherized upon a table'—with water going from this lake to that river to this impoundment to that tunnel through this mountain into leaky main and dripping faucet."

Etherized or not, the Hudson may yet survive all the surgery that has been, and is yet to be, performed on it in the name of economic progress. One of the most hopeful signs is the proliferation of citizen groups determined to defend the river environment, such groups as the Fishermen's Association and the Hudson River Sloop Restoration, first organized by singer Pete Seeger and now headed by John M. Burns, a former assistant to Whitney North Seymour. (Seymour demanded Burns's resignation in 1971 because of the young attorney's brash—some say *justifiably* brash—handling of a Refuse Act preceding against the General Motors plant at Tarrytown on the Hudson.) Under Burns's direction, the Sloop group is assembling data on potential polluters that may be escaping the attention of his former boss. "I think we can save this river," Burns says. "And if we can do that, then we can point the way for the rest of the country and show other people how they can save their own rivers, too."

Al Martinez

Al Martinez has an optimistic view of the future of America based on technological improvements which provide greater physical comfort, security, and freedom. He expects these improvements to be harmoniously blended with the landscape and people's psychological needs by a humane civilization.

CALIFORNIA 2001

Morning comes to California, gleaming off the amber dome of a transpoliner that streaks south out of San Francisco on a cushion of air.

The linear induction motors accelerate smoothly, pressing the multiunit commuter to its cruising speed of 300 m.p.h. just clear of the sprawling San Jose megalopolis.

The six-forty-five is nonstop to Los

Angeles. The trip will take an hour and 20 minutes.

The day is Tuesday, Sept. 25, 2001.

Overhead, on its regular 18-day orbit, the manned station Skylab glides through space, its sensitive scanning equipment geared now to monitor the life of the Golden State in the golden autumn: the rush of rivers and traffic, the purity of air and ocean, the sum of resources and population, the health of crops and forests, the subtle movement of mountains and the barely perceptible erosion of granite.

All of this, translated in a flicker to analog-video-digital telemetry, is flashed to Sacramento as Skylab, its passover done, moves out of range, and as the transpoliner slips by Joaquin-1 on the western edge of the great Central Valley near Polonia Pass.

Joaquin-1 is the first of the cities conceived by a coalition of planners from government and the private sector to relieve the pressure of urbanization from California's overpopulated metropolitan centers, and it is aborning now at the confluence of a network of water and power and transportation, where need and nature destined it should be.

Here business and industry will flourish in a population complex designed to overcome the enigma of wasted space and congestion that still threatens the survival of the big cities. Here new knowledge uses land for capacity and privacy and creates an architecture at peace with nature.

The transpoliner, its computerized acceleration system ignorant of the dream coming true, is past Joaquin-1 in a twinkling and flies through the morning toward its final destination—by towns that appear with disturbing unplanned frequency in the distance, near low hills that mask the nuclear power plants of an energy-hungry state, through the far-flung outskirts of the L.A. suburbs that sprawl into Ventura County.

Finally, Los Angeles.

The transpoliner dips through an underground opening to the mammoth subsurface downtown DOT (Department of Transportation) terminal and glides to a stop, settling gently through the cushion of air to its base.

The doors slide open automatically and the passengers leave their cars. They board electrically operated feeder pods, the so-called people movers, that transport them to key points throughout the big city.

The pods glide with a soft whir on fixed guideways twenty feet aboveground, over the elevated pedestrian walkways and the protected malls and the small clean cars that dart through a shimmery day in a world that has discovered the value of clear air after choking haze.

The city comes to life. The business of the day is beginning.

Thirteen miles northwest of the downtown section, in a multi-use high-rise building near the intersection of Mulholland Drive and the San Diego Freeway, morning has come with the clicking awake of an automated household.

A medium-impact Homemaster, the miniaturized and simplified version of a business computer, has been pre-programmed to bring the essentials of a new day to the six-room apartment.

Indirect lighting spreads automatically through each room, a microwave oven heats up, music plays, a coffee maker turns on and a video screen flashes a reminder of the day's commitments.

A family of three yawns and stretches into the routine of the morning in a scene that is repeated again and again in other high-activity centers and in the suburbs, the New Towns and the desert developments.

The Mulholland high-rise is a relatively new application in urbanized cluster living, part of the movement to utilize space and distance that evolved into multi-use structures.

That family of three, out of the steamy showers now and around their instant breakfast, is but one segment of the building they occupy.

Not only are there other apartments in

the same building—varying as much in price, style and size as homes in a suburban neighborhood—but the unit contains services as well.

School is three levels up, and the bread-winner in the family works in a spacious sub-surface center that assembles instrumentations for the space shuttlecraft at the Vandenberg launching facility.

Other buildings in the Mulholland Cluster are devoted to specific purposes. There is a health-care center that houses a hospital, an out-patient clinic, doctors' offices, laboratories, a rehabilitation unit, a nursing home and an ambulance company.

Another structure combines police and fire headquarters and government offices, and another a wide variety of entertainment facilities from an opera hall to a sports arena. Most of the rooftops are utilized for parks and swimming.

School is without grades and grading, and the six-million public school children of California have emerged as individuals in a system drastically regeared to provide for individual need.

Sophisticated learning machines are utilized in open classrooms, and teachers have become managers of education.

But the human component has not been abandoned in the age of electronic gadgetry.

Senior citizens, a previously untapped reservoir of knowledge and experience, are volunteer teaching assistants. So are housewives and college students.

In the higher grades, the youngsters take a portion of their classes in the centers of communication, government, industry, law and commerce, taught by those involved in the function of society.

It has been a long-evolving dream to integrate learning with society, to realistically equate education with improvement of the culture, to utilize competitive technology for knowledge as well as profit.

The dream comes true not only in the skyscraper world of the high activity centers of Los Angeles, but in the far-flung suburbs as well, drenched now by the mid-morning sun on a blue-sky Tuesday of tomorrow.

The suburbs of California endure around the giant urban centers despite growing efforts to disperse and redistribute the population into the more sparsely inhabited sections of the state.

Growth regulated

An air-cushion rapid transit system, which also ties the high-activity centers together, makes living in the suburbs and working in the cities easier, but suburban growth is regulated by law.

Building permits are frozen or only reluctantly granted in "down-zoning" programs around Los Angeles, San Francisco, Sacramento and San Diego.

For some areas it came too late; the residential clutter is the result along the high-speed transportation corridors of exurbia.

But in other suburban regions, streets have been closed off to provide for the kinds of parks and open spaces only grudgingly granted in the past.

Light industry and warehouse facilities which still exist beyond their specified areas are underground, and the land above them is utilized for public services.

Among the services are transportation terminals. Planners began to realize in the 1960s how instrumental the efficient movement of people would be to the survival of the cities.

They rejected as intolerable expedients the mass construction of additional freeways to meet travel demands.

Instead, state and federal money went into the study, design and creation of air-cushion and electric transit projects, and construction lead-time dissolved in the acid of necessity.

Rapid transport

They had to be built, and therefore they were built.

The long-distance transpoliners, flashing between the cities, evolved along with the interurban systems, the people movers, and the smogless jitneys.

These same ground transportation systems have favored today's continued heavy reliance on jet travel by drastically lessening the time it takes to get from one's home to an airport.

A new generation of jet engines are pollution free and quiet, and their short take-off and landing capabilities have also minimized the environmental impact of airports by limiting their size.

It was the environmental movement generally, a revolution full-blown in the ecology-minded sixties that has resulted in today's smogless cities.

The air snaps with a brilliance predating that era of pollution when the sun shone orange through a deadly haze, when the stars were blurred, when the outlines of the buildings were vague in the brownish density that settled over them.

Now the works of men stand sharply defined against the iridescent sky, and no-where—not piled against the mountainsides nor stagnant in the land basins—is there even a hint of smog.

Water pollution is also only a distant battle—won in the war to preserve the environment.

The victory is evident as the sun at noon shimmers off the revitalized streams and the once dying lakes of California, the level of their purity monitored by instruments 1,000 times more sensitive than they once were.

Pollution is measured in parts per trillion, where yesterday such minutiae was not even detectable.

Natural coastline

But environment involves some abstracts too, and one of them is beauty. Toward esthetic considerations, mansions along with shanties have been removed by law as shore-line barriers to the blue Pacific.

And private vehicular traffic has been permanently barred from the mountain recreation areas in favor of public monorails to help preserve California's forest lands in perpetuity.

All these are triumphs of the environmental wars, a conglomerate name for the crusade to survive that finally unlocked the ecologists and the economists from what had become a private struggle and got them working together for the good of the future.

Their union spawned creation in the early 1980s of the California Committee, an independent, privately financed, quasi-official forum with Sacramento representation and approval.

Initially a coalescence of environmental organizations, the California Committee assumed special status as an advisory body to the Legislature upon successful submission of a master plan for California.

The plan, until then only a long-standing dream, lays out state responsibility for orderly growth and assumes the function of an outline for the more substantive progress of today.

Today.

It begins to fade now as afternoon comes sliding down the western slope of the Cascade Range and flattens out over Mountain Country, the state's newest tourist mecca.

The mecca rises from the brushland southeast of Redding in the shadow of Mt. Lassen, a Disneylandish recreation center half-history and half-carnival.

To draw population

Essentially concerned with re-creating and animating early California, Mountain Country embodies at least one element of a philosophy of population dispersion.

A private undertaking encouraged by tax incentives and a state transportation system, it will hopefully be the nucleus of a whole new population center in a wide-open region.

Until it becomes that nucleus, Mountain Country at least serves to shift a portion of the yearly tourist trade away from those areas barely able to handle the influx of visitors.

Masses of people have long been a critical consideration in California's concept of the future.

Demographers were warning three decades ago that unchecked growth could result in one giant megalopolis covering 50,000 square miles from San Francisco to San Diego and jammed with 40 million people.

Those who feared its inevitability were already calling it San-San and were saying that a total state population as high as 50 million-plus by the year 2000 was not unrealistic.

The population of California today is 33 million.

Even at that, power needs have quadrupled over the last 30 years, urban water needs have doubled, solid waste has increased at five times the population growth, demands on the state park system have doubled.

The needs have so far been met, even to the closed-loop recycling of solid waste into new uses.

But they didn't know then, in the edgy days of the fading twentieth century, that they would, or even could be met.

They called for strict migration control into California, for laws to remove all legal barriers to abortion, for tough marriage requirements among minors, for mandatory birth-control classes.

But as the population boom ended (the birthrate dropped, in-migration eased), the emphasis shifted from control to guidance.

Today, to assure that growth remains at a moderate level, revised income tax deductions discourage large families, a national employment policy has opened new job opportunities in other states and the creation of a uniform welfare system throughout the nation has ended California's reign as one of the places to go for public assistance.

Efforts at dispersion

New energy is being concentrated now in dispersing the population within the state.

One of the results is Joaquin-1 along the route of the San Francisco-Los Angeles transpoliner and in close proximity to Interstate 5, the San Luis Reservoir, the California Aqueduct and a major power tie-in.

Joaquin-1 remains largely experimental to determine whether a so-called New Town, a prepackaged community of homes, services and industries, can survive—and to test how successful it might be in redirecting the state's population away from the cities.

Another effort at population redistribution is also being made in the Mojave east of Barstow where the Desert Campus of the University of California is in fall session.

College in desert

Desert Campus contributes to the birth of a new university town, its creation enhanced by piped-in water, a direct major highway connection out of Barstow, a new jet field for STOL aircraft and the promise of air-cushion feeder service out of the Pasadena substation.

Here, around the tenth campus of the 150,000-student state-wide UC system, tax incentives are again being offered to induce controlled residential and industrial development.

The state hopes that the new campus will have impact beyond education, and that simply by existing it will encourage the establishment of other desert cities—their outdoor activities domed, their transportation underground, their life geared to a blazing sun that hangs low even now over the Calico Mountains this Tuesday in September.

The day is fading over a California in transition.

Much has been done at this moment in time to make the Golden State a better place to live. Much remains to be done through the twenty-first century.

The sins of the past are the problems of the present. Economic ghettos exist even though low-cost housing in any residential development is a fact of law.

Inequities persist

Some forms of animal life continue to face extinction even though hunting has been all but regulated out of existence and game reserves are widespread in the strenuous effort to preserve our wildlife.

There are inequities based on the historic divisions of race and religion and political commitment. Crime plagues the New Towns as well as the old cities. Taxes are high. Prices continue to rise. There is never enough money.

But there is hope. The California Committee will convene tomorrow in Sacramento to consider one more quality of life and to materialize that abstract into manageable substance.

There is talk that the committee itself has become unmanageable, that perhaps there ought to be a North Committee and a South Committee, and the irony of these internal problems is not lost on the members.

But there will be time enough for that tomorrow and the day after tomorrow and all the days after that.

For now the evening has come and the families have gathered and the business of the day has ended.

The night is Tuesday, September 25, 2001.

California sleeps.

Allan Nevins

Allan Nevins (1890–1971), noted historian and winner of two Pulitzer Prizes, looks at contemporary America with all its problems, *divisions, and hostilities as an essentially unified nation always looking to the future with optimistic expectations.*

THE TRADITION OF THE FUTURE

The novelist Henry James once remarked that "Americans are, as Americans, the most self-conscious people in the world." In this self-consciousness is embedded the feeling that Americans are not only different as a peculiar people from Britons as peculiarly British, or from Russians as peculiarly Russian, but are superior. This belief is part of the special American attitude. We pride ourselves on our Americanism. We stigmatize attitudes we dislike, and values we condemn, by terming them "un-American." It would be easy to pick out of our past political history oratory and journalism expressions of Yankee boastfulness, of the Jefferson Brick braggadocio about being ready to whip universal natur' that Dickens satirized after his first visit to the United States. This belongs to our outgrown past. But the attitude persists.

Thus we find Max Lerner declaring in his compendious book *America As a Civilization* that Americanism no longer means a type of nationalism. "To be an American is no longer to be only a nationality. It has become, along with Communism and in rivalry with it, a key pattern of actions and values . . . The American is the archetypal modern man, the archetypal man of the West." This is a bold assertion indeed. No doubt this kind of pride—like Mr. Lerner's belief that "America ranks with Greece and Rome as one of the great distinct civilizations of history"—may really operate as one of the forces making for American unity. But is it important as other forces? Where, then, does the main source of our unity lie?

President Johnson's withdrawal from the 1968 race, his reversal of Vietnam policy, and his sudden alarm over the prospect of our becoming a country full of divisions and antagonism also raise the question: Just what are our principal lines of fission, and how can we act to reduce or abolish them? Is it true, as some say, that our internal conflicts, our schismatic differences, are greater now than at any time since the Civil War? Connected with these questions is another. Did the recent, abrupt change of course by an unexpected exercise of Presidential power indicate that our governmental system is not as adequate to our needs as we had supposed—now that the world has changed so radically in character and our world responsibilities are so much greater than formerly? Johnson's action implied that swift alterations of the course of government may be important. Does this mean that we might well change the character of the Presidency, to make it more responsive to public opinion and more effective in guiding Congress and the nation? Or should we follow our old policy of drift?

An interval of puzzled uncertainty naturally follows any sudden arrestation and deflection of the national course. It is an interval that we can best employ in giving new thought to our national difficulties, as the Executive and Congress pause for thought and study. All nations need these pauses. Britain took one when the electorate defeated Churchill at the height of his wartime prestige, and brought in Clement Attlee. Defeat gave Germany and Japan opportunity for such pauses. India took one, perforce, after the assassination of Gandhi. It is perhaps too seldom that we Americans have sat down to think matters over.

Such a short, sharp political upheaval as we have just experienced ought to let us review at least three important questions. First, we pride ourselves on being a great democracy with liberal outlook and attitude. Just what do we mean by democratic liberalism, and how great a practical hold does it have upon American convictions? Do we have an area of common political beliefs upon which we can place firm reliance?

Unity in American life and political thought certainly does not stem from general agreement on any body of doctrines that can be labeled "liberalism." Most Americans would find difficulty in defining that term, and many, after defining it, would once begin to quarrel with it. We could not define "democracy" without plunging ourselves into a similar quarrel. The meaning of democracy in Oregon is very different from its meaning in Alabama. We are often told that we are held together as a people not so much by our common loyalty to the past—by our patriotic memories of old achievements from Plymouth and Jamestown, Valley Forge and Saratoga, down through the Civil War and the two World Wars—as by our common faith and hopes for the future. It is not the look backward, comparatively short as it is, but the look forward that gives us cohesion. While we share some memories, the much more important fact is that we share many expectations.

Americans have always been an optimistic nation, with a belief that they can hew out a smoother, brighter, forward path. Does this optimistic frame of mind still prevail? Some people would say that our present generation holds a view of the future that has become clouded by pessimism. For this nation-wide and, indeed, world-wide pessimism, they can argue, there exists all too much reason. The memory of two costly world wars is still recent. War still stalks the horizon. The armaments of the nuclear age are more oppressive and threatening than ever. The bombs held by the two great superpowers alone are sufficient to wipe out all civilization, and perhaps all life, on the planet. The grim threat of overpopulation and consequent famine holds a secondary place, but is nevertheless portentous. Still other pessimistic considerations crowd upon us. The decay and death of religious faith seem deeply alarming to many. Allied with it are the lowering of ethical standards and the decline of humanitarian values, the rise of violence throughout the globe, including our own country. These trends discourage all compassionate people, darken our prospect, and chill our once warm faith in meliorism.

Yet optimism still does prevail. The great unifying sentiment of Americans is hope for the future—a belief that, as they made good their bright expectations in the past, they can make good still brighter confidences in coming dawns. After the Second World War, George Macaulay Trevelyan spoke of the view of many Britons that they had been living in "the era of the fall of European civilization." Germans must have felt more strongly that the period from 1914 to 1954 could be so denominated. But we Americans never thought for a moment of the recent era as anything but a period of increasing power, prosperity, and promise for American civilization.

A young man has greater confidence in the future than a mature or aging man; a young nation has greater confidence than a nation past its apogee. We shall never quite recapture the same roseate sense of inexhaustible energy, youthfulness of spirit, and certainty that great gains lie at our fingertips that the generation of Jefferson, Hamilton, and other founders of the Republic had; the delight that they felt in the plasticity of their society; their exaltation of spirit as they realized the enormous wealth of the virgin continent; their rising sense of power as they conquered one obstacle after another. We shall not easily recapture the temper in which men of the Jacksonian era spoke; the temper of William C. Bryant saluting America as "The mother of a mighty race, Yet lovely in thy youthful grace"; or Walt Whitman singing in wartime that beyond the struggle, the wrestling of evil with good, and the temporary defeats, he saw "how America is the continent of glories, and of the triumph of freedom . . . and of all that is begun"; of how Walt Whitman foresaw immense spiritual results, "future years, of the far West."

For national unity it is most important to maintain in the American people this sense of confidence in our common future.

We should feel a sentiment of universality in cultivating this sense. To speak of our minority groups—the Negroes, the Mexicans, the Puerto Ricans—as if they were unhappy chiefly in the present state, with its humiliation, hardships, and deprivations, is an error. Their greatest deprivation is that of faith in sharing on equal terms, in a happier future, a better life, with all other citizens.

Faith in the future does not mean faith in the material gains of coming years; it means faith in ideas—the political, intellectual, moral, and spiritual ideas that will dominate our future. When the United States lay in the trough of "great Depression," with millions discouraged and pessimistic as never before, President Hoover remarked to a caller, "What the United States needs now is a great poet." He meant that it needed somebody who could present a body of central ideas in the enduring values of liberty and equality, as Wordsworth had presented a central sheaf of ideas on the enduring values of British life and thought in his sonnets written during the darkest days of the struggle with Napoleon. Such a voice would speak of the future's mighty promises.

This country has no fear of external foes. As Lincoln said when mob violence, sharp internal dissension, and the murder of Elijah P. Lovejoy by a pro-slavery mob filled him with consternation, no foreign enemy could ever set foot on the Blue Ridge or take a drink from our Western lakes. The real danger, Lincoln declared, was from *internal* foes: men and groups who attack our basic principles and subvert them, tearing the nation apart in the process. He was quite right. After 1816, the question whether our national unity—with which our democratic freedoms had always been closely associated—could survive became doubtful. Disorder overspread the republic. Brother fought against brother. States long welded together under the Compact of 1787 turned savagely against each other.

Happily, that will not happen again. Six hundred thousand young Americans died to settle that question. But the danger of internal schisms and domestic antagonisms that threaten to end in violence may recur. President Franklin D. Roosevelt said in a speech on hemispheric defense that the people of the United States and the New World were determined to keep threats to their peaceful harmony at bay. But forces menacing the life of the United States and the Western hemisphere, though unable to attack from abroad, might crop up from within: "The leaders of these forces," he said, "persist in believing that American lands can be torn by the hatreds and fears which have drenched the battle grounds of Europe for so many centuries . . . Divide and Conquer! That has been the battle cry . . . Malicious propagandists tell us that our old democratic ideals, our old traditions of civil liberties, are things of the past. We reject the thought. We say that we are a people of the future . . . the command of the democratic faith has ever been onward and upward; never have free men been satisfied with the mere maintenance of the status quo, however comfortable and secure it may have seemed at the moment. We have always held to the hope, the conviction, that there was a better life, a better world, beyond the horizon." That was a forceful restatement of the old assertion that Americans are held together not out of pride in the past, but out of faith in the future.

The belief in the future is reinforced by the attachment of the American people to the principle that in their public activities they must cling to moderation, never forsaking it for ideas or attitudes of an extremist character. In all their institutions— political, economic, and social—Americans believe in pluralism, in variety, in competition, and in spontaneity. Long before the essays of John Stuart Mill, Americans were profoundly convinced that there are always two sides to any important question, and that wise action becomes possible only when both sides are heard. Long before the confrontation of the modern dictatorships with liberty, Americans adopted Mill's view that, "The restraints of democracy on the use of power are the last great steps forward in civilization in the last two thousand years."

One by one, the painful causes of national discord are retreating or disappearing. Sectional feeling, once deep and vicious, is dead. The compromises of three-quarters of a century of national life, from the Missouri question in 1820 to the Hayes-Tilden question in 1876, were built to bridge over sectional hostilities. We compromise no longer. The unreconstructed Southerner is a joke. The Northerner who tried to wave the bloody shirt would be confined as a dangerous lunatic. The only sectional feeling is of the trifling kind between Northern California and Southern California, or East Texas and West Texas.

Another dangerous cause of internal discord, the hostility of class to class, was never important in America. It existed everywhere in the Old World. Disraeli lamented in his novel *Sybil* that England was divided by class feeling into two nations. He presented a young Chartist agitator who declared that Victoria ruled over two peoples:

> Two nations, between whom there is no intercourse and no sympathy; who are as ignorant of each other's habits, thoughts, and feelings as if they were dwellers in different zones, or inhabitants of different planets; who are formed by different breedings, are fed by different food, are ordered by different manners, and are not governed by the same laws—the rich and the poor.

But in America we never formed *permanent classes*. The main reasons for this are still valid. We never tolerated laws or customs that would institutionalize class lines. Instead, under Jefferson's leadership, we struck down entail and primogeniture so that property changed hands with the advent of each new generation. We viewed great hereditary estates—whether those of the planters in Virginia, the patroons in New York, or the mill owners in New England—with implacable hostility, and when death did not divide them, we divided them by taxation. Our social mobility exceeded that of any other great nation. Our economic mobility was even greater. Three generations spanned the gap between shirtsleeves and shirtsleeves. The lure of the West called men, decade after decade, into new territories and states. The steady inflow of immigrants helped keep society plastic. Class lines might form among immigrants— the older Irish immigrants looking down on the newer Slovak immigrant; the German Jew looking down on the Russian Jew —but these class lines dissolved overnight. Intermarriage was constant, and Abie's Irish Rose reared a new family completely American in tolerance and faith.

Yet one basis for class lines in America has remained continuously powerful. It is the division between rich and poor, different from that in Europe, but just as strong. The idea that we have not had strong and enduring class lines can be dispelled by a reading of one old book that should be known better than it is, Carleton H. Parker's *The Casual Laborer, and Other Essays.* Parker knew that the color line would be hard to erase in this country, and that the poverty line would be still harder to dim. He found that poverty in America rested on a three-legged stool. One leg was ignorance—the unskilled worker suffered from countless deprivations and injustices, including the hostility of skilled workers. One leg was low wage scales, lowest of all among migratory workers. Still another leg was irregularity of industrial employment. The American coal miner early in the century had to expect unemployment one-third or one-fourth of each year. Hence it was that coal miners, migratory farm workers, and lumber workers often joined the Socialists and the IWW. Parker wrote in 1920 of the roots of poverty:

The combination of low wages, the unskilled nature of the work, and its great irregularity, tends to break the habit and desire for stable industry among the workers. Millions drift into migrating from one center to another, in search of work. In these centers, nearly all saloon keepers run an employment agency business . . . and it is to the saloon that the job-hunter turns. His fee is to drink up part of his pay check. The worker slides down the scale, and out of his industry, and joins the millions of unskilled or lost-skilled who float back and forth . . . These millions form a desperate class.

It is with them in mind that Woodrow Wilson wrote in 1913:

Don't you know that some man with eloquent tongue, and without conscience, and who did not care for the nation, could put this country aflame? Don't you know that this country, from one end to the other, believes that something is wrong? What an opportunity it would be for some man without conscience to spring up, say "follow me" and lead in paths of destruction! We are in a temper to reconstruct economic society, as we were once in a temper to reconstruct political society.

Thus, as far back as Wilson's first administration, a war on poverty and its roots was a war against moral bitterness, class feeling, antisocial attitudes, and national division. The war on poverty is all that today, as our best sociologists, political scientists, and public leaders point out. The crisis has simply become deeper, the exigency more threatening.

Until we attack poverty with all the expert weapons that the latest advances in economics, sociology, and politics have placed within our reach, we shall continue to have a national system that gives 30,000,000 people a life of such limited happiness, such cramping limitations on personal development, and such exposure to sudden onslaughts of fear, deprivation, and misery, that we can expect from our people very little devotion to country, little sense of solicitude for their fellowmen, little expression even of right ethical feeling, and no such manifestations of philosophic wisdom, poetic grace, and determined purpose as will give our national life a higher meaning.

Hope alone is not enough. Meaningful hope has to be given implementation by installments. It is a mere mockery until a first down payment has been made in a substantial step toward truly equal education: then a further step toward fulfillment of promises must be made in the provision of housing worthy of American citizens. After that, meaningful hope will have to be translated into opportunities for employment on a higher and higher plane, less and less menial, and more and more professional. Life without hope is empty. But true hopes are illustrated hopes.

DISCUSSION QUESTIONS

"The American Image"

1. What does Griffith mean by the "immense energy" of America? How is this quality both an asset and a liability? In recent years has there been a change in our belief that "there's more where that came from"?

2. What other qualities make up the American image, according to Griffith? Do you agree? What does he say about immigrants and their children?

3. What is the difference between "the greatest good of the greatest number" and "the greatest pleasure of the most people" (paragraph 8)? How would the distinction in meaning affect our national goals?

4. Is Griffith's portrait of the American woman still true today? If not, what has changed the way women spend their days? What would a portrait of the American man reveal?

5. Is there evidence that Americans have

taken on "duties and responsibilities in return for their privileges"? If not, do you see another alternative to our becoming "indolent" and declining as a culture?

6. Which of Griffith's ideas on the American image are reflected in Ginsberg's "America"? In Sandburg's "The People Will Live On"?

"America" and "The People Will Live On"

1. In what ways does Ginsberg's 1956 poem prophesy some trends of the next two decades?

2. What suggests that Ginsberg may not be totally serious in his views?

3. How could Sandburg provide an answer to Ginsberg? On what is Sandburg's trust based? Out of what American spirit and tradition does his optimism arise?

4. Compare Sandburg's poems elsewhere in this volume, showing how they reflect his dualistic perception of experience.

5. Does Sandburg or Ginsberg more accurately reflect your views of America's future?

"Farewell Address"

1. What is Eisenhower's warning about the military-industrial complex? Are there other areas of bigness which Americans should be wary of?

2. What is wrong with federal grants to colleges for research?

3. What warning about the environment does Eisenhower give us?

4. What is the current status of the influence of the military in both domestic and foreign affairs? Did the war in Vietnam affect the influence of the military permanently? Do Americans need to be concerned about the military-industrial complex today?

"Eisenhower's Visit to Franco, 1959"

1. What side of Eisenhower's Presidency is suggested in this poem?

2. Are the concepts in the poem applicable to more than one President?

3. What is the meaning of Wright's lines "The American hero must triumph/over/ The forces of darkness"?

4. How does the poem suggest both the dream and nightmare of U.S. power?

"Milo"

1. What concepts previously discussed in this volume are brought together in this selection?

2. What things is Heller satirizing?

3. Compare Milo's logic to that of Rockefeller in the Tarbell essay.

4. Milo is upset at the idea of bribery. How can you explain his twisted morality?

5. What is the value of Yossarian's protest? Is it just more idiocy?

6. What does Milo reveal about bureaucracy in general? What are his thoughts on the military-industrial complex?

from *"The Pursuit of Loneliness"*

1. How does the ideal of individualism work against us, according to Slater? What example does Slater use to illustrate and define his rather abstract points? Can you think of other examples which tend either to prove or disprove his thesis?

2. Does Slater succumb to what Bennett Berger calls the myth of suburbia? Explain. What distinction does Slater draw between the culture of the small town and the suburb? Do you think he is correct?

3. How does Rabbit Angstrom in Updike's selection show the same shrinking from interdependence that Slater sees? Why does Rabbit retreat?

4. What connection can you see between Slater's ideas on individualism and Milo Minderbinder's business "ethics"?

5. Are Americans making a greater effort to establish "a viable social context," or is our life becoming increasingly impersonal? Give examples to support your opinion.

"The Changing Place of Women in America"

1. What links does Carl Degler see between women's rights and the frontier?

2. What connections does he draw between industrialization and the rise of the city and the changing roles of both men and women?

3. What comparisons does Degler make between American and European women?

4. Do you see evidence today that a feminist ideology has gained power? Have there been legislative changes brought about by mobilizing power? Have there been changes in social attitudes or mores?

"Restoration of a River"

1. How did the Hudson become cleaner? What complex governmental action took place?

2. How clean was the Hudson in 1972 (according to Mitchell)? What steps does he feel are necessary to clean it up still further?

3. How might the methods used to clean up the river be applied to other areas of society needing improvement?

4. The whole question of environmental protection is still controversial. What do opponents of environmental legislation argue? What is your opinion?

"California 2001"

1. Al Martinez describes an America of the future where the major problems we face have been solved or are on their way to being solved. Choose any one of his problem areas (education, transportation, ecol-

ogy, housing) and discuss whether his solution to the problem is practical.

2. If you disagree with Martinez's solutions, write a short explanation of a more practical solution or show what the results would be if his solution were adopted.

3. What is the political structure of the new California?

4. Would you like to live in a world such as he describes? If not, what do you find disquieting about his description?

5. Is "California 2001" a new American dream?

"The Tradition of the Future"

1. If, as Allan Nevins suggests, America is a spirit rather than a location, where can you find examples of this spirit?

2. In what ways is Nevins's essay optimistic for the future of America? Is his optimism justified?

3. Why does he feel that it is so important to attack poverty vigorously?

4. How does Roosevelt's speech, as quoted by Nevins, reiterate many tenets of the American dream?

5. How does this essay sum up or "crystallize" many previous essays in this text?

SUGGESTED READINGS

ALBEE, EDWARD. *The American Dream.* New York, 1961.

BARTH, JOHN. *Giles Goat-Boy.* Garden City, 1960.

BERNSTEIN, CARL, and BOB WOODWARD. *All the President's Men.* New York, 1974.

BOORSTIN, DANIEL. *The Image, or What Happened to the American Dream.* New York, 1962.

CARPENTER, FREDERIC I. *American Literature and the Dream.* New York, 1955.

DICKEY, JAMES. *Deliverance.* Boston, 1970.

FERLINGHETTI, LAWRENCE. *Coney Island of the Mind.* New York, 1955.

HELLER, JOSEPH. *Something Happened.* New York, 1974.

HOLBROOK, STEWART. *Dreamers of the American Dream.* Garden City, 1957.

KEROUAC, JACK. *On the Road.* New York, 1957.

KESEY, KEN. *One Flew Over the Cuckoo's Nest.* New York, 1962.

MORRIS, WILLIE. *North Toward Home.* Boston, 1967.

PACKARD, VANCE. *A Nation of Strangers.* New York, 1972.

UPDIKE, JOHN. *Rabbit Redux.* New York, 1971.

WEST, NATHANIEL. *A Cool Million.* New York, 1934.

———. *The Day of the Locust.* New York, 1939.

WHYTE, WILLIAM H., JR. *The Organization Man.* New York, 1956.

DATE DUE

GAYLORD | | | PRINTED IN U.S.A.